Central Asia
AND THE Caucasus
after the Soviet Union

Domestic and International Dynamics

Library of Congress Cataloging-in-Publication Data

Central Asia and the Caucasus after the Soviet Union: domestic and
    international dynamics/edited by Mohiaddin Mesbahi.
        p. cm.
    Includes bibliographical references and index.
    ISBN 0-8130-1307-0 (acid-free paper).—ISBN 0-8130-1308-9 (pbk.: acid-free paper)
    1. Asia, Central—History—1991- 2. Caucasus—History. 3. Muslims—Former
Soviet republics. 4. Former Soviet republics—Ethnic relations. 5. Russia
(Federation)—Foreign relations—Asia, Central. 6. Asia, Central—Foreign relations—
Russia (Federation) 7. Russia (Federation)—Relations—Caucasus. 8. Caucasus—
Relations—Russia (Federation). I. Mesbahi, Mohiaddin.
DK859.5.C454   1994
947'.9086—dc20   9416204

The University Press of Florida is the scholarly publishing agency for the State Univer-
sity System of Florida, comprised of Florida A & M University, Florida Atlantic Uni-
versity, Florida International University, Florida State University, University of Central
Florida, University of Florida, University of North Florida, University of South Florida,
and University of West Florida.

University Press of Florida
15 Northwest 15th Street
Gainesville, FL 32611

CONTENTS

Part 4. Russia and the Former Soviet South: The New Geopolitics

Preface

The newly independent Muslim states of the former Soviet Union are grappling with some of the most pressing geopolitical and security issues confronting the post-Soviet international order. Policy makers and scholars of international relations alike face the challenge of dealing with the transformation of these states from parts of a communist superpower to independent nations, under the enduring influences of nationalism and Islam.

This book, a collection of commissioned studies by leading Western, Russian, and Central Asian scholars, originated (with the exception of two chapters) from papers delivered at an international conference, "The Transformation of the Former USSR and Its Implications for the Third World," organized by the editor and hosted by the Institute for Political and International Studies (IPIS) in Tehran, Iran, in March 1992. Given the significance of the Soviet collapse for Iran, especially the opening of a new horizon for Iranian foreign policy, and Iran's status as a link between the Middle East and Central Asia, the sponsorship of this conference by IPIS was a highly important achievement. IPIS, a leading research institute in the Middle East, in addition to producing numerous publications including the *Iranian Journal of International Affairs* and the *Central Asia and Caucasian Review*, holds forums for national and international conferences to provide opportunities for scholarly exchanges.

Co-sponsors of the conference were the Oriental Institute of the Russian Academy of Sciences and the Department of International Relations of Florida International University. The three-day conference brought together more than fifty renowned scholars from the United States, Europe, China, Russia, the Muslim republics of the former USSR, and the Third World. Not only did the gathering generate considerable debate among the participating scholars, it also created a significant contribution to policy debate on the subject.

The chapters in this book have been updated since the conference although by design they were mostly written so as not to be acutely time-sensitive. While they reflect the rich diversity of the contributors' intellectual and cultural orientations, they are also unified under a central theme—continuity and change.

I would like to express special thanks to the IPIS for hosting and sponsoring the impressive international gathering that made this book possible. In that regard the project is especially indebted to Abbas Maleki, Ahmad Hajihosseini, Sohrab Shahabi, and Ali Ghaderi, whose support was essential.

I am grateful to Irina Zviagelskaya of the Russian Academy of Sciences for assisting me in managing the contributions of the scholars from the former USSR. I would also like to express my appreciation to Provost James Mau, Dean Arthur Herriot, and Professor Ralph Clem of Florida International University for the support they rendered to the project. I am also grateful to Michael Senecal of the University Press of Florida for his useful editorial suggestions. Last but not least, I would like to thank Naisy Sarduy, my graduate assistant, whose help both in the organization of the conference and the preparation of the manuscript for this book was indispensable.

Introduction

The Emerging "Muslim" States of Central Asia and the Caucasus

Mohiaddin Mesbahi

For the world that witnessed the dramatic events of the late 1980s in Europe and the dynamics of the eventual collapse of the Soviet Union, there were names, people, places, and historical memories that evoked familiarity, excitement, and—most of all—a sense of anticipation for positive and liberating change. The images of the fall of the Berlin Wall and the "velvet revolution" in Eastern Europe brought home, especially to Western audiences, powerful symbols and images of a familiar historic injustice being undone; the captive nations of Europe were being liberated and the post–World War II historical aberration of Soviet domination was being erased.

The reaction toward the independence drive of the Baltic states was similar: the small, yet brave nations of Latvia, Lithuania, and Estonia were perceived as symbols of legitimate challenge to the yoke of Soviet totalitarianism and became a litmus test of Soviet glasnost and perestroika. Gorbachev's initial hesitation or refusal to accept the Baltic's drive for independence and Moscow's "minor" police operation of intimidation proved to be ineffective, extremely unpopular in the West, and thus costly politically. The Soviet leadership was criticized, and its commitment to the rule of law, democratization, and political reform was seriously questioned.

A totally different attitude was displayed, however, toward Moscow's policy regarding the independence movements in Azerbaijan and Central Asia. When, in January 1990, Soviet special forces brutally put down demonstrations in Baku and declared an indefinite state of emergency, the reaction of the Western world, the media, the public, policy makers, and even scholars was uniformly subdued, often neutral, and at times sympathetic to Moscow's plight. Moscow's concern over the disintegration of the state (the USSR) and Soviet military action in "maintaining" law and order was given considerable weight and legitimacy,

1

while the same had been denied in the case of the Baltics.[1] The collective Western reaction to the Baku massacre and subsequently toward the events in the Central Asian republics since the collapse of the Soviet Union (that is, condoning authoritarian governments in Central Asia) indicated a fundamental Western ambiguity toward the Islamic parts of the USSR, an ambiguity that was mostly connected with the general ambivalence, mutual suspicion, and, at times, outright hostility that has surrounded the Western world's relations with Islam, especially in the 1970s and 1980s.[2]

Perceptions of and attitudes toward the new Muslim states of the former USSR carry all the ingredients of attitudes toward the Islamic world in general. The immediate characterization of the "Islamic threat" that might emanate from Central Asia and the Caucasus has become the umbrella under which policy makers and opinion makers, as well as those in academia, have been operating.[3] The collapse of the Soviet Union and the "demise" of Communism as a competing ideology have given rise to the potential emergence of Islam and the Islamic world as replacements and new challenges facing the Western world in the post–Cold War era.[4]

The emergence of independent states in Central Asia and the Caucasus has led to the significant enlargement of this perceived threat. *Geopolitically*, the black hole of Central Asia now constitutes an expanded part of the new Middle East.[5] *Geoculturally*, few other regions entail a nation-state border system of such potential transparency, where common and cross-border religious, ethnic, linguistic, and collective memories could act individually or jointly as destabilizing or integrating factors.[6] From Kazakhstan to Egypt, dynamics of anticolonial feeling (old or new), economic underdevelopment, uneven development, religious revivalism, arms proliferation, artificial borders, and ethnoterritorially driven conflicts are characteristic. This region now borders a new Russia and China and, above all, has been the focus of intense Western security and economic interests and concerns.

The "Muslim" states of the former USSR thus present a considerable challenge and opportunity for observation and analysis of some of the most pressing ingredients of post-Soviet international relations, ranging from geopolitical and security issues to new areas, such as post-Communist transition. The emerging Central Asia is a gold mine of issues and questions that concern policy makers, scholars, and students of international relations.

What are the geopolitical meanings of the emergence of independent "Muslim" states in Central Asia and the Caucasus? What role will Islam (as a culture and a political ideology) and ethnicity play in the future? How will the issue of post-Communist transition to democracy and market be shaped in this region? What will Russia's role be in the new Central Asia? Will Russia, in view of the Empire's legacy, reassert its role as the dominant core of the Eurasian heartland? How will the United States and regional actors such as Iran and Turkey react and adapt to the new geopolitical and geocultural realities?

This volume, a selection of chapters by leading Western, Russian, and Central Asian scholars, addresses these and other key issues pertaining to the domestic and international dynamics of Central Asia and the Caucasus. It has been divided into four interrelated sections. The first section includes three chapters that address the issues of ethnicity, Islam, and the Soviet legacy in Central Asia and the Caucasus. These chapters will provide a coherent conceptual framework for the analysis of the future trends of ethnicity and Islam in Central Asia and the Caucasus.

The second and third sections will provide individual studies of Tatarstan and the North Caucasus (Russia's "internal Muslims"), as well as of the six Muslim states of the former USSR: Kazakhstan, Uzbekistan, Kyrgyzstan, Tajikistan, Turkmenistan, and Azerbaijan. Each chapter, with different degrees of emphasis and focus, will uniformly consider the key domestic issues facing each republic, in addition to discussing the emerging and nascent foreign policies of these republics.

The fourth section, comprising four chapters, will address the new geopolitics of Central Asia and the foreign policies of Russia—and of key regional actors such as Iran and Turkey—toward Central Asia. In addition to discussions of the foreign policies of individual actors, these chapters will provide a coherent conceptual framework in which Central Asia's place in regional and world affairs will be addressed.

The first chapter of the book, by Sergei A. Panarin, is "The Ethnohistorical Dynamics of Muslim Societies within Russia and the CIS." It provides a comprehensive conceptual framework, termed "ethnoexistential structure," within which seventy years of evolution of Soviet ethnicity have been analyzed. The study details the evolving process of five components of this "existential structure," including geopolitical, intraconfessional, linguistic, ethnic, and settlement structures, from 1926 to the collapse of the Soviet Union. It has been argued that the struggle for the survival of Muslim societies during this period has followed a series of U-shaped curves: an initial and sudden decline, followed by midlevel stabilization and a final, gradual ascent toward the recovery of "collective consciousness." The recovery period of the last two decades, intensified by the dramatic change of the 1980s and the collapse of the Soviet Union, has resulted in a "great outer resemblance between modern existentialist structures and their old (pre-1917) prototypes." Yet the parallel existence of modern and old structures during the Soviet experience has extracted heavy costs from the Muslim societies: a historical distortion—not a synthesis—has taken place. The heritage of the Soviet period "could succumb only partially to the havoc of the breakdown of the USSR."

The chapter by Eden Naby, "The Emerging Central Asia: Ethnic and Religious Factions," examines the ethnic and religious dynamics of the region in the context of increasing tension between rural and urban areas for political control, the uneven role of religion in voicing political dissent, the tension within Islamic forces, and the significant and continuous weight of Russian and Soviet legacies in creating the current ethnoreligious mix in the rural and urban areas. The chapter's focus on Tajikistan and Uzbekistan (largely based on Naby's extensive field study) provides the general comparative context for the study of ethnicity and Islam in other republics. Naby's analysis indicates that while ethnicity and religion should play a constructive role in the long-term stability of Central Asia, they have yet to display such potentialities. The dominant ethnicity of each republic has yet to overcome regional and linguistic differences, while national languages must face intrarepublic linguistic diversity in addition to the challenge of Russian. The significant rural and urban division and the tension between the majority Sunni and the non-Sunni population continue to complicate Islam's task as a stabilizing force.

M. Nazif Shahrani's chapter, "Muslim Central Asia: Soviet Development Legacies and Future Challenges," puts forward a key hypothesis that the Soviet Communist model, while apparently failing to create a progressive modern state in the former Soviet Union, has enjoyed a considerable degree of success in Muslim Central Asia. Shahrani provides a critical analysis of Western Sovietology in both its theoretical and methodological approach toward Central Asia and argues that debate over the success or failure of Soviet development policies should take place within the context of "specific short- and long-term Soviet goals and objectives, both articulated and otherwise." Moscow had accomplished key ingredients of its objectives, including political control, economic exploitation and dependency, and cultural and ideological penetration and fragmentation. As a political, economic, and sociocultural entity, Central Asia was controlled, exploited, and shaped to the extent that it has developed a collective material (objective) and psychological (subjective) dependency on the Soviet Union and its successor, Russia. While the best hopes of the people of the region might lie in finding their own "Islamic alternative," Shahrani warns against unguarded optimism, for "by any measure, the success of Soviet educational, political, and economic achievements in weakening, if not destroying, traditional Islamic cultural forms has been considerable."

The second part of the volume begins with Marie Bennigsen Broxup's study, "The 'Internal' Muslim Factor in the Politics of Russia: Tatarstan and the North Caucasus," which addresses the issues of Russia's multinational empire, namely, "political, territorial, ethnic, economic, and religious complexities that beset the Soviet Union before its demise." Specifically, the chapter focuses on two case studies: Tatarstan in the Volga-Ural region and Chechnia in the North Caucasus. These two autonomous republics, which have opted for full independence, have so far refused to sign the Russian Federation Treaty of March 1992. Broxup provides a succinct historical context for both cases and discusses in detail the process of political colonization and religious repression to which both republics have been subjected for the last century under tsarist and Soviet rule. In the current (post-Soviet) phase, this study puts forward the complex nature of Russia's dilemma and argues that, notwithstanding the case that could be made for an economic explanation, it is Moscow's psychological fear of "encirclement by the Muslim Irano-Turkic world" that remains the key obstacle to the decolonization and eventual independence of these regions. Russia's overall attitude toward the Muslim world, Broxup maintains, will depend to a large extent on Moscow's attitudes toward its "internal Islam."

The chapter by Yuri Zinin and Alexei V. Malashenko on Azerbaijan focuses on discussing socioeconomic and political forces shaping the domestic and foreign policies of Azerbaijan as an independent state. In providing a historical analysis, the authors maintain that—for better or for worse, and regardless of the costs—the profound changes that took place in the life of the republic during the Soviet period were critical in providing the foundations for modern Azerbaijani statehood. The chapter also addresses the critical role of Shiite Islam in the political and social life of the republic and the ambivalent attitude of the liberal forces, intelligentsia, and the current leadership of the republic toward Islam as a potential political rival. The challenges of Nagorno-Karabakh are discussed in the context of Azerbaijan's regional and international policy. A balanced relationship with Russia, Turkey, and Iran and the creation of an international atmosphere conducive to attracting foreign investment are the two key components of Azerbaijan's foreign policy objectives.

Martha Brill Olcott's chapter on Kazakhstan addresses the sociopolitical, ethnic, and economic dynamics of this important republic, in addition to its foreign policy orientation. In the context of Kazakhstan's move toward independence, the analysis signifies the crucial role of Nursultan Nazarbaev, both before and after the collapse of the Soviet Union, and clearly identifies the pivotal challenges facing Kazakhstan; namely, the ambiguous nature of its national identity as "the only former republic of the USSR in which the people for whom the new nation is named, the Kazakhs, are a numerical minority." This ambiguity in the national character has been critical to both domestic policy and foreign policy of the new republic. While Nazarbaev's pragmatic economic programs and his close ties with Russia have been utilized to build a consensus between the Russians and the Kazakh population, the ultimate future of the state as "a multinational state or hybrid half-Russian half-Kazakh, or a sovereign and exclusively Kazakh homeland," remains a structural problem. This internal tension is the primary obstacle to the development and transition of Kazakhstan toward the creation of a civil society. Russian cultural dominance has been confronted by invoking Kazakh cultural heritage, including recognition of the role of Islam, yet Islamization will pose its own problem of becoming an independent political challenge at home. The ambiguity of Kazakhstan's national identity also affects its foreign policy orientation as Alma-Ata tries to place itself, not only as the leader of Muslim Central Asia—tapping into the resources of the Islamic world—but simultaneously presenting itself as a secular/modern nation to the rest of the world.

Zahid I. Munavvarov's chapter on Uzbekistan focuses on the evolution of Uzbekistan's movement toward independence and the future prospects of its sociopolitical developments. A considerable portion of this study is devoted to the role of Islam in the evolution of the sociopolitical character of Uzbekistan and the rich and diverse nature of Islamic movements and institutions in the republic. A critical analysis of the Western and Russian approaches toward the role of Islam, including "the excessive exaggeration of Islamic fundamentalism" and "the focus on the negative aspects of Islam," is presented. Islam will be a major stabilizing factor in Uzbekistan and in Central Asia, while eth-noterritorial irredentism, the "temptation connected with redivision of existing borders," is considered the most important challenge facing Uzbekistan's security.

Alexander Filonyk's study on Kyrgyzstan analyzes and contrasts competing sets of factors of stability and tension in this republic's so-ciopolitical and economic life. The ability of the republic's leadership to manage the acute Kyrgyz-Uzbek conflict, the imperatives of ethnic coexistence, the weakness of Islam as a political force, and the general consensus on the creation of a market economy and ties with Russia have created a promising base of stability. Yet Filonyk points to the re-public's peculiar agricultural setup, including differences between Uz-bek and Kyrgyz traditional settlement systems and social organizations, "the significant role of the unemployed rural youth" in nurturing Kyr-gyz nationalism, and the existing tension between "locals" and "Euro-peans," who compose 45 percent of the population, as key challenges to the future of Kyrgyzstan.

Aziz Niyazi's chapter on Tajikistan focuses on the interrelationship of traditional and modern components of Tajik society and their im-pact on the sociopolitical life of the republic before and after the Soviet collapse. The study provides the historical background of Tajikistan and its birth as a republic and analyzes its contemporary socioeco-nomic problems. One of the key historical legacies of the Soviet period, with far-reaching implications for the future, has been the incompati-bility of Tajikistan's artificially drawn border, which did not coincide with its ethnographical realities. The Soviet national territorial divi-sion of Tajikistan, like other parts of Central Asia, "destroyed the pre-viously existing balance between the Persian- and Turkic-speaking populations of the region." In analyzing the social problems of the re-public, the study focuses on the crucial issues of complex relations be-tween rural and urban sectors, a high rate of population growth, dependency on a Russian skilled labor force, and above all the conflict-prone communal division and clan/tribal loyalties and identities of the republic. Discussing the ongoing political crisis of Tajikistan, the chap-ter investigates the role of the intelligentsia and Islam and concludes that neither the eponymic character (Tajik) nor religious (Islamic) iden-tity has been able to overcome the deeply rooted communal and geo-graphical lines of loyalties, thus extremely complicating the process of nation building in Tajikistan.

Andrei Nedvetsky's chapter on Turkmenistan focuses on (1) the intricate nature of the existing and emerging political culture of the republic; and (2) the economic potential of the republic, especially the central role of the export of gas in shaping both the financial and foreign policies of Turkmenistan. "The most peaceful and stable state of the CIS" characteristically draws its apparent stability from tribal and communal loyalties. The intertwined tribal and communal lines of affiliation have thus far been able to accommodate the emerging national identity, yet the intrinsic tension between these lines of self-assertion and loyalty will remain a source of instability. In the realm of foreign policy, relations with the outside world—especially Iran, Turkey, and Russia—will continue to be dictated by security and economic imperatives.

The last section of the volume is devoted to discussions of the international and geopolitical settings of the Central Asian states. Milan Hauner's chapter, "The Disintegration of the Soviet Eurasian Empire: An Ongoing Debate," provides a conceptual framework for the analysis of the emerging geopolitics of Central Asia and the adjacent regions. The chapter addresses the historical, ideological, and geopolitical significance of Central Asia "as the pivotal region of the new Eurasian commonwealth." Discussions of these three dimensions are presented in the context of a comparative analysis of patterns of disintegration of both the Russian Empire and the Soviet Union and the historical scholarly debate over the defining features of Eurasia. "Can the European and Asian parts of the former Soviet-Eurasian empire still coexist within a commonwealth?" To this central question Hauner provides two parallel scenarios, one based on a "traditional, but reformed geopolitical approach," a post–Cold War version of the eighteenth- and nineteenth-century European system; and the other a complimentary "geocultural approach" (Wallerstein) reminiscent of the integrated thirteenth-century world system, one nurtured by the experience of Central Asia as an "organic part" of Russo-Soviet Eurasia. "The control of the ethnocultural factor will remain the key prerequisite for the emergence of such a scenario."

Arthur Sagadeev's study, "Great Power Ideology and the Muslim Nations of the CIS," provides a historically dynamic and yet critical analysis of the role of Russia's great power ideology as a major factor in shaping Moscow's attitudes toward the Muslim nations during the last two centuries. This ideology shaped the perspectives and policies of both the Russian Empire and the Soviet Union, as well as those of the period of reform under Gorbachev's perestroika and the post-Soviet collapse under Yeltsin. Sagadeev identifies three broad trends within the current Russian leadership: the hardline trends, which unite advocates of Russian nationalism (neo-Communists and neo-Fascists); the second trend, which perceives Russia as a "normal great power" of a democratic nature; and the third trend, which adheres to the concept of modern power with a modern neocolonial character, allocating to Russia the role of an enlightened big brother. The author addresses the role of Islamaphobia as the new external source of threat nurturing the great power ideology of the current Russian leadership toward the Muslim republics of the former Soviet Union, and more specifically toward autonomous republics within the Russian Federation. Human rights slogans, that is, protection of Russian minorities, have become a pivotal component of the current great power ideology.[7]

The chapter by Anthony Hyman, "Central Asia and the Middle East: The Emerging Links," analyzes key trends and dynamics of the burgeoning relations between major Middle Eastern actors and the new Muslim states in Central Asia and the Caucasus. The study provides an overview of religious, cultural, political, and economic links between the two regions since the collapse of the Soviet Union. This includes the expansion of Iranian and Saudi Islamic activities; Turkey and Iran's competition; and major bilateral economic and trade activities and significant multilateral initiatives, such as the expansion of the Economic Cooperation Organization (ECO), which, in addition to its original members (Iran, Turkey, and Pakistan), now embraces the new Muslim states. Although these interregional links and penetrations are bound to expand, Hyman also points to certain constraints and limitations. For example, while the reinvigoration of Islam in Central Asia will be nurtured by contacts with the Muslims of the Middle East, the impact and influence of Islam will be modified by the prevailing secularism of Central Asian elites, who refuse to be confined to either the Turkish or Iranian models and tend to "look everywhere and anywhere for guidance and assistance in solving their severe problem of development." In economic and trade relations, two areas of significant potential will be gas/oil agreements and communication links, yet large-scale and long-term investment remains dubious. The much-discussed Turko-Iranian competition also involves a less noticed element of cooperation, especially under multilateral schemes such as ECO. While relations with Central Asia, Turkey, Iran, Pakistan, and Saudi Arabia have received considerable attention, it is the non-Muslim state of Israel that, given the expected constraints, has made considerable inroads in the region. Future relations between the new Muslim states of

Central Asia and the Caucasus and the Middle East states—especially Iran and Turkey—will also be subjected to the counteractions of the other key regional power, namely Russia. More than ever before, Central Asia plays a pivotal role in mediating and affecting Russian Middle East relations.

The chapter "Russia and the Geopolitics of the Muslim South" focuses on (1) the discussion of prevailing schools of thought in Russian foreign and security policy since the collapse of the Soviet Union; and (2) the place of Central Asia and the Caucasus, both as a collective geopolitical entity and as independent states, each with varying degrees of security challenges and opportunities. Discussions of the domestic, ideological, and geopolitical sources of two main "Euro-Atlanticist" and "Neo-Eurasianist" schools of thought in Russian foreign policy, and in particular their perception of the "Islamic factor," have been given adequate attention.[8] Russia's continuous effort to forge a "collective security system" and its reinforcement by bilateral security treaties have been analyzed. The chapter also addresses the geopolitical significance of Russia's security policy for the adjacent region and argues that, notwithstanding enormous domestic difficulties, Russia intends, both in theory and in practice, to remain a major actor, if not the dominant player, in Central Asia.[9]

The contributions to this volume not only point collectively to the significance of Central Asia in contemporary international relations and the revolutionary changes in the Eurasian plateau after the collapse of the Soviet Empire, but they also direct attention to significant elements of continuity. The collapse of the Soviet Union does not spell the end of Russia's importance, either in its continuous impact on the domestic/regional evolution of Central Asia or, equally important, in shaping its geopolitics. The Russian "core," weak and engulfed in ethnic and economic crisis, is still much stronger than the Central Asian "periphery." Not only will the legacy of the Soviet period—both domestic and external—remain, but, both in intention and practice, Russia displays a clear tendency to protect its historical interests, a tendency that has survived the passage of time, the changes in regimes, and the collapse of ideologies.[10]

From Prince Alexandre Gorchakov's landmark dispatches of 1864, which portrayed Russia's position in Central Asia as a civilizer of a "half-savage nomad population,"[11] to Andrei Kozyrev's elaboration of Russia's role as a force for the enlightenment and democratization of the "Asian wing,"[12] Moscow's colonial and neocolonial fixation and impulse have remained remarkably constant. While hopeful conventional wisdom holds that the Soviet collapse in 1991 and the current Russian weakness have delivered a significant opportunity to both Russians and Central Asians to break the historical cycle of their colonial relations, the lessons of the post-1917 Russian reassertion and dominance call for more cautious prognostication. Historical analogies need not be vindicated by their crude and simplistic repetition in *forms* but rather in their essential continuity in *substance*. The 1990s, which were initiated by the collapse of the empire, will either bring a substantially new relationship or will signify the resiliency of historical legacies manifesting themselves again in new forms.

Notes

1. Moscow's and the West's "double standard" in dealing with the Muslim republics of the Soviet Union was widely noticed and discussed in the media of several Islamic countries, particularly Iran and Pakistan. See, for example, the Iranian coverage of the Moscow crackdown in Azerbaijan in early 1990 in *Resalat*, 7 January 1990. See also *Jomhuri-ye Eslami*, 4, 21, and 22 January 1990. The letter of 160 Parliament (Majlis) deputies and Qom Seminarian Association (Jame'e-ye Modarresin-e Qom) to Mikhail Gorbachev regarding the Baku crackdown is particularly interesting; see *FBIS-NES*, 23 January 1990, pp. 48–49.

2. For a general assessment of the Western view, see Bernard Lewis, *The Political Language of Islam* (Chicago: University of Chicago Press, 1990); also Lewis, "The Roots of Muslim Rage," *Atlantic Monthly*, September 1990, and Daniel Pipes, "The Muslims Are Coming! The Muslims Are Coming!" *National Review*, November 1990.

3. For a good discussion of this issue see Shireen Hunter, "The Muslim Republics of the Former Soviet Union: Policy Challenges for the United States," *Washington Quarterly* (Summer 1992), and Shahram Chubin, "The Geopolitics of the Southern Republics of the CIS," *Iranian Journal of International Affairs* 4, no. 2 (Summer 1992).

4. For a discussion of the post-Communist emergence of Islam as the next challenge to the West see John L. Esposito, *The Islamic Threat: Myth or Reality?* (Oxford: Oxford University Press, 1992); Yvonne Haddad, John L. Voll, and John L. Esposito, *The Contemporary Islamic Revival: A Critical Survey and Bibliography* (New York: Greenwood Press, 1991).

5. For a discussion of the geopolitical inclusion of Central Asia in the Middle East see Bernard Lewis, "The New Middle East," *Foreign Affairs* (Fall 1992); Shireen T. Hunter, "Central Asia and the Middle East: Patterns of Interaction and Influence," *Central Asia Monitor*, no. 6 (1992); and "The Collapse of the USSR and the 'Northern Tier' States," in *Russia and the Third World in the*

Post-Soviet Era, ed. Mohiaddin Mesbahi (Gainesville: University Press of Florida, 1994).

6. For the discussion of geoculture as a "new" concept in international relations see Immanuel Wallerstein, *Geopolitics and Geoculture* (Cambridge: Cambridge University Press, 1991).

7. For the official Russian view on the link between "human rights" and the rights of Russian minorities in the newly independent states see, for example, Yevgeniy Grusarov, "Towards a Europe of Democracy and Unity," *Rossiyskaya Gazeta*, 5 March 1992, p. 7; Andrei Kozyrev interview with *Krasnaya Zvezda*, 26 November 1992.

8. For a discussion of Russian perceptions of Islam during the Gorbachev era see Mohiaddin Mesbahi, "Gorbachev's 'New Thinking' and Islamic Iran: From Containment to Reconciliation," in *Regional Reconstruction and Regional Diplomacy in the Persian Gulf*, ed. H. Amirahmadi and N. Entessar (London and New York: Routledge, 1992); Martha B. Olcott, "Soviet Central Asia: Does Moscow Fear Iranian Influence?" in *The Iranian Revolution: Its Global Impact*, ed. John L. Esposito (Miami: Florida International University Press, 1990). For an assessment of Soviet views on Islam in the earlier periods, see Alexandre Bennigsen and Marie Broxup, *The Islamic Threat to the Soviet Union* (London: Croom Helm, 1984).

9. Moscow's view of Central Asia as a sphere of influence has remained, notwithstanding changes and variations, remarkably consistent throughout the nineteenth and twentieth centuries. See and contrast the following sources: M.I. Venyukov, "Postulpatel'noe dvizhenie Rossii v Srednei Azii," *Sbornik Gosudarstvennykh Znaniy* 3 (St. Petersburg, 1877); D.I. Mendeleev, *K poznaniyu Rossii* (St. Petersburg, 1906); M.S. Gorbachev, *Perestroika: New Thinking for Our Country and the World* (New York: Harper and Row, 1987), pp. 191–98; Igor Malashenko, "Russia; The Earth's Heartland," *International Affairs* (Moscow) (July 1990); Lectures by Ruslan Khasbulatov, Yevgeni Primakov, and Sergei Stenkevich at Moscow Institute of International Relations, in *International Affairs* (Moscow), no. 4–5 (April–May 1992); "Official Draft of Russian Foreign Policy Concepts," in *Interfax* 2 November 1992, *FBIS-Central Eurasia*, 2 November 1992, pp. 11–13; Andrei Kozyrev, "Challenge of Transformation," *Izvestiya* and Boris Yeltsin interview with correspondent of *Izvestiya*, *Literaturnaya Gazeta*, and *Moscow Russian Television* in *FBIS-Central Eurasia*, 15 July 1992, pp. 18–22.

10. Ibid., especially Boris Yeltsin interviews in *Izvestiya*, 15 July 1992 and *Literaturnaya Gazeta*, 15 July 1992; and *International Affairs* (Moscow) (April–May 1992), which carries lectures by Sergei Stenkevich, Ruslan Khasbulatov, Yevgeni Primakov, and Vladimir Lukin.

11. For the discussion of Gorchakov's dispatches of 21 November/3 December 1864 and also Russia's perception and policy in Central Asia, see Firuz Kazemzadeh, *Russia and Britain in Persia* (New Haven, Conn.: Yale University Press, 1968).

12. For Andrei Kozyrev's statements on Central Asia and the Caucasus and the role of Russia as an agent of change see the interview with *Le Monde*, 8 June 1992, cited in *FBIS-Central Eurasia*, 9 June 1992, interview with *ITAR-TASS*, 26 March 1992, in *FBIS-Central Eurasia*, 27 March 1992, and *ITAR-TASS*, 18 January 1994, in *FBIS-Central Eurasia* 18 January 1994, p. 18.

1

The Ethnohistorical Dynamics of Muslim Societies within Russia and the CIS

Sergei A. Panarin

In this chapter, the term *Muslim societies* is used to describe those peoples who, prior to the October Revolution, were listed in the Russian Empire's statistics as Mohammedan populations and who, since 1917, were conferred upon by the Bolshevik leadership with some attributes of statehood named after an ethnonym (or sometimes two ethnonyms simultaneously). As will be shown, this definition's proper confessional meaning has lost its paramount importance, though the other aspect of the term *Muslim societies* is still relevant as it stresses the civilizational similarity, as well as the common propensity of different societies to mobilize Islamic values for serving present-day needs.

Muslim societies within Russia constituted the "former" autonomous republics and provinces. It is important to stress the word "former" because these have all either already achieved or are attempting to achieve a change in their legal-political status. Autonomous provinces have been promoted to the rank of autonomous republics, while some autonomous republics aspire to full sovereignty maintaining a merely nominal link with Russia. There are seven Muslim autonomous formations in Russia. In the Volga-Urals region there are Tatarstan (the former Tatar Autonomous Soviet Socialist Republic [ASSR]) and Bashkortostan (the former Bashkir ASSR). In the North Caucasus there are Adygeya (former autonomous province); Karachayevo-Circassia (another former autonomous province), which now threatens to split into four minirepublics—Karachai, Circassian, Abazin, and one of Russian cossacks; Kabardino-Balkaria (a formerly united autonomous republic now about to split into two); the Ingush and Chechen Republics (which formed the Republic of Chechen-Ingushetiya in 1992); and the multinational Republic of Daghestan (the former Daghestan ASSR). The following Muslim societies, which were formerly Union republics, became independent states of the CIS: in the Transcaucasian region there is Azerbaijan together with the Nakhichevan ASSR; in Central Asia there is Turkmenistan, Uzbekistan with the Karakalpak ASSR, Tajikistan with the Pamiro-Badakhshan ASSR (the former Gorno-Badakhshan autonomous province), and Kyrgyzstan; and between Central Asia and Russia lies Kazakhstan.

In the Caucasian/Transcaucasian region there are four more regions composed of peoples who have remained under the influence of Islam. These are southern (within Georgia) and northern (within Russia) Ossetia, Abkhazia, and Adzharia (both within Georgia). These will not be addressed in this chapter for the following reasons: the historical positions of Christianity in the former three were not less solid than those of Islam, while Abkhazians were also strongly influenced by ancient pagan beliefs; in Adzharia, Muslims do not differ ethnically from other Georgians, and since 1959 they have not been singled out in the censuses. Nor will the Crimean Tatars be discussed because, after losing their statehood in 1944, no attributes of statehood have been restored to date. Thus, this chapter deals exclusively with eponymic (titular) ethnoses (ethnic groups), and generally does not touch upon the ethnohistorical dynamics of peoples without statehood and of ethnic factions beyond the boundaries of their "own" Union republics and autonomies. This limitation has been imposed because of the peculiarity of Soviet official statistical publications, which usually separated data in accordance with the administrative-territorial division of the USSR. As much of the data used in this chapter was compiled from the All-Union Censuses, the ethnohistorical dynamics studied here are restricted to the time period covered by the first and the last Soviet censuses, that is, 1926 through 1989.

Muslim Societies and Their Existential Structures

A significant and complex process—from the "initial absorption" to the new "historical rediscovery"—is prevalent over the entire social fabric of the Muslim societies of the former Soviet Union. For the process to be studied correctly, one must scrutinize the dynamics of historically inherited *existential structures* permeating ethnic consciousness. These structures have been developed by every ethnic group during the course of decades of Soviet (and centuries of pre-Soviet) history, but they are not just withered remains of the past. On the contrary, being inseparable from the present way of life of the ethnic group and its current changes, they are flexible and capable of a partial and often very deep transformation. Despite any negative influence occurring during the course of history, those structures cannot be destroyed completely and replaced by entirely new ones. Their framework is built of very solid bricks—those facts of personal life that, repeated and multiplied in the lives of many men and women of the ethnic group, grow to be the *longue durée* structure, the structure that continuously characterizes and eternally perpetuates the mode of existence of the ethnic group.[1]

Ethnic existential structures determine not only the objective dimensions of the historical action of an ethnic group but also the power of this action, its direction, and the very set of those unconsciously preferred forms of activities in which it expresses itself. It is obvious that the real potential and results of ethnic politicization depend to a great extent on what the ethnic existential structures were before Sovietization, how they changed throughout the Soviet period, and where the balance of their continuity and change is now. This is why the dynamics of these structures offer a valuable, though difficult, task for a researcher to study.

One can envisage numerous ethnic existential structures. It was necessary to revise their inventory to place the study within reasonable limits. The rationale for compiling a list of these structures was their origins as traced back long before recent ethnopolitical developments. Furthermore, whether some statistical data were accessible had to be taken into account. Thus, *geopolitical, intraconfessional, linguistic, ethnic,* and *settlement* structures were selected and analyzed over the censuses period. Their dynamics proved to be complicated. Some of the existential structures demonstrated striking stability, while others were more susceptible to the impact of Soviet history. The following generalizations can be suggested: (1) taking 1926 (or sometimes a more distant benchmark) as a reference point, all structures of any given Muslim society suffered considerable damage, though to different degrees; (2) structural changes were characteristic of all societies, while the deepest ones occurred among the Muslims of Russia; (3) no structures were uprooted, that is, all of them are alive and now determine ethnic politicization.

Geopolitical Structure

The long-term spatial tightening of the geopolitical structure will be addressed first. As late as the eighteenth century, Muslims of the Crimea, Transcaucasia, and the Central Asian khanates formed an integral part of the Islamic world. On their northern frontiers various societies could be found: free communities and ephemeral seminal principalities of Caucasian highlanders and Turanian nomads. Only Bashkirs and Kazan Tatars were under the rule of the "White Tsar." Then, the entire nineteenth century and the major part of the twentieth were marked by Russian expansion. Stalin completed the fifteen-decade-long Crimean saga: in the 1940s the peninsula was de-Islamized and Russianized. Since the Caucasian War and Adygeis' exodus to Turkey, the glorious Circassia of Lord Palmerston's dreams had disappeared, and only tiny fragments survived, surrounded by a growing Cossack population. Muslims of the northeast Caucasus were more successful, yet numerous Russian *stanitsa* (villages) sprang up there as well. Russians also settled and ploughed vast tracts of lands in Beshkiria, North Kazakhstan, and Semirech'ye; they even took root in the Fergana Valley and lower reaches of Syr Darya.

The central authorities used to protect the integrity of the empire vigilantly, thus prior to 1917 no administrative units were permitted to be carved out and treated as national cells. Since the October Revolution however, dozens of national polity formations have been created by the Kremlin leadership. To be sure, their symbolic sovereignty was under the rather malevolent auspices of top officials, yet nationalities did become the legal criteria for organization of territory. Lately the Muslim-Russian line of demarcation has shifted inversely, Crimean Tatars are infiltrating their motherland, and plans for the return of the descendants of the *muhadjirs* (immigrants) are being discussed in the Caucasian capitals, while Russian-speaking settlers are leaving Muslim areas. Concurrently, the administrative hierarchy is being challenged and all Muslim autonomies are promulgating their sovereignty as republics, while Volga Tatars and Chechens, striving for total independence, are threatening Russia's territorial integrity.

It is interesting to look at the impact of geopolitical structure on the political situation. Within Russia, two types of Muslim societies are discernible by virtue of their spatial location. The first group, the societies of Adygeya and Tatarstan together with Bashkortostan, form two classic enclaves. Daghestan with Chechnia and Ingushetiya and Kabardino-Balkaria with Karachayevo-Circassia merge into two Muslim zones of peripheral locations, with Northern Ossetiya separating them. Within the CIS there are two groups of zonal location. The first of these consists of Kazakhstan and the newly born states of Central Asia, stretching from the southern outskirts of the CIS to its geopolitical center. The structural characteristics of both the periphery and the core are present in this zonal location. The second group, separated by the Caspian Sea, is constituted of Azerbaijan, Daghestan, and Chechen-Ingushetiya. Its peripheral location is obvious. Nakhichevan, a small adjunct to Azerbaijan, is certainly an enclave. Adygeya and Tatarstan plus Bashkortostan hold the same position. In addition, Karachayevo-Circassia with Kabardino-Balkaria, besieged by the Krasnodar Territory, Georgia, and pro-Russian Ossetiya, also turn into enclaves.

Finally, and also very important, is the scope of the Middle East. There the picture appears to be pretty familiar, except that Nakhichevan ceases to be an enclave. But one can doubt this spatial impression because of some meaningful dissimilarities. The CIS has its focal point within the Kiev–Moscow–Alma-Ata triangle, while the Middle East fell somewhere between Tehran, Kabul, and Riyadh. Accordingly, if taken as a part of the CIS, Kazakhstan shares its core identity with Russia, while as a member of the Islamic world the republic finds itself playing its ancient role as the Muslim frontier. On the contrary, the geopolitical status of the four southern republics is undergoing a favorable change: in the CIS they form the periphery, but when joining the Middle East they add their spatial strength to the vastness of the Islamic heartland. The Caspian zone also juxtaposes the Middle East, with Azerbaijan gravitating toward its nucleus and highlander societies regaining the status of forefront bulwark. Then, the Ossetian splinter entraps, in enclave, the Muslim people settled over the northwest Caucasus; likewise, the Volga Tatars and Bashkirs continue to be isolated from the rest of the Islamic world.

Intraconfessional Structure

The intraconfessional structure can be described as having three characteristics. The touchstone is the adherence of the ethnos to a particular school or branch of Islam. In this respect, the eponymic Muslim societies of Russia and the CIS are divided into an overwhelming Sunni majority and two minorities—Shia (primarily in Azerbaijan) and Ismaili (primarily in Tajikistan and among the peoples of the Western Pamirs). Sunnis, in turn, are subdivided according to different persuasions and

Sufi orders; the most popular of these are the *Hanafi* and *Shafii maz-haabs* (schools) and *tariqats* (paths) of *Naqshbandiah* and *Qadyriah*.

The division based on the depth of Islamization is of no less importance. The best way to judge this is to estimate the spread of Arabic and Persian book knowledge. In this regard, one can see important distinctions between settled tillers and nomadic-seminomadic societies, between rural and urban dwellers, between ethnoses settled closer to the core of the Islamic world and those close to its periphery, between those converted in the days of the glory of Islam and those who joined the religion in the days of its decline. These distinctions are not absolute, manifested only conjointly. Both the Adygei tribes and the Volga Tatars live on the periphery of the Islamic world, but Adygeis did not develop a strong conviction of the Scriptures, with paganism conspicuous throughout the pellicle of Islam. On the contrary, Tatars, in spite of being exposed to extensive Christianization for centuries, represented by 1917 one of the most deeply permeated Muslim societies of the Russian Empire. In this regard they were superior to the Bashkirs, their next-door neighbors. In the Caucasus, the depth of Islamization increases from west to east—from superficial in the Adygei case to quite considerable in Daghestan and Azerbaijan. In Central Asia, the permeation of Islam was strongest in Maverannahr and weakened while moving away from towns and river valleys to steppes, deserts, and mountains.

There is yet another important distinction: for some Muslims, following the ethical commandments of Islam was of prime importance, while others considered the observance of Islamic rituals most important; some turned directly to Allah in their worship, while others sought the mediation of local saints. The relevant division into "high" ("classical") and "popular" ("everyday") Islam was characteristic of all societies under consideration, though it was more clear in some cases and less clear in others. Moreover, some of the centers of deeply rooted "high" tradition (Kazan, Bukhara, Daghestan) cohabited with vast areas of predominantly "everyday" Islam.

The data on changes of the intraconfessional structures in Soviet times is evidently deficient, but it can be stated with confidence that, under the heavy pressure of the state's restrictive policy, the initial correlation of Islamic branches, mazhaabs, and tariqats has been preserved. The relative equalization in atheism of different Muslim societies occurred simultaneously. Everywhere the bulk of believers was substantially diluted with atheists. In the 1937 census, only twenty years after the revolution, approximately 15 percent of the adult Muslim population registered themselves as nonbelievers.[2] At the same time, illiteracy in matters of religion grew among those who remained faithful. "High" Islam suffered serious damage: the development of traditional religious-philosophical thought was undermined after losing its audience; the modernistic branches were uprooted; Muslim education and Koranic knowledge were strictly localized; and the circle of those who were officially allowed to conduct religious services was greatly narrowed. In contrast to this, "popular" Islam consolidated its positions, and as a result, while the sense of confessional fraternity and knowledge of basic Islamic teachings declined, the rituals and local cults not only survived but became the main distinctive signs of ethnicity.

The function of ethnic identification had long been characteristic of "popular" Islam. The socialistic epoch turned this function into nearly the most effective element maintaining and shaping the intraconfessional structure. But the wide expansion of this function was a novelty provoked by state policy. Presently, post-Soviet nationalistic passions threaten to make this transformation irrevocable. Parallel to this are developments that would have seemed the least probable just five years ago. The tradition of Islamic Scriptures is rapidly reviving; "high" Islam is reaching the levels of "popular" Islam, trying to bring the latter closer to itself through religious enlightenment. While often enough the new missionaries themselves had no systematic religious education, their enthusiasm, combined with radical change in the authorities' attitudes toward Islam and with the opening and legalization of many mosques and *madrassas* (Islamic religious schools), lay down quite a solid foundation for Islamic revival.

This revival will not bring about the complete transformation of the prerevolutionary model of intraconfessional structure. At the same time, authentic repetition of this model is impossible because many grandchildren and great-grandchildren of those once faithful have remained nonbelievers. Still, a tendency toward change is obvious, due both to the different way of life that occurred during Soviet times and to new influences. The Soviet legacy and better communications have eroded the previous boundaries between oasis and steppe, town and countryside, knowledgeable and ill-informed religious teachings. It is symptomatic that a newly born Islamic Renaissance Party claims to represent all Muslims of the former USSR. But beside it, or splitting with it, other Islamic parties appear, accentuating their ethnic basis. It is still too early to conclude which of the two tendencies—toward the simplification of intraconfessional structure or toward its reproduction in the previous, or even more complicated form—will take over, though there is no doubt that this structure is no longer a collection of forcefully separated semifossils but, rather, revived historically established, effective, and interactive subdivisions of believers.

Linguistic Structure

There are three linguistic families that constitute the linguistic structure in the societies under consideration: Turkic (Karachai, Balkar, Nogai, Koumyk, Azerbaijanian, Tatar, Bashkir, Uzbek, Karakalpak, Kirghiz, and Kazakh languages); Iranian (Tajik, Yagnob, Shugnan, and other Pamirs languages); and Caucasian, which is divided into Abkhazo-Adygei (Abkhazian, Abazin, and Kabardian) and Nakh-Daghestanian branches (Ingush, Chechen, Avar, Lezghin, Darghin, Lak, Tabassaranian, and the languages of other smaller ethnic groups in Daghestan).

During Soviet times the main elements of the linguistic structure remained intact. Changes in distributional proportions of different peoples according to their linguistic families were not as noticeable. From 1926 to 1960, the share of Turks among all eponymic Muslim peoples decreased from 87.5 percent to 85.5 percent; the proportion of Iranian peoples increased from 5.8 to 8.0 percent; and Caucasians decreased from 6.7 to 6.5 percent. The changes in intrafamilial proportions were more substantial. Thus, within the Caucasian family the share of Adygei peoples fell from 24.7 to 17.5 percent; within the Turkic family, the proportion of Kazakhs decreased from 26.3 to 18.0 percent and the Uzbeks increased from 25.9 to 36.9 percent.[3] The main cause of this proportional redistribution was the difference in numerical growth of the ethnic groups; intrafamilial linguistic assimilation was negligible. Moreover, differences between ethnic and linguistic self-identification caused by this assimilation have been decreasing. In 1926 they were the largest in the case of two peoples: 12.5 percent of Karakalpaks, conscious of their ethnicity, considered other Turkic languages as their mother tongue; this was also the case with 46.2 percent of Bashkirs, though in their case Russianization was also a factor. By 1970 this gap had already been narrowed to 3.4 percent in the first case and up to 32.8 percent in the second.[4]

Thus, the degree of linguistic assimilation was comparatively low and falling, and that of linguistic endurance was high and rising. But in actuality, linguistic dynamics were even more complicated because, first, bilingualism spread widely, and second, the graphics of the written language were radically changed.

The phenomenon of bilingualism had been well known to Muslim societies long before their Sovietization. First of all, the second language used to be a means of mastering book knowledge; Arabic and Persian languages were chiefly used for this purpose. Furthermore, the second language was a language of record keeping and a colloquial lingua franca. Finally, in the areas where two ethnic groups coexisted an almost equal use of two languages in everyday life was naturally established. Prior to the revolution, the Russian language carried out all the above-mentioned functions. But due to communal self-government, legal procedure in accordance with *Adat* (tradition, habit) and *Shariat* (Islamic law), and the fact that Muslim *makhtabs* (schools run by the clergy) and madrassas continued to exist in the majority of Muslim societies, the permeation of the Russian language was comparatively slow and shallow.

The situation changed radically after the creation of the USSR. The Bolsheviks did not aim purposely at linguistic assimilation, and even lifted the ban on the use of vernacular languages once imposed by the tsar's government. But the Kremlin's policy in other spheres greatly influenced the linguistic situation. The Soviet state was built on a single model leaving no space for local institutions. After the extermination of native schools attached to or established by religious bodies, standard cells of the Soviet school were implanted, and thus the compulsory teaching of Russian became the means for the rapid upbringing of the new internationalistic man. Thus, all obstacles were removed from the path of expansion of the Russian language. The introduction of compulsory military service and secondary education made this expansion rapid and all-pervasive. Having taken a firm hold in the Caucasus and Volga region in the nineteenth century, the Russian language had also been instilled into the thick of Central Asia by the end of the twentieth century. According to sociological surveys in the mid-1980s, 49 percent of high school graduates in Uzbekistan and 90 percent of those in Tajikistan considered themselves fluent in Russian; 63 percent of the Uzbek and 93 percent of the Tajik working youth gave the same answer. Even if the respondents overestimated their fluency in Russian, these figures are significant.

It is important to stress that the tempo and scale of the expansion of the Russian language were much higher than the expansion of the Russian culture, which was in poor condition. Actually, this expansion was one of cliché-ridden "neo-lang"; the language of Russian humanism crawled along the side of the road leading to the East. Almost everywhere the Soviet version of Russian has adopted all the functions of the previous bilingualism.

The Soviet-Russian language, once the keeper of bureaucratic records and ideological maxims, had become at once a lingua franca, a language of record keeping, and a language of book knowledge. The former bilingualism used to be an intrinsic possession of Muslim civilization; the bilingualism of the Soviet times, having put an end to the "stagnant" cultural autarky of Sovietized Muslims, also damaged the integrity and endurance of their linguistic structure. This has had the strongest effect on the administrative elite and intelligentsia, that is, those social groups that articulate ethnopolitical tasks and provide for their enforcement. They both have to act with the help of the Soviet-Russian vocabulary, phraseology, connotations, and stylistic cliches. Even when speaking their native language, the mouthpieces of politicizing ethnicity express it as if copied from Russian, borrowing as a rule particles of meanings inseparable from the imported verbal forms.

The transition of written languages from the Arabic to the Cyrillic alphabet, introduced during Stalin's time, accompanied and worsened sociocultural ruptures because, unlike the adoption of the Russian language, the latter process was completely oppressive and momentary. Whatever the defects of the Arabic alphabet might be regarding the phonetic orders of the Turkic, Iranian, and Caucasian languages, proof of its undoubted merit rests in its centuries-long duration. The new alphabetic systems cut off Soviet Muslims from their own cultural heritage, from the heritage of the whole Islamic world, and from the cultural movements of Muslim peoples outside the USSR, which took place in the twentieth century.[5] The new alphabet allowed linguistic endurance in oral speech alone, but in taking into consideration the peculiarities of the spread of the Russian language one might say that only one, although the strongest, substratum of ethnicity turned out to be truly enduring—the colloquial language.

In recent years this situation has begun to change. Languages of eponymic ethnic groups have acquired state status; the transition of record keeping to those languages has been completed; and their importance has grown in the educational sphere, where the hours previously allotted to Russian lessons, physics, chemistry, and biology have been reduced in order to give pupils more time for learning their native languages. At the same time, the teaching of classical Arabic is being revived in schools. All this, however, testifies not so much in favor of the genuine revival of vernacular languages and the extension of their functions and capabilities but in favor of an artificial contraction of the sphere where Russian has traditionally been used, a process dictated by the present political and nationalistic interests. There is little doubt that a reverse movement towards the prerevolutionary linguistic structure exists in general, but it has only manifested itself on a small scale.

Ethnic Structure

The advent of imperial reign did disturb the ethnic structure of Muslim regions, but changes were not uniform. In short, the higher the barriers to be surmounted by Russian officers and colonists—both natural (landscapes, climates, soils, and crops) and societal (well-established ways of economic life, indigenous social institutions, cultural idioms, strength of adherence to Islam)—the smaller the damages suffered by the original ethnic structure. And save the Circassian and some minor cases, all structural innovations issued from slow development, not abrupt changeover. Even there, where newcomers outnumbered natives, both parties usually had enough time to provide mutual adaptation and ethnocultural continuity. In the course of constructing the Soviet Union, the authors of the design followed, though with many retractions, one general rule: the larger portion of the population entitled to have its own republic or autonomy was to be eponymic. Politically, the new formations were hardly noticeable, yet in one sense they were to assume actual importance: within their boundaries incipient national feelings would consolidate and outweigh—or at least equal—traditional loyalties to the local entities and to the totality of the *umma* (community of believers).

Stability was necessary for the process to evolve without much delay, but the initial Soviet decades were turbulent. The ethnic structure had to withstand fierce and recurrent onslaughts when borders of republics and autonomies were recarved, multiethnic capitals raised, entire peoples deported, enormous labor immigration encouraged, atrocities committed against peasants, collectivization established, and sedentarization of nomads achieved before ethnic elements could arrange into a new order. All these developments stirred up ethnic elements before they could arrange into a new order. The ethnic structure appeared to be on the way to radical transformation, but almost all eponymic peoples managed to redeem their structural weights.

In 1926 the ratio of eponymic ethnic groups amounted to 57.1 percent in Kazakhstan, 62.1 percent in Azerbaijan, 66.6 percent in Kirghizia, 70.2 percent in Turkmenia, 74.2 percent in Uzbekistan, and 74.6 percent in Tajikistan.[6] By the end of the 1930s the ratio had plummeted dramatically: it ranged from only 30 percent in Kazakhstan to 62 percent in Uzbekistan.[7] Nevertheless, in 1989 the 1926 figures were exceeded by two republics (87.2 percent in Azerbaijan, 72.0 percent in Turkmenistan), nearly recaptured in Uzbekistan (71.4 percent), and were on the rise in Tajikistan (62.3 percent), Kyrgyzstan (52.3 percent), and Kazakhstan (39.2 percent).[8] Trends in the autonomies are less clearcut, but five of them exhibit a similar trajectory of changes. In Daghestan, Tatarstan, Azerbaijan, and Turkmenistan the eponymic ratio exceeded the 1926 level.

What were the reasons for this remarkable recovery from the damages? According to the most widespread explanation, it was a mixture of traditions, continued preferences for large families, and innovations such as modern health services that somehow produced high birth and low death rates and, finally, the rapid growth of the Muslim population in the USSR. Approached from the perspective of ethnic behavior, an endangered ethnicity often seeks unconsciously to establish its rank in a popular taxonomy of ethnic groups, because this rank is perceived by the people's collective memory as one of the primordial characteristics of ethnic identity. The official hierarchy of Soviet quasi states was, to some extent, the caricature of the same historically approved taxon gradation. It is no wonder, therefore, that the existence of quasi states and the numerical superiority of eponymic ethnic groups within the states contributed, in people's minds, to the validity of claims for sovereignty and independence.

This is confirmed by the fact that as soon as the worst of Stalin's purges had passed the spontaneous self-gathering of Muslim peoples began. Many of those who found themselves in a foreign Soviet Union republic or autonomy—even Muslim—migrated to resettle within their own national formation. Since 1985 the tempo of migration has accelerated under the pressure of political circumstances, that is, interethnic conflicts, as in the case of Azerbaijan, or appeals to return to the "ancestral land" propagated by nationalist media and parties among those settled abroad, as in the case of the Kazakhs.

Settlement Structure

The dynamics of Muslim urban-rural distribution are an appropriate blueprint for the shifts within the settlement structure. On the eve of the Revolution, a great proportion of urban dwellers was of non-Muslim origin. Muslim urban life flourished only in Azerbaijan and in some parts of Turkestan. Even there, Muslim citizens constituted a small fraction of the indigenous people, the highest ratio being observed in the Bukhara emirate: perhaps 12 to 14 percent.[9]

The post-Revolutionary period was characterized by the upsurge of urbanization in the regions of the Soviet East and the significant increase in the numbers of urban dwellers. But the transition from traditional rural ways to urban ones seems to be close to completion only in Tatarstan and, with some reservations, in Azerbaijan. Kazakhstan and the majority of autonomies are en route, while Chechnia and Ingushetiya and all republics of Central Asia are turning back. Indeed, in 1989 their ratios of urban population were slightly lower than those reported by preceding censuses. So we witness the ascendancy of a unique group of Muslim societies; being rural for the most part, they tend to become rural once more in the future.

With regard to Chechnia and Ingushetiya, there are as yet insufficient materials to allow a scholar to arrive at any trustworthy conclusion. Yet it is almost certain that the diminution of the percentage of citizens has roots in the history of urbanization there. In 1926 urban dwellers of the Chechen and Ingush autonomous regions (then separate) totaled four thousand, and hardly a quarter of them were locals. In 1929 the town of Grozny was assigned to the Chechen region as its capital. Obviously, it was hoped that two birds would be killed with one stone: the autonomy would jump onto the industrialization train with the acquisition of the Grozny oil fields, urbanization would increase by twenty-five times, and the number of its urbanized natives would double.[10] As a result, rural and urban sectors declined. Urban growth focused on the town of Grozny. In 1989 nearly one-third of the total population of Chechnia and Ingushetiya (then one republic) and three-quarters of all citizens lived in the capital.[11] Perhaps it is this hyperconcentration of urbanization, artificial from the very beginning, that makes urban dwellers too dependent on the welfare of only one city.

The analysis of the Central Asian experiences is more rewarding. Uzbeks and Tajiks were among the most urbanized subjects of the tsar, but the degree of Kirghiz and Turkmenian urbanization was insignificant. Despite strong distinctions in the past, all four societies showed the same pattern of urban development toward the end of 1970. They rejected the model of settlement structure forced on them from Moscow. The rural-urban settlement structure, having suffered the accommodations necessary in the general frame of the Soviet society, did not undergo an overall transformation. As before, rural ways of life continue to determine people's demographic behavior, their world view, and daily customs, and consequently the pattern of their ethnic reproduction and identification.

Many points confirm this line of argument. As far as one can judge, and based on the analysis of available statistical data, there were two successive waves of urban development during the Soviet years. From the 1920s to the 1960s it was the inflow of Russian labor migrants that took the lead; afterwards, the steadily mounting birthrates of the eponymic urban population made for the lion's share of the increase. And what is often referred to as the main human stock of city replenishment—the stream of rural-urban migration—is almost drying up. On the other hand, the original settlement structure, which survived the assaults of socialist reconstruction, contributes to the restoration of pre-Revolution patterns. Thanks to agrarian overpopulation, many *kishlaks* (villages) outgrow the quantitative boundaries of rural settlement and need formal change of their status to towns and townships. Local authorities, who welcome the expansion of the urban sector as a sign of social progress, do their best, primarily in Uzbekistan, to augment this sector with swollen village agglomerations.[12] In addition, towns such as Bukhara, as examples of early Oriental urbanism, have kept intact their traditional social and spatial organization, and their inhabitants are bypassed by the modernization process inherent in a Europeanlike megalopolis such as Tashkent.

Surely, Tashkent, Dushanbe, Navoi, Nurek, and other urban centers built and rebuilt according to the Soviet standard must not be ignored altogether. However, because of the rapid natural increase of their populations and a rather rigid ethnic division of labor, they have very limited capacities to ensure would-be rural migrants of remunerative wages and salaries. Even if Russians leave, the problems of unemployment and underemployment now haunting urban youth could not be

properly resolved. It is not incidental that the number of people resid-
ing in their birthplace is increasing in the rural areas of Central Asia.

Some features of urbanization common in other Muslim societies
should also be mentioned. Adygeya, which was bestowed with a capital
in the same manner as Chechnia, is imitating the Chechen settlement
structure. Within Daghestan some peoples have already become urbanized, whereas others still cling tenaciously to rural settings. In Azerbaijan, the only indication of further changes is an increase in the share of
eponymic nationality in the total number of the urban population. Between 1959 and 1989 the share of the Azerbaijanis in the urban population of the republic grew by an impressive 25 percent, increasing the
propensity of Azerbaijani cities and towns to become monoethnic.
Only the multiethnic Tatarstan-Bashkortostan enclave, strongly influenced and penetrated by Russian people and Russian culture, can be
cited as a relatively reliable instance of actual, not false urbanization;
only there do the traditional patterns of settlement structure seem to
have been definitely reversed.

Conclusion

The evolution of the existential structures of Muslim societies can be
presented graphically as a series of curves. All of them tend to become
U-shaped. Indeed, every structure has undergone two great cycles of
change. First came destabilization and decline, which could be depicted
as a swift descent of the left branch of the parabola. At a certain point
this descent becomes more and more gradual. Second, at the minimum
point the breakdown comes, giving the impulse to the accelerated ascent of the right branch of the parabola, the reverted upward movement. The process shows a new consolidation of pre-Soviet structural
elements and reinstitutionalization of their cohesion, damaged by Soviet power. If anything, a great outer resemblance between modern existential structures and their old prototypes has been reached.

To a great extent, this was achieved because the trends for change of
various structures overlapped and reinforced one another in terms of
the general search of the societies to recover their ancient structural
order. But the societies of zonal location with coherent geopolitical
continuity have fared better than those of the enclaves. The ascending
branch of the former type has come closer to that initial level of structural stability where the descent started. This fact alone gives an indi-

cation that the recovery has failed to be absolute, the conclusion being valid for both zonal and enclave types of societies, although to different degrees. And there is another telling point. The very shape of the evolutionary curve prevents its starting and finishing points from being superimposed. The horizontal line joining these two points has been broken by those irreversible changes of seventy years that the Muslim peoples of the former USSR were forced to go through. Put another way, the developments of the Soviet era gathered their own momentum, their legacy being only partially nullified by the havoc of the breakdown of the USSR.

I do not, however, pretend that this social engineering brought about a symbiosis between the old and newly introduced elements in the fabric of these societies in a state that could be ever-growing and self-sustaining. Instead, these elements coexisted—sometimes for mutual benefit, sometimes at each other's expense. There was a rough side to the partnership: the continuous inflation of inherited and implanted elements brought structural constraints and set the stage for an overt conflict.

One can say that during coexistence with Russia and the Soviet Union, Muslim societies managed to correct the most serious disjunctions of their sociocultural institutions, which had been condemned in the original ethnopolitical blueprint of the Kremlin. This remarkable ability—to accommodate or adapt to unfavorable historical circumstances without too much of a loss of identity—could be seen as a sign of hope for Muslim societies in their search for full liberation from the Soviet legacy.

The prospects, however, are more complicated in the long run because the results of Muslim societies' experience as "subjects" in history are at best ambivalent, if not gloomy. All Muslim societies paid a high price to keep the balance between continuity and change to the benefit of the former: the vulnerability of geopolitical status; vulgarization of life and indigenous linguistic forms, including vernacular; agrarian overpopulation and pockets of rural poverty; interethnic tensions and aggressive nationalisms; and false urbanization, with its familiar concomitants—urban-rural disintegration, unemployment and underemployment, and deterioration of the environment and the physical infrastructure. And there is also the rapid rise of ostentatious consumption, criminalization of tribal/clan structures, and the decay of traditional moralities and folk culture; the list can go on. It is more important to stress once again that all these historical losses could not pass without leaving a trace; altogether they preclude a smooth transition between the past existential structures and the present ones. Thus, the U-shaped curve of ethnohistorical dynamics never transforms into the classic closed circle, which used to be identified as the very motion of history in the scriptures of the old Muslim Orient.

Notes

1. Paraphrased from Fernand Braudel, *Les structures du quotidien* [from the Russian translation: *Structury povsednevnosti: vozmozhnoye i nevozmozhnoye*] (Moscow: Progress, 1986), 35, 39.

2. For the results of the All-Union Census of 1937, see *Sbornik statisticheskikh materialov 1990* [Collected statistical materials, 1990] (Moscow: Finansy statistika, 1991), 28–39.

3. V.I. Kozlov *National'nosti SSSR: etnodemograficheskii obzor* [Nationalities of the USSR: Ethnodemographical survey] (Moscow: Statistika, 1975), 249–350; *Soyuz* no. 34 (August 1990), no. 39 (September 1990).

4. Kozlov, *National'nosti SSSR*, 211–12.

5. This subject has been studied by several authors. See, for example, Sharif Shukurov, "Yazyk i pis'mennost': razryv traditsii" [Language and script: break of the tradition], in *Ozhog rodnogo ochaga* [Burn of the family health], ed. G. Guseinov and D. Dragunskii (Moscow: Progress, 1990), 109–19.

6. Kozlov, *National'nosti SSSR*, 111–12.

7. Ibid.

8. *Soyuz* nos. 34, 39.

9. Kozlov, *National'nosti SSSR*, 211–12.

10. Computed by: *Poselenniye itogi perepisi 1926 g. po Severo-Kavkazskomu krayu. Rosto-na-Donu: Severo Kavkazskoye krayevoye statisticheskye upravleniye, 1929* [Settlements, results of census of 1926 related to the North-Caucasian region] (Rosto-na-Donu: North-Caucasian Regional Department of Statistics, 1929), 404, 440.

11. *Naseleniye SSSR 1988. Statisticheskiy ezhegodnik* [Population of the USSR: statistical yearbook] (Moscow: Finansy i statistika, 1989), 16, 32.

12. In Uzbekistan the threshold for requalification was leveled down in 1973 by 3,000 residents. As a result, the number of settlements officially classified as urban mushroomed from 42 in 1970 to 124 in 1989. See *Pravda Vostoka*, July 18, 1990.

2

The Emerging Central Asia

Ethnic and Religious Factions

Eden Naby

Issues of ethnicity and religion in Central Asia, for at least the next several decades, must be regarded in the context of Russian imperial expansion, both under tsarist rulers from St. Petersburg and under Soviet Communist ones from Moscow. The reason is that although Russian expansion was motivated by greed for land, trade, and military might, hand in hand with generals and governors marched teachers, priests, and other representatives of a culture whose presence has profoundly affected Central Asian life. In order to understand the trends of current ethnic and religious movements, we need to keep in mind this historical background and its effect on the social psyche of Central Asian societies.

Central Asia today is a society split along political boundaries imposed in the Soviet period. Large and powerful immigrant populations hold key economic power and skilled positions that they are reluctant to give up to local professionals. Significant segments of rural populations effectively live in cultural frames divorced from urban developments. Such patterns may not be confined to the Central Asian successor states of the old Soviet Union, nor to other developing pockets of the world, but in Central Asia it is political artifice and social engineering that have produced the sociocultural mix we see today. Moreover, in Central Asia the tsarist colonial period and subsequent domination by Soviet Russians have exerted greater pressure on society than in any other comparable colonial and postcolonial region of the world other than South Africa.[1] In order to understand the mix, we need to examine its ingredients, for without this understanding we may misread the actual and latent turmoil brewing in the region.

In the following pages I will examine the ethnic and religious factions in Central Asia from my perspective as a resident in Dushanbe,

Tajikistan, from the fall of 1990 almost continuously until December 1991. During this period, Tajikistan became transformed from one of the fifteen republics of the USSR—firmly allied to Moscow and presided over by a pro-Russian leadership—to a politically volatile independent country in the throes of establishing politically legitimate governing bodies. I witnessed the emergence of new religious forces, the competition among them and with secular forces, and, to some extent, the play of ethnicity in political relations. As at this juncture the rigorous and bureaucratic binds loosened considerably, I had the privilege of village visits and extended tours in the eastern parts of both Tajikistan and Uzbekistan. I should note that my past research, too, has been focused on the sedentary indigenous populations of Central Asia and not on those with recent nomadic histories.[2] For these reasons, my focus is on Tajikistan, and to some extent on Uzbekistan, but not on Kazakhstan, Kyrgyzstan, and Turkmenistan, except for purposes of broad contrast and comparison. Moreover, because I have had considerable experience in Afghanistan and with its culture since the 1960s, I shall draw some comparisons with regions of that country as well.[3] In all, what I aim to present are arguments in support of the thesis that the emerging Central Asia can be characterized in its ethnic and religious aspects as follows: (1) the strength of rural forces is relatively unmarked by seventy years of Soviet domination; (2) demographic trends will give political and religious voice to rural forces at the expense of more secularized urban ones heretofore in complete political control with the aid of Moscow; (3) tensions among religious elements pit reformers against traditionalists and political activists against cultural moralists, thus creating a disunified religious picture; (4) ethnicity is emerging as a lesser political force among rural people, while religion is gaining in its overall unifying possibilities; and (5) trends toward confrontation between rural and urban forces can be negotiated more on the basis of religion than on the basis of ethnicity or of its political manifestation as nationalism. To provide a more detailed basis for the discussion, I will begin with a background summary.

The Structure of Ethnicity among Central Asians

Central Asia can be defined as a cultural region that stretches in a northeast line from Khorasan to the Gobi Desert. Definitions of Central Asia based on linguistic affinities, historical relationships, and political spheres may be wider or narrower. But the region from Khorasan to the eastern limits of Xinjiang shares historical culture, a linguistic Irano-Turkic present and past, and similarities in twentieth-century political fate. In its expanse are included modern sovereign states such as Afghanistan and parts of larger states such as the Xinjiang Uighur Autonomous Region of the Republic of China. The additional term *Inner Asia* has been defined far more broadly to include not only the Irano-Turkic culture of Central Asia but also the Tibetan and Mongolian cultures of the region, as well as many less well known ones such as the Yaqut to the east or even the Manchu, and the Chuvash and Gagauz and the Estonians to the west.[4] For our purposes, I shall confine my discussion to those areas included within the scope of this book; that is, the part of Central Asia that tsarist armies had conquered by 1868 and which remained within the Soviet orb after the defeat of local attempts to gain independence after 1917. Despite this narrow geographical definition of Central Asia, in a discussion of ethnicity and religion it is necessary to make a mental note of historically related areas, although at present these areas fall outside the international boundaries of the CIS, the (probably temporary) successor to the old Soviet Union.

One note is needed here to supplement the geographic definition. In Soviet works, the term *Central Asia* has been applied only to the four southern republics of Turkmenistan, Tajikistan, Uzbekistan, and Kyrgyzstan, and not to Kazakhstan. The large, powerful, and compact non-Kazakh population of the latter, as well as a slightly different pattern of inclusion into the tsarist state, continues to make Kazakhstan susceptible to a sufficiently different set of cultural and ethnic forces to warrant its separate treatment in terms of potential political stability and ethnic/religious development. The southern four republics of the old Soviet Central Asia, on the other hand, though divided along nomadic and sedentary traditional social structure, terrain configuration, and historical political activism, nonetheless share several important features that indicate a basically similar political ethnic future: (1) the demographic dominance of the eponymous republic ethnic group to a degree allowing the *possibility* of indigenous political control;[5] (2) relatively uniform Sunni Islamic sect affiliation; (3) a history of interrelationship flowing from the role of the Bukhara as a political pivot; and (4) relatively stronger retention of their cultural identity as apparent through language use and historical pride.

Within southern Central Asia, the Tajiks and Uzbeks share a far greater degree of culture and history than the Kyrgyz and Turkmen do with them or with each other. Despite the difference in language—

Persian for Tajiks and Turki-Uzbek for Uzbeks—the two formed in the past a coherent group that even today retains a unique closeness and, at the same time, competitiveness. The futures of the two republics, now countries, will remain intertwined because of geographical, communications, and trade necessities, regardless of the outcome of the cultural and population issues.

Two Brothers, Two Nationalities

To gain an understanding of ethnicity in Central Asia, it is important to remember the ethnic picture prior to the imposition of Soviet nationality. Basically, the indigenous people can be divided into sedentary and pastoralist, with the pastoralists as well as the sedentarists attached in differing ways to land. Therefore, the Kazakh, Kyrgyz, and Turkmen (and some Uzbek and Karakalpak groups), though nomadic pastoralists, nonetheless had distinct territoriality. In the same manner, inhabitants of the oasis towns and surrounding villages lived on the land, and in more outlying areas hardly experienced political change when rulers changed from Iranian Samanid in the tenth century to Turkic and subsequently from Turkic to tsarist in the nineteenth century. The Mongol conquest, immigration of the Uzbek tribes, the formation of competing political centers and empires, the decline of international trade after the sixteenth century, and the religious division of Khorasan into Shiite and Sunni spheres did disrupt centralizing political organization, the military situation, and the legitimacy of aristocracies. But they did not shake the traditional Islamic society or the life and identity of villagers. No ruling group deliberately determined to change the lives or identities of every member of Central Asian society until the installation of Soviet nationality policy by Stalin, and the continuation of that policy by Moscow since then.

Prior to this, an official, politically significant ethnic identity was important insofar as extended sedentary families or clans and tribes in pastoral nomadic areas were partially based on ethnic association. The confounding of terms such as *Kyrgyz* with *Kazakh*, the invention of terms such as *Kara-Kyrgyz*, and the developing usage of Sart (away from its original use for Indian merchants, to Tajiks, to urban Turkic merchants) all attest to the difficulty that tsarist officials met with in trying to apply their own understanding of ethnic politics to Central Asians. Scholarly discourse notwithstanding, a political identity associated with the Bukharan, Khivan, or Kokandi khanates (the first two

lasted in altered form until 1924) did not exist outside the narrow circles of political power.⁶ Throughout the tsarist period, sedentary Central Asia remained free from imposed ethnic appellations. Bukhara,
ruled until 1920 by descent within an Uzbek clan (the Manghit), insisted on no particular ethnic-based patriotism, although, socially speaking, individuals within the Bukharan khanate could be identified as
being of Tajik, Turk, Tatar, or similar background. In the Samarkand
area, ruled since 1868 directly by tsarist officials centered at Tashkent,
the population was mixed, with some, such as the Urgut, unwilling to
identify themselves with any major group, Uzbek or Tajik, and totally
bilingual. In towns such as Khojent (Leninabad until 1991), the second
largest city in Tajikistan, populations are so intermixed and bilingual
that two brothers born of the same parents in the same location can be
different ethnically today: one can be Uzbek and the other Tajik. Baba-
jon Ghafurov (d. 1977), the well-known Tajik head of Soviet orientalists
from 1956 until his death, is an example of such a situation.⁷

Even if the case of persons in Ghafurov's situation can be dismissed
as belonging to the formative period of Soviet history and therefore
susceptible to ethnic confusion, middle-aged siblings today are found
with the same pattern of ethnic diversity. In such cases, Tajik and Uzbek, as well as Russian, are spoken in the home with equal frequency.
In the many cases of Tajik-Uzbek mixed marriages, the father's nationality and language are often assumed. But particularly when families have moved from one republic to another, one meets siblings
officially registered as different nationalities often enough to give
pause to assertions that ethnic identity is a meaningful source of political allegiance.

In Central Asia hyphenated identities have no place; that is, Soviet
Uzbek distinguished an Uzbek to the north of the Amu Darya from
one to the south, but the term *Tajik-Uzbek* does not exist. Therefore,
during the Soviet period one could be identified as a Tajik in official
documents and live in any part of the Soviet Union without a political
need to reidentify as a Ukrainian if living in Kiev, or a Kazakh if living
in Alma-Ata (the one exception appears to have been that of Tajiks living in Uzbekistan, as discussed below). With the breakdown of the Soviet system, the pressure on non–Central Asians to reidentify or migrate
out of a Tajikistan and Uzbekistan appears to be intensifying, while at
the same time certain groups are using this period of change as an opportunity to assert their ethnic identity as part of a new political
agenda. Because the whole concept of a hyphenated identity has not

existed, Russians or other non–Central Asians who wish to remain in Dushanbe, Tashkent, and other Central Asian towns, and even learn the local language, find themselves in a state of political nonexistence. They cannot become Russian-Tajiks or Uzbek-Russians, because the concept of republic (now state) is rooted in the recognition of ethnicity as the basis of nationality. The argument is often made that Russians (and other non–Central Asians) are departing the area under the threat of wholesale social change toward an Islamic society. Yet even if the eventual Islamic direction of Tajikistan, for example, is not a factor, the underlying assumption that the eponymous ethnic group deserves the privileges of citizenship would effectively prevent nonlocal people from remaining in Central Asia.

Given both the historical uniqueness of the Tajik/Uzbek relationship and the almost haphazard official identities carried by many people in geographically intermixed towns and regions, discussion of the structure of ethnicity among Tajiks and Uzbeks must be treated cautiously. Claims of territoriality and historical legitimacy by Tashkent or Dushanbe require close examination to see what issues—besides ethnic identity—motivate such claims. Some currently identifiable motivations are regional power play within the republic (for example, Khojent's struggle for power within Tajikistan) and economic gain (as in the case of Samarkand, a potential economic dynamo within Uzbekistan whose lucrative future Tajiks may wish to share). Territorial and historical issues have been and continue to be prejudiced by political struggle for power. In the Uzbek and Tajik case, the problems are (1) a blurred historical precedent for the Tajik/Uzbek distinction of culture and ethnicity; (2) the fabrication of historical precedent for ethnically associated issues such as language and culture; (3) a climate of competition for resources as the Soviet Union has disintegrated; (4) the positioning of each former republic to meet border challenges; and (5) the possibility of ethnic purification.[8]

Language, Religion, and Ethnicity

Turkic and Iranian languages have dominated sedentary Central Asian culture for the historical period. This fact reflects the movement of Iranian and then Turkic people within the region as a whole. Whether local people in Central Asia developed from pure Iranian or Turkic stock is immaterial to understanding the role of language in ethnicity.[9] The fact remains that Persian was the cultural language of sedentary

Central Asia into the beginning of this century. Despite the efforts of that grand man of letters, Mir Ali Shir Nawa'i (Fani) (d. 1501), "Turki" (as sedentary Central Asian Turkic was called until the 1920s) did not overtake Persian as the cultural language, though it incorporated a prodigious number of Persian words and phrases. Into the early Soviet period in Bukhara and in Samarkand (as well as in Kashgar, in eastern Turkestan), historians and poets employed Persian. This language usage was not a reflection of ethnicity but a reflection of the prestige and cultural wealth of Persian. Nor did the Uzbek conquests of the sixteenth century and the cleavage of Khorasan into Shiite and Sunni affect the status of Persian. *Tazkiras* (anthologies) even from as late as the early twentieth century attest to the dominance of Persian usage. In those cases where authors chose to write poetry in Turki (as well as Persian) they were always of Turkic background; rarely did persons of non-Turkic background actually write in Turki.

If the past pattern has been that language usage and ethnicity (defined as self-identity or attributed identity) did not necessarily coincide, can we assume that today, also, ethnicity (a politically enforced identity) may exist without a coinciding language component? The answer appears to be a cautious yes, but perhaps for reasons quite different from those of the pre-Soviet period.

In contemporary Uzbekistan and Tajikistan, as in the past, ethnic identity and language usage are distantly related, especially among urban elites. The widespread introduction of Russian into Central Asian society separates members of an ethnic/nationality group in two ways. First, Soviet nationality policy was constructed on the premise that a nationality had a distinct language. If this premise had been strictly applied to individuals, a person who did not speak the ethnic language would no longer have belonged to that nationality group. However, due to the additional premise that Soviet nationalities would converge or even merge to create a single Soviet culture in which Russian would dominate naturally, many Central Asian elites effectively became Russian native speakers without the possibility of adopting Russian nationality. In Central Asia this dichotomy is manifested among many professionals whose working, thinking, and cultural language is Russian but who are officially regarded as, for example, Tajik or Uzbek. Even people among these elites who are still able to speak their own language employ regional dialects limited in vocabulary and stunted in scope. They can no more comprehend a law written in their nationality language than understand a newspaper article or a radio program. The level of alienation that such persons feel during this period of emphasis on the gradual, exclusive use of local language is comparable to that of their Russians friends, who at least have the option to emigrate to Russia, even at great economic disadvantage.

Second, Russian language proficiency became a necessity for education, culture, and advancement in all urban professions. Among some Central Asians, this language proficiency, coupled with immersion in Russian/Western culture, bred a negative attitude toward native culture and language, a Russophile habit shared with immigrant Russians. Thus, although they can never become accepted as Russians, a significant number of middle-aged professionals in Central Asia not only cannot function in their ethnic language but also regard with contempt a language and culture that they associate with rural folk. Comparable cultural alienation in neighboring Iran has been termed *Western-struckness (gharbzadagi)*. The problem may also be conceptualized as similar to the notion of Ottoman (that is, sophisticated and cosmopolitan) as opposed to Turk (country hick) prevalent at the period of the formation of the modern Turkish state. In Central Asia, Russian served as the window to the international world. It was not equivalent with ethnic identity. Ethnicity, in turn, is not a reliable means of evaluating allegiance and political networks.

If language is not a dependable feature of identification, how did people in the past identify themselves, and how do they do so in the shifting present? In both cases, the answer, broadly stated, is the same: through religion, region, and social position. Although the Russian presence makes a decided difference, as in the formation of Russophile elites and the use of Russian instead of the local language, the basic and effective political networks follow the historical pattern to a surprising degree.

Throughout Central Asia, the dominant religious affiliation has been and is Islam. Because Central Asia preserved its religious affiliation faithfully, if not assiduously, it served as a place of refuge for Muslims fleeing persecution. The Hue or Dungans of China, though Chinese in language, took refuge in Central Asia during the nineteenth century persecutions, and large numbers of them now live in communities from Alma-Ata to Komul. In like manner, Central Asians, when faced with a tsarist or Soviet (or Chinese) threat, fled to neighboring Muslim areas for refuge. Until the upheavals in Afghanistan, Central Asian *muhajirs* (Muslims who seek refuge in an Islamic state when their own community is threatened by non-Islamic rule) were to be found in northern Afghanistan.[10] Religion, then, was the main identifying force among sedentary Central Asians vis-à-vis outsiders, especially until the Soviet period.

Within this broad Muslim identity, differentiation existed chiefly along regional lines, a factor only partially erased after seven decades of social engineering. First, the oasis identities were of primary importance: Bukhara, Samarkand, Termez, Marv, Khiva, Khojent, and Kokand. These are the major locations with which people identified even if they or their ancestors lived in villages outside the immediate towns. Those who do not identify with major oasis towns identify with large villages or river valleys, then the smaller village name. By the 1930s patterns of regional identification altered due to the political refocusing of capitals and cultural centers. The newly important cities informally divided to reflect *mahaleh* (quarters) or sections representing the old regional identities. Dushanbe, a village of five hundred persons in 1929, received many immigrants as it became Stalinabad, the capital of the Tajik SSR. To this day, those who emigrated from in and around old Bukhara maintain a formal association and live in proximity if housing is available. This allows them to participate in the life cycles of regional members.[11] For example, when a Bukharan family member dies the mourning meals and services are announced (not by a town crier any longer, but by telephone) to the entire Bukharan community in Dushanbe. Each extended family sends at least one male representative to the male ceremony and a female to the female ceremony. It is important to stress that this community is not necessarily related through marriage, language, or ethnicity but by *region* and *religion*. Indeed, today the language of this transplanted Bukharan community is often a mixture of Russian and Tajik, as well as Uzbek.

Sunni Islam, though the dominant form of Islam in Central Asia, is not the exclusive Muslim affiliation of indigenous people. In Bukhara a large and important Shiite community exists with historical ties in Iranian Khorasan. Many in this community trace their origins to merchant families, others to the raid and enslavement practices of the eighteenth and nineteenth centuries. Though the Shiite community is small (no more than about 100,000), it has been influential in maintaining the Persian language and relationships with Iran. This particular Shiite community, which is Ithna Ash'ara, or Twelver, has always lived in a compact neighborhood in a part of Bukhara called the Juybar. *Tazkiras* of the last century give prominent space to writings of judges and seminary professors from this region. With the thaw in restrictions on Islamic practice, this community has been permitted to reconstruct its mosque, which at present also serves to provide religious instruction for children and adults.[12]

A politically more significant Shiite community (and one that tends to confuse many of those newly entering the Central Asian field) is the large Ismaili-professing multilingual community of Gorno-Badakhshan (Mountain Badakhshan). Located in the Pamir mountains and spilling over into the People's Republic of China (PRC), Pakistan, and Afghanistan, these people belong to the majority Ismaili sect (called Khojas in India, as opposed to the Bohras) whose living Imam is the Agha Khan. Although they form the majority of the population of Gorno-Badakhshan, the Ismailis share this remote setting with the Kyrgyz, who profess the loose Sunni practices of Central Asian pastoralists. During the Soviet period, small urban communities of Ismailis have spread out into Samarkand and Bukhara, as well as Dushanbe, where many have entered the educational and administrative institutions in addition to the Communist, then subsequent parties. Particularly active in the Rastakhiz (Resurgence) and Democratic parties that emerged semilegally during 1990 to challenge the power of the existing Communist party structure, Davlat Khodanazarov, the son of a former mayor of Dushanbe, ran as the major "democratic" opponent of Rahman Nabiev in the controversial 1991 elections.

The Ismaili population was prevented from contact with the Agha Khan since 1927, the last year in which they were able to send their annual tithe to him. It is only with the breakdown of Soviet power that they have reestablished open ties with Ismailis in Afghanistan and neighboring parts of China and are moving toward eventual renewal of ties with the Ismaili community worldwide. Historically often considered heretical by mainstream Islam (even as late as the last century), Ismailis were persecuted and discriminated against under the Amir of Bukhara and by neighboring local rulers. Following World War II, prominent Ismailis began acquiring positions of political power within the Communist party structure of Tajikistan, and today they form one of the contending political forces in Dushanbe, with a strong network of support among the bureaucracy and former Communist party cadres.

Within Tajikistan, the Ismailis represent a special ethnoreligious position for several reasons. First, because of their strategic position in the Pamir mountains on crucial Soviet borders with South Asia and China, they became the focus of attention from Moscow. Initially, their distinct Iranian languages (Shugni, Wakhi, Ishkashimi) were encouraged, but by 1937 all publications in local languages had ceased. The distinct languages remained only on the spoken level until now, when attempts to revive them as written languages are being allowed.[13]

The Ismailis of Tajikistan are among the staunchest supporters of the propagation of Persian and Tajik. Three reasons have persuaded them into this position: (1) Persian, rather than Arabic, is the liturgical language of the Ismailis; (2) Persian/Tajik has served as the interethnic language for the multilingual Ismaili community for much of its history; and (3) Ismailis suffered disproportionately from Uzbek overlords who discriminated against them on religious grounds and, according to Soviet period writings, exploited the Ismailis economically. For these reasons, but especially the last, Ismailis lead the effort to preserve Persian/Tajik, to build ties with fellow Persian speakers, especially among the Iranian postrevolutionary diaspora, and to oppose compromise with Uzbeks.[14] Ismailis naturally remain suspicious of Islamic revivalist activity, and, if anything, favor a secular state and culture. They have already begun the process of forming a politically autonomous republic in eastern Tajikistan out of the old autonomous Gorno-Badakhshan district.

The recent history of the Ismaili community demonstrates how, though distinct in language and religion from other Persian-speaking inhabitants of the area, Ismailis became subsumed into the Tajik nationality. The appellation "Tajik" has traveled over the Pamirs into China, where the religiously similar but linguistically diverse groups around Tashgurghan are also uniformly called "Tajik." This term has gained in usage in Afghanistan for this same religious community and may be spreading to Pakistan as well, where there is little likelihood that the Ismaili community will adopt the language associated with Tajik, that is, Persian, as its general interethnic language. As with other groups in Central Asia, the case of the Ismailis illustrates also the genesis of nationality names, which tend to confuse rather than clarify the complicated relationship between language, religion, and politics.

Likewise, Central Asian areas that were bilingual and nonethnic became ethnically and linguistically distinguished in the Soviet period. Two problems that were suppressed on Moscow's insistence were regions of mixed ethnicity and towns that were predominantly of one or another ethnicity.

The Khojent area of Tajikistan is inhabited by both Tajiks and Uzbeks, or, more accurately, by families who were bilingual and sedentary without concern for belonging to either group. Khojent became a part of Tajikistan in 1929 to give the new republic an economic base. In the midst of internal Tajik political turmoil and conflict with Uzbekistan, the danger that Khojent would break away frightens Dushanbe, while its retention has required a political compromise with supporters of Nabiev and subsequent leaders from his camp that is intolerable for persons from other regions.

Samarkand and Bukhara are prime examples of submergence that, after the breakdown of Soviet power, are emerging as potential areas of ethnic conflict. The populations of these two towns have been historically Tajik, but the two areas are within the boundaries of Uzbekistan. Moreover, the Tajik populations have been culturally and politically suppressed because, despite Soviet law, the tendency has been to force Uzbek identities upon the population. In a campaign led by the first Tajik association to exist in the contemporary period, 35,000 Uzbeks reregistered as Tajiks in Samarkand within one month in 1991.[15] The pressure to become or remain Uzbeks is very strong, however, a pressure made all the more forceful by the presence of large numbers of Uzbeks who have been appointed to government posts and taken up residence in the suburbs.

Chances are slim that Tajikistan will acquire Bukhara and Samarkand, or that other border shifts will take place (for example, Khojent and Osh to Uzbekistan).[16] In large part, even the Uzbekistan Tajik populations, such as similar Uzbek populations in Tajikistan, represent families who have inhabited their area for many generations. They are bilingual, even trilingual with Russian. When they had a chance to move to the newly formed Tajikistan, they chose not to do so. Many claim today that they registered as Uzbeks in the 1930s and 1940s because they were threatened with deportation to the wilds of the Pamirs if they did not. But the likelihood that they will emigrate to Tajikistan is remote. Therefore, the emerging ethnicity of these Tajiks will continue to be a political factor but, in all likelihood, will not lead to redrawing of borders, shifts of population, or ethnically induced bloodshed.

Language and the Alphabet Issue

For most of urban Central Asia and for most professionals, Russian is still an indispensable language. It continues to be important for people who are at the most productive stages of their lives, between the ages of twenty-five and sixty-five. They use Russian for communication, particularly outside their own republics. Although English is gaining rapidly as necessary for international trade and discourse, it will take at least one generation for it to become widely and easily known, even given current enthusiasm for learning it.

A distinct set of problems occurs as the language issue has spilled over from intellectual debate into the political forum. These problems, briefly, are (1) the elevation of local languages to the status enjoyed by Russian; (2) the vocabulary; (3) the relationship to other related languages within the Turkic and Iranian region; and (4) the alphabet.

The first problem emerged with the formal appointment in 1989 of the language of the ethnic majority in each republic as the official and national language. Except in Kazakhstan, all the republics/countries operate under the assumption that Russian will eventually be replaced by the national language. Forcing the local language to function as the language for all fields, from agronomy to diplomacy, has put a great deal of pressure on languages that had receded into the increasingly narrow confines of creative literature. Academies of science, which had shunned publishing works in languages other than Russian, have adopted the reverse policy and now exclude manuscripts that are not in local languages. A by-product of this is the relegation to secondary roles of those nonindigenous scholars who cannot function in the local language.

The second problem occurs as pressure mounts on local languages to substitute non-Russian vocabulary for political and scientific terminology. This has led to the creation of committees similar to the Academie Francaise or the Farhangistan in Iran.[17] These committees debate and decide among usages, such as whether the word for the Russian *respublika* (republic) should be the Iranian-used *jumhuri* or the Turkish (and Arab)-used *jumhuriyat*.[18]

The third problem arose as committees formed to translate all government documents and forms from Russian into local languages. The dilemma is, should the documents be simply translated from Russian, thus retaining the Soviet format, or should Turkish and Iranian documents, based on international standards, be adapted for local usage? At the same time, the proliferation of publications, especially newspapers, together with the widespread opportunities to read and hear related languages from outside the Soviet sphere (from Turkey, Iran, and Afghanistan, specifically), has resulted in a breakdown of the standards of language as it had been defined following the delineation of republics. In Uzbekistan, acquisition of Turkish polite conversation and common forms has become desirable, while in Tajikistan the influence of Iranian Persian is becoming increasingly apparent on the printed page and other media. While this shift toward the adoption of terminology and even syntax from Iran and Turkey is appealing to urban intellectuals, an unanticipated problem of comprehension is appearing; namely, the breakdown of standard written forms of Uzbek and Tajik means that in the countryside, where the village dialects were already relatively removed from the standard Tajik studied in schools, an added barrier to media comprehension is being created by the Tehranization of Tajiki, or the Istanbulization of Uzbek. This distance created in language may further alienate urban and rural populations from each other.

The fourth problem is the alphabet. The modified Cyrillic alphabet, used in a slightly different form for each of the Central Asian languages, has come under attack as a vestige of Stalinism, unsuited to Central Asian languages, a barrier to pre-Soviet culture, and an impediment to communication with neighboring areas such as Turkey and Iran. Aside from its having been imposed by Stalin during the 1940s, this alphabet enforces a closeness with the Russian language that many resent. Moreover, it creates orthographic barriers among Turkic people who may be able to comprehend each other's written words (better) with a uniform alphabet. As a consequence of these arguments against Cyrillic, proponents of the Latin and Arabic alphabets have pressed for the adoption of one of these. For the Latin alphabet, two advantages are apparent: knowledge of this alphabet would make entry into the Western world language and alphabet systems simpler (for students, businessmen, and so forth), and interacting with Turkey would become that much easier. For the Arabic alphabet the strongest arguments are historical and religious: knowledge of this alphabet would open the door to reading the rich Central Asian culture of the pre-1923 period, and the Arabic alphabet would help in reading the Koran and other religious materials. Additionally, the adoption of the Arabic alphabet would facilitate communications with the rest of the Islamic Middle East, with the exception of Turkey.

For Tajikistan, the Arabic alphabet appears to present the fewest problems, since the rich resources of books and materials from Iran provide an incentive. The teaching of Tajik in the Arabic orthography is gaining ground daily.[19] For Uzbekistan, the alphabet decision cannot be made in light of pressures from religious elements that are balanced by secular arguments for closeness to Turkey.

It remains clear that the alphabet decision, even when made, can be implemented in measured steps to avoid creating illiteracy. In societies that have lost much local autonomy of culture in the Soviet period, with almost universal literacy as one of the few real advantages, rapid alphabet dictate could be as crippling as the previous dictates to Latin in 1928 and Cyrillic in 1940 have been. Universal literacy remains a cultural, economic, and political advantage not to be lightly discarded. Therefore, the implementation of alphabet policy will require a transitional period, even after the political decision is taken. For this reason, the Cyrillic alphabet, like the Russian language, will function for at least one generation, not as a signal of ethnic or political identity but for purely practical reasons.

Ethnicity and Nationality Realities

The general outlines of the Soviet nationality policy are well known, since they have been studied widely as part of the Cold War dissection of the Soviet system.[20] In Central Asia, the realities of the system functioned differently from its formalities. In form, each of the five republics of Central Asia had the political assets of territoriality and sovereign structure constructed around a core nationality that in most cases represented the majority of the population. Immigration by Western populations, voluntary and as part of political prison groups, shifted the proportions of local to outsider quite dramatically in the administrative centers throughout, and, in Kazakhstan, in the countryside as well. It is because of this large Russian, Ukrainian, and German population manning mineral exploitation resources in northern Kazakhstan that the ethnic and religious picture in this northern republic emerges differently from areas to the south. All of the Central Asian republics can claim, with President Akaev of Kyrgyzstan, that several dozen nationalities are represented in the republic.[21] But what does this mean for ethnicity and religion and for future trends?

Today Central Asia faces a very different attitude toward nationality than that formally embraced during the Soviet period. First, the emergence of religious practice and institutions into the open, the restructuring of these institutions, and the political role of religious figures all begin to overshadow not only the defunct Communist party but also the nationality system it supported. For example, the newly formed Islamic Renaissance party (IRP) in Tajikistan has as a key plank in its platform the irrelevance of ethnic and national identity. Although it is true that this party formed initially as an all-union organization—and therefore, on the pattern of the "Soviet man," aimed for integration as

Muslims—the party formed with local republic-based units, which at the same time are divorced, in theory, from the ethnicity of each republic. In the same manner, the *madrassas* in Bukhara and Tashkent, though functioning in Uzbekistan, were not ethnically associated but rather served the need for trained leaders throughout Soviet Islam.

Though the importance of these two madrassas is diminished by the emergence of many madrassas throughout Central Asia, even the new ones in capital cities (as in Dushanbe) function not as Tajik madrassas primarily but as Islamic ones. Uzbek students also attend (though it must be said that the curriculum emphasizes Arabic, then Persian, with no Turkic component).[22] The revival of Islam in Central Asia confronts the same dilemma of universalist religions everywhere; this is the danger of becoming an ethnic preserve.

With the structure of imposed Soviet nationality policy coalescing into a formal sovereign national structure, it is even more important to distinguish between state and ethnicity. In the old system, ethnic identity was given paramount place and was enshrined as nationality. After seventy years, nationality is emerging as a nation-state. In this process, the weakness of ethnic identity may become even more apparent as the nation-state accommodates the diversity of ethnicity within its borders—even local indigenous diversity.

Rural and Urban Forces

Notable throughout sedentary Central Asia is the fact that local populations are scattered in the countryside, while outsiders tend to live in the cities. The difference in the life-style and worldview of city dwellers and country dwellers, then, is in part shaped by the presence of influential foreigners, among whom the Russians are demographically the most important.[23] Tatars, also largely urban, represent a slightly different issue because they march in the forefront of the Islamic revival when they are not secularized.

The presence of Russians has deeply affected the cultural picture over the past decades, but rural populations have remained immune to foreign presence. True, cinema, radio, and now television have had some effect on rural cultural life, but the effect has been minimal, whereas in the cities the Russian presence and Soviet insistence has meant the expenditure of large sums for the maintenance of opera and ballet troupes, performance sites, and the entire support network for the establishment of Western culture in Central Asian garb.[24] Today, as

Central Asia emerges from its Soviet past, financial support of such institutions is being questioned by a public that is no longer afraid to withstand Russian insistence. As Russian presence and power diminish, so too will the voices of those local people, largely secular in culture, who supported urban, Soviet-style culture. Without passing judgment on the value of these institutions, it is clear that local populations do not participate in these manifestations of Western culture. Rather, local populations prefer entertainment from neighboring regions, such as India or Iran, or locally influenced programs by music and dance ensembles.

In the countryside, traditional forms of culture persist. The teahouse served as a meeting place for men, and women's culture took place within the family and among neighbors, as it still does. After the breakdown of Soviet power, the ubiquitous teahouse served regularly as a surrogate for mosques, which were either shut down or taxed out of existence. Over and over, when mosques were closed, local leaders accommodated the new Communist structure by holding prayers in teahouses and clubs, however surreptitiously.[25] Although this may have been true even in parts of towns, it certainly was true in the villages and smaller towns.

With the political freedom to again openly construct mosques, in much of the Tajik countryside from Panjikent to Aini mosques are being constructed utilizing donated work time by craftsmen, in-kind contributions of materials, and money collected and extracted door to door.[26] This is also true in Syr Darya towns and villages, as well as in the Fergana Valley.

The effect of the surfacing of religious life is that village and *kolkhoz* (collective farm) dwellers find themselves once more at odds with city dwellers, who often are secularized and culturally Westernized. Since the majority of local populations live in the countryside, the force of religious culture is beginning to make itself felt in the large towns and especially at teaching institutions that draw their students from the countryside. At Dushanbe schools of higher education, the observance of fasting during Ramadan is becoming widespread, as is the observance of *hijab* (modest female dress).[27]

Such activity creates tension between those of rural origin and urban dwellers. The tendency is for urban dwellers to worry about the departure of Russians (also Russian Jews and Tatars), which removes the support for secular culture. Although this emigration creates professional opportunities (especially for urban Tajiks and Uzbeks), in Dushanbe the fear of the emergence of an Islamic culture as in Iran or Afghanistan haunts many households, especially those who are anxious about the future of their daughters. Rural dwellers appear to regard the changing sociopolitical conditions as an opportunity to reinvigorate local language, culture, and positions of power voluntarily or involuntarily being vacated by Russians, Russophiles, and entrenched, though renamed, Communist party cadres.

Conclusion

While ethnicity and religion configure into the prospects for stability in Central Asia, with the loosening of Moscow's restrictions on political and religious expression we see a reactive response on both of these issues rather than a creative one. Small groups such as the Ismailis are voicing their grievances and desires at the same time that religious leaders on local and republic levels are attempting to reconstruct institutions, forge an Islamic society (moral or political), or simply compete for power. Whereas before the Soviet period ethnicity did not serve as a major source of identity and language use was not a major issue, today, in the nation-states that are emerging on the territories of the republics, ethnicity must translate into patriotism and language must serve as a communications tool on many sophisticated levels. The questions that Central Asians confront in terms of ethnicity and religion are basically three: (1) To what extent has the dominant ethnicity of each republic overcome regional and linguistic differences? (2) Can the individual languages survive as national languages in light of linguistic diversity and without the scientific and educational strength of Russian? (3) Given significant divergence between rural and urban elements, roughly divided into secular and Islamic perspectives on the future, and the minority but politically potent non-Sunni population of southern Central Asia, can the introduction of Islamic politics bring stability in the aftermath of the Communist party's disintegration?

The focus on ethnicity as a key to understanding Central Asian politics follows from the political importance of Soviet nationality policy in studies of Central Asia. With the breakdown of the Soviet Union, the assumption that ethnicity would automatically translate into "national" identity, with the eponymous republics being transformed into "states," is being challenged. The main challenge currently is evident in Tajikistan, where there is a weak self-identity of regions with the Tajik republic. These regions do not wish to be transformed into a Tajik state on the terms hitherto dictated by Dushanbe. Islamic leaders have joined and indeed lead in the political struggle, less as regional or ethnic figures than as religious leaders commanding respect across ethnic lines. Despite the homogeneity and therefore consensus possible under an Islamic umbrella, secular and Ismaili competitiveness threaten any unity forged by Islam. Appeals to Tajik ethnicity offer little hope for rescuing the situation from chaos, because the Tajik ethnic components are heavily mixed with Uzbek components in nearly all respects except language. Appeals to Islamic identity may also be defeated due to secular and Ismaili interests. Thus a stalemate has emerged that—if nothing else—can lead to the hasty departure of non–Central Asians (including the hundreds of Russian military families along the Afghan border). The fear of a close working relationship with related people across international borders, especially in Afghanistan and Uzbekistan, which would influence the political balance in southern Central Asia, may mean that Moscow will relinquish its military position reluctantly for the time being. In the short run, Tajikistan's significant economic problems can only be aggravated by the political stalemate as Western aid and trade missions steer a wide path away from Dushanbe.

Notes

Author's note: This material was first presented in conference in spring 1992. Subsequently, two versions of the article were printed, in the *Iranian Journal of International Affairs* (1992) and the *Central Asian Survey* (1993). The present article has additional modifications, though it basically adheres to the arguments and conclusions presented in 1992.

1. Similarly, Eastern Central Asia, or the Xinjiang Uighur Autonomous Region, as it is known in Chinese parlance, which came under direct Chinese colonial pressure also during the last quarter of the nineteenth century, continues to be governed as a colonial outpost.

2. The research I conducted in Tajikistan concerned cultural transition during the early twentieth century as Soviet cultural patterns became imposed on Tajik and Uzbek society. See also Eden Naby, *Central Asian Literature in Transition: Tajik and Uzbek Prose Fiction, 1909–32* (Ph.D. diss., Columbia University, 1975).

3. See, for example, my article "The Ethnic Factor in Soviet-Afghan Relations," *Asian Survey* 20, no. 3 (1980): 237–56. See also, coauthored with Ralph Magnus, *Mullah, Marx and Mujahid* (Boulder, Colo.: Westview Press, forthcoming).

4. See a comprehensive discussion by Guy G. Imart, *The Limits of Inner*

Asia: Some Soul-Searching on New Borders for an Old Frontier-Land (Bloomington: Indiana University Press, 1987).

5. The official census shows that Kazakhs form only 39 percent of the population of Kazakhstan, whereas the following proportions exist in the southern
republics: Kyrgyz, 75 percent; Tajik, 78 percent; Turkmen, 82 percent; Uzbek,
86 percent (of 20 million total).

6. Timur Khocaoglu has argued that by 1924 a Bukharan nationality had
begun to emerge which included the several ethnic groups that lived in the old
Khanate, including Tajik, Uzbek, and Turkmen. See "The Existence of a Bukharan Nationality in the Recent Past," in Edward Allworth, ed., *The Nationality
Question in Soviet Central Asia* (New York: Praeger Publishers, 1973), 151–58.

7. For an English language biography of Ghafurov, see my "Bobodzhon Gafu-
rovich Ghafurov, 1908–1977," *Slavic Review* 37, no. 2 (1978): 283–85.

8. The towns of Bukhara and Samarkand, awarded to Uzbekistan under
Stalin, were largely populated by Tajiks (Persian-speaking people). Today these
two towns are dominated by in-migrating Uzbeks who have settled into government positions and the high-rise suburbs of the two towns. Altogether
about one million Tajiks live in Uzbekistan. Similarly, 24 percent of the population of Tajikistan is identified as Uzbek. For a Tajik perspective on Samarkand and Bukhara see James Critchlow, "Tajik Scholar Describes a Source of
Ethnic Discontent," *Report on the USSR* 2, no. 8 (1990): 19–20.

9. Not surprisingly, perhaps, a war of words about the authenticity of Uzbek
or Tajik ethnic identity has engaged otherwise respected scholars from Dushanbe and Tashkent. The Tajiks argue for the Iranian origins of Central Asian
culture, while the Uzbeks lay counterclaims to a historically unsupported pre-
Iranian Turkic settlement of Central Asia. For background to the historical relationship between Tajik and Uzbek see A. Samatov, *Uzbek-Tajik adabiyoti:
Usaro aloqalar-Uzaro Ta'sir* [Uzbek Tajik literature: Mutual relations, mutual
influences] (Tashkent: 1990), also Muhsin Umarzoda, "Ma'nii Tojik'," in *Darsi
Kheshtanshinosi* (Dushanbe: 1989), 68–87. For the medieval relationship between the two see the excellent article by Maria Subtelny, "The Symbiosis of
Turk-Tajik," in *Contemporary Central Asia in Historical Perspective*, edited by
Beatrice Manz and Alexandra Vacroux (Boulder, Colo.: Westview Press, forth-
coming, 1994).

10. See especially the research of Audrey Shalinsky on this subject, as in "Islam and Ethnicity: The Northern Afghanistan Perspective," *Central Asian Survey* 1, no. 2 (1984): 77–85.

11. I am indebted to Mr. Kamoluddin Sadriddinovich Aini for alerting me to
the existence of Bukharan, Samarkandi, and Khojandi *mahaleh* and accompany-
ing networks in Dushanbe.

12. The mosque is popularly known as the *husayniya*, normally the term
used for the special compound in which the memory of the second grandson of
the Prophet is commemorated through pageant and services. That the sur-

rounding Sunni community uses this name indicates the emphasis on the eschatological separation between Sunni and Shiites.

13. Due to the small numbers within each of the Ismaili language groups, the prospects for the propagation of the languages in written form remain dim *without* cross-border cooperation among all the speakers of the particular language. Thus far the Ismailis of Afghanistan pose the only viable community with hopes of interacting with the Tajik Ismailis.

14. A Pamiri historian, Rahim Masov, director of the Tajik Institute of History, has published an especially vindictive account of the republic division of the 1920s in which he has highlighted Uzbek duplicity in acquiring the city of Samarkand. See *Istoriia Topornogo Razdeleniia* (Dushanbe: Irfon, 1991).

15. This information comes from my meeting with leaders of the group in Dushanbe in February 1991.

16. During May 1992, a crucial month in which demonstrations in Dushanbe threatened to dislodge the Khojandis from power, Khojent threatened to secede to Uzbekistan. President Karimov of Uzbekistan immediately issued a statement from Tashkent eschewing Uzbekistan's wish to include Khojent within its boundaries. *FBIS-SOV* 92-138, p. 10.

17. For a discussion of the work of the Tajik Terminology Committee see John R. Perry, "Tajikistan's Language Law: Two Years On," *Association for the Advancement of Central Asian Research Bulletin* 5, no. 2: 3–4.

18. In Tajikistan the Iranian form was chosen, while in Uzbekistan the Turkish/Arab form has been adopted.

19. Dushanbe received from Tehran twenty thousand alphabet primers in time to distribute for use during the 1992–93 academic year. Some of this number were intended for schools in Bukhara and Samarkand. Personal communication from K. S. Aini on 7 October 1992 in Cambridge, Mass.

20. Among the first to examine nationality issues in Central Asia was Edward Allworth, ed. and contr., *Soviet Nationality Problems* (New York: 1971).

21. Akaev has been admired for this seemingly magnanimous attitude because he speaks in terms considered correct by his Western observers and because he may well represent the more ethnically tolerant attitude of Kyrgyz intellectuals as opposed to Tajik or Uzbek ones. Nonetheless, this does not diminish Uzbek anxiety about perceived Kyrgyz ethnically directed barbarism against Uzbeks during the 1990 clashes in the Fergana Valley. Despite the widely circulated conciliatory statements from Tashkent about the historical brotherhood of Uzbeks and Tajiks, Bukharan and Samarkandi Tajik delegations to the major Tajik cultural conference in Dushanbe were prevented from attending, according to Tajik intellectuals from Dushanbe. For President Karimov's statement on this occasion see, *FBIS-SOV* 92-178, p. 36.

22. This information is derived from an interview with Mulla Jafarov at the madrassa in Dushanbe, conducted in November 1991.

23. Even when Russians live in rural areas, they tend to live in closed pro-

fessional communities such as those around hydroelectric installations or chemical, mining, and other technically advanced projects. Census data indicates that rural Russian residents, like rural Chinese residents in Xinjiang, are far more segregated from their indigenous neighbors than the situation that exists in the urban environment.

24. For a study of nonliterary urban culture in Tashkent and Dushanbe, see my "Tajik and Uzbek Nationality Identity: The Non-Literary Arts," in Allworth, *Nationality Question*, 110–22.

25. I am grateful to my students at the Pedagogical Institute in Dushanbe for hosting visits to small towns and rural areas where opportunities to meet with elders revealed information about the preservation of Islamic life. These interviews took place during March 1991.

26. Door-to-door collections may not always benefit the local mosque as claimed, but may be scams. Resentment was tempered by fear of reprisal among secular Dushanbe residents in March 1992 when, during the fasting month of Ramadan, neighborhood collection increased. Based on personal observation.

27. I observed and discussed these matters with university-age students during the spring of 1991 in Dushanbe and Tashkent.

3

Muslim Central Asia

Soviet Development Legacies and Future Challenges

M. Nazif Shahrani

The collapse of the Soviet regime following the failed coup of August 1991 in Moscow marked the end of a long and, for the most part, agonizingly painful era in the history of Muslim peoples of Western Turkestan (former Soviet Central Asia). More specifically, it marked the end of centuries of gradual and systematic incursion, penetration, and, eventually, total control of the region by the economically motivated, ideologically driven, and technologically and militarily powerful Russian and Soviet colonial powers. These prolonged and often traumatic encounters of Turkestani Muslims with the agents and forces of tsarist Russia and, since the 1917 Bolshevik Revolution, with the overwhelming and oppressive force of the Soviet state, represent a form of colonial experience that has had distinctive, powerful legacies and lasting transformative effects upon the region, its peoples, and its cultures.

In the wake of euphoric celebrations of the failure of Communism and the recent declaration by Francis Fukuyama of the "end of history" heralded by the apparent triumph of Western capitalism and liberal democracy,[1] it is easy to overlook or even dismiss the considerable "developmental" policy successes and legacies of the Soviet system, especially in post-Soviet Muslim Central Asia.[2] The full extent of the impact of Soviet rule (both positive and negative, constructive and harmful) and its real and potential effects upon post-Soviet Central Asian societies and cultures may not be known for some time yet. It is crucial for us at this juncture, however, to examine why many Western Sovietologists assume that Soviet policies in Central Asia failed, especially in view of the fact that these scholars and experts of Central Asian affairs loudly and repeatedly warned that Islam and Muslims of

Central Asia posed the most serious challenge to the Russian-dominated Communist system of the former USSR.[3] With perfect hindsight we now know that the former Soviet Central Asian Muslims did not play any significant part in the demise of the Communist regime in Moscow, but the prevailing political and economic realities in post-Soviet Central Asia are quite the opposite of what experts predicted. That is, the national Communist parties continue to rule in all the independent Central Asian republics, albeit under altered party names. The emergent opposition movements are relatively weak, ineffectual, and lethargic, and the Central Asian public, while reacting rather passively to the fall of the Communist regime in Moscow, apparently supports the continuation of Communist rule in their home republics. Why? It is argued in this chapter that these patterns of political responses among Communist party leaders and opposition movements in the independent republics, as well as the reactions of the Central Asian public to the historic events in Moscow, testify to the considerable success of the Soviet "modernization" and "development" policy goals in the region, and not their failure.

It is argued in this chapter that, in spite of the apparent dismal failure of the Russian-formulated and -implemented Communist model for the construction of a progressive, modern, industrialized, socialist system in the former Soviet Union, Soviet developmental policies in Muslim Central Asia have enjoyed a considerable degree of success economically, politically, and culturally. This is particularly so when the consequences of Soviet policies are viewed from the perspective of the Central Asians themselves—the targets and objects of Soviet Russian development policies. It is important to note, however, that while Russian and Soviet developmental policies succeeded in furthering Russian national interests in Central Asia, these policies were not necessarily advantageous to the peoples of the region.

The problems with the generally pessimistic assessment of Soviet policy achievements in Central Asia by Western Sovietologists are twofold: theoretical and methodological. Theoretically, the discussions of Soviet policies in Central Asia are either couched in terms of theories of colonialism or theories of modernization and development based primarily on the experiences of the so-called "developing" societies of the "free world." Those analyzing the Central Asian situation from the standpoint of theories of colonialism have often acknowledged manifestations of considerable changes due to the heavy-handed enforcement of Russian policies in the region, but they may also have exaggerated the extent of cultural and attitudinal resistance to change. For example, one well-known authority, with obviously a great deal of sympathy for the Muslims of Central Asia, has asserted that "the twelve decades of Russian rule may have altered the ways people in the region work, behave and think, *but not the basic values and beliefs that pervade the society and create its attitudes*" (emphasis added).[4] Nevertheless, it is important to point out that values and beliefs are neither entirely detached from what people think and do nor are they immune to the forces of cultural change, especially when change is attempted through the systematic intervention of a powerful modern state such as the former USSR.

On the other hand, those who have applied the yardstick of theories of modernization to evaluate Soviet political and economic achievements in Muslim Central Asia have often judged, and indeed misjudged, the Soviet efforts as failure because these observers measured the outcome of Soviet policies in Central Asia in terms of their deviance from the presumed path taken by Western "developed" societies, or imagined Soviet ones, rather than in terms of Moscow's own goals and objectives in the region.[5] Therefore, advocates of "failed modernization" in Central Asia, while considerably empathetic to the peoples of the region, also appear to misconstrue Soviet accomplishments in the area. For instance, another well-known authority on former Soviet Central Asia states that, "stripped of political rhetoric of the 'achievements of socialism' and 'benefits of fraternal assistance,' the fate of Soviet Central Asia represents perhaps the most tragic and least reversible example of the failure of the Soviet experiment that, in the name of ideological goals, led to near destruction of a region, its people, and its culture."[6] Indeed, the facts that are lamented as revealing the failure of the Soviet experiment in Central Asia may have been the very fulfillment of significant aspects of Soviet Russian objectives in Central Asia.

Methodologically, scholarship on Muslim Central Asia has traditionally been Moscow-centered and Russian-dominated—the researchers have looked at Central Asia primarily from the perspective of Russian and Soviet ideologies and interests, based on data from Russian and Soviet sources, and for the most part excluded native voices and interests. As a result, the combination of these methodological and theoretical approaches appears to have helped shape the academic discussions by directing attention to questions regarding whether Soviet hegemony in Muslim Central Asia was colonialist and whether Soviet modernization programs have failed, rather than urging researchers toward the explication of specific Russian and Soviet policy goals and objectives, and their consequences, especially from the vantage point of the Muslim Central Asians themselves. Adequate assessment of the successes and failures of Soviet development policies and practices in Central Asia is possible only in reference to specific short- and long-term Soviet goals and objectives, both articulated and otherwise. It is to these issues I would like to turn next.

Legacies of the Soviet Development Policies

The Soviets' developmental goals in general and their objectives in Central Asia in particular were formulated during the early years after the Bolshevik Revolution.[7] Strong and systematic measures taken to achieve these ends were implemented relentlessly throughout the Soviet period. These goals and strategies differed radically from those of national development and modernization programs in other societies outside the Soviet orbit. Some of the most significant components of Soviet policies in Muslim Central Asia consisted of the following closely linked elements: (1) absolute control of political and military power by Russian Bolsheviks; (2) large-scale economic extraction, as well as creation and promotion of long-term economic and technological dependency upon Russia and Russians; (3) systematic destruction of traditional Muslim Central Asian societies and cultures; and (4) the creation and establishment of a new alternative Soviet (Russian) society and culture to replace the old. It is therefore in reference to these specific Soviet policy objectives that we need to discuss and assess Soviet developmental policy successes and/or failures in the present post-Soviet Central Asia.

Political Control: Centralized State Power

The fundamental project of the Bolshevik Revolution was to capture political power and concentrate it in the sole control of the Communist party–state apparatus of the former USSR. "Dictatorship of the proletariat" was the necessary instrument for the construction of the socialist system and realization of other revolutionary objectives through the management, control, and mobilization of all social forces, natural resources, and means of production in society. Indeed, the working class organized important social institutions "in preparation for the revolution, such as the soviets, trade unions, factory committees, newspapers, and militias," which were incorporated with the goal of fusing state and society into a "combined societal-state dictatorship that would eliminate its class enemies and create the economic, cultural, and political environment for socialism."[8] With the consolidation of the Bolshevik "mobilization regime," as Thomas Remington asserts,[9] the foundation for the creation of a particular kind of "dual society" within the former Soviet Union was laid:

> One society was a walled fortress of state power, with its official doctrine and its bureaucratic solidarity; the other was the "little world" outside the state made up of individualized endeavor and reward, of small-scale production and trade, of hermetic pockets of unauthorized culture. Over the decades of Soviet rule, [however,] the more that the regime has sought to realize its early dreams of a fused and centralized authority stretching across state and society, the greater the bifurcation between the realm in which the state held sway and that of the private action.

In Turkestan, the establishment of the Russian Bolshevik revolutionary government as the successor state to the tsarist colonial empire was entirely a Russian affair.[10] Soviet power in the region was consolidated with the help of large Russian settler communities, both urban and rural. Challenged by a widespread, badly organized, but strongly motivated anti-Bolshevik Muslim resistance movement, the *basmachi*, the Soviet Russians defeated the opposition by about 1924 through a combined strategy of withholding food from the starving Muslim population and applying massive military force. By 1925 the peoples of Central Asia had lost all traces of political autonomy, and Central Asian politics and economics were managed from Moscow and by Russians and/or Russified natives loyal to the Soviet Russian regime.[11] Centralized control of military, police, political, and economic power in Muslim Central Asia by the Russian Communist elite was complete and undeniable. The possibility of any challenge to Soviet installed power was minimized through a systematic series of purges, liquidations, and decapitations of potential or actual native leaders, and as a result no credible opposition was ever allowed to emerge. Therefore, the Soviets were able to deploy the overwhelming power of the state in Central Asia to achieve their other three principal objectives in the region.

Economic Control: Extraction and Dependency

The second most important objective of Soviet policy in Central Asia has been economic extraction and the creation and promotion of long-term economic and technological dependency. The economic importance of Central Asia as the source of essential raw materials for Russia—hence its significance for the Soviet empire—is widely discussed and debated in the literature.[12] The most clear and succinct expression of Soviet economic aims perhaps appears in the following statement made by Lenin's comrade in arms, Zinoviev, in September 1920: "We cannot do without the petroleum of Azerbaijan or the cotton of Turkestan. We *take* these products which are necessary for us, not as the former [tsarist Russian] exploiters, but as older brothers bearing the torch of civilization" (emphasis added).[13]

Satisfaction of the former USSR's cotton needs resulted in what has been termed a "superspecialization" in cotton production in Central Asia. Supported by the region's favorable climate, a very heavy investment in a specialized extractive infrastructure in cotton production has proved extremely successful; that is, Central Asian Muslim republics produced about 95 percent of its vegetable oil, 100 percent of its ton and cotton fiber, 15 percent of its vegetable oil, 100 percent of its machinery and equipment for cotton growing, more than 90 percent of its cotton gins, and a large quantity of looms, and equipment needed for irrigation."[14] Although Central Asia contains considerable coal and mineral deposits, ranks as "one of the richest and most promising regions in the USSR" in oil and hydroelectric power, and "stands second only to Western Siberia in the volume of its holdings in natural gas," Rumer suggests that until the demise of the Soviet state, Central Asia's "productive capacity . . . [was] defined exclusively by the production and export of cotton and its by-products."[15] Approximately 96 percent of the raw cotton produced in Uzbekistan is shipped out for processing and manufacturing to the former RSFSR (Russian Soviet Federated Socialist Republic), the Ukraine, Byelorussia, and other republics, to Eastern Europe, and elsewhere. In effect, Central Asia has been excluded from textiles manufacturing and rendered dependent on Russia even for cloth manufactured from its own cotton.

With more than 70 percent of Central Asia's best arable lands (in principal cotton growing areas of the region) under cotton, dependency on Russia for staple foods has been another major effect of cotton monoculture. By the late 1980s the overwhelming success of the Soviet "agrarian-colonial" approach to development in Central Asia and its tragic consequences for the environment and peoples of Turkestan reached embarrassing proportions, even by the former Soviet standards. A statement published by the Moscow weekly *Literaturnaia Gazeta* shows the magnitude of the "superspecialization" problem in the Republic of Uzbekistan:

> Specialization should be reasonable. In Uzbekistan it has degenerated into a dictatorship of a single crop, . . . cotton. It first became a monoculture in a psychological sense, when it drove all the other needs of the region from the minds of certain leaders [in Moscow]. Then it crowded the normal crop rotation from the fields and pushed everything else out of the plan. By being transformed into virtually one great cotton plantation, Uzbekistan embarked on a long, tragic experiment— to determine the capacity of a monoculture to corrode not only agriculture, but also industry, education, health, and finally public morality [that is, charges of official deception, corruption, and bribery].[16]

Industrialization, whether extractive or productive, has been another important means for the former Soviet Russians to create and perpetuate Central Asian dependency. All modern industrial development in Central Asia came from outside; that is, all equipment and machinery were brought to the area from Russia and run primarily by the Slavic operators and managers. The high degree of industrial, manufacturing, and marketing dependency in Central Asia remains virtually unchanged after seven decades of Soviet rule. The full extent of the economic dependency of the newly independent Muslim republics upon Russia and the challenges it presents for the future of the peoples of this region are only now becoming visible.

Toward Cultural and Ideological Control: A Struggle for Recognition

The remaining two interrelated goals of the former Soviet regime in Central Asia, that of cultural and ideological transformation and control, are by far the most challenging aspects of Soviet development and modernization to assess. For the purposes of this discussion, however, and from the perspective of both Soviets and Central Asians, the outcome of Soviet policies and practices toward cultural and ideological transformation and control might be most critical.

After literally taking control of Turkestan's "products" (that is, petroleum and cotton) which were deemed necessary for Russia and the Bolshevik Revolution, and having taken them "not as the former [tsarist Russian] exploiters" had done, as Zinoviev stated, "but as older brothers bearing the torch of civilization," the Soviets took it upon themselves to enlighten, modernize, and civilize the backward Central Asians.[17] It was assumed, in the mold of classical colonialist tradition, that the peoples of Turkestan, like other Orientals, could not represent and rule themselves.[18] Therefore they had to be represented and ruled by the Russian Bolsheviks. Central Asians had nothing to say about setting the goals, the criteria, or the means for the development and modernization of their own society and culture. Thus, the Russian "older brothers," the bearers of the "torch of civilization," armed with a new, revolutionary Marxist-Leninist ideology and the powers of modern science and technology, Western rationalism, and industry, embarked upon modernizing Central Asians to save them from the "feudal oppression" of their native rulers and their own presumed cultural and religious ignorance. Efforts toward the achievement of these goals commanded much of the resources and energies of the former Soviet state, often with mixed, but significant results.

Soviet policy makers considered the existing Muslim Central Asian cultural values, institutions, and traditional identities (personal and collective) incompatible with the ideological goals and objectives of the revolutionary Soviet state, which claimed it intended to create a modern socialist society. Therefore, the Soviets considered it essential to undermine and destroy all forms of traditional Islamic social and cultural identities, loyalties, and institutions in Muslim Central Asia and to replace them with new Soviet (Russian) ones. To realize these objectives, the Soviet policy makers adopted and relentlessly carried out a three-pronged attack on Central Asian traditional social and cultural systems: (1) fragmentation of Turkestan territorially, politically, and ultimately culturally; (2) cultural isolation of the peoples of Turkestan, both from their historic past and from other Muslim and Turko-Persian speaking areas in the region; and (3) defamation and destruction of religious beliefs and values, especially those of Islam, and devastation of Islamic institutions.

Fragmentation of Turkestan. One of the most successful and obvious legacies of Soviet domination of Muslim Central Asia is the territorial and political fragmentation of the area, which has radically, perhaps even permanently, altered the geopolitical complexion of Turkestan.

The policy of fragmentation began in 1924 with the implementation of Stalin's infamous "Territorial Delimitation" and "Soviet Nationalities Policy" dividing the area into a number of artificially drawn titular Soviet Socialist Republics and Autonomous Regions based on alleged linguistic and dialectical distribution. Terms such as *Turkestan* (homeland of the Turks or Turkic-speaking peoples), implying larger and more inclusive political and cultural identity of the Turkic speakers inhabiting the vast area, suddenly disappeared from public discourse. Instead, new language-based "nationalisms" were invented, bestowed, and promoted through competition for access to strategic resources among nationalities at all levels of social articulations. The effectiveness of the Soviets' policy of political fragmentation is proved by the emergence, in 1991, of five independent republics in former Soviet Central Asia: the new states of Kazakhstan, Kyrgyzstan, Tajikistan, Turkmenistan, and Uzbekistan.

Cultural Isolation. The former Soviet regimes applied several means to undermine traditional cultures of Central Asia through effective cultural isolation, both from their historical literary and scientific heritage, the closely related neighboring Turko-Persian Muslim societies, and the wider Muslim world. The Soviets achieved this by two extremely effective means: drawing an "iron curtain" across the southern borders of the former USSR to deny outsiders, especially Muslims, access to the region; and by introducing a series of alphabet changes as part of their language reforms and nationalities policy.

These alphabet changes included an initial switch from the standard Arabic-Persian alphabet, which had been used for centuries in writing the Turkic (Chaghatai) language,[19] a literary form of Central Asian "Turkish," to a reformed Arabic-Persian alphabet, then to Latin (1929), and eventually in 1939–40 to modified forms of the Cyrillic alphabet. To enhance the official recognition of the distinctiveness of each of the many "autonomous national republics and regions," Soviet Russia adopted differently modified forms of Cyrillic alphabets for writing each of the various officially designated languages and dialects, thereby further isolating even related linguistic groups within the area. Adoption of Cyrillic alphabets in Turkestan had two important consequences: it made "enrichment" of Central Asian languages through Russian loan words possible, and it rendered the literacy skills of the educated Central Asians obsolete and denied the new generations of Central Asian youth access to their considerable literary heritage written in Arabic-Persian script as well as to contemporary writings and literature in the languages of Central Asia produced outside the former

USSR. This situation amounted to the effective intellectual and cultural isolation of Central Asian Muslims from the rest of the world in general and the Muslim world in particular.

Destruction of Islam and Muslim Institutions. The motivations of Soviet policy makers in attacking Islam and institutions responsible for its social reproduction and maintenance were both ideological and pragmatic. Ideologically, Islam and religions in general were considered incompatible with the requirements of the modern (secular, individualistic, egalitarian, rational, and industrial) socialist way of life, and therefore Islam could not be tolerated.[20] Pragmatically, Islam provided the only common cohesive intellectual and organizational framework for the ethnolinguistically heterogeneous peoples of Turkestan. Muslim leadership (*ulama* and *sufis*), closely linked to the traditional ruling circles as well as the public, posed the only credible source of challenge to Soviet hegemony in the region. Indeed, almost all resistance to Russian penetration of the area, including the anti-Bolshevik *basmachi* movements, was mobilized and led in the name of Islam.[21]

Therefore, Islam and Muslim practices in Turkestan became the target of a multifaceted, intense, systematic, and sustained attack by the Soviet state. Among other things, it consisted of killing countless Muslim scholars and local leaders; destroying Islamic texts and literature; demolishing and reallocating mosques, madrassas, and *khanaqas*; confiscation of *waqf* (endowment) properties; closure of religious institutions of learning (makhtabs and madrassas); outlawing all public forms of Muslim worship, including performances of life crises rituals; changing Muslim components of personal names; and abolishing all *Shari'a* courts. The Soviets also attacked traditional kinship- and religion-based structures of communal authority, gender, and family relations, and all Islamic norms governing rights of private property and inheritance.

In addition, numerous new Soviet institutions were put into place in order to discredit Islam and agitate against its "pernicious" effects on Central Asian society. These included major educational institutions such as Soviet schools, as well as many other institutions of socialization and community services, such as peasant unions, Pioneer and Komsomol youth organizations, "Red" Chaikhanas (teahouses), women's clubs, the Red Army, illiteracy campaign groups, atheist clubs, the press, and electronic media. These institutions served simultaneously as "agenc[ies] of education and secularizing changes."[22] Schools and affiliated organizations served as the principal instruments of desirable social change, including diffusion of "modern culture" and Soviet morality (secularism, atheism, strong labor ethic, sacrifice for the collective, and absolute loyalty to the state), dissemination of Marxist-Leninist ideology, science, and technology, socialistic-communistic principles of social and economic organization, and belief in materialism.[23] Schools, together with numerous agencies aimed to inspire social and political conformity to Soviet norms and policies through systems of reward and punishment, have succeeded, especially in urban Central Asia, in creating a substantial number of obedient, docile, and loyal servants who run the mammoth centralized bureaucracies of the various republics. The Soviet attacks on Islam and Muslim family structure and function, as well as Soviet sponsorship of an alternate code of Soviet morality based on Communist ideology, are reportedly less effective in rural Central Asia.[24] Thus, in much of rural Central Asia, the Soviet system, instead of replacing traditional Islamic ideals and institutions, operated parallel to the Islamic system of values, but the Soviet system alone offered all the rewards.[25] By any measure, the success of Soviet educational, political, and economic achievements in weakening, if not totally destroying, traditional Islamic cultural forms has been considerable. As a result, the powerful legacies of Russian and Soviet rule and policies of "modernization and development" in Central Asia are bound to have significant effects on the future regional political dynamics of southwestern Asia and the Middle East for decades to come.

Future Challenges and Prospects

The sudden and unexpected demise of the Russian-dominated Soviet state has given birth to quintuplets—independent Muslim Central Asian nation-states that are economically weak, technologically dependent, politically fragmented, and socioculturally bifurcated. These legacies of the seven decades of Soviet rule present powerful challenges to its newly emergent successor states in Turkestan. As John H. Kautsky points out, *"the end of colonialism comes not with political independence but with economic independence,* which is a matter of degree, as is political independence, too" (emphasis added).[26] For Central Asian states, however, gaining economic independence in the post-Soviet era may be highly contingent upon whether and when these states would be able to earn, psychologically and practically, their real political independence and national sovereignty.

Unlike most other postcolonial nation-states in Asia and Africa, Central Asian republics did not have to fight anticolonial wars of liberation to gain their freedom. Independence was thrust upon them suddenly and unexpectedly due to the internal collapse of the colonizing Soviet Russian empire. No credible opposition movements in any of the five republics called for political independence from the former USSR. The only squabbles mentioned by outside observers were those of the highly Russified Central Asian bureaucratic elite, who competed with their Russian masters over gaining greater personal access to the higher sanctum of power within the Communist party and/or asking for larger collective access to greater shares of the Soviet Union's total economic pie.[27]

Relationships between the Central Asian urban native elite and their Russian overlords remained tense and guarded for a variety of reasons. For example, although the Soviet Russians conferred positions of power on members of the native elite in the governance of their own republics, those in Moscow never trusted Central Asian leadership and gave Central Asians little voice in planning for their national republics. As a result of this refusal by the Slavs to acknowledge and recognize the common humanity of Central Asians—even those of their elite who were willingly serving the Soviet system—Central Asians harbored considerable resentments toward Russians, other Slavs, and Europeans. Powerless to alter the political and military situation favoring the Soviet state, the native elite continued to cooperate with the Russians in order to reap some personal benefits from their association.

As a result, the postindependence governing elites have little credibility in the eyes of their own people, because they were servants of the former Soviet power, especially in predominantly rural areas. As Rakowska-Harmstone points out, these leaders "have never been allowed a real share in the Soviet model, yet find themselves connected to it by a network of dependency ties they seem unable and unwilling to break."[28] This is particularly true in light of the fact that "the Central Asian Muslim leaders have yet to articulate a blueprint for their sovereign future."[29] As shown by the unfolding events of early May 1992 in Dushanbe, the capital of Tajikistan, the position of those in power at this time in the Central Asian republics seems highly precarious indeed. At the same time, a well-organized alternative political structure with a clearly formulated vision of a postindependence social and political system to replace the ruling Communist power structures in the Central Asian nations remains conspicuously absent. What is required at this juncture in the processes of state formation in Muslim Turkestan is the reestablishment of an organic relationship between the long-bifurcated Russified bureaucratic elite and the reluctant rural masses in Central Asia. Without closing this gap, the prospects for the future socioeconomic and political development of this critical region will remain uncertain.

The conditions for gaining true political and thus economic independence, however, seem more problematic in view of the heightened nationalisms within each republic as well as between and among the new states. Although Moscow has unilaterally broken the cord of political dependency, leaving Central Asians in charge of their own republics, the question remains: Are the leaders of the independent titular republics willing to allow their minority citizens a real share of the power and resources in their domain? The promise of earning real sovereignty and independence for the peoples of these multiethnic nations rests in large measure upon the answer their leaders give to this question. Repetition or imitation of Russian practices of ethnic inequality in the former USSR by the leaders of its successor states in Central Asia could wreak havoc in the region. In this age of highly politicized ethnicity, the need, and the power of struggles for recognition and equity by each and every one of the multitude of nationalities invented and nurtured to maturity by the former Soviet system, cannot and should not be underestimated.[30] Only freedom from potentially debilitating internal communal strife, sustained peace, popular participation in governance, and cooperation within each state as well as among various Muslim nations in Central Asia and contiguous regions could afford the peoples of Turkestan the opportunity to strive for economic, technological, and cultural freedom and independence. The challenge of diversifying agricultural production from the superspecialization of cotton monoculture, reclaiming land, water, energy, and mineral resources for a balanced and internally and interregionally sustainable system of economic extraction, production, processing, manufacturing, and distribution is immense, but so are the opportunities for success. Over seven decades of isolation—spatial, social, cultural, generational, intellectual, and ideological—from the Muslim societies of southwestern Asia and the Middle East have taken their toll on both communities, giving rise to feelings of mutual doubt and suspicion. Central Asians and neighboring Muslim societies need to make concerted efforts through educational reforms and ideological and moral reorientation to promote a healthy environment of mutual understanding and respect amongst the Muslim peoples and nations of Central Asia and surrounding areas.

Overcoming these powerful legacies of the successful Soviet developmental policies will be only part of the future challenge for Central Asian Muslims. The real challenge will be the formulation and implementation of a culturally appropriate alternative model for future development of Turkestan that would ensure economic growth, political freedom, and social justice for the long-oppressed peoples of this region—a kind of development that, as James Lamb puts it, "should be a *struggle* [a *jihad?*] to create criteria, goals, and means for self-liberation from misery, inequity, and dependency in all forms . . . it should be a process a people choose, which heals them from historical trauma, and enables them to achieve a newness on their own terms."[31]

Muslim peoples of Turkestan have suffered the trauma of more than one hundred and twenty years of oppressive, degrading, and suffocating colonial rule. They are among the last nations in the twentieth century to gain their national freedom and independence. These new nations, progeny of the sudden demise of a once-powerful revolutionary Soviet empire, are by no means homogenous political entities. Diverse in population, natural and human resources, and potentials for economic growth, each is capable of charting distinct strategies for its own national development. They have the opportunity to choose from a wide array of alternative development models, approaches, ideologies, and strategies, tested and untested. And the course each of the Turkestani states adopts "will be determined by the performances of those involved in its politics, not by the preferences of those who analyze it."[32]

Notes

Author's note: A draft of this article was originally delivered at the international conference on *The Transformation of the Former USSR and Its Implications for the Third World* (2–4 March 1992, Tehran). I would like to express my appreciation to the Institute for Political and International Studies, Tehran, Islamic Republic of Iran, the conference sponsor, and especially to Dr. Mohiaddin Mesbahi of Florida International University, Miami, Florida, the North American coordinator of the conference, for their kind invitation and warmest hospitality both in Tehran and Esfahan.

1. Francis Fukuyama, "The End of History?" *The National Interest* 16 (Summer 1989): 3–18.

2. During the conference in Tehran (which at times sounded like a postmortem of the former USSR), most participants, especially the Russian participants of the CIS, dismissed the development and modernization policies of the former Soviet regimes as an utter failure. Undoubtedly, with the benefit of

hindsight combined with the personal and professional disappointments of former Soviet scholars with a regime that had promised so much and delivered so little, especially in European Russia, this is understandable. However, I argue in this chapter that Russian and Soviet policies in Muslim Central Asia, when observed in the light of objectives set by Moscow regimes for the region, may have enjoyed a considerable degree of success, albeit with serious negative consequences to the peoples and cultures of the region.

3. See for example, Michael Rywkin, *Moscow's Muslim Challenge: Soviet Central Asia* (Armonk, N.Y.: Middle East Sharpe, 1990); William Fierman, ed., *Soviet Central Asia: The Failed Transformation* (Boulder, Colo.: Westview Press, 1991); Edward Allworth, ed., *Central Asia: 120 Years of Russian Rule* (Durham and London: Duke University Press, 1989); and Alexandre Bennigsen and Marie Broxup, *The Islamic Threat to the Soviet State,* (New York: St. Martin's Press, 1983).

4. Allworth, *Central Asia,* 572.

5. See for example, Samuel Huntington, *Political Order in Changing Societies* (New Haven and London: Yale University Press, 1968); and Fierman, *Soviet Central Asia,* 290–308.

6. Teresa Rakowska-Harmstone, "Foreword," in Fierman, *Soviet Central Asia,* ix.

7. Thomas F. Remington, *Building Socialism in Bolshevik Russia: Ideology and Industrial Organization, 1917–1921* (Pittsburgh, Penn.: University of Pittsburgh Press, 1984).

8. Ibid., 17.

9. Ibid., 21.

10. See A.K. Park, *Bolshevism in Turkistan, 1917–1927: A Study in Colonial Rule* (New York, 1957); and Richard Pipes, *The Formation of the Soviet Union* (Cambridge: Harvard University Press, 1957).

11. Donald S. Carlisle, "Power and Politics in Soviet Uzbekistan," in Fierman, *Soviet Central Asia.*

12. See Boris Z. Rumer, "Central Asia's Cotton Economy and Its Costs," in Fierman, *Soviet Central Asia;* Boris Z. Rumer, *Soviet Central Asia: "A Tragic Experiment"* (Boston: Unwin Hyman, 1989); and Alec Nove and J.A. Newth, *The Soviet Middle East: A Communist Model for Development* (New York: Fredrick A. Praeger, Publishers, 1967).

13. Quoted in Merle Fainsod, *How Russia Is Ruled* (Cambridge, Mass.: Harvard University Press, 1953), 304.

14. See Rumer, "Central Asia's Cotton Economy," 63. For more details see Rumer, *Soviet Central Asia.*

15. Rumer, "Central Asia's Cotton Economy," 63, 69.

16. Ibid., 80.

17. Fainsod, *How Russia Is Ruled,* 304.

18. Edward Said, *Orientalism* (New York: Vintage Books, 1978); and Johannes

Fabian, *Time and the Other: How Anthropology Makes Its Objects* (New York: Columbia University Press, 1983).

19. Until the 1920s in Central Asia the term Turkic, as in *"Turkic ketab"* (book written in Turkic language), referred to the literary form of the Uzbek language that was in use throughout both Western and Eastern Turkestan and among all Turkic speakers, including Kazakhs, Kirghiz, Turkmen, and Uighurs, as well as Uzbeks. Western authors have applied the term *Chaghatai* to identify this literary form of Central Asian Turkic language, or "Turkish."

20. See William K. Medlin, William Cave, and Finley Carpenter, *Education and Development in Central Asia: A Case Study of Social Change in Uzbekistan* (Leiden: E.J. Brill, 1971); and Muriel Atkin, *The Subtlest Battle: Islam in Soviet Tajikistan* (Philadelphia: Foreign Policy Research Institute, 1989).

21. Marie Broxup, "The Basmachi," *Central Asian Survey* 2, no. 1 (1983):57–83.

22. Medlin, Cave, and Carpenter, *Education and Development in Central Asia*, 75.

23. Ibid., 66, 178, 188–89.

24. See Atkin, *Subtlest Battle*.

25. For details see, Medlin, Cave, and Carpenter, *Education and Development in Central Asia*, 86–89.

26. John H. Kautsky, *The Political Consequences of Modernization* (New York: John Wiley and Sons, 1972), 63.

27. See, for example, Carlisle, "Power and Politics"; and James Critchlow, "Prelude to 'Independence': How the Uzbek Party Apparatus Broke Moscow's Grip on Elite Recruitment," in Fierman, *Soviet Central Asia.*

28. Rakowska-Harmstone, "Foreword," xiii.

29. Ibid.

30. See Fukuyama, "End of History"; and *The End of History and the Last Man* (New York: Free Press, 1991).

31. Quoted in Kenneth P. Jameson and Charles Wilber, *Direction in Economic Development* (Notre Dame, Ind.: University of Notre Dame Press, 1979).

32. Kautsky, *Political Consequences of Modernization*, 13.

4

The "Internal" Muslim Factor in the Politics of Russia

Tatarstan and the North Caucasus

Marie Bennigsen Broxup

Since the disintegration of the Soviet empire, the fact that Russia—the Russian Federation—has remained a multinational colonial empire has conveniently been forgotten by many of Russia's foreign interlocutors. Russia is facing the same nationalities problem—with all its political, territorial, ethnic, economic, and religious complexities—that beset the Soviet Union before its demise. In this chapter I will present case studies of Tatarstan in the Volga-Ural region and Chechnia in the North Caucasus, two "autonomous" republics that have refused to sign the Russian Federation Treaty of 30 March 1992 in a bid to gain independence and sovereignty. Relations with these two deeply Muslim, strategically important areas may influence Russia's future foreign policy toward the newly independent Central Asian states, Turkey, and Iran. Both regions are important for several reasons: (1) Tatarstan and the North Caucasus are among the oldest territories conquered by Russia. They have influenced Russian anti-Muslim ideology and, more generally how Russians identify themselves vis-à-vis Islam and the East. (2) They are primary examples of the failure of the Russian imperial policies. As opposed to Central Asia, the North Caucasus was temporarily subdued only after a century-long, painful war of conquest, while the Volga Tatars have successfully resisted all of Russia's attempts to assimilate them over four centuries. (3) In both regions Islam is particularly strong and totally identified with the idea of nation. For the Tatars, Islam served as a protection against assimilation by the Russian milieu, while in the case of the Chechens it helped them defy extermination during Stalin's deportations by keeping the idea of nation alive. In neighboring Daghestan, divided between some twenty nations, national unity is only possible around Islam as it was at the time of Imam Shamil. (4) The Volga-Ural region and Chechnia are oil rich and produce a considerable percentage of Russia's oil requirements (25 percent in the case of Tatarstan alone).

It may be worthwhile to recapitulate the different tactics that Russia used in the past to conquer, subdue, pacify, or win over the populations of its neighboring Muslim states and colonies. Despite the propensity for self-justification among Russian political leaders and intellectuals who blame the Communist leadership for the eruption of national unrest, colonial policies were elaborated and perfected by successive Russian rulers since the sixteenth century. The Soviets did not innovate but merely applied the same methods with greater brutality than their tsarist predecessors. In simplified form, this strategy may be summarized as follows:

Settlement of Russian Peasant Colonies. From the North Caucasus to the Tatar Volga region, Siberia, and Kazakhstan, and to a lesser extent Central Asia, Russian military conquest was preceded, accompanied, or followed by settlements of Cossacks and, in the nineteenth century, Russian peasants. The colonists provided armed militias who helped to expel the natives. From the Russians' point of view, colonial settlement made conquest irreversible; the lands became part of "Russia." Today this opinion still prevails and is related to the size of the Russian colonies in a given area. Thus, for instance, it is difficult for even educated Russians to admit that Kazan, which has a majority Russian population, was not a Russian city since time immemorial.

Assimilation. Two contradictory methods were used under the tsars: conversion to Orthodox Christianity followed by full assimilation by the Russian milieu, a policy moderately effective among the elites alone; or conversion without linguistic and cultural Russification. The latter policy was favored in the Volga region in the eighteenth and nineteenth centuries, with some notable results. The Soviets used this method, merely changing Orthodoxy to Marxism with the slogan "national in form and socialist in content," with rather less success than the tsarist administration.

Cooptation of Elites. This was practiced from the sixteenth century in Kabarda in the North Caucasus to the 1970s and 1980s in Afghanistan. In the case of the North Caucasus, as in Afghanistan, this policy was usually counterproductive because of the lack of strong centralized political or dynastic power. Among the Tatars, however, cooptation of the Muslim religious elites, inaugurated by Catherine II, enjoyed spectacular success and gained the Romanov dynasty the loyalty and cooperation of the Tatars for more than a century.

Destruction of Islam. Under the tsars, serious efforts to destroy Islam as a religion were only attempted among the Tatars, under Tsar Feodor (the son of Ivan the Terrible), Peter the Great, and Tsarina Anna (1738–55). Under the Soviets, the antireligious campaign affected all the nations of the USSR. In the Muslim territories the aim was to destroy not only the faith but also the Muslims' way of life, which was considered a handicap to the merging of Soviet nations. In the North Caucasus and Tatarstan the campaign was set in motion in 1924, earlier than in the rest of the Soviet Union, where the full-scale attack on Islam was only launched in 1928. In the North Caucasus the offensive was directed against the Sufi *tariqat* (brotherhoods), who inspired the political opposition to Sovietization. The revival of religious fervor throughout the Muslim territories of the former Soviet Union is the best illustration of the short-lived impact of this policy.

Expulsion, Deportation, and Genocide. To expand its colonies, Russia experimented with several more or less effective methods of genocide in Muslim territories. One practice consisted of cutting a population off from external contacts, thereby condemning it to extinction. This policy was applied with some success in the Volga-Ural region from the sixteenth to the eighteenth centuries, as well as in the Kazakh steppes in the nineteenth and early twentieth centuries. Genocide through slaughter was attempted unsuccessfully by General Skobolev against the Turkmen tribes at Gök Tepe in 1881. Genocide through forced exodus, a crude but effective tactic, was applied consistently in the North Caucasus against the Cherkess and the Chechens.

These policies were usually abetted by the Russian elites at the time of their implementation.

The Case of Tatarstan

Historical Background

The Volga Tatars are not a small minority. They are the fourth largest Muslim population of the former Soviet Union and the second largest nation in Russia.[1] The Tatars have an ancient tradition of statehood going back to the Bulgar Kingdom, to the Golden Horde which ruled over medieval Russia, and its successor state, the Kazan Khanate. The Tatars offer a unique example in the history of Dar al-Islam, that of a

nation that has survived more than four centuries of foreign domination. Since the conquest and destruction of the Khanate of Kazan in
1552 by the army of Ivan the Terrible, which marked the beginning of
the Russian conquest of Muslim lands, Russia has persistently tried to
convert or assimilate the Tatars in order to eliminate this alien Muslim body in its midst.

Military conquest was followed by a systematic policy of colonization. The ruling classes were ruined, Tatars were expelled from Kazan,
and their richest lands were confiscated and distributed among Russian
colonizers. At the end of the sixteenth century the former territory of
the Kazan Khanate already had a mixed population, and by the end of
the eighteenth century the present territory of the Republic of Tatarstan had a majority Russian population. Soon after the fall of Kazan
Tsar Feodor launched an energetic missionary campaign, and as a result a relatively large group of Tatars became Christian Orthodox.
They have survived until today as a separate community, the Kryashens. From the Times of Trouble until the reign of Catherine II
(1762–96), various measures were taken to eradicate Islam: mosques
were destroyed, waqf (religious endowments) properties were confiscated, and Muslims were expelled not only from the cities but also
from villages where groups of converts had been formed. Special
schools were opened for Tatar converts, while Muslim proselytism was
punishable by death. Religious persecutions reached a peak in the mid-
eighteenth century: between 1740 and 1743 alone, 418 out of 536 of
the Kazan guberniia (provinces) were destroyed.[2] These policies, reminiscent of the Spanish reconquista, resulted in a massive exodus of the
Tatars toward Turkestan, the Kazakh steppes, and Siberia in frequent
armed uprisings and active participation in the two great Russian popular rebellions of Stepan Razin and Pugachev (1670s and 1773–75, respectively).

Catherine II corrected the errors of her predecessors. She halted the
anti-Muslim campaign and established the Central Muslim Spiritual
Board in Orenburg in 1783 to care for the needs of her Tatar subjects.
For a century afterward the Tatar merchant class cooperated loyally
with the Russian government. Their trading colonies served as scouts
in parts of Central Asia still closed to the Russians, Siberia and China.

The conquest of Central Asia put an end to this partnership, and
new economic and religious pressures were brought to bear by the
Russian government. In 1863 Nikolai Il'minsky of the Religious Academy of Kazan devised a program aimed at creating a new Tatar intelli-

gentsia converted to Orthodoxy but speaking and writing Tatar. The aim of the Orthodox missionary school was to stem the flow of revolutionary ideas that were rapidly spreading among the Russian intelligentsia by creating a new class of obedient subjects for the Orthodox monarchy. The results of this Christianization campaign were momentous—Il'minsky estimated that 200,000 Tatars were converted, 130,000 in the guberniia of Kazan alone.[3] Despite the success of Il'minsky's scheme, the tsarist administration rejected it because it felt more confident of the ultimate loyalty of Russian revolutionaries than of Tatars, even when they were devoted Christians. Even more than economic harassment—a decree of 1886 forbade the Tatars to own property and companies in Central Asia—the community viewed this policy of religious assimilation as a deadly threat, and the Tatar elites were quick to react. They understood that in order to survive they had to regain intellectual and economic equality with the Russians, preserve Islam as the basis of Tatar society, and reject all social conflicts within the community. Their efforts to this end gave birth to the first modern reformist movement in the Muslim world—Jadidism. The movement flourished thanks to the remarkable unity of purpose among all layers of Tatar society, and on the eve of the 1905 revolution the Tatars were a developed nation with a sophisticated capitalism, some industrial experience, and a higher degree of literacy than the Russians in the Kazan guberniia.

The defeat inflicted by Japan on the Russian army in Manchuria in 1905 prompted the rise of all the nationalist movements in the Russian Empire. The Tatars were in the forefront of the movement, providing ideas and leadership to the Muslim nations of the empire. Three Muslim congresses were held in rapid succession in 1905 and 1906, and a Muslim Union (Ittifaq) was founded under the aegis of the Volga Tatars to achieve equal civic rights for Muslims—freedom of religion, education, and the press. However, hopes for liberal reforms and national equality were frustrated in 1908 when the Russian government adopted a hard-line attitude toward nationalist demands. As a result, the leadership of the national movement became more radical and revolutionary. Confrontation was inevitable, and at the time of the October Revolution the Tatar struggle against Russian centrism was at its height. Because of the intransigence of the White generals during the Civil War and their refusal to compromise on the notion of "one indivisible Russia," the Bolsheviks were seen as a lesser threat to national aspirations. While the outcome of the Civil War was uncertain, Lenin's and Stalin's clever concessions to the Muslims—the adoption of the April Thesis by the Bolsheviks in the spring of 1917 and the Appeal to the Muslim Workers of Russia and the Soviet East of November 1917, which promised the right of secession and self-determination to all the peoples of the old Empire—won the support of the Tatar nationalists to the Soviet cause until 1921.

On 23 March 1918 a decree of the NARKOMNATS (People's Commissariat of Nationalities) proclaimed the creation of the "Tatar-Bashkir Soviet Republic of the Russian Soviet Federation," but the outbreak of the Civil War in May 1918, with the Tatar-Bashkir territory at the heart of the confrontation, rendered the decree meaningless. The hopes of the nationalists for a large state on the Volga were crushed with the creation on 23 March 1919 of the Bashkir Autonomous Soviet Socialist Republic, followed by the Tatar Autonomous Soviet Socialist Republic on 27 May 1920. The *razmezhevanie* (parceling) of the Tatar Volga territories was especially drastic—the borders of the republics were drawn arbitrarily, leaving 75 percent of the Tatar population outside the boundaries of their nominal republic, while in the Bashkir ASSR Tatars represented the majority ethnic group.

From 1921 the tenets of Muslim national Communism dominated Tatar political life and dissent. Its greatest exponent was Mirsaid Sultan Galiev, who argued that all the classes of the Muslim colonized peoples had the right to be called "proletarian" because of the colonizers' oppression. Priority therefore had to be given to national liberation, with the cohesion of the Muslim society preserved and the class struggle postponed. Sultan Galiev's ideas have since inspired most of the national liberation movements of the Third World. Accused of "counterrevolutionary nationalist conspiracy against the power of the Soviets," he was arrested in May 1923 on the personal initiative of Stalin and executed in January 1940.[4]

Between 1924 and 1939 the political battle within the Communist party in Tatarstan was fought by the "right," Tatar partisans of Sultan Galiev, and the "left," almost exclusively Russian Communists. The conflict broke out at the Ninth Regional Conference of the Communist party (b) organization of Tatarstan in May 1924. The issues at stake were collectivization, confiscation of kulak lands, and the introduction of class struggle in Tatar society. The Tatar "right" was reminded that "one should not confuse the objectives of World revolution with the aspirations of the Tatars. Without denying the importance of the rise of oppressed nationalities, one must not forget that the future of the revolution depends on the West alone."[5] Furthermore, it was stated that Russian chauvinism could not exist among Russian Communists and that it was merely an invention of the Tatar nationalists aimed at disguising their own subversive activities. For the next four years, the Tatar Communists, themselves divided into right and left factions, united in a desperate effort to block the policy of the party and of the Russian Communists, whom they accused of leading "an imperialist policy contrary to the national interests of Tatarstan."[6]

The trial of Sultan Galiev in 1928 was followed by systematic purges, beginning with the Tatar Communists and ending with the liquidation of all the political, intellectual, and religious elites. By 1933 organized opposition had ceased, but the purges continued until 1939 and affected all those who defended the political and cultural autonomy of the native Tatars.

In the postwar period, Tatarstan underwent intensive industrialization, mainly in the defense sector. This served to justify a new, massive import of Russian manpower while Tatars wishing to return to their homeland from other parts of the USSR were forbidden to settle within forty kilometers of the capital, Kazan. Society became dangerously polarized along ethnic lines, with the Tatars representing mainly the rural, peasant communities, and the Russians the urban industrial workers and technical cadres, controlling key sectors of the economy and the local government and administration.

The Present Conflict

Some commentators have been surprised that national protest in the USSR did not start among the stronger and larger nations such as the Uzbeks. With hindsight one sees that it was the nations who felt most threatened—by a stronger neighbor, assimilation, a disastrous ecological situation, and so on—or those among whom Russian presence and central control were particularly heavy who reacted first and most vigorously. In the case of the Tatars it was the loss of their language and cultural identity and the threat of assimilation that prompted them to political action.

Perestroika and the debacle of Afghanistan had the same catalyst effect on the rise of the national movements in the USSR as the Russian defeat in the war against Japan in 1905. In 1984–85 Tatar intellectuals began to campaign for the rehabilitation of the Tatar language and cautiously raised the question of federalism and sovereignty in the hopes of upgrading the status of their republic from "Autonomous" to "Union"

(Federal). They were the first to address such issues, which were considered dangerously disruptive and nationalistic at the time. With the degradation of the Soviet economy and increasing distrust of Moscow's ability to administrate, the issue of the republic's status also had a practical implication—federal republics were allowed to retain between 8 and 10 percent of their national produce and revenues, while autonomous republics could hope at best for a meager 2 percent.

In 1989 nationalist demands gained momentum. Two factors contributed to channel national forces: first, the establishment of TOTs (Tatar Public Centers) in 1988, the first important political group with a distinct pan-Tatar character to emerge in the Republic after perestroika; and second, the celebration in August 1989 of eleven centuries of Islam since its official adoption by the Bulgar Kingdom in 922. This anniversary was greeted as "the first true national festival since the fall of the Kazan Khanate." As events began to precipitate in the USSR, Tatarstan declared sovereignty on 30 August 1990, the first autonomous republic to do so. The Declaration of Sovereignty made no mention of Tatarstan being part of the RSFSR (Russian Soviet Federation of Socialist Republics). On 17 March 1991 Tatarstan (together with Chechen-Ingushetiya, North Ossetiya, and Tuva) refused to hold the RSFSR referendum on the institution of the post of a popularly elected president.[7] Preparations for the presidential elections of the RSFSR due to be held on 12 June 1991 were met in Kazan by massive demonstrations and a hunger strike led by deputy Fauzia Bayramova. As a result, on 28 May 1991 the Parliament of Tatarstan announced that it would hold its own presidential elections instead and forbade civil servants to take part in the RSFSR elections. On 12 June 1991, on the same day that Boris Yeltsin was elected president of Russia, Mintimer Shaymiyev was elected president of Tatarstan.[8]

Relations between Tatarstan and Russia continued to deteriorate after the August 1991 abortive coup in Moscow. After the CIS had been set up in December 1991, Tatarstan announced that it wanted to be admitted as a founding member, an intention equivalent to a demand of recognition as an independent state. Kazan was in the grip of demonstrations and strikes of a magnitude that surprised the nationalist leaders themselves, provoked, among other reasons, by Yeltsin's attempt to remove Shaymiyev for his lack of support during the coup and replace him with a Russian proxy.[9] Until that time the demands of the Tatar nationalists and of the Russian democrats—such as greater decentralization of power, control of the national produce, and ecology—

had coincided to some extent. It was the referendum on independence and the refusal to sign the Federation Treaty that brought the government of Tatarstan in direct conflict with Moscow and divided the two communities irrevocably. On 21 February 1992 the Tatarstan Parliament, under pressure from the radical nationalists, declared that a referendum would be held on 21 March 1992. The question to be put to the voters was: "Do you agree that the Republic of Tatarstan is a sovereign state, a subject of international law, building its relations with the Russian Federation and other states on the basis of treaties between equal partners?" After initial acquiescence, Moscow virulently challenged the referendum when it became clear that the response would be positive. On 5 March the Russian Parliament issued an appeal to Tatarstan cautioning against the danger of interethnic strife and separatism and asked the Russian Constitutional Court to decide on the issue. On 13 March the Constitutional Court duly ruled that the latter part of the referendum question was unconstitutional. For good measure, those sections of the Declaration of Sovereignty that limited the application of Russian laws in Tatarstan were also declared illegal. The chairman of the Constitutional Court, Valery Zorkin, accused the leadership of Tatarstan of dishonesty but nevertheless stated on Central Television on 18 March 1992 that the referendum "created the legal basis for secession." The Parliament of Tatarstan retorted that the Constitutional Court judgment was "the fruit of a judicial travesty." On 19 March Yeltsin warned that the referendum could tear the Russian Federation apart, and the Russian Parliament proclaimed that the vote would have no juridical basis. On 20 March, in a final effort to influence the outcome, Yeltsin appealed personally to the people of Tatarstan to vote no, an injudicious action that convinced many of those who were hesitant to vote in favor of independence. The results of the referendum, as indicated by ITAR-TASS on 22 and 25 March 1992, showed that 82 percent of the electorate took part. Of those who voted, 61.4 percent gave a positive reply.[10]

The Case of the North Caucasus and Chechnia

Two Centuries of Warfare

In 1783 Azaq and the Crimean Khanate fell to Russia, opening the way for the annexation of the North Caucasus. Totally divided linguistically and socially, the small nations of the North Caucasus seemed doomed. What happened instead was an epic struggle that united the North Caucasian Mountaineers in the longest and fiercest armed resistance of any Muslim nation to a foreign Christian invader. It drained Russia's military power, contributed to Russia's defeat in the Crimean War, discredited the Romanov dynasty, and provided inspiration to all the subjugated nations of the empire. The fighting was led by the Sufi *tariqat*, at first by the Naqshbandiya and later jointly with the Qadyriah. The *tariqat* gave the necessary cohesion, discipline, and jihad ideology to sustain the North Caucasians in their century-long combat.

Sheikh Mansur Ushurma, a Chechen Naqshbandi sheikh initiated by a Bukharan *haji*, was the first to lead the North Caucasus, from Chechnia and north Daghestan to Kuban, in a holy war against the Russians. In 1785 Mansur's warriors encircled an important Russian force on the bank of the river Sunja and completely annihilated it—the worst defeat ever inflicted on the armies of Catherine II. However, the Russians were able to crush the North Caucasians after the fall of the Ottoman fortress Anapa in 1791. Sheikh Mansur was captured and confined in Schlusselburg prison, where he died in 1793.[11] The Naqshbandiya disappeared from the North Caucasus, but the jihad left the memory that resistance and unity around Islam were possible. Thirty years later it would rise again to provide the ideology and inspiration for the Murid movement and to Shamil's *imamate*.

The Russian offensive continued after 1791. The piedmont of the Caucasus range was occupied, and inroads were made deep into the mountains. After victory in the Napoleonic wars, Russia threw her best generals, such as Ermolov, into the conquest. Russian action was ruthless, and for the first time genocidal tactics were applied against the Caucasians. In 1821 General Aleksei Petrovich Ermolov wrote to Alexander I, "The subjugation of Daghestan begun last year is now complete; and this country, proud, warlike and hitherto unconquered, has fallen at the sacred feet of Your Imperial Majesty."[12] But, as remarked by a contemporary Russian source, "he did not note that although the crater of the volcano had been cleansed, the internal fire was far from extinguished."[13] In 1825 the volcano erupted and war consumed Daghestan and Chechnia. For over thirty years afterwards, under the leadership of the three imams of Daghestan—Ghazi Muhammad, Hamza Bek, and Shamil—the Mountaineers, surrounded and isolated because Transcaucasia was already subjugated, managed to halt Russia's advance. In 1859 the imamate fell when Prince Bariatinsky deployed 40,000 troops to capture Shamil and his fifty remaining *murids* in their last strong-hold of Gunib.[14]

The North Caucasus was defeated but undaunted. After 1859 resistance was carried on by the Cherkess tribes until their tragic mass exodus to the Ottoman Empire in the 1870s. In Daghestan and Chechnia, the ideology of Muridism exemplified by Shamil—military jihad combined with the age-old traditions of freedom of a democratic, clanic mountain society—inspired the Mountaineers to rise again in 1877–78, and once more in 1920–21. In this latest great uprising, led by the militant *tariqat* and fought to regain the independence that the short-lived Mountain Republic (Gorskaia Respublika) had failed to obtain in the turmoil of the Civil War, Daghestan and Chechnia were subdued only after the intervention of two Red armies.[15] The Soviet period witnessed several sporadic but violent rebellions in protest against the antireligious campaign and collectivization in 1926, 1929–30, 1940, and 1942.[16]

During World War II, Russia tried to impose a final solution on her unruly Caucasian dominion, the most brutal attempt yet—genocide through deportation of entire North Caucasian nations. Six Muslim nations were deported in 1944, four of them from the North Caucasus: the Chechens, Ingush, Karachays, and Balkars, as well as some Cherkess, Muslim Ossetians (Digors), and Daghestani Avars. Approximately one-third of the nations perished during transportation alone.[17] Solzhenitsyn wrote that in the camps "only one nation refused to accept the psychology of submission," and that this applied "not to individuals, nor to insurgents, but to the nation as a whole—the Chechens."[18] After Stalin's death the North Caucasians were permitted to return to their homeland but were not entirely rehabilitated. In Chechen-Ingushetiya the control of the local organs of power and the Communist party remained firmly in Russian hands without even a modicum of outward concessions allowed for national cadres, as in other republics.[19] Furthermore, in an attempt to eradicate Islam completely, all mosques were destroyed after the deportation. It was only in 1979 that the Soviet authorities allowed the opening of a few mosques in an unsuccessful attempt to stem the growth of the clandestine Sufi brotherhoods.

The Path to Independence

The National Chechen Congress held its inaugurational meeting on 23–25 November 1990 in Groznyi. Its purpose was that of a popular front—to unite all the republican opposition political movements. On 27 November 1990, under pressure from the Congress, the Chechen-

Ingush Supreme Soviet proclaimed the republic's sovereignty. The aims of the Chechen nationalists, like those of the Tartars, were originally fairly modest—mainly to escape from the fold of the RSFSR and raise the status of their country from autonomous to federal republic, which would have enabled them to sign a union treaty with the USSR on an equal par with the former fifteen union republics of the Soviet Union.

Less than a year later, in June 1991, the National Chechen Congress held its second convention. By then the stand of the opposition had hardened. General Dzhokhar Dudaev, the chairman of the National Congress, hailed the imminent fall of the colonial empire that had robbed the nation of its "religion, language, education, science, culture, natural resources, ideology, mass media, leadership cadres, and rights to freedom and life." He rejected any "hybrid" version of sovereignty for the sake of economic stability, as advocated by the republican establishment and the Supreme Soviet in Moscow, and argued that "the price of genuine sovereignty is so great that to expect to achieve it cheaply is as absurd as to presume that the Chechens will ever be reconciled with their present miserly colonial freedom. . . . There is only one question to raise today: Do we want to be free or shall we willingly sell our future into serfdom? The time has come to make our choice."[20] He added that a slave who did not wish to free himself of his chains deserved his slavery. Significantly, he identified Islam as the only force able to unite the Caucasian nations and to resist foreign ideology and creeds.

The demands of the Chechen Congress included free elections, a new constitution and citizenship law, institution of a post of president, a referendum to determine the status of the republic vis-à-vis Moscow, and a referendum among the Ingush to decide on their relations with Chechnia. It was stressed, however, that a peace treaty was necessary between Chechnia and Russia before any agreement could be signed with either the USSR or the RSFSR, in view of the fact that the two countries had been continuously at war since the end of the eighteenth century. Certain preconditions had to be met: unconditional recognition of the right of the Chechen nation to sovereign independence; trial of those guilty of genocide against the Chechen nation; payment of compensation for the crimes against the nation and the return of the national patrimony; and finally, establishment of a proper government structure based on democratic principles.

The coup of 19 August 1991 in Moscow was met in Chechnia by nationwide resistance organized by General Dzhokhar Dudaev and Zelimkhan Yandarbiev, chairman of the Vainakh Democratic party. Dudaev was one of the few political leaders of note in the republics, along with the Kirghiz President Askar Akaev, to oppose the junta in the early hours of the putsch. The Soviet leadership of the republic absconded to Moscow or went into hiding. Protesters gathered opposite the government buildings for what turned out to be an unprecedented three-month-long demonstration. After the failure of the coup, on 22 August 1991, the Chechen opposition demanded the resignation of the local government and new elections. There was nothing exceptional in these demands—similar developments were taking place simultaneously throughout the Soviet Union. However, whereas in most of the Soviet republics and administrative units the defeat of Yanaev's junta allowed a transition, if not complete change, to a more genuinely national or democratic order with the agreement of Boris Yeltsin and the Russian Parliament, this was not to be the case in Chechnia. On 27 August the all-union radio reported an "uprising" in the Chechen-Ingush Republic.[21] Delegations from every town and village overtook the capital, Groznyi, to support the demonstrators; barricades were erected; the center of town was closed to traffic; the road to the airport was blocked; government buildings, radio and television stations and the telephone exchange were seized; and the parliament—besieged by demonstrators—went into permanent session for two weeks. Finally, two weeks later, on 6 September 1991, the Supreme Soviet was stormed by the National Guard units of General Dudaev and disbanded.

What followed until the election of Dzhokhar Dudaev as president on 27 October 1991 is still unclear. If one disregards Moscow's hysterical disinformation about Chechen "bandits" and Muslim fundamentalists, what stood out was the refusal of the Russian leadership to accept that what was right for Russia was also right for Chechnia—free elections, political pluralism, and democracy. The timing of the elections was the main point of discord with Moscow and the former establishment, who tried desperately to prolong the transitional period in order to recoup their forces. The Russian Parliament, on the advice of Vice President Alexander Rutskoy, issued a resolution on 8 October 1991 demanding that elections to the Supreme Soviet be held "on the basis of existing legislation," thus condemning Chechen-Ingushetiya to the status quo ante and denying the republic the same rights to change that had been gained by the federal republics of the USSR—in some cases effortlessly. The resolution allowed for "unconditional" use of force to ensure law and order.[22] The next day, Alexander Rutskoy recommended that General Dudaev and his "political clique" be arrested as criminals and terrorists.[23] The resolution was received in Chechnia as a virtual declaration of war. On 18 October, as Russian troops were massing in North Ossetiya and Daghestan, General Dudaev warned that war might be unavoidable. He reported that 62,000 Chechens had signed up for the ranks of the National Guard and militia and that volunteers from the neighboring Muslim North Caucasian republics were pouring into Groznyi to support the Chechen resistance. The conflict continued to escalate. On 19 October President Boris Yeltsin ordered the Chechen opposition to submit unconditionally within three days; on 23 October the RSFSR Procuracy ruled that Chechens were subject to criminal law for public appeals to overthrow the state and the establishment, for "violating the integrity of the RSFSR," and for whipping up national or religious differences. The Procuracy further threatened to close the local newspapers and to ban "any associations of citizens, . . . political parties, public organizations or mass movements." Yeltsin's *ukaz* (decree) was vividly described on Chechen television as "the last belch of the Russian Empire."[24]

Despite the turmoil, the elections went ahead, and on 27 October 1991 Dzhokhar Dudaev was elected president over three other candidates.[25] He was sworn in on the Koran. Moscow made a last, inept attempt to intervene directly: on 8 November 1991 Yeltsin declared a state of emergency and airlifted some two thousand troops to Groznyi to arrest Dudaev. Chechnia was put on war alert, and the capital became a fortress. All political factions in Chechnia, putting aside their differences, rallied behind General Dudaev; the neighboring Daghestani mountain clans proclaimed *Ghazawat* (jihad) and pledged to fight alongside the Chechens. Mobilization of volunteers began throughout the North Caucasus as far afield as Azerbaijan. Significantly, the old-guard, supposedly pro-Russian Daghestani government, one of the most conservative and unreformed in the USSR at the time, backed the call for Ghazawat and promised its assistance to Chechnia in the event of a Russian intervention—an indication of where real loyalties stood. The Russian troops were unable to move from the airport and were ignominiously dispatched back to Russia the next day.

Implications for Russia

What are the reasons for Russia's refusal so far to grant CIS status to Tatarstan and Chechnia? Strangely enough, economic concerns do not appear to prevail, despite the fact that Tatarstan produces 25 percent of Russia's oil and that a two-week-long embargo from Chechnia in early 1992 wrought havoc in the south of Russia. Furthermore, regional decentralization has gone far enough since the beginning of 1992 to ensure de facto economic autonomy to the republics and regions of the Russian Federation. For example, Prime Minister Sabirov of Tatarstan signed an agreement on 22 January 1992 with his Russian counterpart, Gaidar, that effectively canceled Russia's right to raise federal taxes in the republic, although officially Moscow continues to refute the principle of one-channel taxation. The agreement, valid for five years, gave Tatarstan control over its natural produce. Under a special clause, Tatarstan agreed to deliver 50 percent of its oil production to Russia in exchange for drilling and refinery equipment.[26]

I would argue that Moscow's objections to decolonization are of a psychological order and therefore more difficult to overcome. They lie in Russia's perceived danger of encirclement by the Muslim Irano-Turkic world, the possible loss of strategic outlets on the Black Sea and the Caspian, and the fear of pan-Islamism and pan-Turkism. The Muslim political leaders who were liquidated in the Stalinist purges in the 1930s were accused indiscriminately of nationalism, pan-Islamism, pan-Turkism, and even pan-Turanism in the case of Sultan Galiev. In the postwar period nationalism among non-Russian peoples of the empire was equated with chauvinism, while pan-Turkism and pan-Islamism were judged utter evils. The situation has not changed with the demise of the Soviet Union. If anything, the Russians' sense, real or imagined, of a Turkic and Islamic threat to their national "integrity" has increased proportionately to their loss of control. It is a determining factor in the Russian government's attitude toward the Tatars and Chechens because (1) they are more rebellious, politicized, and inimical to Russian interference than the Central Asians, and (2) their sense of identity and nationalism have a supranational and extraterritorial dimension. And this may have very practical implications.

In the case of the Chechens, the supranational notion of being Caucasian "Mountaineers" (Gortsy) overrides any disputes they may have with their fellow Muslim neighbors. This sense of communality of the North Caucasian mountain peoples has been forged through fire and battle against the common enemy since Mansur's first jihad against the Russian invader. The national heroes—Mansur, Ghazi Muhammad, Hamza Bek, Shamil, and Uzun Haji[27]—be they Avars or Chechens, belonged to all the Muslim North Caucasus. Furthermore, the Republic of the Mountain,[28] which survived as an independent state recognized by Germany, Austro-Hungary, and Turkey for a tragically short time in 1918, showed that a confederate state of the North Caucasus Mountaineers was possible. General Dudaev described it as "one of the most important efforts to create a common Caucasian home." During the second Chechen Congress he stated, "We must not forget that we bear a responsibility for the fate of our sister nations in the Caucasus. The union of all the Caucasian nations on an equal basis is the only possible way for the future. As we hold a central geographic, strategic and economic position in the Caucasus, and have the necessary human potential, we must be the initiators of this future union."[29] To this end, one of Dudaev's first moves after coming to power was to give his support to the Assembly of the Peoples of the North Caucasus, whose aim is to resurrect the Mountain Republic.

The Assembly of the Mountain Peoples was formed in 1990 on the instigation of the Abkhazians after relations with Tbilisi began to deteriorate. The first objective of the assembly is to encourage the establishment of independent government structures among the nations of the North Caucasus. Once this is achieved these nations would form a confederation that would eventually secede from Russia. Meanwhile, the national congresses of the nations forming the assembly have signed an agreement to support each other in case of danger. Despite its "informal" basis, the assembly provides a nascent political and national framework for a future North Caucasian confederation.[30] The escalation of the Georgian and Abkhazian conflict has shown the effectiveness of the Mountaineers' solidarity by allowing the small Abkhaz nation (97,000 people) to resist the onslaught of the Georgians (four million strong) and their regular army with the help of a handful of volunteers from the assembly. (Despite Georgian claims, not only Russian weapons but also intervention explains the Abkhaz military success.) This latest confrontation in the Caucasus emphasizes the historical opposition of the Muslim North Caucasians against Russia and Georgia. It was under the pretext of defending Christian Georgia from the attacks of the Muslim Daghestani and Chechen "bandits" that Russia embarked upon the conquest of the Caucasus. This conflict is potentially extremely dangerous, especially since Georgia's entry into the CIS. It could embrace the whole North Caucasus and leave the door open for Russian military intervention. On the other hand, it could speed up the process of pan-Caucasian unity. Indeed, attacks and ethnic violence inflicted on the nations of the assembly by Russia or Georgia would lead to a political awakening among those peoples, such as the Daghestanis, who have not yet raised the issue of independence and sovereignty and whose participation is strategically essential for a viable independent North Caucasus.

In the Tatars' case a pan-Turkic vocation is almost inevitable. They are the only Muslim diaspora nationality of the former Soviet Union with colonies from Romania and Finland to China and Japan; 75 percent of the Volga Tatars live outside Tatarstan. Until the October Revolution Kazan served as a political, cultural, and religious center for other Tatars—Siberian, Astrakhan, Crimean, Lithuanian, and Polish—and other Turkic peoples, such as the closely related Bashkirs, as well as the non-Muslim Turkic peoples of the Volga region: Chuvash, Mordvins, Maris, and Udmurts. All the prerevolutionary Tatar Jadids were convinced pan-Islamists and pan-Turks. It was among the Tatars of Russia and not in the Ottoman Empire that the ideology and tenets of pan-Turkism were originally elaborated, understandably so because it was a question of survival. The Jadids believed that only the unity of the 'Umma could allow the Muslims to resist assimilation by Russians. On the eve of the revolution they advocated national and cultural extraterritorial autonomy for all Muslim nations of the empire within a unified but decentralized and democratic state. The Tatar national Communists followed in their footsteps and reasoned that in order to escape dying out as a nation in the Russian environment—to control their destiny and influence the politics of the Soviet Union—they needed the support of all the Tatar communities and Turkic and Muslim nations of the USSR.

Similarly, today the three Tatar organizations that aspire to represent the Tatar nation—TOTs, Milli Majles, and the International Tatar Congress—all claim an extraterritorial authority. When TOTs was set up in 1988 as a cultural body—because political claims were still unacceptable at the time—its manifesto stated that "it is essential to elaborate and put into effect a legal mechanism regulating the relations of the republican cultural, educational and scientific bodies with the Tatar diaspora in order to ensure the cultural consolidation of the nation." The manifesto clearly described TOTs as "a movement based on two principles, the territorial and the national (non-territorial). The first principle unites citizens . . . from all groups of the population of the Tatar Republic, while the second brings together initiative groups from the Tatar population living beyond the borders of the Tatar ASSR."[31] The main opposition of state organs to the establishment of

TOTs was over this very issue. The Tatars are also the most active proponents of the Assembly of the Turkic People, founded in 1990 in Astrakhan, a loose organization but one that may well come to sudden prominence, as did its counterpart, the Assembly of the Peoples of the North Caucasus. At any rate, this assembly serves to keep the ideals of pan-Turkism alive.

The question of Idel-Ural and Bashkortostan is, however, of more pressing concern than the hypothetical unity of the Turkic peoples. As in the Caucasus with the Mountain Republic, the dream of resurrecting a large Turkic state in the Volga-Ural region has been kept alive. Today a Tatar-Bashkir confederation would be an economically viable and politically practical solution: both republics are highly industrialized; Bashkortostan has the oil refineries Tatarstan lacks, while Tatarstan has the agricultural produce needed to feed its neighbors; the two nations were well on the way to assimilation before the revolution; and the Tatars are the majority nation[32] in Bashkortostan, where they live in compact settlements in the richest oil-producing lands bordering Tatarstan. They can control the parliament, where they have the majority of seats, and although the government of Tatarstan firmly denies having any irredentist claims on neighboring republics, the territorial question is bound to be raised sooner or later. Russia succeeded in convincing the Bashkirs to sign—although after some hesitation—the Federation Treaty, with pledges of devolution of power and economic privileges. However, the promises have failed to materialize and discontent is growing. A national opposition that doubts the wisdom of this decision is increasingly willing to work with the Tatars toward independence. Finally, Kazakhstan, not Russia, would be a natural pole of attraction for Tartar-Bashkir confederation, strengthening the Turkic and Muslim character of that Republic and weakening its dependence on Russia.

Conclusion

Russia is fighting a rearguard action to remain "one and indivisible" and to preserve its Muslim colonies. As Russia has little to offer, there can be little doubt that sooner or later the Chechens and the Tatars will convince their neighbor sister nations of the advantages of cooperation, thus bringing the prospect of genuine independence closer. For Russia this will mean the loss of its southern territories in the Caucasus, with the perspective of a strongly Muslim and by no means friendly southern bloc looking for ties to Turkey and Iran. In Tatarstan, the republican government is committed to working toward full independence and is slowly gaining concessions in negotiations with Moscow. The Russian opposition has been unable to mobilize the Russian masses in Tatarstan and to articulate an attractive alternative program to independence. However, the Tatars themselves say that "we were the first to be colonized and will be the last to be free." But when Tatarstan wins independence it will be quickly followed by Bashkortostan. The other Volga republics where the Tatars have begun to spread the idea of a Volga-Ural confederation will naturally gravitate toward Kazan. At stake for Moscow is the loss of a large territory that controls trade routes and communications between western Russia and Siberia through the Volga.

Because Russia is the only colonial power that humbly suffered the yoke of the peoples it claims to rule today—(the modern Tatar descendants of the Golden Horde), because Russians were always defeated in the East—twice this century, in Manchuria in 1905 and Afghanistan in 1989—they are unable yet, unlike other colonial and multinational states, to envisage a pragmatic and fair principle such as a confederation or a genuine commonwealth on which to build future relations with their colonies. To lose Kazan is compared to disembowelment, and thus Russian energies are geared to an intellectual, political, and propaganda campaign: (1) Among the intelligentsia, efforts are being made to revive the concept of Eurasianism, which would combine the best of East and West, to find a completely novel nationality theory and redefine the role of Russia—to build a "revolutionary" new order, yet again. (2) The Russian democrats' approach is less sophisticated. They proclaim that "democracy," "pluralism," "privatization," and "human rights" must take precedence over narrow and selfish national issues. It is implied that these worthy ideals can only be safeguarded by greater Russia. In the 1920s it was the defense of "world revolution," "Bolshevism," "Marxism," and "collectivization" that was used by Russian Communists to curtail the power of their Muslim comrades. The catchwords are different, but the rationale remains the same. However, "democracy" as reinterpreted by Moscow holds little attraction for the nationalities. (3) The press propaganda is the most crude. It stresses Russia's messianic role in civilizing the wild "Asiates" and defending Christendom from their invasions. A new danger now faces Christian Russia in the guise of her own home-grown Muslim fundamentalists— no distinctions are made between the very liberal and secular Tatar Islamic tradition and the Sufi-inspired brand of Islam among the North Caucasians. Muslim political leaders who oppose Moscow, such as Dzhokhar Dudaev, are branded as enemies of Russia and, therefore, of the West, and compared indiscriminately to Colonel Qaddafi, Saddam Hussein, and Ayatollah Khomeini. The Tatar radical leader Fauzia Bayramova is vilified as a bloodthirsty fundamentalist, while according to the former speaker of the Russian Parliament, Ruslan Khazbulatov, President Shaymiyev should be brought to Moscow in an iron cage. These persons are accused, sometimes in the same breath, of being unreformed Communists, fascists, rabid nationalists, and Islamic extremists. Apocalyptic visions are drawn of ethnic conflicts and persecutions of Russians. The notion that only Russia can prevent barbarism is frequently inferred. The fact that ethnic tensions are to a great extent the legacy of Russian and Soviet government is never addressed. Such attitudes serve to justify the new Russian military doctrine toward the "near abroad" and within the Russian Federation the need for drastically increased centralization of political power in Moscow in Russian hands. It does not augur well for stability in the region.

Thus, after four centuries of imperial rule, the Russians have not learned to understand their Muslim subjects, and this augurs ill for the future of the Russian Federation as we know it today. As important as the future shape of Russian frontiers is the question of the role that Russia will want to play in the Muslim world as a regional power that will remain even if it loses its colonies. Since perestroika Russian leaders have given priority to establishing the country as a respectable fellow European, but this does not mean that Russia has discarded its oriental ambitions forever. When the hopes of economic recovery with Western help are not fulfilled, Russia will reconsider its Eastern policy. When this happens, the hysteria that is deliberately or unconsciously fanned against the Muslims of Russia will prevent Moscow from making a realistic assessment and engaging in a sensible and pragmatic foreign policy. This will be felt particularly in relations with Iran and Turkey—the other two great powers in the region closely connected by historical, cultural, and religious ties with the Muslims of Russia—and its traditional opponents now vying for influence in Central Asia and the Caucasus.

Notes

Author's note: I wish to thank the Lynde and Harry Bradley Foundation for supporting the research reflected in this chapter.

1. According to the 1989 All-Union Census, the population is 6,648,760, which places them after the Uzbeks, Kazakhs, and Azerbaijanis. The Tatars believe, however, that their real numbers are much higher because many Tatars living in a Russian environment, or children of mixed marriages, used to hide their nationality.

2. Azade Ayse Rorlich, *The Volga Tatars: A Profile in National Resilience* (Stanford: Hoover Institution Press, 1986), 41.

3. Many of these new converts, Novo-Kryashens, remained crypto-Muslims, as opposed to the early Kryashens converts, and reverted to Islam after 1905.

4. Sultan Galiev was released in 1924 and rearrested in 1928. In 1929 he was condemned to death and spent six months on death row. He was reprieved and sentenced to ten years hard labor in the Solovki camp. Released once again in 1934, he was arrested for the final time in 1937. For Sultan Galiev's theories of Muslim national communism, see Alexandre Bennigsen and Chantal Quelquejay, *Les Mouvements nationaux chez les musulmans de Russie: Le "sultangalievisme" au Tatarstan* (National movements among the Muslims of Russia: "Sultangelievism" in Tatarstan) (Paris: Mouton, 1960), *Sultan Galiev, Le père de la révolution tiers-mondiste* (Sultan Galiev, the father of Third World revolution) (Paris: Fayard, 1986). For biographical information based on newly released archival material, see Sh. F. Mukhamedyarov and B.F. Sultanbekov, "Mirsaid Sultan Galiev: His Character and Fate," *Central Asian Survey 9*, no. 2 (1990): 109–18.

5. *Stenografichekii otchet IX-oi oblastnoi konferentsii Tatarskoi organizatsii* R.K.P. (b) (Stenographic report of the Ninth Regional Conference of the Tatar Organization of the Russian Communist Party [bolshevik]), 113–14.

6. Gerhard von Mende, *Der Nationale Kampf der Russland Turken* (The national struggle of the Turks of Russia) (Berlin: 1936), 158–59.

7. The All-Union referendum to decide on the future of the USSR was held the same day.

8. Thirty-six percent of the population of Tatarstan took part in the RSFSR elections, and only 14 percent voted for Yeltsin. Sixty percent of the electorate voted in the Tatarstan presidential elections, out of which two-thirds voted for Shaymiyev.

9. Shaymiyev, usually a cautious politician, unwisely supported the junta during the first day of the August 1991 coup in Moscow. When Yeltsin tried to remove him, the alternative would have been somebody from Yeltsin's team or the vice president of Tatarstan, Vasily Likhachev, a Russian. Despite the fact that Likhachev has taken a position in favor of Tatarstan's independence, is married to a Tatar, and heads the Tatar team negotiating with Moscow, he is not entirely trusted by the nationalists, who in any case do not want a Russian president for Tatarstan whatever his affiliation. The situation could be compared to Kazakhstan in December 1986 when Brezhnev removed the first secretary Din-Muhamed Kunaev—who had, totally undeservedly, become a symbol of Kazakh nationalism—and replaced him with the Russian, Kolbin.

10. Altogether, 50.3 percent of the electorate voted in favor while 30.5 percent voted against. The votes in the predominantly Tatar rural areas were 75.3 percent in favor, and in the cities, which have a greater ethnic mix, 55.7 percent. In Kazan 51.2 percent voted against.

11. See Alexandre Bennigsen, "Un mouvement populaire au Caucase au XVIIIe siècle. La 'Guerre Sainte' du sheikh Mansur (1785–1791), page mal connue et controversée des relations russo-turques" (The 'Holy War' of Sheikh Mansur [1785–1791], a little-known and controversial aspect of Russo-Turkish relations), *Cahiers du Monde Russe et Soviétique* 5, no. 2 (April–June 1964): 159–205; also the first-ever history of Mansur published in the Caucasus and Russia by a young Chechen historian, Sharipuddin B. Akhmadov, *Imam Mansur: Narodo-osvoboditel'noe dvizhenie v Chechne i na Severnom Kavkaze v kontse XVIII v.* (Imam Mansur: The national liberation movement in Chechnia and the North Caucasus at the end of the eighteenth century) (Groznyi: Izd. Kniga, 1991). Akhmadov worked on his biography of Mansur for the last twenty years, but was prevented from publishing it because the subject remained taboo. Symbolically for the Chechens, the book was delivered to the printers on 20 August 1991, the day of the attempted putsch in Moscow.

12. Quoted by Moshe Gammer in "Russian Strategies in the Conquest of Chechnia and Daghestan, 1825–1859," in M. Bennigsen Broxup, ed., *The North Caucasus Barrier: The Russian Advance towards the Muslim World* (London: Hurst and Co., 1992), 47, from John F. Baddeley, *The Russian Conquest of the Caucasus* (London: 1908), 137–38.

13. Moshe Gammer, "Russian Strategies," 47.

14. John Frederic Baddeley, *The Russian Conquest of the Caucasus* (London: Longmans, 1908) and *The Rugged Flanks of the Caucasus* (Oxford: Oxford University Press, 1940), remain the main sources in English on the history of the North Caucasian *Ghazawat*. See also W. E. D. Allen and Paul Muratoff, *Caucasian Battlefields: A History of the Wars on the Turco-Caucasian Border* (Cambridge: Cambridge University Press, 1953); and forthcoming by Moshe Gammer, *Muslim Resistance to the Tsar: Shamil and the Russian Conquest of Chechnia and Daghestan* (London: Frank Cass).

15. The two Red armies that participated in the liquidation of this uprising were the 11th Army from Astrakhan (the "Terek-Daghestan Army") and the 9th Army (the "Kuban Army"). For a detailed description of this war, see my chapter "The Last *Ghazawat*: The 1920–1921 Uprising," in *The North Caucasus Barrier*, 112–145.

16. The detailed history of this period is still to be written. The only available source in English so far is Abdurahman Avtorkhanov, "The Chechens and Ingush during the Soviet Period and its Antecedents," in *The North Caucasus Barrier*, 146–95.

17. The other deported nations were the Buddhist Kalmyks, the Crimean Tatars, the Meskhetian Turks, and the Volga Germans. See on this subject Robert

Conquest, *The Nation Killers: The Soviet Deportation of Nationalities* (London: Macmillan, 1970); and by the same author *The Soviet Deportation of National-ities* (London: Macmillan, 1960). For the deportation of the Chechens and In-gush, see Avtorkhanov, "Chechens and Ingush," and his *Narodoubistvo v SSSR* (Genocide in the USSR), a special memorandum to the United Nations written in 1948. More recent data and figures are provided in "Deportatsiia. Beriia dokladyvaet Stalinu. . . ." (Deportation: Beria reports to Stalin. . . .) *Kommu-nist* (February 1991): 101–12.

18. A. Solzhenitsyn, *Arkhipelag Gulag* (Paris: YMCA Press), 420–21.

19. On this subject see Michael Rywkin, "The Communist Party and the Sufi Tariqat in the Checheno-Ingush Republic," *Central Asian Survey* 10, nos. 1/2 (1991): 133–45.

20. A precise agenda was formulated setting up conditions and a timetable for negotiations with Moscow. They were published together with Dudaev's speech in the Groznyi independent newspaper *Bart*, no. 6 (June 1991).

21. Monitored by the BBC, SWB SU/1163 ii, 29 August 1991.

22. Tass World Service in Russian, 1920 GMT, 8 October 1991, SWB SU/1199 C1/2, 10 October 1991.

23. Under Article 218 of the Criminal Code and Articles 67 and 68 on ter-rorism against the lawful authorities.

24. The full text of the Procuracy statement is reproduced in SWB SU/1212 B/4, 25 October 1991. For the Chechen television comments see the report by S. Asuev in SWB SU/1208 b/5, 21 October 1991. For the detailed description of events following the Moscow attempted coup and the election of Dudaev, see my chapter "After the Putsch, 1991," in *The North Caucasus Barrier*, 219–40.

25. The other candidates in the presidential elections were R. Gaitemirov, leader of the Green movement, M. Sulaev, an agronomist, and B. Umaev.

26. The agreement was published in the Tatar press, but the clause regarding the oil industry remained secret. In July 1992 Tatarstan was considering slow-ing down the deliveries of oil because Russia was late in fulfilling its part of the contract. Prime Minister Sabirov thought that this was due mainly to inef-ficiency rather than deliberate pressure to bring the Tatar government to com-promise in the negotiations for independence (reported by P.M. Sabirov during an interview with the author). The Tatars want their relations with Russia sealed by a treaty and incorporated in the two countries' respective constitu-tions. Only in this way will they feel secure that Russia will not renege on present and future agreements.

27. Sheikh Uzun Haji was an Avar, but his military activity was centered mainly in Chechnia, where he is particularly revered. He inspired the uprising of 1920–21.

28. See Haidar Bammate, *Le Caucase du Nord et la revolution russe. (Aspects Politiques)* (The North Caucasus and the Russian Revolution: political issues) (Paris, 1929) republished in English translation by *Central Asian Survey* 10, no.

4 (1991): 1–29. Haidar Bammate was the foreign minister of the Mountain Republic.

29. *Bart*, no. 6 (June 1991).

30. Among these conflicts one can mention those opposing the Chechens and the Ingush over a division of territory, the Ingush and the Ossetiyans over Vladikavkaz, the Chechens and the Daghestanis in Khasav Yurt, and the Kabardians and the Balkars, who have refused to take part because of the anti-Balkar sentiments of the president of the Assembly, Musa Shanibev.

31. *Tezisy k podgotovke platformy tatarskogo obshchestvennogo tsentra* (Thesis for the preparation of the platform of the Tatar Public Centre) (Kazan: 1989).

32. According to the 1989 All-Union Census, 1,120,000.

5

Azerbaijan

Yuri N. Zinin and Alexei V. Maleshenko

Azerbaijan in the Soviet Period

The republic of Azerbaijan, with a population of 7.1 million, is situated in Transcaucasia and occupies a territory of almost 87,000 square kilometers. Its indigenous population, the Azerbaijanis, make up 83 percent of the total population, with Russians accounting for 5.6 percent and Armenians (up to 1990) for 5 percent. The other minorities include Ukrainians, Kurds, Tatars, and various peoples of Daghestan. Several hundred thousand Azerbaijanis live in neighboring Georgia, and about as many lived, until 1990, in Armenia. The number of Azerbaijanis living in neighboring Iran is estimated at over ten million.

The territory of Azerbaijan has been the birthplace of various civilizations and has formed part of different states and empires. Ethnically, Azerbaijan is predominantly Turkic, its inhabitants by and large the descendants of the Oguz and Seljuks who settled in the region as early as the eleventh century. Spiritually and culturally, Islam, introduced by the Arabs in the seventh century, has had the strongest impact. Since the sixteenth century, the territory of Azerbaijan was the birthplace of various khanates dependent on either the Ottoman Empire or Persia. Then, as a result of Russia's wars against Turkey and Persia, those khanates became part of Russia. In 1918, after the demise of the Russian Empire and the October 1917 revolution, the Azerbaijan Democratic Republic was proclaimed. In 1920 Soviet power was established in Azerbaijan with the Bolsheviks' help, and the Azerbaijan Soviet Socialist Republic was formed within its present borders.

Over the years of Soviet power, in the course of industrialization, collectivization, and the cultural revolution directed from Moscow, Azerbaijan underwent a radical demolition of its traditional ways of life and structures and became fully integrated into the USSR's socioeconomic and administrative system. The rate and the character of these changes, however, differed from those in the neighboring republics of Transcaucasia and Central Asia. This was due, first of all, to the republic's huge oil and gas reserves and the traditional specialization of Baku in oil production (as early as the 1880s the area accounted for up to 50 percent of the world's oil output). Secondly, these distinctions stemmed from the fact that the republic bordered Turkey and Iran. These countries were seen by Moscow as satellites of the West and, during the Cold War period, as military allies to the West directly on the southern borders of the USSR. A third factor has been Azerbaijan's fertile soil and subtropical climate, which are perfect for large-scale cultivation of cotton, tea, tobacco, grapes, and other foods and technical crops.

All this made Azerbaijan a priority republic from the perspective of Russia's intensive industrialization and investment policy. From the 1920s to the 1940s, the republic produced 50 to 60 percent of all oil extracted in the USSR. According to *Soviet Azerbaijan: Myths and Reality*, published in Baku in 1987, the average annual rate of growth of investments in its economy were higher than the average figures for the USSR. Specifically, they were 8 percent higher on average between 1928 and 1941, and 18 to 140 percent higher during the 1980s.[1]

As a result, a considerable industrial potential, represented by 100 different production sectors, was built in Azerbaijan during the seventy years of Soviet power. Leading among them were oil production and refining, the manufacture of oil equipment, chemistry, metallurgy, and instrument making. As in the other republics, the economy of Azerbaijan was deeply integrated into the Soviet economic system and followed the common centralized plan. In the beginning of the 1990s the republic produced 1.5 percent of the gross industrial output of the former USSR, although it accounted for only 0.4 percent of the country's population. In the late 1980s, just before perestroika, Azerbaijan shipped about 50 percent of its industrial products to other republics and regions of the former USSR by way of natural exchanges. In turn, its entire demand for sugar, coal, tractors, cars, metallurgical equipment, wood, and chemical products, and part of its demand for flour, dairy products, butter, fabrics, and other products, was met with reciprocal deliveries from other republics.[2] According to estimates by Azerbaijani economists, in the interrepublican exchange Azerbaijan's imports slightly exceeded its exports, with Russian goods accounting for 55 percent of the essential products brought into the republic.[3]

Other consequences of the seventy years of Soviet reign were the profound social and cultural changes in society. Regardless of how they were achieved, the fact remains that those decades have contributed to the assertion of modern Azerbaijani statehood and the ethnic consolidation of Azerbaijanis into a single nation with a defined territory. The modernization of society, cultural uplift, proliferation of modern knowledge, and familiarization of the masses with the advances of modern science and technology may also be attributed to Soviet rule.

This is confirmed by a literacy rate of 100 percent and a high educational level in a republic that houses 4,300 schools, sixteen institutes and universities, and 100,000 students. It is also manifested by the large contingent of top-grade engineers and skilled workers, the local school, which trains personnel in the spheres of oil production and petrochemistry, which were among the most reputable in the former USSR. Many of them occupied key positions in the Soviet petrochemical industry.

At the same time, as in the other republics, Azerbaijan developed by the canons of the heavily ideologized administrative command system and, consequently, went through the same trials and tribulations—forced collectivization in the 1930s and 1940s with mass purges and repression. Among its victims were the "bourgeois nationalists," the "religious establishment," whose mosques and *madrassas* (Islamic religious schools) were closed, the "national intelligentsia," and the "proponents of antisocialist ideas."

In the European republics of the USSR, the authorities waged a vigorous struggle by way of bans and intimidation against the "pernicious influence of capitalism and the Western way of life." In Azerbaijan the official propaganda was particularly vociferous against the influence of pan-Turkism and pan-Islam, especially after the beginning of the Islamic revolution in Iran and the events in Afghanistan.

The party bureaucracy reigned supreme in all spheres and sectors of society and, in the last few decades, began to merge with the mafia and the local "shadow" economy. According to one of the leaders of the Popular Front of Azerbaijan, the well-known writer Yusef Samedoglu, people in the provinces and in the countryside were "on the authorities' hook."[4]

Any top district executive (normally, a member of the Communist party) was a small local *allah*. With the ban on private trade, he was all-powerful in deciding whether or not to let a farmer set out to sell his harvest in another district or republic. If the farmer was not allowed to leave, his family simply could not make ends meet. This slavish dependence eroded society from top to bottom.

These were not just occasional deviations or shortcomings but mani-festations of the deep moral, social, and economic crisis that affected the entire system. The extensive model of development fully outlived its use and became a stumbling block to progress. Social problems such as unemployment (0.5 million people were unemployed), the flagrant corruption among officials at all levels, the shortage of goods and hous-ing, and ecological problems grew worse with each passing year. More-over, after the discovery of large oil deposits in Siberia in the 1960s, Azerbaijan began to lose its unique and privileged role as the country's oil treasury. By the end of the 1980s it accounted for only 2 percent of the production of oil and condensate in the USSR, or twelve million tons per year in physical terms.[5] This naturally affected the general fi-nancial situation in the republic and exacerbated social tension.

Perestroika in Azerbaijan

Perestroika, proclaimed in Moscow by Mikhail Gorbachev, was ac-cepted by the Communist leadership of Azerbaijan as yet another cam-paign from the center, leaving intact the foundations of the old system. Its slogans did not find immediate acclaim in the republic as they did in Russia. According to Samedoglu, "there wasn't a single emigrant dissi-dent in the republic before 1985."[6] This was not only because the au-thorities cracked down on dissent but because of the psychology of a traditionally law-abiding and God-fearing people.

The problem of Karabakh, however, triggered the participation of dif-ferent forces, including the intellectuals, in the process of perestroika. The attempt by the Armenian leadership of the Nagorno-Karabakh au-tonomous region to annex that territory in February 1988 and make it part of Armenia brought about fierce resistance by the Azerbaijanis. The slogans in defense of the sovereignty and national interests of the republic united the most diverse forces, including prominent intellec-tuals, public leaders, and scholars. Relying on mass support, these forces started the struggle against the official power structures for greater independence for Azerbaijan in the economic, political, and social spheres, and for the acceleration of the reform process.

It is evident that the Azerbaijani leadership has yet to develop a comprehensive economic model for the republic, and this has become the subject of acute debates. The participants in these debates have made negative assessments of Azerbaijan's relations with Moscow (nonequitable exchanges and prices to the detriment of Azerbaijan, pilferage of its wealth, and other losses). The task is to break free from the centralized system, dispose freely of the goods and products manufactured in the republic, and establish direct links with other republics and foreign countries. Although there is general support for the market model with diverse forms of ownership and an open economy, experts differ on the pace and scope of the reforms.

It is believed that Azerbaijan has more prerequisites for success than the other eastern republics because of its oil and gas reserves and other natural resources, especially cotton, advanced industry, and qualified personnel. In particular, according to the weekly *Azerbaijan Panorama*, of the thirteen million tons of oil produced in the republic, after laying aside six to seven million tons for internal needs, the rest can be sold at world prices for about a billion dollars.[7] As of the beginning of 1992 there were 864 registered participants in foreign economic relations in the republic: enterprises, cooperatives, and joint ventures.[8] Statistics point to the growing export of raw materials: petroleum products, hydrocarbon wastes, detergents, and cotton fiber, mostly in exchange for flour, sugar, butter, and other foodstuffs and consumer goods. The republic badly needs consumer goods because they account for only a quarter of its overall industrial output.[9] For example, the "Azerbintorg" foreign trade association has exported 21,000 tons of diesel fuel and a large amount of rolled nonferrous metals in exchange for 6,000 tons of flour and 1,800 pairs of shoes.[10]

Azerbaijan hopes to reorient a number of defense installations of the former USSR located on its territory for its own needs. A special industrial research center has been set up for this purpose that unites more than twenty former defense installations. A national aerospace agency, ANAKA, has also been formed. It comprises three institutes for space research, several design bureaus, and an experimental space technology plant.[11]

Nevertheless, the full-scale independent entrance by Azerbaijan into the world market is restricted by its heavy dependence on what was once a centralized Soviet economy. It should be noted, for example, that Azerbaijan brings in a considerable amount of oil for its refineries from Russia, and the same applies to gas and to the deliveries of other semifinished products and accessories.

The disruption of the old intersectoral links between Azerbaijan and the other republics of the former USSR has had a detrimental effect on the Azeri economy. The president of Azerineft has described the situation in the oil industry as catastrophic. This includes a production slump, general technological backwardness, and the absence of investment for the development and modernization of production assets, which formerly came from the centralized federal budget.[12]

Today, according to the republican press, only 20 to 50 percent of the capacity of the enterprises in the leading sectors of the republic's economy are utilized, while on the whole, plants and factories are on the brink of closure.[13] Instead, just as in the other republics of the former USSR, brokerage activities and the opening of cooperative shops reselling imported goods are on the rise.

The Azerbaijanis see the attraction of foreign capital for the development of new oil and gas fields and the modernization of old ones as a way out of this situation. There have been offers from the international arena to assist in the development of a large Azeri offshore oilfield. The Amoco Eurasia Petroleum Company, from the United States, was granted this opportunity. The contract has yet to be signed, but under its terms Amoco is to invest six billion dollars in the project.[14] Negotiations are also under way with British Petroleum, Pemco Penzoil, and a number of German and Turkish companies.

As announced by the prime minister of the republic, oil production is to be raised over the next few years to twenty million tons per year with the participation of foreign companies.[15] Most significant will be the construction of a regional oil pipeline north of the Caspian, with assistance from Oman, for the pumping of Azerbaijan's and Kazakhstan's oil into the Black Sea and Mediterranean ports.

It was apparently in the hope of becoming energy self-sufficient that Azerbaijan decided against joining the CIS, and it does not participate in the economic and financial agreements within its framework, or is doing so only partially. At the same time, two prominent economic leaders of Azerbaijan, S. Gadzhiyev and A. Azizbekov, have warned that because of the lack of coordination in the CIS—each member tries to operate independently in the world market—the prices of fuel and cotton have dropped—to the detriment of all member states of the former USSR.[16] In June 1992 the deputy prime minister of the republic for the affairs of the former USSR, Azerbaijan's ambassador to Moscow, Khikmet Gadji-zade, said that his republic had no intention of joining the CIS, but he did not rule out the possibility in the future. "All of us," he said, "have the same 'Soviet' economy, so we will have to coordinate our actions with the CIS states in implementing reforms."[17]

One should also note the impact of the Karabakh problem on the course of the reforms. The war has already caused great economic damage to the republic, estimated at twenty billion rubles over the past five years of the conflict. Over one-third of the territory of Azerbaijan is affected by the hostilities in one way or another. As a result, large areas of cotton, wheat, and other crops have been lost, not to mention the vast capital outlays on the accommodation of the refugees and unemployed and the treatment of the wounded.[18]

The Problem of Nagorno-Karabakh: Its Roots, Its Present, and Its Future

The problem of Nagorno-Karabakh is of utmost concern in Azerbaijan's domestic and international policy. The Nagorno-Karabakh autonomous region, with a territory of 4,000 square kilometers, has been part of Azerbaijan since 1921. It is separated from the republic by a strip of mountainous Armenian territory and is peopled by a mixed Armenian-Azerbaijani population. This problem is the bone of contention between Azerbaijan and neighboring Armenia and the cause of the war that has been waged by them since the end of the 1980s.

The roots of the problem go back many centuries and stem from the variegated ethnic and religious composition of the population of Transcaucasia. According to Azerbaijani historians, before the annexation of Karabakh by Russia in the course of the Russo-Persian wars of 1804–13 and 1826–28, Azerbaijanis made up the bulk of the population of the local khanates. After the annexation, Armenians from Iran and Turkey were allowed to settle freely on the territory of the present Armenia and Azerbaijan. According to the historians' conclusion, this fact contributed to the expansion of Armenians and their settlement on the fertile lands of Karabakh. They confirm their arguments with statistics of the fast growth of the Armenian presence in Karabakh and of their conversion from a minority into an overwhelming majority of the area's population.

In contrast to this, Armenian historians deny the existence of Azerbaijani statehood and regard the Azerbaijanis as a migrant population in the area. They also see these lands as historically Armenian even though they had fallen at some point under the yoke of either the Ottoman or Persian empires. In maintaining this point, they refer to the surviving documents and historical landmarks of the Christian period.

In 1920 and 1921, after the establishment of Soviet power, the present borders of Azerbaijan and Armenia were delineated. Under an agreement between the two sides, Karabakh, with its prevailing Armenian population, was placed under the jurisdiction of Azerbaijan and became an autonomous region within its format. It was unwise to divide it because both the valley and the mountain areas of Karabakh, with alternating Armenian and Azerbaijani villages, made up a single economic whole.

During the Soviet period the borders between the constituent republics of the USSR had a purely formal meaning. Azerbaijan, and especially Baku, was home to many Armenians, while hundreds of thousands of Azerbaijanis lived permanently in Armenia, mostly in the countryside.

The era of perestroika and glasnost illuminated the hidden contradictions, miscalculations, and breaches of law made in the past, notably in the ethnic sphere. Under the influence of these sentiments, in February 1988, the leadership of the autonomous region yielded to pressure from the Armenian MPs and appealed for a transfer under the jurisdiction of Armenia. This, however, aroused protests from the Azerbaijani side, which resulted in armed attacks on Armenian villages in the areas with mixed populations. The Armenians began to arm, and the flow of Armenian troops and weapons for self-defense into Karabakh has been growing ever since.

In response, there were mass pogroms of the Armenian population in the Azerbaijani city of Sumgait. They left the entire population of Armenia inflamed with wrath, and very soon all Azerbaijanis were expelled from Armenia. About 200,000 Azerbaijanis fled Armenia and flooded Baku and other cities, forming an inflammable mixture that is fertile soil for nationalist organizations.

The attempt by the top authorities of the former USSR to resolve the problem by setting up the Special Administration Committee, an arbitration body for the disengagement of the warring parties, failed. Having become a target for attacks from both sides, by the autumn of 1989 the committee was disbanded.

As the clash for Karabakh grew more intensive, the influence of the forces favoring a more radical course in curbing the "Armenian aggression" became more tangible. The lead among these forces was taken by the Popular Front, which was officially registered in autumn 1989. It brought together a wide range of movements and activists, from democrats and nationalists to die-hard Islamists. The Front criticized the Communist authorities for inaction and compliance with Moscow's line on the Karabakh issue and spoke up for the sovereignty and renewal of Azerbaijan. A prominent scholar, Abulfez Elchibey, headed the Front.

In that overstrained situation, mass Armenian pogroms erupted in Baku in January 1990, where hundreds of thousands of Armenians lived at the time. After the entry of regular troops and interior ministry forces in the city as a result of the decision made by Gorbachev to curb further violence, there were clashes in the city that left dozens of peaceful civilians dead.

Although the presence of the army somewhat stabilized the situation, it played into the hands of the Front, which exploited the situation to discredit the authorities as accomplices of the Centre. Using mass rallies and strikes, the Front exerted even stronger pressure on the republican leadership headed by the Communist party chief, Ayaz Mutalibov, gradually forming parallel power structures.

In the autumn of 1991 the Armenian part of the Nagorno-Karabakh leadership proclaimed a Nagorno-Karabakh Republic (NKR) and called for its recognition. This step added fuel to the fire, and the military hostilities on the territory of Karabakh became even more fierce than before. In March 1992, after the success of the Armenian troops (the seizure of the city of Khodjaly on the territory of Karabakh), President Mutalibov resigned under pressure from his opponents. The Azerbaijani forces, disjointed and poorly organized, suffered defeats, and the Armenians managed to seize two cities of strategic importance: Lachin and Shusha.

In June new presidential elections were held in Azerbaijan and were won by the leader of the Popular Front, Abulfez Elchibey. The new president proclaimed as his primary task the assertion of Azerbaijan's statehood and territorial integrity and the settling of the Karabakh problem. With his coming to power, urgent measures were taken, including the reorganization of the armed forces and mobilization of the population. This was followed by operations to regain the towns and villages seized by Armenians, some of which have been recaptured.

The fifty-four-year-old President Abulfez Elchibey (a specialist in medieval Arabic studies) is a proponent of reforms emphasizing three principles: democracy, Turkism, and Islam. He is pinning great hopes on the settlement of the Karabakh crisis through its internationalization, with the participation of the United States, Britain, France, and, especially, the CSCE (Conference on Security and Cooperation in Europe). It was probably to win a favorable image in the West and to dispel suspicions of fundamentalism that the president has criticized Iran several times.

According to Elchibey, his country expects a major breakthrough on the foreign policy front to take place soon. The image of a "civilized state" is important for Azerbaijan if it is to counter the influence of the pro-Armenian lobby in Europe and the United States. That lobby has been instrumental in instilling in the West the traditional image of Armenia as "a victim of Moslem fanaticism." After all, the Armenian diaspora, which commands considerable financial and information resources around the world, has for decades exploited the subject of the 1915 genocide against Armenians in Turkey.

Mindful of these realities and, notably, of the sensitive attitude of the West to the Armenians' position, the new Azerbaijani authorities are persistently calling for a peaceful settlement of the Karabakh problem. At the same time, they are determined to secure military parity with Armenia in order to speak to it "on equal terms." Azerbaijan is building its own army and hopes that with time its manpower and material resources will nullify the present military superiority of the Armenians and that the hard blockade (most transport routes to Armenia go through Azerbaijan, which also supplies fuel and energy to its western neighbor) will force the Armenian economy to its knees.

On the domestic level, the Karabakh problem is a crucial factor in the consolidation of all national forces and movements. In the republic a broad campaign has been launched that can be characterized by the slogan "Everything for the Front." It includes the collection of donations, medicine, clothes, and material resources for the fund against the "aggression." Awards for the title of "Hero of the Azerbaijan Republic," which are conferred (often posthumously) on those who distinguish themselves in the operations in Nagorno-Karabakh, have been granted. The press judges the Azeri people's patriotism and loyalty to the motherland and its ideals through their attitudes toward the Karabkh conflict.

The leader of Azerbaijan is displaying caution and pragmatism, maintaining a pluralism of views and civil concord in the face of a common enemy: Armenia. Thus, of the 5,000 officials who worked under the previous regime he replaced only 120 with his own people.[19] Elchibey's emphasis on the reversal of the setbacks in Karabakh, which hurt the national sentiments of the Azerbaijanis in the republic, has raised his prestige as a popular leader.

But the patience of the masses is limited, especially among the hundreds of thousands of Azerbaijani refugees. They wish to be returned to their homes, both in Karabakh and in Armenia, from where they were expelled, or at least for some improvement in their situation.

If that does not happen, the desperate people led by the opposition may demand more resolute actions. In that case, Elchibey will have to choose between uplifting their nationalism and maintaining his allegiance to democracy, of which he has spoken so much.

Islam in Azerbaijan

The Azerbaijanis profess the Shiite version of Islam. Over the centuries, their formation as a distinct ethnic entity has occurred under the influence of and in close contact with neighboring Turkey and Iran. In the genetic and linguistic sense they have been part of the Turkic ethnos, and in the spiritual sense they have accepted the creed and doctrine of the Shiites in Iran. These Shiite values largely determine the behavioral norms, lifestyle, and psychological distinctions of the Azerbaijanis.

During the Soviet era, the Azerbaijani nation, as a result of contact and close coexistence with other peoples, namely Russians, underwent modernization in many aspects of life. This was accompanied, as in the other Muslim regions of the former USSR, through the forceful expulsion of Islam and Islamic culture from social life (for example, the closure of many mosques, the virtual elimination of traditional religious education, physical destruction of religious leaders and scholars, and the monopoly of atheism). Whereas before the revolution there was a mosque in practically every town and village, today there are only two mosques in Azerbaijan. Before perestroika, the supreme authority in charge of religious affairs in the republic, which was controlled by the official power structures, was the Muslim Board for Transcaucasia. Only a few believers could afford the *hajj* (pilgrimage), and visiting Shiite holy places in Iran and Iraq or celebrating Shiite holidays was practically banned.

After perestroika, the new authorities stopped suppressing Islam and set the course for returning religion to its natural place and role in society. The doors of the Islamic world have been opened for Azerbaijan. Since late 1991 Azerbaijan has been a member of the Organization of the Islamic Conference (OIC) and of the Islamic Development Bank.

In this atmosphere of religious revival, as elsewhere in the Islamic republics, Azerbaijan has begun to restore old mosques, build new ones, and establish religious societies and theological schools and courses.[20] All this amounts to the institutionalization of Islam and its structures within the framework of a sovereign republic. The liberal strata of the intelligentsia, who are the backbone of the ruling authorities, fear the rise of Shiite Islam as an independent factor in Azeri politics. They prefer the moderate brand of Islam, which predominates in Turkey. This is why they are promoting the view that the Turkic states of the new commonwealth belong to a very specific region in the Islamic world. Their main distinctive feature is a European orientation, decided by the fact that they have undergone the lessons of Russian moderni- zation and religious tolerance toward other cultures and creeds.[21]

The head of the Muslim Board for Transcaucasia, Sheikh ul-Islam Hadji Allah Shukur Pasha-zade, who occupied this post even before perestroika, keeps abreast of the present-day realities as a proponent of educated, moderate Islam. He supports the official position of the au- thorities and condemns the Armenian aggression against Azerbaijan. In one of his addresses to the OIC he urged the Muslims of the world to "denounce the aggression and display solidarity with Azerbaijan."[22] He rejects the notion that the root cause of the conflict in Karabakh is Islam. Speaking at a roundtable on religious problems in Moscow at the end of 1991, Sheikh Pasha-zade stated that Islam was not the cause of the ethnic conflict, but that it was precipitated by sharp social prob- lems, scarcity of land, and unemployment.[23]

The Islamic renaissance is connected with the emergence of a number of fundamentalist groups and parties. According to some sources there are a total of six of these. The Islamic Party of Azerbaijan (IPA) is the only one among them that is registered with the authori- ties. The membership of these parties is not large, ranging from several dozen to several thousand (according to the information distributed by IPA, this organization has a membership of sixty thousand). The fun- damentalist movement in Azerbaijan is not united and cemented. The ties between its different groups remain weak. Moreover, it may be stated that a kind of rivalry exists between its local branches.

The idea of Islamic revival has become both the ideological and spir- itual basis of the "Towbeh," an organization composed of several thou- sand young men and headed by Mashadi Haji Abdul Islami, who asserts that the salvation of Muslim society lies in the decisive improvement of social and individual morality created by the return toward the path of God. The activities of the "Towbeh" are similar to those of the famous Muslim Brothers in the Middle East.[24]

The authorities in Baku, likewise, deny the existence of religion- based causes for the Karabakh conflict. In June 1992 the Plenipoten- tiary Mission of Azerbaijan in Moscow denied a report published in the Russian press that Baku Radio had broadcast appeals for a jihad

against the "infidels" living in Karabakh. The Azerbaijani authorities
noted that this was nothing but an attempt to portray the war between
Azerbaijan and Armenia as a religious conflict between Christians and
Muslims.[25]

Referring to the revival of Islam in the republic, Sheikh Pasha-zade
has not denied the existence of great difficulties surrounding this process. He has admitted that, for all the upsurge of interest in the revival
of the Islamic religion, "we have a great shortage of reputed theologians
and serious religious literature on the ethics of Islam, even on fasting.
The number of religious schools and various courses is growing fast,
but the quality of education there is a big question."[26] The main reason
for this is that for the past seventy years Islam in the republic has been
isolated from the rest of the Islamic world. This has affected the general
standard of Islamic culture in Azerbaijan by both common believers
and their spiritual mentors.

Apparently worried by this situation, the sheikh has urged the state
to render effective assistance to religious organizations. Most significantly, during his meeting with President Elchibey, he suggested setting up a board for religious affairs with the government, opening an
Islamic university with a theological department, and stepping up the
publication of religious literature and textbooks.[27]

There is no reliable information so far on the existence and operation of any Shiite parties or groups opposed to the authorities and to
the officially recognized religious structures. The provinces, however,
have not had their say yet. After all, 46 percent of Azerbaijan's population lives in the countryside. The totalitarian ways have overlaid the
traditional lifestyle there, creating a remarkable structure where, un-
derneath Communist slogans, there are strong religious sentiments.
These sentiments may become a source and nutrient for real fundamentalism. In this regard, one must always bear in mind the moral and
ideological influence of neighboring Iran.

Foreign Policy

The foreign economic policy of Azerbaijan's current administration has
not been fully elaborated. The forces that came to power in Baku were
taken aback, as it were, by the speedy disintegration of the Soviet
Union. Apparently, they expected Azerbaijan to become an object of
long disputes between the CIS, Turkey, and Iran, in the course of which
Baku would seek to benefit from Moscow's policies rather than come
up with independent initiatives. Indicatively, the chairman of the re-

public's Supreme Soviet, Yagub Mamedov, who was a member of Ayaz Mutalibov's team, observed that Azerbaijan's independence came "out of thin air" thanks to the collapse of the Soviet empire.[28]

The analysis of the Azerbaijani administration's foreign policy moves testifies to the fact that it relies primarily on imparting an international character to the Nagorno-Karabakh issue and on creating a political foundation for integrating the republic into the world market, receiving aid, credit, technology, and know-how.

Azerbaijan has become a member of the UN and has established diplomatic relations with the United States, Great Britain, France, Turkey, Iran, and other states. Embassies from these countries have been set up in Baku. Since it joined the CSCE, Azerbaijan has considered itself a member of the common European process and a link between the East and West. (Incidentally, all the Central Asian republics of the former Soviet Union claim such a position.)

Primary emphasis is being placed on the vigorous development of Azerbaijan's relations with Turkey at all levels. An increasing number of delegations of Turkish MPs, journalists, politicians, businessmen, and, in particular, U.S. and European entrepreneurs of Turkish origin, are coming to Baku.

The cultural aspect of these relations is stressed as well. About one thousand Azerbaijani young women and men went to study in Turkey this year, and a number of diplomats received advanced training at the Turkish Foreign Ministry. Moreover, Turkey has published textbooks for Azerbaijani schools, since the republic has recently shifted from the Cyrillic to the Latin alphabet.[29]

Turkey's official circles do not conceal siding with Azerbaijan in the Karabakh issue. However, while supporting the idea of Azerbaijan's territorial integrity, Ankara advocates peaceful settlement in Karabakh and denies any kind of military involvement in the conflict, which in fact has been confirmed by the Turkish Ambassador to Russia, Volkan Vurual, in an interview.[30] Turkey's attachment to NATO's strategies limits its possible interference in the conflict and freedom to maneuver.

Iran is religiously closer to Azerbaijan than Turkey, but less welcome politically. This neighboring country, whose twenty million Azerbaijanis do not have their autonomy, is not interested in a strong Azerbaijan. Furthermore, the Azerbaijanis are concerned about the clout the Shiite clergy has in the Iranian administration and their anti-American attitudes.

Iran's mediation effort in Karabakh has thus far yielded no results. An Azerbaijani leader commented on this by stating that Tehran's stand is different from the UN's and the CSCE's, and gives Armenia another chance for political maneuvering.[31]

Yet Iran provides a source for significant financial cooperation, and Azerbaijan has signed a number of agreements with Tehran, particularly on economic and cultural cooperation. A branch of Iran's National Bank opened in Baku. An agreement was signed for the annual supply of one billion cubic meters of gas to Azerbaijan with payment in hard currency, or for barter supplies of diesel fuel. Azerbaijan, the Ukraine, and Iran signed an agreement on setting up a joint venture, Iranukrazer, to build and use a 4,000-kilometer-long gas pipeline to Western Europe across Azerbaijan, the Ukraine, and Russia.[32]

Azerbaijan's relations with Russia have gone through two distinct phases since the collapse of the USSR. Baku initially had discarded Russia's previous authority within the former USSR, had gravitated toward Turkey and the Western world in general, and had championed the cause of total independence from Moscow and the CIS structure. The initial Azari optimism, however, was dashed amidst continuous economic crisis, a losing war with Armenia over Nagorno-Karabakh, and the increasingly evident limitations of Turkey as an alternative to Russia. A general national crisis came to a head when in August 1993 Elchibey was overwhelmingly defeated in a referendum (93 percent of the voters were against him) and subsequently replaced by Geider Aliev, the former first secretary of the Azerbaijan Communist Party. Facing national humiliation by not only losing Nagorno-Karabakh but also territories beyond the autonomous republic, desperately in need of economic aid and military hardware, and recognizing the continuing significance of Russia, the new Azari leadership opted for a closer relationship with Moscow. Russia's mediating role in the conflict with Armenia was accepted,[33] and the decision was made to join the CIS structure.[34] In addition, the new government also expanded and improved its relations with Turkey and Iran. The triangle of Iran, Turkey, and Russia will, in the foreseeable future, be the focus of Azerbaijan foreign policy. In the triangle, Russia, for intricate sets of economic, political, and security factors, will play a predominant role.

Conclusion

The political situation in Azerbaijan has been as dynamic as the situation in other post-Soviet republics: presidential leadership has rapidly changed, and interethnic conflicts and civil wars have erupted.

Meanwhile, society itself has been changing at a far slower pace. Its main values, mentality, modes of behavior—what collectively could be called political culture—have remained practically intact.

In the immediate months after independence, Azerbaijan's political dynamics indicated a determined desire to break with old communist structures and adopt democratic ideals and institutions. Azerbaijan's chance for democratization seemed, in contrast with the more conservative Muslim states of Central Asia, to be promising. Azeri nationalism appeared to be well developed in its conceptual, political, and even psychological aspects. The events of summer 1993, however, indicated the resiliency of the strong authoritarian trend inherent in the traditional Muslim societies of the former Soviet Union and its significant impact in shaping the sociopolitical dynamics of the new republic. The local democrats displayed all the birthmarks of traditional society, and their influence and popularity proved to be weaker than long-existing clan and local ties. Even Elchibey, a former Soviet dissident and a popularly elected president, failed to introduce any reliable preconditions for a democratic regime.

It would be wrong to see the events of summer 1993 and the emergence of a former communist leader as the return of communism in Azerbaijan, however. The Aliev triumph was welcomed by the general public, the army, the head of the Muslim community of Azerbaijan, and the fundamentalist Islamic Party of Azerbaijan. The popularity of the new leadership has less to do with its previous communist credentials than with the public's frustration with the Elchibey government's failure in Nagorno-Karabakh and its approval of the image of strength that the new government projects. The survival of the current regime, like that of the previous one, will depend on the same factors: it must stabilize the economic crisis and, above all, come to an honorable solution to the conflict in Nagorno-Karabakh.

Notes

1. *Sovetskiy Azerbaidzhan: Myfy i deistveetel'nost* [Soviet Azerbaijan: myths and reality] (Baku: ILM Publishing House, 1987), 67–68.

2. *Bakinskiy Rabochiy* [Baku's worker] (Political and social daily), 27 April 1991.

3. *Sovetskiy Azerbaidzhan*, 90.

4. *Literaturnaya Gazeta*, 29 May 1991.

5. *Panorama Azerbaizana* [Azerbaijan panorama] (a weekly published in Moscow in Russian since 1991 by the Permanent Delegation of the Azerbaijan Republic), no. 2, 23 January 1991.

6. *Literaturnaya Gazeta*, 29 May 1991.

7. *Panorama Azerbaizana*, no. 2, 23 January 1991.

8. *Bakinskiy Rabochiy*, 17 March 1992.

9. Ibid., 17 June 1992.

10. Ibid., 17 March 1992.

11. Ibid., 10 April 1992.

12. Ibid., 20 June 1992.

13. Ibid., 12 June 1992.

14. Ibid., 20 June 1992.

15. Ibid., 7 July 1992.

16. Ibid., 31 March 1992.

17. Ibid., 19 June 1992.

18. *Panorama Azerbaizana*, no. 4, 16–22 March 1992.

19. *Bakinskiy Rabochiy*, 7 July 1992.

20. *Islamskiy Vestnik* (Fortnightly published by Russian Information Agency Novosti since 1992), no. 1, 15 January 1992, p. 10.

21. *Panorama Azerbaizana* no. 4, 16–22 March 1992.

22. *Bakinskiy Rabochiy*, 13 June 1992.

23. *Islamskiy Vestnik*, no. 1, 15 January 1992, p. 10.

24. *Melodioj Azerbaizana*, 8 August 1992.

25. *Bakinskiy Rabochiy* 13 June 1992.

26. *Islamskiy Vestnik*, no. 1, 15 January 1992, p. 10.

27. *Bakinskiy Rabochiy*, 3 July 1992.

28. Ibid., 18 March 1992.

29. Ibid., 6 June 1992.

30. Ibid., 31 March 1992.

31. Ibid., 2 June 1992.

32. Ibid., 7 July 1992.

33. For Baku's view on Russia's mediation see *AZERTAC*, 28 January 1994, in *FBIS-Central Eurasia*, 31 January 1994, 75–76.

34. *FBIS-Central Eurasia*, 27 December 1993, 14–29.

6

Kazakhstan

Martha Brill Olcott

If any one factor bears primary responsibility for the course of Kazakh politics in the evolution toward independence, it is that Kazakhstan is the only former republic of the USSR in which the people for whom the new nation is named, the Kazakhs, are a numerical minority. Most recent census figures suggest that Kazakhs make up about 40 percent of the population, with just slightly fewer Russians, but even this is a recent phenomenon. From formation of the Kazakh SSR in 1936 until the mid-1980s Kazakhs did not make up even the largest ethnic group in their republic. Perhaps more important, Russians remain culturally dominant in that there are nearly half again as many native speakers of Russian as there are of Kazakh. Although most Kazakhs know Russian, there are virtually no Russians, even third- and fourth-generation residents, who know Kazakh.

Russians and Ukrainians came to what is now Kazakhstan in three distinct stages: as settlers and "homesteaders" in the late tsarist period (1890–1910); as deported *kulaks* (private farmers) prior to and during collectivization (1920s); and as volunteers during the Virgin Land agricultural campaign (1950s).[1] Despite their agricultural origins, most Russians live in Kazakhstan's cities and are concentrated primarily in the industrial regions of the north and east, which demographically are indistinguishable from the Russian Siberia, on which they border. Equally, the Kazakhs are clustered in the southern, western, and central provinces; even so, Kazakhs are the majority population in only eight of Kazakhstan's oblasts.

Being nomadic in genesis, the Kazakhs have a vaguely defined historical territory, comprising more traditional migration paths than of land controlled. These include not only what has become Kazakhstan, but also parts of modern Uzbekistan, Turkmenistan, Kyrgyzstan, and western Siberia. Administered as part of Central Asia under the tsars, after the revolution Kazakhstan became an autonomous republic within Russia. It did not achieve full republic status until 1936, and the borders continued to be shifted about until as recently as the 1960s.[2]

Despite this somewhat arbitrary territorial history, the Kazakhs today reject all claims to land within their present boundaries, particularly claims based on arguments that the western part of the republic was Ural Cossack territory and so properly belongs to Russia. Many Kazakhs, including those who are not otherwise identified with nationalist causes, do not even accept that Russians living within Kazakhstan should enjoy the same civil rights as do the Kazakhs.

Some of this hostility is a product of the Kazakhs' conviction that they became a minority in their own land because of the brutal policies of the Russian-dominated Soviet government, and of the Russian Empire that preceded it. However, for most Kazakhs it is not enough that, as the prominent Kazakh poet and leading political actor Olzhas Suleimenov phrased it at the first Congress of Peoples' Deputies, "Kazakhstan must no longer be a colony of Moscow."[3] Millions of Kazakhs were killed or starved to death during the collectivization,[4] millions more were impoverished by the disruption of the Virgin Land agricultural campaign, and thousands of hectares and an unknown number of lives have been polluted and destroyed by more than thirty years of unrestrained Soviet nuclear testing on Kazakh territory. Not surprisingly, Kazakh sentiments for retribution and restitution are common and strong.

Until the failed coup of August 1991, political stability was preserved in Kazakhstan primarily because the republic was part of a much larger multinational state. Kazakhstan's secession from the USSR was not proposed by any politician of standing in the republic. Indeed, Kazakhstan's President Nursultan Nazarbaev remained a staunch supporter of some form of revamped Soviet Union even after the August 1991 coup, when he introduced a proposal for a new form of union government to the Supreme Soviet of the USSR.[5] Nazarbaev remained an advocate of continued republic membership in the Soviet Union until 8 December 1991, when Russia, Ukraine, and Belarus withdrew from the USSR, effectively ending it, and making further support of a continued union pointless. Kazakhstan was the last of the former Soviet republics to declare independence, on 16 December 1991.

Perestroika and Its Legacy

The final period of Soviet history may be said to have begun precisely five years before that, when D. A. Kunaev was forced to "retire" as Kazakhstan's Communist party first secretary and de facto leader. Fifteen years a member of the Politburo of the CPSU (Communist Party of the Soviet Union) and an intimate crony of Leonid Brezhnev, Kunaev had reached the highest political rank ever attained by a Kazakh, which made it all the more bitter that his replacement, Gennadi Kolbin, was both a Russian and, far worse, from outside the republic.

Although the move was depicted as part of a new Communist party policy to rotate cadre from region to region within the country and so prevent development of local loyalties,[6] the Kazakhs of Alma-Ata understood the move as a political and cultural insult. Within hours of the announcement demonstrators took to the streets of Alma-Ata, where they met with dogs, sharpened shovels, and fire hoses (in sub-zero temperatures). Although official casualties were put at only two, unofficial accounts put the death toll as high as 168.

Despite concerted attempts to portray the Alma-Ata incident as drunken hooliganism, this demonstration was the Soviet regime's introduction to the significant difficulties that would accompany attempts to introduce political and economic reforms in non-Russian areas of the USSR. Gorbachev and his key advisers drew some of the necessary lessons from the Alma-Ata demonstrations, so that, for example, rotation of cadre irrespective of region and nationality was reduced. More substantively, Moscow also began to permit the republics more latitude in controlling their own cultural policies.

President Nazarbaev

In 1989 Kolbin was replaced as first secretary of the Kazakhstan Communist party by a Kazakh, Nursultan Nazarbaev, the man who had led the attack on Kunaev. An adroit politician, Nazarbaev was able to straddle the gulf separating Kazakhstan's two largest nationalities at a time when nationalism was growing ever more important in the USSR; his popularity rose even further in 1990, when the republic legislature named him Kazakhstan's president,[7] reaffirmed in 1991 by a nearly unanimous popular vote.

Support for President Nazarbaev's economic program, which calls for the creation of private property and a free market, seems equally strong among Kazakhs and Russians, who both share Nazarbaev's reluctance to privatize agriculture extensively. Kazakhs and Russians also support the notion of a sovereign Kazakhstan.

Where the two groups differ sharply is on the question of whether the Kazakhstan of the future is to be a multinational state, a half-Russian, half-Kazakh hybrid, or a sovereign and exclusively Kazakh homeland. Thus far Nazarbaev has managed to avoid defining Kazakhstan by asserting that it is all three, as the situation demands. Nevertheless, Kazakhstan has inevitably had to become more Kazakh, and Nazarbaev has understood this. The difficulty, which he also appreciates, has been to increase the role and prominence of Kazakh culture, language, and history in the republic without alarming the non-Kazakh populations, especially the Russians.

The most intractable problem in Kazakhstan is that of economic control. Republic economic sovereignty first emerged as an issue indirectly following bloody ethnic riots in the far western town of Novy Uzen in June 1989. Novy Uzen is a Soviet-era town, created to service nearby oil and gas fields during a brief development boom in the 1970s, which imported Azerbaijani and Daghestani oil workers to the area. At that time the region was divided into two oblasts. A decade later Moscow withdrew funding from the development, but the non-Kazakh workers remained, with better housing and better-paying jobs than those of the local Kazakhs. A bad situation turned much worse when Gennadi Kolbin reunited the two oblasts, naming distant Gurev as the oblast capital. At a stroke this halved the number of available patronage jobs, as well as cutting considerably republic investment in the area. By 1989 conditions made civil disturbances almost inevitable.[8] Later that same summer, coal miners in Karaganda followed the example of their Siberian and Don Basin colleagues, striking for higher wages and better conditions and raising the spectre of further unrest, with possible violence.

The unequal relationship between Moscow and the republics all but tied Nazarbaev's hands because there was little that he could grant the strikers beyond promises of better wages. For the moment that was sufficient, and the miners returned to work in less than two weeks.[9] The two events made clear, though, that the republic had to gain greater control of its own economic resources if it was to have any hopes of solving the significant economic problems that underlay the unrest. By the end of summer 1989 Nazarbaev began to call openly for moving Kazakhstan's mineral resources to republic control.[10]

This did not mean, however, that Nazarbaev had broken with Moscow. In fact, throughout 1989 and most of 1990 Nazarbaev and Gorbachev seemed almost to speak with one voice, arguing that power sharing would come on a schedule to be determined among the leaders, following Gorbachev's judgment. Nazarbaev shepherded the party through local and republic elections of 1989 and 1990 with measured calls for republic "self-rule" and "self-financing,"[11] balancing the obvious necessity of elaborating a new relationship between Moscow and the republics if the union was to hold with the equally obvious instabilities Kazakhstan would face if independence were pushed too far. Although he modified the wording of the statement a bit in the direction of greater autonomy for Kazakhstan, Nazarbaev became one of the major public advocates of a yes vote on the 17 March 1991 referendum on the continuation of the Soviet Union.[12]

Through spring and summer 1991 Nazarbaev increasingly became Gorbachev's second for the principles elaborated in the Novo-Ogarevo meeting between Gorbachev and republic leaders, which mandated the drafting of a formal union treaty among "sovereign republics." Nazarbaev also argued that the transition to a market economy could only be accomplished within a USSR that was "a single economic space."[13] This vigorous support of the Gorbachev position enhanced Nazarbaev's prestige at home by greatly increasing his national profile; his articulation of Gorbachev's propositions also transformed Nazarbaev into an international figure.

This strong support of the center was balanced by Nazarbaev's ever-greater claims for republic economic authority, which Moscow began to cede, for example, by turning over partial control of Kazakhstan's mines and mineral resources to Alma-Ata in June 1991.[14] A more substantial reward was initiated in negotiations between Moscow and Chevron Oil for development of the Tengiz fields in western Kazakhstan, although preliminary agreements favored Moscow far more than they did Kazakhstan, and Nazarbaev was only brought into the deal after negotiations were far advanced.

The issue of political sovereignty seemed to catch Nazarbaev by surprise, for all his understanding of issues of economic control. The demand for complete republic autonomy came to the forefront with Boris Yeltsin's election as chairman of the Russian Federation Supreme Soviet in June 1990, following which Russia declared its own sovereignty. Gorbachev countered with his call for a formal Treaty of Union to be agreed on by sovereign republics; this then obligated all the republics to elaborate statements of republic sovereignty.

Two different statements were put on the floor of the Kazakhstan legislature. The government version called for complete republic control of Kazakhstan's political and economic life, including full rights to and profit from the republic's natural resources, and mandated that Kazakh be the official state language. The draft also affirmed that the Kazakh people had a historic claim to their territory.

An even stronger statement, demanding separation of party and state, equal rights for all citizens, and formation of a market economy,[15] was formulated by a Democratic bloc of more than one hundred legislators that had formed during summer 1990. Soon afterward a Communist bloc appeared to defend the government position; it was headed by Nazarbaev's second secretary and claimed 128 legislators.

Several weeks of intense debate followed. The sovereignty decree that was finally adopted on 25 October differed little from the original government document. Kazakhs were declared primus inter pares in the republic, with a right to defend and preserve their cultural institutions; however, Russians were given virtually the same guarantees for their language as Kazakhs were for theirs, and the equality of all citizens was also established. In the economic sphere, however, the Democratic bloc's version had pushed the final bill to an even stronger declaration of economic sovereignty than had been the case in the government draft.[16]

Once that statement was secured, Nazarbaev moved into an aggressive declaration of his own political agenda, establishing the legal framework to substantiate the republic control of resources he had claimed and the powers he had exercised in claiming them. In the eight months following the declaration, more bills were put to and passed by Kazakhstan's legislature than had been introduced in the entire previous decade; among them were bills for privatization of industry, regulation of foreign investment, delineation of rights and responsibilities of local government organs, and extension of social benefits within the republic.

However, similar autonomies were being claimed elsewhere in the USSR, as one part of which the USSR's ban on Cossack military and social organizations was lifted. The Cossacks of Ust-Kamenogorsk and Uralsk, in western Kazakhstan, served as the nucleus of a growing Russian separatist movement that the Kazakhstan press began to cover with growing alarm.[17] The Kazakh intellectual establishment responded with renewed defenses of the inviolability of Kazakhstan's present borders, on both historical and pragmatic grounds.[18]

As a response to increasing Russian nationalism, Kazakhs of all stripes, including those sympathetic to the growing Kazakh nationalist party, Azat (Freedom), began to swing behind Nazarbaev, accepting the premise that they would increase political instability in the republic if they failed to support the president. With Gorbachev's prestige in obvious and increasing eclipse, Nazarbaev wisely decided to resolve his well-publicized differences with Yeltsin, who was in Kazakhstan on the eve of the abortive August coup to sign a memorandum of agreement between Kazakhstan and Russia that also recognized the existing 3,000-mile-long border between the two republics.[19]

The Coup and Beyond

The prescience of Nazarbaev's fears about the stability of Kazakhstan's northern border was demonstrated just days after the coup when a Yeltsin press aide spoke of possible Russian claims to northeastern Kazakhstan. Although Yeltsin quickly distanced himself from such claims, even sending his vice president to Kazakhstan to reaffirm his government's commitment to the existing borders,[20] obvious cause for concern remained; demonstrators under Russian flags took to the streets in the Kazakhstan city to celebrate a Cossack tetracentenary.

Along with new dangers, the aftermath of the coup also gave new opportunities for Nazarbaev to increase his domination of republic politics. There were many local party networks of which he had never been in full control, so that the unionwide abolition of the Communist party gave grounds on which Nazarbaev could replace local officials with men loyal to himself. He also named a new vice president (Erik Asanbaev, until then chairman of the Supreme Soviet) and a new prime minister (Sergei Tereshchenko, a Russian, but a Kazakh-speaking one who had grown up in the southern, and therefore more Kazakh, city of Chimkent).[21] Just as important, he solidified his own mandate for the presidency in a popular election, in which he got over 98 percent of the votes cast, with more than 80 percent voter turnout. The only other person in the republic who had wished to run against him, from the Zheltoksan group, was unable to collect the 100,000 signatures necessary to put his name on the ballot.

For all his public support and his control of the *apparat*, Nazarbaev had difficulty creating a political body to incorporate his program of economic reform and to back his government. A socialist party, created on 7 September 1991, was meant to inherit the dissolved Communist party, but Kazakh politicians and former party members did not join in large numbers. As a result the new party became predominantly Russian and Russified Kazakh. Nazarbaev sought to counter this by creating a Popular Congress of Kazakhstan, formulated 6 October 1991 and headed by prominent Kazakh poets Olzhas Suleimenov and Mukhtar Shakhanov. Nominally open to all citizens, the party was intended to be Kazakh dominated.

In the year following, neither party enjoyed much public support, but neither did any nonofficial party or group, which were slow to form, probably inhibited in part by the existence of the two official parties. This seems indeed to have been Nazarbaev's design, for he has stated on a number of occasions that the people of Kazakhstan do not yet have the political maturity to sustain a democratic system based on a multiplicity of parties.[22]

The discrediting and banning of the Communist party has left an administrative vacuum in the republic, a vacuum that Nazarbaev has largely filled with himself. In the late Soviet period there were essentially two Communist parties functioning in Kazakhstan; one was the republic party, which derived its power from the oblast and lower-level organizations, and the other was the party represented in the huge industrial plants, whose administrators and leaders were tied to and often directly subordinate to the all-union party organization in Moscow. The first was dominated and controlled by Kazakhs to the extent that the Russians who were active in this "party" became subsumed into the clan- and region-based networks that controlled the respective oblasts. The second was exclusively Russian because Russians controlled the economy, managing and directing the large industries, answering directly to the all-union ministries and the CPSU bureaucracy in Moscow, which permitted them to ignore the local party authority at their convenience. All that is now gone, and with it the central ministry system; with independence the Kazakhstan government has also inherited the responsibility for regulating and transforming public life.

For the present, as well as for the foreseeable future, that government is effectively the person of Nursultan Nazarbaev, who essentially rules by decree. Nazarbaev talks of the necessity of creating a civil society for Kazakhstan in which the rights of all citizens will be respected regardless of nationality, but he demonstrates no vision of how that might be achieved, nor has anyone succeeded in defining what it would mean to be a "Kazakhstanets," or citizen of Kazakhstan, as opposed to a Russian, a Kazakh, or other nationality.

Nazarbaev's unarticulated hope is that the solution, and the political allegiance it requires, will grow from the general prosperity that a market-based economy is presumed eventually to create. For the moment Nazarbaev enjoys wide support among both Russians and Kazakhs, so the republic is relatively stable and Nazarbaev's government has legitimacy. However the transition from a centrally planned command economy that is tightly integrated within a single all-union economy to a market-based, private-sector economy would have been difficult enough within that integrated all-union economy. With the near collapse of the all-union economy and with serious economic problems facing all of Kazakhstan's trading partners, Nazarbaev's task seems more than daunting.

Kazakhstan among the Other Republics

One of the lines Nazarbaev has pursued to fill the vacuum created by the collapse of the Soviet all-union systems is to position Kazakhstan as the regional leader for the five Central Asian republics. This began with a meeting of the republic heads, hosted by Nazarbaev, on 23 June 1990 at which a series of five-year agreements were signed mandating cooperation in matters of the economy, the environment, and scientific development. Initial work was also done on establishing a permanent coordinating council of Central Asian leaders.[23] Parallel to the government meeting, Olzhas Suleimenov met with leaders of "informal" organizations from the five republics, with an eye to coordinating nongovernmental Central Asian activities as well.[24]

For the first year of its existence the Central Asian coordinating council was little more than a paper entity, but at the second annual meeting, held in Tashkent just before the August coup, plans were announced to expand the council's function, as well as to include Azerbaijan.[25] The council served as a convenient vehicle a few months later when the Slavic republics unexpectedly dissolved the Soviet Union. The Central Asian leaders convened in Ashkhabad, Turkmenistan, to affirm their intention of joining the CIS.[26]

The creation of this council has been an important preliminary step in the evolution of a genuine regional mediating body because it further ratifies existing borders among the new nations, while demonstrating a shared preference for regional cooperation rather than conflict. At the same time, however, the council has yet to elaborate mechanisms for dealing with the many problems that all the nations of the regions share, nor has it developed any that help individual republics deal with internal problems. The decision to include Azerbaijan may provide the necessary additional motivation to transform the council into a functional entity, for the Azerbaijanis have argued strongly the need for a vigorous regional association around the Caspian, including Iran and Turkey.[27] However, the more nationalist government of Elchibey, which is pursuing the conflict with Armenia more vigorously than did its predecessor, may see the council as less of a priority.

Indeed, for all their attempts at cooperation, none of the five republics' leaders place much faith in the ability of regional networks to solve the development problems of their countries, which require resources greater than any of them possess individually, or even collectively. Nazarbaev's position is especially delicate because Kazakhstan's large Russian population requires him to portray the republic as a secular, multinational entity rather than as a Central Asian one of Turkic and Muslim pedigree. Not coincidentally, a pluralistic, nondemoninational Kazakhstan is also more attractive to the potential foreign investors Nazarbaev courts with considerable energy.[28] However, for all the time and attention he devotes to international and internal public relations, Nazarbaev is shrewd enough to know that image is at best a short-term substitute for a stable political base in the republic. One of the ways he is seeking to achieve that is through the Kazakh poet and public figure Olzhas Suleimenov, who achieved wide notoriety in 1976 by advancing the thesis that the Turkic and Slavic tribes of early medieval times had shared one culture, and so were a kind of brother peoples. If widely accepted, this thesis would provide the ideological underpinnings necessary for stabilizing Kazakhstan's binational makeup.

Suleimenov's history, however, suggests how unlikely such a melding of nationalities is. When Suleimenov, already a well-known young poet, first made his ideas public with the publication of his book *Az i ia* (the title is a complex pun on "Asia"),[29] Russian opinion was scandalized and Suleimenov was forced to renounce his book on threat of expulsion from the party and the Writer's Union. The book was reissued in 1989, but rather than serve as something to stitch Russian and Turkic Asia together, as Suleimenov may have wished, the poet and his ideas have become a rallying point for Muslim intellectuals throughout the entire former USSR. Although Suleimenov has actively argued that Turks and Slavs can and should work together to create a great confederation of separate states, or a single secular state, based on their shared heritage, history, and culture,[30] the result has been, if anything, to make the people of Turkic extraction even more confident in their cultural identity, and thus the chances of this Turkic-Slavic melding grow correspondingly smaller.

It must be said, however, that such chances were never large. Such a state would of necessity be without a religious identity and would require that Russians and Turks function as equals within a single state; neither nationality seems likely to accept either condition, at least in current conditions. Russians have never been noticeably tolerant of alien cultures, but their understanding has fallen still further as Central Asians undergo a cultural revival. After happily accepting for decades Soviet practices that made Russian the de facto legal language, Central Asian Russian communities are now aggressive in their condemnation of new laws that mandate Central Asian languages as official or as the language of education,[31] calling such laws "violation of human rights."

Realistically, Nazarbaev seems aware that he has little chance of achieving the allegiance of Russians in Kazakhstan on ideological or patriotic grounds, and so has worked hard to forge pragmatic grounds for their support, continuing the Soviet-era philosophies for developing Kazakhstan. What that means, in short, is that any development plans must deliver as much for Russia and the Russians as they will for Kazakhstan and the Kazakhs.

Kazakhstan and the World Outside

The task of creating an international identity for itself once the coil of the dead USSR is shuffled off has presented Kazakhstan with a curious dilemma. There are obvious immediate benefits and large potential ones to positioning Kazakhstan as a part of the common Islamic heritage, but there are equally obvious dangers, both internally and internationally. Nazarbaev, a declared atheist, has hewn a delicate line between issues strictly of religion and those of national heritage. He has encouraged an official Kazakh nationalist party, led by establishment figures, as a way of slowing the growth of Azat, a legally established noncommunist Kazakh party, and of Alash,[32] an illegal Muslim party (Alash was the legendary "first Kazakh"). For the time being at least, Nazarbaev has managed to prevent the even more religious Islamic Revolutionary party from getting a toehold in the republic.

Nazarbaev is attempting to keep Islam itself in administrative check. In 1990 he removed Kazakhstan from the jurisdiction of the official Central Asian Spiritual Directorate of Muslims (SADUM), establishing instead a separate Kazakhstan "muftiate."[33] That there is some resistance to this office may be deduced from what followed after the Ka-

zakh *qazi* (head cleric) Ratbek Nysanbaev spoke out against formation
of an Islamic party in Kazakhstan, which he styled "a breach of the
peace"; a group of believers then broke into Nysanbaev's office and attacked him, breaking his leg. Nysanbaev, though, has remained in office, with Nazarbaev's support.[34]

Internationally, Kazakhstan has shown more enthusiasm for a Muslim identity, which it can claim now for the first time in modern history. Delegations have participated in meetings of Islamic nations in
both Dakar and Tehran, so far only with observer status. Kazakhstan
has seen considerable activity from both Saudi Arabian and Iranian nationals because of the possibilities of combining economic interests
with religious proselytizing.

Turkey also has demonstrated increased interest in Kazakhstan, but
with somewhat greater caution because of Turkey's ties to Russia. As
Russia's influence has waned in the area, Turkey's presence has increased. Indeed, since 1989 the desire to improve ties with the Caucasian and Central Asian republics has been an open part of Turkey's
foreign policy,[35] and was reaffirmed by the incoming Demirel government.[36]

Influential people in Central Asian governments and in Turkey, including, very publicly, President Ozal, have spoken of Turkey as a natural developmental model for the four new Turkish-heritage states of
Central Asia, as well as for Azerbaijan. President Ozal made state visits
to Azerbaijan and Kazakhstan in the spring of 1991 and hosted a return
visit by President Nazarbaev in fall of that year, during which a number
of bilateral agreements on economic and technical cooperation were
signed.[37] Although it is pro-Western and democratic and has a market-
based economy, Turkey is also Islamic. Committed to a secular Kazakhstan, Nazarbaev has taken some pains to balance "Muslim" investment with those from non-Muslim foreign partners. Probably the
single largest deal concluded to date is one with Chevron Oil to develop the Tengiz fields of western Kazakhstan. Apart from that, however, U.S. firms have no great presence in the republic. Some sizable
projects, both oil and nonoil, have been announced with Western European partners; nevertheless, European interest in Central Asia has not
been much greater than that of the United States.

At least for the visible future, Kazakhstan's biggest foreign trading
partner will be China, with Korea a distant second. Direct rail links
have been opened between Kazakhstan and China, facilitating movement between Chinese factories and Kazakhstan sources of raw mate-

rials.[38] Korea has emerged as the major supplier of "high-tech" investment in Kazakhstan, in part through the offices of Chang Yung Bang, a Korean-American with close ties to several major industrial families in Korea, whom Nazarbaev appointed vice chairman of Kazakhstan's Council of Economic Experts.

Even Kazakhstan's most enthusiastic trading partners, however, treat the republic, and Central Asia in general, with considerable caution because of the huge potential for various forms of economic and political instability, which make any investment highly speculative at best. Before Kazakhstan can be viewed as anything other than a risky investment, President Nazarbaev and the other Kazakh politicians must demonstrate that Kazakhstan is a genuine entity of which they are in real control, rather than a creature of the moment, a whim of Russian sufferance.

Notes

Author's note: This paper was prepared for publication in September 1992 and reflects developments up through that date. Funding in support of this project was received from the U.S. Institute for Peace.

1. Unfortunately, precise breakdowns of the relative makeup of each community are unavailable.

2. At that time the boundaries with Uzbekistan were shifted somewhat in Kazakhstan's favor.

3. *Kazakhstanskaya Pravda*, 8 June 1989.

4. Nazarbaev has now officially claimed that four million Kazakhs died during the collectivization drive; *Izvestiya*, 2 July 1991.

5. *Kazakhstanskaya Pravda*, 27 August 1991.

6. Ibid., 18 December 1986.

7. Ibid., 25 April 1991.

8. For a lengthy discussion of the abysmal living conditions in Novy Uzen, published a month prior to the riots, see Ibid., 17 May 1989.

9. *FBIS USSR Daily Report*, 26 July 1989, 69.

10. Ibid., 28 August 1989, 71.

11. *Kazakhstanskaya Pravda*, 22 November 1989.

12. *Izvestiya*, 13 February 1991.

13. *FBIS-SOV 91-116*, 17 June 1991, 101–3, a transcription of a Central Television broadcast from 14 June 1991.

14. *Radio Liberty on the USSR*, 9 August 1991, 13–15.

15. *Kazakhstanskaya Pravda*, 13 September 1990.

16. Ibid., 28 October 1990.

17. Ibid., 20 June 1991 and 3 August 1991.

18. Ibid., 16 May 1991. This article was in answer to one that appeared in *Literaturnaya Rossiia*, 8 March 1991.

19. *Kazakhstanskaya Pravda*, 21 August 1991.

20. *FBIS-SOV 91-169*, 30 August 1991, 125, a translation of a Russian Radio broadcast of August 29, 1991.

21. *Soiuz* 44 (1991): 88.

22. *Vremiia*, 2 December 1991.

23. *Kazakhstanskaya Pravda*, 23–24 June 1990.

24. *Literaturnaya Gazeta*, 22 August 1990.

25. *Kazakhstanskaya Pravda*, 17 August 1991.

26. *Turkmenskaya Iskra*, 18 December 1991.

27. *Vyshka*, 27 June 1991.

28. Nazarbaev is reported to have retained public relations firms in London and Washington to help popularize this picture of his republic.

29. *Az i ia* (Alma Ata, 1976, reissued 1989).

30. Suleimenov has been a member of the USSR Supreme Soviet, president of the Nevada-Semipalatinsk Anti-nuclear Movement, and the behind-the-scenes force in a short-lived Assembly of the Peoples of the East.

31. The leading national literary journal, *Literaturnaya Gazeta* now has a rubric, "Children of Russia," in which it details the hardships such people are undergoing.

32. Alash is named for the Kazakhs' legendary founder.

33. *Kazakhstanskaya Pravda*, 6 September 1990.

34. *Komsomolskaya Pravda*, 17 December 1991.

35. *FBIS-WEU-220*, 20 November 1991, 60.

36. *FBIS-WEU-235*, 6 December 1991, 40.

37. *Kazakhstanskaya Pravda*, 25 September 1991.

38. *FBIS-SOV 91-100*, 23 May 1991, 16.

7

Uzbekistan

Zahid I. Munavvarov

It is impossible to speak of the political, socioeconomic, and ethnic changes taking place in the former Soviet Central Asian republics without considering those processes that marked the beginning of a new era of radical change. Until April 1985 these changes were retained somewhat artificially and by force. They were stirred to greater activity with the accession to power of the forces that dared to abandon the obsolete dogma that led this vast country to inevitable disaster.

The current political changes impetuously developing in the former republics of the Soviet Union became the essence of the global process. These changes sped up the disintegration of the Soviet Union and ran through all ensuing political, economic, social, cultural, and spiritual consequences. An analysis of the radical reasons and peculiarities of this historical event is an undertaking for scholars of the social sciences, economists, and others. This essay will suggest a vision of the evolutionary process of the USSR's disintegration and will define its four basic stages.

The first stage began in April 1985 with the proclamation of the program of reconstruction of Soviet society. These policy changes in both foreign and, primarily, domestic affairs favored the beginning of a new international atmosphere. The internal political situation became such that the possible secession from the USSR by individual republics, as well as their right to do so, was a matter of definite concern.

The Baltic states were the most receptive to the prospect of secession. This was largely the result of the freshness of the moral and political trauma connected with their "annexation" to the Soviet Union, and, to a lesser degree, of the integration of their economies into the all-union national economy. Their previous experiences in state organization served to stabilize their bourgeois development, which was sim-

ilar to the Western European model. Consequently, the logical end of
the first stage was that these states adopted Declarations of Sovereignty to reestablish their national sovereignty. As was subsequently
seen, the leaders of the reconstruction (perestroika) policy were totally
unprepared for such a turn of events, since they had been confident
about preserving the unity of the "unbreakable union."

The drastic actions of the Baltic states were a powerful incentive for
the partisans of the strict totalitarian system. They took the offensive
against democratic movements and relinquished their doubts concerning the cardinal renewal of the essence and structure of the USSR.
They wished to combat the tendency toward the expansion of rights
and the sovereignty of the republics, as well as the contraction of the
functions and powers of the central authorities.

The second stage was marked by an intensified conflict between
these forces. The logical end of this clash was the August coup, which
marked the end of the second stage. Its distinctive feature was the
growth and stirring up of centrifugal tendencies, along with increased
aspirations by the republics to secede from the USSR. Despite numerous efforts by the CPSU (Communist Party of the Soviet Union) to hold
the union together, the Baltic states were followed by, among others,
Moldova and Georgia, and the Ukraine was also inclined to follow suit.
Furthermore, similar movements began to emerge in other republics,
including those in Central Asia.

The third stage covered the period from the August coup to the
Minsk meeting of the leaders of the Slavonic republics. This period
dispelled any illusions about the possibility of there being some former
Soviet republics in the structure of an indivisible state with some central governing bodies. The result was a radical change in the political
situation in the Soviet Union, manifesting itself in actual political disintegration and complete abolition of the central governing structures.
Both the August coup and the Minsk meeting played important roles
in the fundamental changes and future development of the Central
Asian states. The August coup was reflected in the mass consciousness
of this region's peoples as an attempt at the restoration of a strict, totalitarian system. Moreover, the Minsk meeting was perceived by the majority of the Islamic population in Central Asia as a step to a split on
the ethnic and confessional basis. At this time, Uzbekistan declared its
sovereignty.

The fourth stage—most likely the last one—has been the complete
disintegration of the USSR and the formation of independent states on
its territory. This began at the Minsk meeting and was further devel-

oped in Ashkhabad and Alma-Ata, but has not been completed. Because of their history and the close integration of their economic potentials, all newly formed states will face a great number of practical problems. These include, among others, the transition to new forms of economic cooperation, the reorganization of the army, and currency and financial factors.

This essay will analyze how the disintegration of the former USSR influenced the evolution of events in Uzbekistan and will consider the prospects of socioeconomic development and spiritual progress in the new state.

Sociopolitical Dynamics

Despite groundless allegations, supported by some foreign Sovietologists[1] that Central Asia has achieved high levels of industrialization, its economy has remained agrarian and raw material oriented. By the beginning of the 1990s this region produced 90 percent of the total volume of raw cotton—7.7 million tons—including 1.5 million tons of fine-fiber cotton.[2] Close in its quality to natural silk, the latter was grown only on the territory of the Central Asian republics. Until the 1990s over 90 percent of the raw cotton was exported to other regions in the Soviet Union. This was done at very low prices and under extremely unfavorable economic and social conditions for Central Asia.

According to statistical data, the population of Uzbekistan increased by almost seven million from about 1970 to the mid 1980s. The growth rate of the national income, however, was reduced from 5.7 to 3.1 percent. When the average indices per capita in the USSR were 1168 rubles in production of consumer goods, 465 rubles in foodstuffs, and 703 rubles in manufactured goods, the same indices in Uzbekistan were, respectively, 470, 202, and 268 rubles.[3] There is a considerable portion of truth in the comment of the Arab scholar Mukhammad Ali-al-Barr that Central Asian republics are "mere Russian provinces or colonies governed by representatives from the Kremlin. They are even deprived of the opportunity to settle their domestic problems on their own."[4]

At the end of 1991 Uzbekistan witnessed important political events that favored the achievement of genuine independence. To begin with, this period marked the beginning of international recognition for the Republic of Uzbekistan.

Turkey began this process. Turkey and Uzbekistan are connected by a number of elements, including ethnolinguistic, religious, and cultural factors and a common historical past. As of 1992 more than 120 states have recognized the Republic of Uzbekistan as an independent international subject. In addition, it has been admitted to the UN. For the first time, the leader of Uzbekistan has paid official visits to the Turkish Republic, Saudi Arabia, the People's Republic of China, the Korean Republic, Indonesia, and Malaysia. Moreover, foreign countries have begun opening embassies in Uzbekistan.[5]

It is of great importance that the United States established the first foreign embassy in Tashkent. The above factors, in addition to Uzbekistan's membership in the Organization of Regional Development, founded in 1964 by Iran, Turkey, and Pakistan, have become important indices in gaining and strengthening Uzbek independence. They have greatly influenced the consciousness of the republic's citizens, giving rise to national self-consciousness among the native representatives and inducing them to become more politically active. At the same time, they generated and intensified anxiety among the nonnative nationalities, including, but not limited to, the Russian-speaking population.

International recognition of Uzbekistan as an independent actor is gaining still more concrete outlines. By the beginning of February 1993, the republic of Uzbekistan had high-level diplomatic relations with sixty-six states, twenty foreign ambassadors presented their credentials to the president of Uzbekistan, and twelve more states established diplomatic representation in Tashkent. Uzbekistan, however, has embassies only in Russia and Turkey and consulates in about ten other countries as of February 1993.[6]

The first alternative presidential elections in the republic were an important event in the republic's domestic political life. Despite a small number of candidates and the inequality in starting conditions, the elections showed the availability of, or more precisely the beginning of, the formation of legal political opposition in the republic and its recognition by the political forces in power. The candidate from the Democratic party "Erk" (Will), Mukhammed Salikh, was behind due to many factors, including inexperience in the political struggle and being relatively unknown as a political figure. Other factors included the strong positions held by the People's Democratic party of Uzbekistan (whose membership consists of most of the former Communist party of Uzbekistan) in the social and political structure of the society and the reputation of Islam Karimov as a political figure and competent economist, one who is well aware of the most important issues concerning the republic's development.

It should be noted that a multiparty system is entering the republic's political life. The Democratic party "Erk" has become of importance in political life. This party, together with the people's movement "Birlik" (Unity), can be considered one of the main forces of the functioning political opposition in the republic. The party has been officially registered and is engaged in the active work of setting up its branches on the territory of the republic. In addition, "Birlik" carries on legal political activities and has its own weekly, *Erk*.[7]

Under the changed conditions engendered by the USSR's disintegration and the formation of independent states on the basis of the former Soviet republics, Uzbekistan has a great opportunity to be a potential partner for mutually beneficial cooperation with foreign countries.

Economic Prospects

There are six factors on which the assertion of Uzbekistan's value as a partner for foreign countries is based. First, the cotton wealth of Uzbekistan is certain to become one of the most important items of foreign economic activity, capable of securing considerable revenues for the state treasury. Moreover, it is the basis of economic relations between Uzbekistan and the countries of Europe and Japan. Thus as of the beginning of 1993 contracts for sale, in the absence of intermediary structures, have been concluded with, among others, France and Italy.

Cotton is not only a profitable export; it also attracts foreign technology and investment. Countries with highly developed textile industries, such as India, Pakistan, China, South Korea, and Japan, will find favorable prospects for investment in the republic. Therefore, along with strengthening the sovereignty of Uzbekistan, it is necessary to set up legal structures and norms that are reliable and which meet international standards recognized for protecting foreign investment. Other projects will be developed in the near future.

Second, Uzbekistan has the potential to promote the development of bilateral economic relations, especially with developing countries. For example, it is a large-scale producer of nitric and phosphate fertilizers and pesticides, as well as agricultural techniques and mechanisms that are in high demand throughout the developing world. Moreover, the republic has a great deal of experience in hydrotechnical and irrigation construction, which may also be of use for developing countries. The list of the republic's scientific and industrial means is far from small. For instance, deposits of gold, other precious and semiprecious metals, and precious stones are abundant. These resources provide the basis for setting up large enterprises for the production and export of jewelry.

Third, more than twelve hundred springs of mineral and thermal water have been discovered in the Central Asian region. With the overwhelming majority of these containing medicinal properties, the opportunity exists for them to be turned into international spas and clinics. With the investment of foreign capital, this branch of the economy has the potential to bring in high revenues. However, foreign assistance is needed to organize these services according to international standards. India has already begun to render aid by constructing a number of complexes for international tourism in Uzbekistan. It is also expected that a number of Islamic countries will participate in this task due to similarities in their geography, religion, customs, and traditions.

The fourth factor is the existence of a vast labor market. This is despite the fact that under the Soviet system labor sources—in theory, though not in practice—stopped being a commodity because the term "labor market" was considered seditious. The presence of a great number of administrative, legal, and economic restrictions was an insurmountable obstacle to the free sale of labor forces under conditions most favorable to the workers themselves. Regions with labor surplus, such as Uzbekistan with its population of twenty million, particularly suffered from the unbalanced labor market under the Soviet regime.

It is expected that the future introduction of true market principles into the economy will remove the above-mentioned restrictions. The republic is examining the possibility of exporting labor to those countries close to Uzbekistan both geographically and religiously and in need of highly qualified workers and technicians. It is appropriate to mention here a possible forthcoming competition between workers in Uzbekistan and those in South and Southeast Asia, North Africa, and the rich, oil-extracting countries of the Persian Gulf.

The fifth factor is the presence of gold in the republic. It has been estimated that the Soviet government extracted 20–30 percent of its gold from Uzbekistan.[8] The republic has large gold-extracting enterprises and is ranked among the top ten countries worldwide in volume of gold output.[9] The gold from Bukhara has been famous since ancient times, but under the Soviet regime the republic was deprived of controlling this wealth.

In 1993 Uzbekistan began to create its own gold fund and work on defining markets for high-standard gold.[10] It is important for Uzbekistan to have—at least for a short period of time—its gold fund at a level that will allow it to take its place in the world gold balance as well as to create the basis necessary for introducing its own currency.[11] This will increase the level of confidence of potential foreign partners in the republic, and will also strengthen its international prestige.

The last factor is the discovery of an oil field in the Namanghan region of the Fergana Valley. This gives a new impetus to the republic's quest for economic sovereignty.[12] According to estimates by the *New York Times*, Uzbekistan's quota in the total extraction of oil in the former USSR was 0.4 percent in 1991.[13] For oil products, the republic was greatly dependent on external resources, namely those in Russia. The discovery of a new oil field engendered the hope of ridding the republic of its dependence on Russia and the prospect of developing an external market for this resource.

It should be noted in defining the prospects of the new state's relations with the world community that the tendency of certain circles to restrict connections, including economic ones, with Russia, and their compensation at the expense of similar relations with other foreign countries, will play a negative role in the development of the republic's economy. This perspective was born more out of the euphoria of sovereignty than out of real concern for the economic welfare of the state and its citizens. Furthermore, it may lead to the worsening, at least for a short while, of the economic situation in the Republic of Uzbekistan.

Islam and Spiritual Revival

One should think that to facilitate integration into the world economy it is necessary to assume the development of economic, political, cultural, and humanitarian relations with foreign countries, and particularly with the Islamic states, based on equal and mutually beneficial cooperation with their largest northern neighbor.

The Central Asian republics of the former Soviet Union are undergoing a revision of their spiritual, ethical, and cultural values. Islamic culture is considered the basis of this process for the majority of the region's population. The past seventy years of Soviet rule in Central Asia have proved false the Marxist-Leninist tenet that "religion is the opiate of the masses." All efforts made by the host of atheists attempting to erase Islam from the people's memory have failed, but they are not traceless. For instance, the population of Tajikistan, about four times smaller than that of Uzbekistan, listened to some 74,000 lectures on scientific atheism from 1976 to 1981.[14] The struggle against religion led to spiritual impoverishment, degradation, an increase in crime, corruption, and other negative social and ethical behavior.

Sociological analysis carried out to please the existing political institutions showed that Uzbekistan's population is almost entirely atheist.[15] Islam and its culture, however, did not become alien to the people of Central Asia.

Foreign Sovietologists, often labeled as "bourgeois falsifiers," were more objective in their estimations of the real religious situation and the prospects for its development in Central Asia. As far back as the early sixties, an English Sovietologist, W. Kollarz, wrote that "the Soviet authorities have and will have to take into consideration the exceptional religious character and resistance of the Islamic population of the Soviet Union, particularly in Central Asia and the Northern Caucasus," and that "to eradicate it [i.e., religion] is next to impossible."[16]

Recent events, the starting point of which was set up by the policy of perestroika, became a prelude to a new epoch of progress for the peoples inhabiting one-sixth of the world's land mass. Besides the purely economic aspects of development, which are far from obtaining their final form, one should also consider the spiritual, cultural, and ethical factors. The first results are clearly observable. The main contributions of Mikhail Gorbachev are manifested in the fact that he was the first to declare the absurdity of following the dogma of forced unification of the sociopolitical and economic development of different countries and peoples. The people of the former Soviet Union seem to have forgotten that the key to progress is found in the diversity of sociopolitical development and the diversity of human thinking. The experience of Uzbekistan confirms that such an opportunity has appeared as a result of the reconstruction policy.

The most significant event in the cultural and spiritual life of Uzbekistan since the mid-1980s was the return of Islam to its proper place in society. At last it can be stated that liberty of conscience and religion has become a reality. During the seventy-year reign of the Soviet Union this was declared but never put into practice under the totalitarian Communist state.

The Muslim clergy was persecuted for decades but was able to preserve its spiritual influence within society. Now it has, to a degree, been legalized, and Islamic values have been returned. Moreover, all the holidays of the Islamic fast and sacrifice have become official and are celebrated in Uzbekistan. At the end of the 1980s an age-old dream of the country's Muslims came true: they have been allowed to go on the pilgrimage to the holy places for all Muslims—the cities of Mecca and Medina. For example, twelve hundred men from Uzbekistan made the hajj in 1992. The number of mosques is increasing, and the official number of five hundred is probably low.[17]

But do these processes mean that everything is returning to the medieval, fundamentalist norms, as some foreign sociologists on Central Asia predict? E. Arron of the Heritage Foundation does not doubt such developments and writes, "There is a strong conviction that the forthcoming events will repeat the experience of Iran: the rise of a fundamentalist movement, the exchange of pro-Western intellectuals for Islamic clergymen as the source of leadership and inspiration and . . . after the inevitable victory over Moscow, the formation of several fundamentalist Islamic states, with the exception, perhaps, of Russified Kazakhstan."[18] Some Moscow publications also intimidate with the prospect of an "Uzbek Islamic Republic."[19]

The main mistake of estimating the events developing in Central Asia is the fact that these authors consider the religious movement in Central Asia, including Uzbekistan, as something homogeneous. The example of Uzbekistan shows that such generalized conclusions are inaccurate. They are even dangerous and may generate misperceptions both about the present-day reality and the prospects of social, political, and economic development in the republic.

The religious movement in Uzbekistan absorbs a number of trends different in their social, regional, and philosophical nuances. Taking into account the nuances connected with the evolution of each can help in objectively estimating the current religious situation as well as the prospects of new religious revival in the country.

There is no doubt that the most influential center remains the former spiritual Islamic Board of Central Asia and Kazakhstan, which was reorganized into the Spiritual Board of the Muslims of Mavarannakhr at its *kurultai* (congress) in February 1992. Having considerable means (for example, profits from mosques, donations from the faithful, assistance on the part of foreign Islamic organizations, compatriots), its leaders hope to avoid any of the governing bodies and aspire to more independence in their daily activities. This state of affairs became possible thanks to the considerable liberalization of social life and the rise in democratic trends in the country.

Side by side with the Islamic Board, religious movements in Uzbekistan include a number of other trends that disagree with the policy of the board's leaders, as evidenced by their position on some questions.

Three of the most notable among these will be considered. First is the Islamic fundamentalist movement, known in the republic as Vakhabits for their aspiration to return to the norms of elementary Islam. The center of this movement is the Fergana Valley, particularly its Namanghan Region. Until recently, the Vakhabits have been opposed to the official clergy on the board. The group of pilgrims in 1991 included only about fifty representatives of the Vakhabits, and over one hundred went on the pilgrimage via Ufa. However, the sharpness of disagreements between the board leaders and Vakhabits has dulled somewhat.

Second, a notable place in defining the religious situation in the republic belongs to the clergy of Tashkent, and to the region itself, for trying to rid the former board of its influence and control. The representatives of this trend are ready to cooperate with the authorities under the condition of reliable guarantees for the performance of religious rites.

Third, one of the constituents of the religious movement is represented by a sufi order, the brotherhood Naqshbandiah.[20] In 1993 plans were made to celebrate the 675th anniversary of Naqshbandi's birthday. The main center of this trend is Bukhara, where B. Naqshbandi was born. The Naqshbandiah are more moderate in their program purposes than the Vakhabits of the Fergana Valley. This movement is small in numbers, but one can expect that the celebration of Naqshbandi's birthday will give it more dynamism and increase the number of its followers.

The composition of the religious movement in Uzbekistan is not confined to those mentioned above. For instance, the republic has a branch of the all-union Islamic Renaissance Party founded in Astrakhan and registered in Moscow before the USSR's disintegration. Despite the negative attitude by both the authorities and the official clergy, who consider that "religion must not govern the government's activities, as it has its own role and purposes,"[21] it has certain influence in the towns and cities, particularly among students. However, the influence of the Islamic Renaissance Party, as well as other minor movements, cannot be compared with those emphasized above.

Regarding the possible repetition of the Iranian experience in its Central Asian version, it should be said that linking the process of religious revival in the Central Asian republics with the problem of power and obligatory transition to an Islamic fundamentalist government is a result of insufficient and superficial knowledge of the historical past and the reality of the region and its Muslim peoples.

It should be noted that, on the whole, experts concerning themselves with politics, history, culture, and other problems connected with Central Asia observe the intensification of the Islamic factor in the social and political life of the region. It is important to realize what this means and how it is interpreted in conformity with the situation in the former Central Asian republics. Even superficial analysis of the publications on the subject shows that there is a tendency to overemphasize the negative aspects of the phenomenon. At the same time, the causes that gave rise to the negative aspects—whose roots date back to our relatively remote and quite recent history—are ignored.

Islam for the Central Asian region is not a new phenomenon but a basis for the unique civilization of the peoples inhabiting the region. The attempt to eradicate Islam—along with Christianity—in Russia was an unnatural effort doomed to failure from the very beginning. It should be admitted as erroneous what some scientific-analytical centers suggest—that the present-day religious renaissance in the Central Asian region is exclusively the result of a sharp rise in Islamic fundamentalist activities. Here one should speak about the ways of returning to the truly *national* culture, in the finest sense of the word. We cannot do without Islam in this case.

It is also a mistake to look for only black spots in the religious movement. And it is erroneous to compare Islam to Western civilization, as each is the product of its own independent and unique phenomena, as a thorough study of the experience of Islamic states shows. Turkey is the most characteristic example in this respect. We should also take into account that the image of other states where Islam is the state religion was disfigured by an official Soviet propaganda. We are still held captive by confrontational thinking, so it is necessary to strive to achieve reasonable and useful harmony between secularism and religion. Excessive exaggeration of the question of fanatic Islamic fundamentalism cannot eliminate the great positive ethic and moral potential of Islam, but it might provoke or radicalize the more fanatical groups.

At the same time, in the republic it has been realized that turning religious trends—particularly Islamic ones—into political trends is very dangerous. The well-known developments in neighboring Tajikistan, which were mainly the consequence of the struggle for power between the former administrative system and different clans, obviously showed the danger in turning Islam into a political trend and involving the clergy in active political life. The evolution of the political situation in

Tajikistan affected the development of constitutional law in Uzbekistan. Article 12 of the first Constitution of the republic of Uzbekistan, adopted in December 1992, emphasizes that "no ideology can be considered as the state ideology."[22] Striving to create a secular social system and do justice to religious values, Article 31 of the Constitution accentuates, "Everybody has the right to confess any religion or to not confess any at all. It is inadmissible to propagate religious views in a compulsory way."[23]

A more complex factor capable of exerting its negative influence, under certain circumstances, upon the state of social and political stability in the Central Asian region may be the territorial and frontier issues in relations among the republics of the region. Owing to the links of interrelations among peoples, this factor may be referred to as interethnic problems, but cannot be seen as the strengthening of nationalistic sentiments of any people or nationality living here.

The Leninist-Stalinist division of the Central Asian republics is known to have been carried out with complete disregard for the important social and political factors linked with the notion of "common cultural territory." When the frontiers among the Central Asian republics were defined, everything had been done to create the conditions for the destruction of the ethnocultural units of this region. The most characteristic example of this phenomenon is the most densely populated part of the Central Asian region—the Fergana Valley. Historically, it was a common ethnocultural territory and was divided among the republics of Uzbekistan, Kyrgyzstan, and Tajikistan. As a result, 13 percent of the population of Kyrgyzstan are now Uzbeks. The 1990 tragedy in Osh, as well as the unsettled Kyrgyz-Tajik conflict, have shown the potential danger of this factor, not only for this area but for Central Asia as a whole. Moreover, there are disputable territories and problems among practically all the newly independent states. The transformation of the former Soviet republics in Central Asia into independent states will certainly sharpen the feelings of the people that find themselves outside their national territory and will intensify their anxiety over their future. Furthermore, a certain percentage of the Russian-speaking population of these states feels less at ease under the present-day conditions. It is believed that this factor may result in destabilizing circumstances for political life in the region.

But what should be done? How should these sensitive and delicate problems be dealt with? First, it is necessary once and for all to get rid of the temptation to change the existing borders. This process would hamper the process of change and development more than any other action. This is the way to set off a chain reaction capable of throwing the Central Asian peoples into war.

Second, the search for foreign partners (quite justified and necessary under the present conditions) must not turn into a competition among the new states of the region. Moreover, it is inadmissible for them to intensify the pro-disintegration processes in the Central Asian region. On the contrary, it is very important to enhance the existing economic, political, and cultural ties, and it is necessary to provide the economic basis for their development. The benefit of such a policy is twofold. On the one hand, the former Soviet Central Asian republics have already formed a common economic space capable, in the future, of providing great dividends for everybody in its sphere. On the other hand, close economic, political, and cultural ties among the republics of Central Asia will take away the acuteness of interethnic relations in each of them, and therefore important groundwork will be laid for the preservation and strengthening of political stability in the whole region.

Third, it is very important that all the native peoples of Central Asia are connected through Islam. This factor is capable of becoming one of the main stabilizing forces in the social and political life of each republic and in the region as a whole. It is evident that Uzbekistan's leaders fully realize the importance of the religious factor in creating a social and spiritual environment, as well as for providing the foundation for reform in the republic. This is manifested in a number of specific steps taken by the Republican leadership. For example, the Law of Liberty of Conscience and Religious Organization, for the first time in seventy years, stated that "religious organizations have the right to take part in social life" (Article 5).[24] The law also officially recognizes the citizens' rights to receive religious education: "The citizens may receive religious education in the language of their choice. The religious organizations that have registered statutes have the right to set up educational institutions and groups. These groups will provide religious education for adults and children and will carry out instruction in other forms using the premises belonging to them or granted to them for such use."[25]

Much work on the revival and popularization of Islamic values is being carried out. These include the translation of the Koran from Arabic to Uzbek; comments made on Islam as well as on Kaddish, a Jewish prayer; mass publications of religious literature; and the printing of the Islamic newspapers *Islam nuri* (The light of Islam) and *Islami madaniyat* (Islamic culture) in Uzbek. Broadcasts and telecasts with leading theologians have become ordinary events. Moreover, celebrations honoring great Central Asian theologians have taken place: in 1990 the 1200th anniversary of Al-Khakim Abu Abdallah Makhammad bin Abi at-Tirmizi was celebrated, and it is expected that celebrations will take place for Nakshbandi and Makhmud bin Umar Abu-l-Kassim as-Zamakhsharis. This indicates that the political leadership of Uzbekistan realizes that Islam is of importance and has a great moral role to play in the formation of a new society.

These factors indicate that the situation in Uzbekistan cannot be compared to what took place in Iran in the 1970s. There may be a certain analogy between the religious movement in Iran and the movement of the Vakhabits in the Fergana Valley, but despite some common factors there are a number of others quite different in essence. First, the Vakhabits of the Fergana Valley do not strive for political power. Their purpose is mainly to change the spiritual and social character of education, culture, and everyday life and to inculcate Islamic norms. Despite some radical notions, they are not opposed to the goals of the present authorities. Within the limits of the current legislation, they are active businessmen and take an active part in the economic development of the country.

Second, despite their common religion, the fundamentalists in Iran and in the Fergana Valley are the followers of different sects: Shiism and Sunnism. Third, the lack of experience of the theocratic states, including Islamic ones, in the present-day world does not promote the rise in the fundamentalists' aspiration for attainment of political power in the country. And finally, the increase of religious awareness in Uzbekistan and in Central Asia as a whole bears a similar impetus, characteristic of the anticolonial struggle in the countries of the Islamic East.[26] This does not include, however, the Iran of the 1970s.

A number of speculations can be made regarding the path that Uzbekistan will follow. One possibility is the Turkish model of development, due to its great vitality and the fact that it is believed to have advantages over the others. The former Soviet Central Asian republics cooperated with their Islamic neighbors, but this cooperation was limited within the Soviet Union's cooperation with these countries. Other models include Iran and Saudi Arabia.

It is dangerous to simplify the problem of choosing a developmental model for the Central Asian states, and it is a mistake for experts to maintain that a given republic should follow a certain model. Uzbekistan and the other Central Asian states should not follow any model blindly, regardless of how worthy it may be. The tragic errors of history should not be repeated.

Notes

1. For example, a well-known Sovietologist, J. Willer, who headed the Central Asian Islamic Center in England, in his speech at the international symposium in 1966 in London, alleged that thanks to the policy of industrialization and collectivization the Islamic people of the USSR, formerly backward and oppressed, made a great advance from patriarchal economy to a modern civilization; this region has a developed industry and agriculture, and the living standard of the population is higher than in Japan, a highly developed country. See *Problems of Communism* 4 (1967): 87.

2. Kh. Umarov, "Sovietskaya Srednyaya Aziya vneshneekonomichesky potentzial" (Soviet Central Asia: its external economic potential), *Sovincom Business Review* 4 (1990): 14.

3. *Khalk Suzi* [People's word], 19 April 1992.

4. Muhammad Ali Albar, *Al-Muslemoon fi-Ittihad al-Sofiyeti* [Muslims of the Soviet Union], vol. 1 (Jedda, Saudi Arabia: 1983), 35.

5. According to President I. Karimov, the republic of Uzbekistan has been officially recognized by 120 states, and 45 of them have already established diplomatic relations. See his *Istikbol Yuli: Muommalar va Rezhalar* [The path of independence: problems and prospects] (Tashkent, Uzbekistan: 1992), 2.

6. *Turkestan*, 4 February 1993.

7. Out since March 1990, with a circulation of 100,000 copies (in Uzbek).

8. According to Uzbekistan President Islam Karimov, the quota of Uzbekistan in the total extraction of gold in the former USSR had been 25 percent, which made up ninety tons annually. See O. Sultonov and M. Muminov, "Mustakillikning iktisodiy negislary," *Fan va Turmush* 1 (January 1992): 2.

9. *Turkestan*, 4 February 1993.

10. *Narodnoye slovo* (Tashkent), 22 January 1992.

11. Uzbekistan's need to introduce its own currency has the general support of the public, including prominent businessmen. See, for example, *Turkestan*, 12 March 1992.

12. The output of oil from the drilled well was 10,000 cubic meters per day, making it comparable, according to some experts, to the most efficient oil wells in Iran and Kuwait. *Uzbekistan Ovozi* [The voice of Uzbekistan], 15 April 1992.

13. *New York Times* (Weekly) (Russia), 19–25 March 1992.

14. "Islam v SSSR" (Islam in the USSR), Moscow *Mysl* (1983): 142.

15. For example, I. Jabbarov claims that the results of the specific sociological analysis in four provinces of Uzbekistan showed that 88.3 percent of

workers and 70.6 percent of peasants were atheists. See "Social System, Mode of Life and Religion," Tashkent *Fan* (1973): 82.

16. W. Kollarz, *Religion in the Soviet Union* (London: 1961), 309.

17. The newspaper of the Spiritual Board of Muslims of Mavarannakhr, *Islam Nuri* 24, no. 42 (December 16–30, 1991), states that only in the Namanghan region are there more than 1000 mosques functioning today. However, it should be taken into account that an absolute majority of these are not traditional mosques, but rather meeting houses. According to vice mufti of the Spiritual Board of Muslims of Mavarannakhr, Sheikh Zakhid Abdel Kader, there are six hundred large and some thousands of small mosques currently functioning in Uzbekistan.

18. *Izvestiya*, no. 240, 9 October 1991.

19. See, for example, *Kommersant* 2 (January 1992).

20. Naqshbandiah is a sufi brotherhood that got its name from Bakhautdin Mukhammad bin Burkhaniddin Mukhammad al-Bukhari (1318–89), who revived and supplemented it with a number of theses and theory and practice borrowed from Akhmad al Yasavi's school. It is one of twelve Sunni brotherhoods, deriving its spiritual traditions and *silsila* (geneology) from Abu Bakr on the one hand, and on the other hand from Ali ibn Abi Talib. The genealogy of Naqshbandiah is called *silsilat az-zakhab* (golden chain), which means that brotherhood is connected with the Prophet, both spiritually (Abu Bakr) and physically (Ali ibn Abi Talib).

21. For example, the head of the Spiritual Board of Muslims of Mavarannakhr, mufti Mukhammad Yusuf Mukhammad Sadyk. See *Izvestiya*, 9 January 1992.

22. *Constitution of the Republic of Uzbekistan* (Tashkent: Uzbekistan Publishing House, 1992), 11.

23. Ibid., 15.

24. *Narodnoye Slovo* (July 1991).

25. Ibid.

26. See for example, Shireen Hunter, "Nationalist Movements in Soviet Asia," *Current History* 89 (October 1990): 325.

8

Kyrgyzstan

Alexander O. Filonyk

Kyrgyzstan, formerly part of the Soviet Union and geographically part of Central Asia, has inherited many problems common to the newly independent states in the area. At the same time, however, its development is characterized by certain peculiarities that have resulted in a degree of stabilization. This stability is determined by several factors. First, due to the republic's leadership—namely, the role played by President Askar Akaev—the country has managed to overcome an acute Kyrgyz-Uzbek conflict and secure a basis for democratic reform. Second, the ethnic composition of Kyrgyzstan, which consists of a large non-Kyrgyz population engaged in different spheres of economic activity, makes interethnic coexistence an imperative for the survival of the state. According to the national census in 1989, the population was divided as follows: Kyrgyz, 52.4 percent; Russians, 21.5 percent; Uzbeks, 12.9 percent; Ukrainians, 2.5 percent; Germans, 2.4 percent; Tatars, 1.6 percent; and the remainder, which consists of Uigurs, Kazakhs, Tajiks, and Dungans.[1] Despite the bloody clashes in the Osh region, which will be discussed later, the Kyrgyz have been known for their tolerance. Moreover, recent history, with the above-mentioned exceptions, knows of no interethnic controversy. Third, the role of Islam is weak, and the domestic secular policy has been in line with the general mood of the population. Fourth, the republic's orientation toward market economy, and its ties with Russia, Kazakhstan, the West, and the developed Asian and pro-Western Muslim states also add to a reserved optimism. Askar Akaev stated as early as 1989 that he was a supporter of market economy. According to him, the market economy has negative aspects of its own, such as unemployment and the division of society into the rich and the poor. However, there are rich and poor countries among those with a market economy, but there isn't a single rich country among the states with command economies."[2]

These positive trends are not necessarily irreversible. The fact is that

Kyrgyzstan, like the other former Soviet republics, is in a period of transition. It faces the daring tasks of becoming a sovereign state, overcoming economic backwardness, and acquiring international status. These tasks, difficult as they are for any national entity, are even more complicated for Kyrgyzstan, which has additional burdens as well.

Socioeconomic Dynamics

Kyrgyzstan has always been an agrarian republic whose share of agriculture and industry in the national income was about 37.6 percent and 36.8 percent, respectively.[3] This made the republic very dependent on external sources, especially agriculture. Under the Soviet regime, Kyrgyzia, as part of a unitarian state, was automatically included into the division of labor and could rely on supplies from the other Soviet republics. However, many economic ties inside the former USSR have been severed as a by-product of the Soviet Union's collapse and the quest for sovereignty among its integral parts. In this respect Kyrgyzstan is no exception, and its old problems are becoming more painful.

The most acute problem in the countryside is covert and overt unemployment. According to some sources, the number of unemployed reached 150,000 in 1992.[4] There are many *kyshlaks* (villages) with populations exceeding 20,000 of which a large percentage is unemployed. A number of factors account for this, including the high rate of growth of the rural population. National traditions, which praise a large family as a symbol of prosperity and blessings from God, are still very strong in the villages. For the Kyrgyz, who for centuries were nomads combining cattle breeding with the cultivation of land, large families were a prerequisite for survival.

The second reason is a surplus of publicly owned cattle, which resulted in a lack of land for private farming. In the Soviet Union, increasing the number of cattle had always been encouraged. For instance, in 1989 the amount of sheep and goats was 8,397,600 head, and meat cattle reached 744,700 head.[5] Due to primitive methods of breeding, the yearly loss of cattle was substantial and compensation was needed. This clearly had negative consequences.

Apart from the lack of pastures, it led to the low quality of cattle breeding and productivity. The workers' lack of interest in their work, characteristic of the *kolkhozes* and *sovkhozes*, also played its part. A decree on the privatization of cattle, however, may help to solve part of the problem.

The annulment of the restrictions limiting the amount of cattle in private property does not mean that young people will automatically become involved in agricultural production. The rural populations in Kyrgyzstan, Russia, and the other republics have experienced not only economic but also psychological handicaps. During the years of socialism, agricultural workers became accustomed to the low, but guaranteed, incomes of collective farms where labor was never very intensive. Thus, it is difficult to train the new generation about the notion of property, the importance of being responsible for the results of one's work, and of the need for initiative and readiness for certain economic risks.

The situation in Kyrgyzstan is paradoxical because the youth in the rural areas, despite their low level of education, do not want to breed cattle. At the same time, the lack of appropriate qualifications does not permit other alternatives. The urban way of life is now more attractive, and hence a high level of migration by the rural population of Kyrgyzstan to the urban areas is expected.

It is quite evident that administrative restrictions may not improve the situation. Another problem lies in the potential danger of a social explosion in the rural areas where there is a highly concentrated unemployed and frustrated population. The situation is still aggravated by the existing interethnic tensions. Rural youth took an active part in the interethnic conflict in Osh in 1990 and in anti-Russian demonstrations in the Issyk-Kul area in July 1991.

The social and ethnic tensions were eased by the government's decision to distribute plots of land in the suburbs to the new migrants from rural areas for house building. At the same time, however, the possibility of using financial support from the state for the construction of private homes (credit, loans) is not very feasible due to the lack of building materials. Preferential taxation in rural areas, lowering the pensionary age, and special credits for peasants and cattle breeders are also not very effective due to the crisis in the supply system.

Kyrgyz cities face problems typical of the former Soviet Union: a high infant mortality rate (32.2 per 1,000), lack of housing (12 square meters per capita, according to the official data of 1987), and poor public transportation (in Bishkek one can wait for a bus endlessly in the evening).

The course of speeding up the industrialization of Kyrgyzstan in the Soviet era did have some positive effects. However, it also led to the concentration of industry exclusively in the larger cities. Hence, the possibility for employment in small-and medium-sized towns is low. According to President Akaev, the dispersal of industry could not only help solve housing, ecological, and other problems in the big cities but could also create a kind of buffer between the urban and rural areas.

At the same time, the government is interested in creating small processing enterprises in rural areas. This will help lessen the losses of agricultural production during transportation and long-term preservation on the one hand, and will solve a number of social problems on the other.

One of the most difficult problems for Kyrgyzstan is its Russian-speaking population. This problem pertains predominantly to urban areas. The "Europeans" (Russians, Ukrainians, Byelorussians, Germans, and other Russian-speaking people who have arrived from the European part of the USSR and Siberia) account for 45 percent of the population in cities and 65 percent in the capital. In the cities they form an elite sector: Kyrgyz account for only 8 percent of the skilled workers and only 3 percent of engineers and technicians. It should not be forgotten that the greater part of the "Europeans" arrived in Kyrgyzstan as settlers, not as migrants in search of work. Many of them are fifth-or sixth-generation natives of Kyrgyzstan.

Both the Europeans and the Kyrgyz are taking a rather active part in public movements. The first (parliamentary) election for the president, in October 1990, when the pressure of the Bishkek students on the parliamentarians ensured in many respects Akaev's victory, has shown that democratic sentiments are strong among the Kyrgyz youth in the cities. Another important factor behind the success of local democrats is the absence of a political split between the "European" and the Kyrgyz parts of the urban population.

The absence of open interethnic tensions between the Kyrgyz and the Russian-speaking population does not mean that there is no danger of ethnically based unrest in Kyrgyzstan. There are no sociological studies, however, providing information on the current trends in this respect. It seems evident that the policy of the Soviet regime within the framework of a united state gave the Russian-speaking citizens the opportunity to adjust to the non-Russian milieus of the outlying oriental districts of the former USSR. There was, for example, no need to learn the local language. Even more, there were no easy ways to do it. Local cultural traditions remained strange and alien. This resulted in very superficial integration and the creation of enclaves.

Only 1.2 percent of the "Europeans" (1 percent in cities and 1.85 percent in the villages) speak the language of the indigenous population. Moreover, they are badly informed about the intertribal relations among the Kyrgyz. The situation is quite different, however, from that of the Russian Empire, where Russian and indigenous communities were completely isolated from one another.

After the disintegration of the USSR and the formation of independent states, the rate of migration from Central Asia to Russia greatly increased. In Kyrgyzstan, however, there are practically no immediate causes for such migration.

In the past few years an increasing number of "Europeans" left the republic. However, this group accounts for just a small percentage of the "Europeans" living there. Incidentally, some of those who left the republic returned, after some time, to the area where they previously lived. The main reason for the emigration is that in 1989 the republican leaders proclaimed a gradual (up to 1998) transition to the Kyrgyz language in all state institutions and educational establishments.

Interethnic conflicts in the other former Soviet republics have had a destabilizing effect on the situation in Kyrgyzstan. There are widespread fears that domestic policies will become more nationalistic and that the problem of self-identification in a new, drastically changed cultural context will become morbid. Of course, very few emigrants may rationalize along these lines. The cumulative factor (many have already left, hence it is more dangerous to stay), the lack of will or ability to adjust oneself to the new conditions of life, and the economic situation are the main psychological reasons for emigration.

As mentioned above, the best nutrient for nationalism is the unemployed rural youth who have migrated to the cities but are still out of work. They are restricted by episodes of everyday life. Thus, it is important to remember the demonstrations, mentioned above, in Osh and Issyk-Kul. A nationalistic party, "Asaba," was created in Kyrgyzstan in the early 1990s. It consists of about one thousand members, but has thus far been unable to influence the situation in the republic. But, for those who have found themselves in a foreign country, after the disintegration of the USSR, even minor symptoms of nationalism are scary enough.

The situation is also being destabilized from the opposite side. There is a movement within the Russian-speaking community of Kyrgyzstan for the introduction of dual citizenship. This movement is also working toward the establishment of an ethnically based proportion in the leading bodies of the republic, corresponding to the share of each ethnic group in the population. These nationalistic ideas are forwarded in Russia exclusively by right-wing extremist organizations opposed to the present administration. Various organizers of the migration to Russia are very active. They collect money from would-be migrants with the promise of helping them get an allotment of land and start a new life in the different regions of Russia. The foundation "Russian Community" is one such organization. It promises all future migrants the possibility of becoming farmers in the Rostov region. Even if there are no doubts about the wishes of the foundation to assist the Russian population of the former outlying districts to emigrate, the question remains whether the situation in the Rostov region is favorable for the newcomers. In this region the Kazaks (not to be confused with the Kazakhs), who are very influential, are hardly interested in strengthening the economic positions of the new settlers and thus their capacities for competition.

There is one more aspect to this problem that should not be neglected. It has been pointed out by many scholars that the Russian population of the oriental republics gradually formed a particular subethnic group in terms of cultural characteristics, traditions, and everyday living that differs from the Russian population of Russia proper. These local Russian populations are evidently considered "Russians" in Kyrgyzstan, but they might as well be treated as "Kyrgyz" or some other ethnic group in the Rostov region. This factor may seriously complicate the process of reintegrating the representatives of these subethnic groups into the Russian community.

As for Kyrgyzstan, massive emigration of the Russian-speaking population will create many problems and should be avoided. Qualified workers and specialists in the local enterprises are mainly Russian speaking. Furthermore, Kyrgyzstan's industries are utterly dependent on Russia and the Ukraine. Interethnic conflicts causing a forcible emigration of the Russian-speaking population may lead not only to an economic crisis but also to tensions in relations with Moscow and Kiev. The leaders of Kyrgyzstan are fully aware of these dangers. Askar Akaev vetoed the land-law act, which stated that the land was the property of the Kyrgyz (that is, the titular nationality), not the peoples of Kyrgyzstan. This law would have infringed upon the rights of other ethnic communities.

The president of Kyrgyzstan also put forward the idea of creating a Slav university in Bishkek. According to the *Moscow News* correspondents, "the nomination of Felix Kulov as the vice president of the republic was an unambiguous signal to the nationalists. Felix Kulov, while being the commandant of Frunze (now Bishkek), ordered strict measures, following the Osh events, to stop interethnic conflicts there."[6]

According to Akaev, human rights are more important than the rights of an ethnic group or of a nation: "In another case humanism, democracy, and legal state are empty words. I am on the side of those who stand up for a civic union among nations and for joint actions of people of different nationalities."[7]

Akaev faces a rather complicated heritage as regards the potential for ethnic conflict, particularly between the Kyrgyz and the Uzbeks. Economic competition has served as the basis of these conflicts. When the Kyrgyz Autonomous Soviet Socialist Republic was created in 1924 (since December 1936, Kyrgyz Soviet Socialist Republic) the territories of Uzbekistan and Kyrgyzstan were delimited in such a way that the present Osh region of Kyrgyzstan included some parts of the Fergana Valley with an overwhelming Uzbek population. The Uzbeks also formed the majority of the population in Dzhelal Abadt, Maile-Sae, and Kyzyl-Kiya.

While the Kyrgyz and the Uzbeks in Kyrgyzstan occupied their particular economic niche there were no conflicts between them. The Kyrgyz were predominantly nomad cattle breeders and dwelled mainly in the mountains and foothills. The Uzbeks, being the main tillers and artisans, concentrated in the valleys, where their urban and rural settlements came into being. The relations between the two ethnic groups were based on this even separation of economic functions and territories.

Later on the situation began to change. After the creation of the kolkhoz and sovkhoz systems, a growing number of Kyrgyz were forced to settle and, thus, to change their traditional way of life. They started to move from the mountains to the valleys and from the mountain villages to the cities. This process led to their involuntary competition with local residents. Since the 1960s the Kyrgyz began settling in parts of the Fergana Valley, including towns and settlements that had been founded by the Uzbeks and Russians. Nevertheless, the Uzbeks still constituted an absolute majority in the towns of Osh and Uzghen, while the Kyrgyz became predominant in the suburbs. Since the Kyrgyz were newcomers in these regions, their positions were less favorable than those of the Uzbek population. This inequality embraced housing conditions, as well as spheres of economic activity. Service and com-

merce were considered prestigious and profitable, and the Uzbeks occupied predominant positions in these spheres: they constituted 51.6
percent in state commerce and 79 percent among the taxi drivers in
Osh.[8]

The Kyrgyz population was subdivided into two main groups. The
first, small in number, included office employees working in the state
and party structures. This was the result of nominating representatives
of the titular nations in the republics to leading posts. This principle
was always in force under the Soviet regime, but in the 1970s its importance increased. Thus, the Uzbeks could not lay claim—even in the
Uzbek districts—to the leading posts. A large percentage of the Kyrgyz
in the urban centers consists of recently arrived rural migrants, who
preserve ties with their places of origin. The majority of these were
semiqualified or unqualified workers, forming marginal groups in the
urban workplace. These social groups have lost their traditional values
and principles. Moreover, they are devoid of their roots but cannot adjust to the new conditions of urban life. They are easily roused, prone
to primitive nationalistic slogans, and always ready to place blame on
other ethnic groups for their problems.

It was easy for the Kyrgyz migrants to react this way, given the fact
that economic and housing conditions, as well as other social problems, were much worse for them than for the Uzbeks. It is necessary to
work for years in the same enterprise in order to get an apartment. A
private house with a small parcel of land—a standard Uzbek dwelling—
is beyond imagination. Consequently, the urban lot for many Kyrgyz
families with numerous children was a room in a hostel. It should be
pointed out that in traditional Uzbek settlements the *mahalla* system
of social organization is usually well preserved. This system makes it
practically impossible for non-Uzbeks to get a parcel of land in Uzbek
quarters. The Kyrgyz were no exception to this rule.

As a result, a very dangerous social situation was created. Social and
economic inequalities were moved into the sphere of interethnic relations. In response to the bloodshed and the demands of Kyrgyz youth
in May and June of 1990, the local authorities decided to distribute
land for house building in the suburbs of Osh. However, it turned out
that the land belonged to the Lenin Collective Farm, where 95 percent
of the members were Uzbeks. At their meeting on the collective farm
field, the Uzbeks demanded autonomy on the territory of the Osh region. During the meeting, fighting started between Uzbeks and Kyrgyz.
Similar fighting occurred in Uzghen in which Uzbeks, a majority of the

population, ousted Kyrgyz residents from the town. The latter set up a "refugee camp" nearby. Later, Kyrgyz from the countryside joined the urban dwellers and in several days burst into Uzghen and started Uzbek pogroms. After that, troops were brought into the conflict-ridden regions.

The bloodshed in Osh accelerated the process of political change in the republic. It also strengthened the positions of the national democratic forces. The pressure of these forces helped Askar Akaev rise to power. After the Osh events, First Secretary Massaliev of the Central Committee, who had a reputation as a militant conservative, was relieved of his post. In October 1990 the first presidential election took place in the Supreme Soviet of the republic, and Akaev defeated Massaliev by four votes. The opposition, claiming changes in political orientation, gave its support to Akaev. Later, Akaev noted that he owed his victory to the support of the democratic opposition in the Supreme Soviet.

During the elections, the partisans of reform posted pickets around the building of the Central Committee, where the session took place, in order to deprive Massaliev and his faction of power by pressuring the deputies. Soon after Akaev was elected president, his political rival left the post of chairman of the Supreme Soviet of Kyrgyzstan.

The election of Akaev reflected not only the balance of political forces in the republic but also the interaction of clans and regions. A struggle for power between the Issyk-Kul and Osh groups has traditionally determined the political situation in the republic. The claims to power of the Issyk-Kul group are in line with similar historical claims made by the Bugu and Sarybagyshese—two of the most powerful Kyrgyz tribes—in the mid-nineteenth century. The chief Manap of the Sarybagyshese, Ormon, even proclaimed himself the khan of all the Kyrgyz in 1850. The two Issyk-Kul tribes have always fought for power. The claims of the Osh group date back to the Kokand Khanate when the southern Kyrgyz played an appreciable role and, by 1840, placed under their control nearly all of present-day Kyrgyzstan.

For over twenty-five years the power in the republic belonged to the former first secretary of the Central Committee, T. Usubaliyev, a Sarybagyshese. At the same time, a large role was played by representatives of the Solto tribe from the Chui Valley: Chairman of the Council of Ministers B. Mambetov (1961–68) and KGB Chief D. Asankulov (1967–91). T. Kulatov, from Osh, was chairman of the Supreme Soviet presidium. He was apparently promoted to the post by I. Razzakov, also from

Osh, who headed the Council of Ministers from 1945 to 1950 and was first secretary of the Central Committee from 1950 to 1961. In 1981 Usubaliyev succeeded in making T. Kh. Koshoyev and A. Duishayev president and prime minister, respectively. Both are Sarybagyshese from the village of Kishi-Kemin in the east of the Chui Region.

In 1985 Usubaliyev was replaced by A. Iolasaliyev, from Osh. However, the Sarybagyshese fought against him and succeeded in removing him from the post in 1990. Akaev, a Sarybagyshese, was appointed head of the republic. After the August 1991 coup, KGB Chief Asankulov, who supported the coup, was removed from his post. Apparently the intertribal rivalry should not be underestimated, but at the same time, all political reshuffles, especially from the most recent period, should not be reduced to such rivalry. Akaev's victory was not the victory of the Sarybagyshese alone, but was also a victory of the more democratic north over the more conservative, traditionalist south.

It was not possible for Akaev to ignore the traditional relations between the different clans, as well as the strength of the old nomenclature. All *akims* (heads of the local administrations), without exception, are former party officials. Akaev commented on this situation as follows:

> I agree with my critics, when they accuse me of not following the best path in terms of nominations. The representatives of the old guard are, indeed, on many key posts. But if I ignore the reality of life, it would be possible to suffer a general defeat. For instance, I may nominate a democrat, but he will not be accepted by the region. He will be rejected. And there will be no progress in reforms. It is much easier for me to nominate a conservative akim, than a democrat, but later to suffer, because he is not accepted by the people.[9]

A nominated head of the republican Radio and TV Committee, belonging to the democratic wing, was compelled to resign because he failed to establish normal contacts with the personnel. Local democrats interpreted this as a victory for the conservative forces and as a next-in-line concession by the president. It is quite evident that the president is obliged to make compromises and to take into account the interests of the different political, ethnic, and economic forces. This policy demands much tenacity from the president, since it makes him a target for attacks from the side of his supporters during the presidential elections. According to *Izvestiya* correspondent Nicolai Andreev, a fierce attack on the president has been unleashed by the local press. The public is being warned against "the bloody dictatorship" of Akaev, who is being compared to the overthrown Georgian president Gamsakhurdia. The destiny of the latter is increasingly mentioned to Akaev.[10]

Projections of this kind are obviously far from reality, but they aggravate Akaev's position, which is already very complicated. The leaders of Kyrgyzstan face the complex problems of building a new independent state. Among these problems one should mention the restructuring of the political system, the transition to market economy, the elaboration of the concept of national security, and the development of foreign relations. The program of economic reforms was elaborated with the collaboration of International Monetary Fund experts and adopted by the parliament on 7 July 1992.

The debates on the new constitution are at the center of political life in Kyrgyzstan. In order to prevent the transformation of presidential power into a dictatorship, the new constitution of the republic needs to be based on the parliamentary rather than the presidential pattern.

Islam in Kyrgyzstan

The relative weakness of Islam in Kyrgyzstan may be attributed to the following factors: (1) the country's significant non-Muslim population; (2) a presidential policy that is not geared toward pleasing the local nationalists; and (3) Islam's short history in the republic. The Islamization process was completed only in the nineteenth century, and since then the Kyrgyz have never been considered true believers.

The Islamization of the Kyrgyz underwent different stages, and Islam acquired different forms in the state's various regions. In the south, primarily in the Fergana Valley, where the population was sedentary, Islam was established as early as the eighth and ninth centuries. In the tenth and eleventh centuries splendid mosques and mausoleums were built, and the Arabic script was introduced. In the thirteenth and fourteenth centuries the development of Islamic culture suffered major setbacks under the Mongol conquerors. From the seventeenth to the twentieth centuries the Kokand rulers implemented a policy of forced Islamization that was extended to the northern regions of present-day

Kyrgyzstan. The nomads in the north resisted Islamization for over three centuries and were conquered not by the sword but rather through the work of Muslim missionaries.

The process was helped by the fact that a great number of nomads from the north were forced by the Dzungar rulers into the vicinity of the Fergana Valley, where they established contacts with the Uzbeks, who strictly observed Muslim traditions. After the collapse of the Dzungar khanate the nomads returned, but they did not cut ties with the Uzbek settlers. The Uzbek mullahs often traveled to the north in search of support and to convert the Kyrgyz to Islam.

The Kyrgyz adherence to Islam, and especially their knowledge of the Koran and Muslim rites, have remained very superficial. In addition, the Kyrgyz maintained many of their pre-Islamic traditions. According to a Kazakh traveler, Ch. Valikhanov, who visited the Kyrgyz in the 1880s, "Islam among illiterate people without mullahs cannot have roots; it is nothing but a sound, a phrase which conceals the old shaman notions."[11]

In 1924, according to the delimitation of Central Asia, the Kara-Kyrgyz autonomous area was formed within the Russian Federation. In 1926 it was given the status of Kyrgyz Autonomous Republic, and in 1936 Kyrgyzia became a constituent republic of the Soviet Union. The official atheist ideology could not but alienate the Kyrgyz even further from religion. Islam was regarded as a remnant of feudalism that should be mercilessly uprooted.

With this in mind, it is obvious that Bishkek will hardly become prey for the Islamists. When the Islamic Renaissance Party was founded it had practically no supporters in the republic. The situation has slightly changed under the impact of the Tajik events. Military hostilities forced several Islamist armed groupings across the border into Kyrgyzstan. They found themselves in the Fergana Valley, where the Uzbek population is far more religious than the titular nation. The Uzbeks and the Kyrgyz of the Osh region cannot forget the bloody massacre of their relatives in 1990. Each year the authorities guard against potential revenge. In such tense situations, the appearance of the Tajik Islamists, who might add fuel to the developments, was an unpleasant surprise for the Kyrgyz government.[12]

The Islamic Center was set up in Kyrgyzstan. Its head, Sakykjan-hadji Kamalov, does not conceal his sympathy for the fundamentalists.[13] Manifestations of political Islam in Kyrgyzia remain marginal. The Islamists are being chased out, not only in Tajikistan but throughout all of Central Asia where the rulers do not want the "Tajik infection" to spread in any form. For the time being, political Islam has been held back in the region. This has happened not because it is alien to the local population but rather because Islamist leaders have not gained enough political experience. Many observers do not dismiss the idea of a new Islamic revival in Central Asia in the future. If it develops, its impact on the society of Kyrgyzstan will be much more substantial. It will also affect interethnic relations, first and foremost between the Uzbeks and the Kyrgyz.

Foreign Policy

National security is one of the most substantial problems facing Kyrgyzstan. At the beginning of the 1990s the State Committee of National Security, organized on the basis of the former KGB, has begun to work out the necessary documents. According to V. Verchaguin, vice chairman of the State Committee, relations between Kyrgyzstan and China, as well as with Turkey, Iran, Afghanistan, Pakistan, and other countries, are considered most important in this respect. At the same time, the officials of Kyrgyzstan are fully aware that it would not be possible to ensure stability without taking into consideration the traditional interests of the United States, other Western countries, and Russia.[14]

The armed forces are not only the means to ensure state security but are also a symbol of sovereignty. The disintegration of the USSR led to the need to reconsider the former defense doctrine. The approach to the problem of the national armed forces varies in different republics. The situation in Kyrgystan is the most difficult. The new independent republic had to declare its intention to create a national armed forces, as did the other members of the former USSR, but it lacks financial and other means to achieve it. Thus it was announced that at present the national armed forces would be confined to an aviation regiment, but financial sources are still unclear.[15]

The formation of new independent states and the changes in the geopolitical situation caused by it provoked changes in the existing system of regional international relations. As a Soviet republic, Kyrgyzstan had no independent part in international life. Now the new country must formulate its own national interests and priorities in international relations. The development of relations with its close neighbors is one of these priorities. Kyrgyzstan organized the first free trade zone on the border with China. The Chinese factor is of prime importance in politics as well as in the economy. Kyrgyzstan is interested in balanced relations with China. But quite unexpectedly, at the end of July 1992 the constituent conference of the party "For independent Uighurstan" was held in Bishkek. The goal of this party is the formation of the Uighur state on the territory of the Xinjiang-Uighur autonomous region of China, neighboring Kyrgystan. An appeal to the peoples and governments of the world, with a request to assist the will of the Uighurs in creating its national statehood, was adopted at this conference. This activity may be considered an attempt to provoke tensions with China.

Of course, one should not overestimate declarations of this type, but it is important to point out that the ideas of ethnically based self-determination and sovereignty characteristic of many regions of the former USSR are also widespread in Kyrgyzstan. If these trends escalate the domestic situation in multiethnic Kyrgyzstan may become even more complicated.

The development of economic relations with foreign states is of prime importance to Kyrgyzstan. In order to modernize its economy, Kyrgyzstan needs foreign technology and investment. Akaev increased the adoption of foreign laws in order "to guarantee foreign firms and companies that there are no risks in investing in Kyrgyzstan."[16] The organization of joint enterprises with the participation of foreign companies is encouraged. In this domain, the leaders of Kyrgyzstan have to struggle against local "ultrapatriots" who claim that "the land is being sold out to capitalists."

The development of relations between Kyrgyzstan and South Korea has been successful. A TV and VCR factory is being constructed on the territory where Koreans are settling.

At the same time, foreign economic relations are still limited. The scantiness of financial possibilities, underdeveloped infrastructures, absence of respective laws and guarantees, and lack of highly qualified specialists are among the main factors hindering the development of relationships between foreign countries and Kyrgyzstan, as well as other Central Asian republics. Of course, different countries interested in establishing relations with the new Central Asian states (for example, Turkey, Iran, Pakistan, Saudi Arabia, Japan) due to their respective political and/or ideological orientations may grant loans, subsidize particular projects, and so forth, but private business, which is the basis of all economic activity, prefers to act under safer conditions.

The attempt to establish Kyrgyzstan as an independent partner in international relations and an equal member of the world community has been very difficult. In this context the consolidation of relations within Central Asia is now regarded in Bishkek as a shock absorber to the pressure exerted on Kyrgyzstan by various domestic and external problems.

Notes

1. *Kyrgyziya v tsyfrahk* [Kyrgyzia: basic data] (Kyrgyzstan: Frunze, 1990), 3.
2. Abidin Bozdag, "Kurzbiographien: Askar Akayev," *Orient* (Hamburg) 3 (September 1991): 340.
3. *Kyrgyziya v tsyfrahk*, 9.
4. *Moscovskiye Novosti*, 19 July 1992.
5. *Kyrgyzia v tsyfrah*, 8.
6. *Moscowskie Novosti*, 19 July 1992.
7. Bozdag, "Kurzbiographien," 344.
8. *Mezhnatsional'nyye problemy i konflikty: poiski putey ihk resheniya* [Inter-ethnic problems and conflicts: a search for settlement], Part I (Bishkek: 1991), 105.
9. *Izvestiya*, 24 June 1992.
10. *Izvestiya*, 24 June 1992.
11. Ch. Valikhanov, *Collected Works*, vol. 1 (Alma Ata: 1961), 470.
12. *Nezavisimaya Gazeta*, no. 429 (1993).
13. Ibid., no. 426 (1993).
14. Ibid., no. 137 (1992).
15. *Moscovskiye Novosti*, 9 August 1992.
16. Bozdag, "Kurzbiographien," 342.

9

Tajikistan

Aziz Niyazi

The process now under way in the politico-ideological life of Tajikistan represents above all a natural response by traditional society to accelerated modernization introduced from outside. The political process and political behavior are intertwined with and greatly influenced by ethnic psychology, historically established ways of life and communication, and the enduring complexes of ethnic concepts.

The reform impulse propagated from the center, having reached the Muslim areas of the USSR and come across their historic heritage and peculiar cultural values, partially faded and partially engendered a complicated and unpredictable reaction, which came as a real surprise to the Kremlin reformists. The Muslim societies, where traditional relationships and concepts are still strong, met the changes cut out after the same pattern for the entire Soviet Union with suspicion.

Between 1980 and 1991 there has been a significant body of study in the former USSR (based on the experience of Asian and African countries) on the problem of the interrelations of traditional and modern components in culture, state construction, law, politics, social thinking, and mass consciousness.[1] This chapter has used the findings of such studies to shed some light on the social and political processes that have taken place in the Muslim republics of the CIS in general and in Tajikistan in particular.

The first part of the chapter will provide a short historical synopsis of the republic and will then discuss the sharp social and economic problems which to a great extent determine contemporary ideological and political processes in the republic.

The Birth of the Republic

After the Samanid period, Tajiks had no state organization of their own until Soviet power was established in Central Asia. Formed as a nationality in the nineteenth and twentieth centuries, the Tajiks lived in

the states of Tahirids and Samanids from the tenth through the thirteenth centuries; in the states of Gaznevids, Karakhanids, and Khorezm
from the thirteenth through the sixteenth centuries; in the state of
Timurids from the fifteenth century; in the Bukhara Khanate (later in
the Bukhara Emirate); and in a number of small, feudal domains. In
1868 the northern areas of contemporary Tajikistan joined the Russian
Empire (a part of the Fergana and Samarkand *oblasts*).[2] The central
and southwestern areas, known as Eastern Bukhara and the Western
Pamires, remained in the Bukhara emirates. Administrative division
into *bekanates* prevailed in these areas. The bekanates of Hissar, Bal-
juan, Darvaz, Karategin, Kabadiyan, Kurgan-Tyube, and Kulyab were
parts of Eastern Bukhara. The Western Pamires were composed of the
Rushan, Shugnan, and part of the Vahan bekanates.

A part of modern Tajikistan within the limits of the Leninabad and
Murghab administrative oblasts of the Gorno-Badakhshan administrative *rayon* belonged to the Samarkand and Fergana oblasts. The Samarkand oblast consisted of eighteen *volosts*. Among them were the territories of contemporary Naus, Proletarsky, Khojent, Zafarabad, Matchi,
Ura-Tyube, Ganj, and Pendjikent rayons. The Asht and Bobodarkhan
volosts (currently known as the Asht rayon) were parts of the Na-
mangan *uezd*. Kanibadam and Isfara as independent volosts were parts
of the Fergana oblast.

The Tajik Autonomous Soviet Socialist Republic (ASSR) was founded
on 10 November 1924 as part of the Uzbek SSR. Its borders embraced
mainly former Eastern Bukhara. There were 2.1 million Tajiks at the
time, but only 739,503 were among the population of the national republic. Two-thirds of the Tajiks remained outside the borders of the
Tajik SSR.[3] This situation meant that the Tajiks acquired statehood
only on the periphery of their historical motherland, that is, in the
mountainous, economically backward regions. The ancient cities of
Bukhara, Samarkand, and Khojent, which had been the centers of Tajik
economic and political life for many centuries, remained outside the
new republic. This situation was partly changed in 1929 when Khojent
was added to the republic. The border problem between Uzbekistan and
Tajikistan was finally settled in 1930: on February 3 the Central Executive Committee (CEC) of the USSR declined the application of the Tajik
SSR concerning transferring the *okrugs* of Samarkand and Bukhara to
Tajikistan, and a short time afterward the CEC declined its previously
confirmed resolution of transferring the Surkhandarya okrug to the
Tajik SSR.[4]

Thus, Tajikistan's borders were marked artificially and did not coincide with ethnographical realities. The Bolshevik Revolution and the national-territorial division of the Central Asian peoples that followed destroyed the previously existing balance between the Persian- and Turkic-speaking populations of the region. That balance had provided sufficient harmony in fulfilling the social and economic functions of the settled and nomadic peoples. The former contradiction between the settled (agricultural) and nomadic cultures was replaced by one of national character.

It would be impossible to mark a precise border between the Tajiks and their neighbors, taking into consideration the mosaic settling patterns. Bilingualism was widespread in many regions, and there were many mixed families. The Tajiks formed the majority of the urban population, whereas the Turks prevailed among the rural population. Nevertheless, it must be admitted that a certain injustice took place in solving the problem of Samarkand and Bukhara.

From the perspective of Tajik intellectuals, the established borders are an injustice. The unfair territorial division and the planned "Uzbekization" of the Tajik population of Uzbekistan that followed were primarily the consequence of implementing a pan-Turkic ideology. Some followers of this ideology denied the very existence of Tajiks as an ethnic community.[5] Others considered only the inhabitants of Gorno-Badakhshan to be Tajiks.[6]

Unfortunately for the Tajiks, the only political force the Bolsheviks could unite with in their struggle for power in Central Asia was the revolutionary wing of the Jadid movement[7]—a group with a vividly pan-Turkic character. Russian revolutionaries were attracted by the Jadids negative attitude toward tsarist Russia and by their desire to put an end to the despotic rule of Alim Khan in Bukhara. But having gained power, the new companions in arms faced the dilemma of how to harmonize the incompatible. While the Jadids were still dreaming of a united, modernized Turkic nation, the Bolsheviks proclaimed: "Workers of the world, unite!"

With the Bolshevik victory the class dictatorship began to gain the upper hand, while the ethnic dictatorship had to step back. The strength of the former was in its claim of internationalism, an idea that had already captured the minds of millions of common people, irrespective of their national borders or ethnic background. Furthermore, the idea was backed by the military might of the Red Army. Along with internationalism, the Bolsheviks proclaimed the right of nations to self-determination and granted a national formation such as a union or autonomous republic, autonomous *kray*, or oblast to each nationality. This promoted the process of national self-determination of people on the one hand, while developing their consciousness as citizens of one big country—the USSR—on the other.

Thus, the logic of forming a strictly centralized multinational state determined the developments in the spheres of social life in Central Asia. Pan-Turkism gradually gave way to the nationalism of the people of the republic for which it was named. Local nationalisms were naturally less dangerous for the central/Moscow power than the ideology of pan-Turkism, which embraced a vaster community. One by one, yesterday's pan-Turkists began to publicly recant their former delusions, and many of them adopted narrow, nationalistic positions. In the late 1930s almost all of the participants of the Jadid movement in Central Asia, Azerbaijan, and Tatarstan were sent to concentration camps or were shot. Indeed, the revolution ate its own children! The repression was a major blow at local nationalisms. Joseph Stalin's evil genius acted without mistakes. An all-embracing state dominating national consciousness was becoming firmly established in a multinational state.

The principle of ethnoterritorial division did not affect the political life of society much as long as the state remained a unitary one with an all-embracing and flourishing ideology. The borders between the republics were mainly of a conventional/superficial character, as it was the center that made most of the decisions. Yet, the ethnoterritorial principle proved much more significant, much to the dismay of the center. As soon as the Soviet Union collapsed and new independent national states appeared, the national egoisms of the latter began to manifest themselves. The ethnoterritorial divides, having been marked conventionally and mostly without an objective base, are now viewed by many people as natural partitions. The new states themselves began to champion primarily the interests of the title-ethnic groups of which the republics assumed the names—that is, the interests of the Uzbeks, Ukrainians, Moldavians, Azerbaijanis, Tajiks, and so on—rather than the interests of Uzbekistan, the Ukraine, Moldova, Azerbaijan, Tajikistan, and so on, and ethnic passion began to prevail in the inner and "international" relations of these states. This happened because Communist ideals, destroyed by perestroika, were replaced in many cases not by democratic ideals but by nationalistic ones.

Public consciousness, having been formed under Soviet totalitarianism, was not ready to accept the values "common-for-all-mankind," which had been preached by the advocates of perestroika; collectivist ideals gave way to communal or nationalistic ones. In Central Asia, as elsewhere in the former Soviet Union, collectivist consciousness made a quick switch to communal or nationalistic ideals rather than to democratic ones, thus paving the way for its effective manipulation and use by the emerging political elite in the region.

Contemporary Social and Economic Problems

The Soviet regime, though established by force, nevertheless greatly stimulated the economic development of Central Asia. There was also great improvement in the spheres of health care and education. Tajikistan received sufficiently large subsidies from the Soviet Union budget,[8] but already in the 1970s the general recession experienced by the entire USSR began to manifest itself in the republic. During this common economic crisis Tajikistan faced sharp social and economic problems, as the republic had been included into the Soviet economic complex primarily as a supplier of agricultural products and raw materials.

By the end of the 1980s the living standards in the republic were the lowest in the USSR. In 1989 the poverty mark in the USSR ran at 78 rubles per month per person (apparently an understated figure). In Tajikistan 58.6 percent of the population had an income below this (in comparison to Russia's 6.3 percent). The average annual income growth rate per person decreased 3.8 times between 1989 and 1991, while the public consumption funds decreased 3.9 times. Thus the statistically registered personal consumption rate in Tajikistan amounted to only 63.3 percent of the all-union rate (for 1989). Just before the collapse the ration of foodstuff consumption had become considerably lower than that prescribed by the standard.

The situation in industry and agriculture has steadily worsened. The reasons for this are obvious: the inertia of the past, the break of economic ties, the uncertainty in choosing an economic model, and political instability. The national income in the first quarter of 1992 decreased by 5 percent, production of consumer goods by 19 percent, and heavy industry production by 13.2 percent. The volume of construction building decreased 2.2 times.

According to other no less pessimistic data, during the winter and spring of 1992 the common recession in production amounted to 25 percent every month, while food production fell 30 percent. State purchases of meat amounted to only 57 percent of those of the previous year. Only 50 percent of spring agricultural works were fulfilled. There was great scarcity of oil (the republic does not have oil resources of its own), gas, and coal. The budget deficit was estimated to be sixteen billion rubles.

Under such unfavorable circumstances, the natural population growth rate remained high (now it is more than 3.4 percent per year). Ten years ago the population of Tajikistan was 3,806,000, and by 1989 it reached 5,093,000. According to demographic forecasts, the population of the republic will reach nine to ten million people in fifteen years, that is, twice its present size. With such a large population and unfavorable economic trends, it is extremely difficult to anticipate normal living standards.

The problem of land shortage is already acute with a proportion of only 0.1 hectare per person. The weakness of the industrial infrastructure has also become evident. Hence unemployment is quickly growing in Tajikistan. In 1992 there were 100,000 unemployed in Tajikistan, 90 percent of these in rural areas.

It is particularly in rural areas that there are great difficulties in creating new jobs for the younger generation. In 1989, 68 percent of the population of Tajikistan lived in the countryside. Forty-five percent of the rural population were capable of working, and among these 71 percent were young people between the ages of fifteen and twenty-nine. The annual birthrate of 4 percent in the rural areas was a record figure in the Soviet Union.

The rural areas of Tajikistan suffer from a surplus of manpower. At the same time, country-to-town migration is very slow. As a matter of fact, since the 1970s the process of deurbanization, that is, reduction of urban population (which is actually the lowest in the CIS), has steadily increased. The greatest sectors of new manpower are staying in the countryside. Young people are not at all enthusiastic about moving to the towns, notwithstanding the fact that incomes in the rural areas are low. Many of the young people are bound by family ties, as it is not easy to get parental consent for moving away. The main reason for this is that Tajik peasants cultivate their personal plots—the main sources of food for their families—without machinery. Thus, the effectiveness of labor in this case depends mainly on the quantity of manpower. Furthermore, scarce migration is also a function of the low educational and professional training levels in rural areas, which do not provide much opportunity for getting jobs in town. Traditional fields of occupation such as agriculture, processing enterprises, trade, and services prevail among Tajiks, Uzbeks, Kirghiz, and Pamiris. In June 1992, for example, there were six thousand positions available in enterprises and construction sites in the republic, but people of local nationalities showed no desire to work there. Thus, it is no mere coincidence that three-fourths of Tajikistan's working class are people of nonlocal nationalities.

Moreover, the quality of urban life is far from attractive. The social problems of Tajik towns and cities are horrible, even in comparison with some of the worst in the former USSR's towns and cities. For example, the capital of the republic, Dushanbe (population of over 600,000 people), is second among the CIS capitals (after Ashkhabad) in the number of children who die before reaching one year of age—38.4 per 1,000 born in 1988. Dushanbe is last among the CIS centers in the allocation of average provision of dwelling space per person (11.4 square meters in 1988) and last among the thirty largest cities in terms of the number of flats built (only 294) per year for every 1,000 people. And this in view of the fact that 20 percent of the city's families are in "perpetual" waiting for their turn to be allotted a flat.

Social problems both in the rural and urban areas of Tajikistan are most acute for young people, who constitute a large and ever-growing portion of the population. In 1989, 53.3 percent of the population was under the age of nineteen. Among these, 58 percent were not engaged in the labor force. According to official data, there were 13,000 young people in Dushanbe alone who neither studied nor worked; this growing population has become the breeding ground for illegal activities, including drug trafficking.

All these factors determined the social structure of the rioters' ranks in February 1990 and of the participants of the 1992 spring and autumn demonstrations and clashes in Dushanbe. The rioters were basically young people from the towns and countryside. The former were represented mainly by students of professional technical schools, technical schools, and institutions of higher education, as well as workers and clerks. It should be noted that the participants were mostly former villagers who had recently moved to the capital and were working or studying there, and also inhabitants of microregions—specific settlements arising from villages bordering the towns.

The population of these microregions consists partly of descendants of townspeople who got flats there and partly of former villagers who moved into new blocks of flats that replaced their traditional small houses. The latter, in spite of the changed conditions in their lives, retained stable communal structures and links. Alienated from the soil, having lost traditional sources of income, and without the essential professional training to join the urban work force, these people formed a sort of axis of the marginal Dushanbe population, which was further augmented by the unemployed youth from old city blocks.

It should be pointed out that the mentality of these people retained many traditional features not only in the first but also in the second and the third generations. As a result, notwithstanding the scarce migration to Dushanbe, the city came to be filled with people alienated from modern city culture, to say nothing of those cultural influences in the city, which were imported from abroad. This stratum of the Dushanbe population, though respectful of the city's norms of behavior and forming part of the town's work force, disapproves of the city's morals and manners and is dissatisfied with the city's occupations. This is why they retain a strong impulse for continuing their traditional way of life even within the city's precincts: they seek to reestablish the traditional environment, do not accept innovations, and are often aggressive, as they are subconsciously aware that their tiny world is doomed.

Another peculiarity of the structure of the urban population directly informs the political behavior in Tajikistan, and that is the national-professional division of townsfolk. The Russians constitute 7.6 percent of the population of Tajikistan. Most live in the urban areas (22.3 percent of the townspeople are Russian). Together with the so-called Russian-speaking people—the Ukrainians, Russian Germans, Jews, Armenians, and so on—they hold the leading positions in industry, especially in such an important branch of the national economy as energy. They are mainly highly qualified workers, engineers, managers, teachers, scientists, and people of the arts and literature.

The Soviet Communist environment made it easy for Russian-speaking settlers to integrate into the oriental frontier areas of the country. Such integration did not exist in tsarist Russia—the Russian and native communities lived absolutely separately. The process of integration was also promoted by the structure of towns (their division into certain regions or areas) and by settlement principles that prevented the formation of monoethnical regions. At the same time, a certain ethnic-cultural separation of the nonnative population, which became the professional elite due to their knowledge of skills the natives did not possess, took place. Most of the Russian-speaking people do not know the Tajik language and customs. Moreover, they are infected with Islamophobia.

The state law on the status of the Tajik language adopted in 1990 under the pressure of the opposition, the February events of the same year which were partially anti-European in character, the ideas of some national democrats on the national exclusiveness of the Tajiks, and the official press attack on the Islamic and secular opposition all had a cumulative effect. The bulk of the European population did not and does not back the opposition. The nonnative population saw the party autocracy—which was obedient to the Kremlin and at least verbally devoted to internationalism—as the only force that could defend their civic rights.

Yet another important peculiarity of the social life in the republic deserves attention, namely, the local regional consciousness of the Tajiks. Though the Tajiks constitute one people, they are divided on the basis of local-territorial communities. Ethnographers distinguish five or six types of such communities, beginning with the inhabitants of neighboring villages to the inhabitants of mountains and valleys, "northern" and "southern" Tajiks. It is important to recall that before the Bolshevik Revolution the northwestern area of contemporary Tajikistan was more developed, both culturally and economically, than its southern or southeastern areas. Khojent, together with the adjacent oblasts, formed one cultural area of influence with Samarkand, Bukhara, and Fergana. Currently, the Samarkandi, Bukhari, Khojenti, and Pendjikenti Tajiks constitute one "valley subculture" (with the exception of the inhabitants of mountainous regions or old Matchi).

The Tajiks of Eastern Bukhara and the Western Pamires, who are divided by mountain ranges and administratively among bekanates, lead a more independent and isolated life. Inclement climate and difficult mountain life have formed their firm character.

A mountaineer was also always more frank and naive than his valley brother. Even ethnically mountainous Tajiks differ from the northern valley Tajiks: the latter have inherited the blood of Genghis Khan's descendants. At the same time, unlike the valley Tajiks of the northwest, the mountainous southern and southeastern Tajiks are strictly divided into local subcultures (Garmi, Kulyabi, Darvazi, Badakhshani, and Pamiri) with their own dialects, customs, traditional clothes, and food. As to the Badakhshanies, they have two more important distinguishing features: (1) they belong to the Ismaili branch of Islam, whereas the rest of the Tajiks are Sunnis; and (2) they speak languages that other Tajiks do not understand.

The inner divisions of the Tajik ethnos, that is, the existence of local subcultures, stipulate a regional factor in politics. Tajik sentiments for local cultural self-identification are often exploited by people greedy for power, thus preventing the consolidation of the society.

Dynamics of Domestic Political Life

The dynamics of domestic political developments in Tajikistan, a process full of constant instability, sprang in 1990. It was then, during the days of "hot February," that the tragic, blind, uncontrolled social protest burst out in one of the quietest republics of the Soviet Union. Unexpectedly for the local and central powers, an artificially compressed spring of public contradictions and dissatisfaction with everyday life poured into the streets of Dushanbe.

The phenomenon of the February events in Dushanbe was caused by diverse and complicated factors. The natural explosions of social dissatisfaction, which took shape as a spontaneous, cruel, and to a great extent senseless riot, the march of the national democratic forces, and an unsuccessful coup d'etat in the top power echelons, occurred simultaneously. The instigators of the tragedy of 11–18 February were corrupt party *apparatchiks* (officials of the top bureaucratic structures of the Communist party, legislative and executive power) and operators of the shadow economy. The main executors were mafia groupings. Among the allies, there were some, but not many, radical mullahs and secular opposition members.[9] If successful, the groups expected to receive large pieces of the power pie and generous material benefits. The scriptwriters were inspired mainly by clan and career interests and hardly by ideological motives. The social diversity of the "conspirators" is vividly reflected in the structure of the Temporal People's Committee they created. It was joined by high state officials, leaders of the Rastokhez (Renaissance) organization, representatives of the intelligentsia, businessmen, an Islamic leader, and a worker.[10]

The committee was headed by Buri Karimov, head of the state Planning Committee and vice chairman of the Council of Ministers (a Garmi). The idea of changing the republican leadership was backed by the Minister of Culture Nur Tabarov (a Garmi) and by the head of the Political Department of the Ministry of Domestic Affairs of the republic, Abdullah Khabibov (a Kulyabi). Soon after "hot February," G. Pallayev (a Badakhshani), chairman of the Supreme Soviet, resigned. The reasons for his resignation have yet to be explained. The organizers of the coup d'etat were unable to foresee that they could lose control over the people. The artificially caused impulse (the rumors about the arrival of Armenian refugees and their allotment with flats and work-places) resulted in the burst of such wide social protest and caused such a demolishing energy of social-psychological outburst that the preplanned actions sank in the mass psychosis.

The riots occupy the leading position in the complicated composition of the February events. They reflected the social problems rooted deep in people's consciousness, as well as the contradictions between traditional and modern ways of life, intensified by perestroika and closely connected with the above-mentioned problems.

As has been the case with many oriental countries, the symbols of power, luxury, wealth, and European civilization were among the first objects of the rioters' hatred. The diversity of calls and slogans during the meeting reflected the different directions and vagueness of the goals and interests of separate groups participating in the events, the spontaneity of the actions of the bulk of the participants, and the vagueness of ideas on finding the way out of the social crisis. It is necessary to stress that the actions as a whole were not aimed at demolishing the existing power structure. In mass consciousness, social disasters turned to be closely connected, not with the political system, but with the "detractors of national interests."

The pyramid of the party and state power itself remained stable. Its vitality and unity (which can be observed in Uzbekistan, Kazakhstan, and Turkmenistan) can be explained, first of all, by the peculiarities of traditional relations and connections within an oriental society. They nearly perfectly match the structure of the party and state power pyramid. In the 1920s the supreme despotic power of the Bukhara Emir, the Khiva Khan, and the Russian colonial administration were replaced by Soviet power. But basically nothing changed for the natives, as the less despotic form of power had inherited many of the functions of the former rulers. The Bolsheviks changed the form of the state by installing a wide network of party organizations into the state's system; however, the historically formed structure of Central Asian society was changing extremely slowly and in many cases was adapting socialist innovations to its own notions.

The institutions of power introduced in the 1920s and 1930s, which were uniform for the entire country, did not change the centuries-old communal, tribal, clan-paternalistic, fellow-countrymen relations in Central Asia. Periodic purges of all sections of the state bureaucracy practiced until the mid-1950s, however, prevented elite groups from being formed. But changes in the following years gave them an opportunity to emerge. The endurance of such groups was based not only on tribal-land relations but also on the tradition of giving "gifts" and of respect for ranks, loyalty, and connections with individuals of power and wealth. The structure of the state government began merging with the legal, semilegal, and illegal private business, widely spread in the region. Consequently, corruption and protectionism flourished and the operators of the shadow economy, politicians, and bureaucrats became linked in the circle of activities. At the same time, the lower echelons of power were, and are still, successfully based on traditional forms of communal local government in *kishlaks* and *mahallahs* (rural and urban residential quarters).

Cemented both vertically and horizontally with informal and strictly formal economic, administrative, and party links, the pyramid of power is still satisfying the society, or, to be more exact, is perceived by it as something natural and indispensable, as it adopts a considerable number of traditional institutions (though often destroying and deforming their original essence). Thus, this kind of political structure still corresponds to the social psychology and specific Central Asian social organization, and especially to Tajikistan.

The party bureaucracy of the Central Asian republics, having easily excused itself from the Communist ideology, is still successfully controlling, if not political, then at least economic life. It remains the main component of the administrative-economic structure. If its experience, economic ties, and interests are taken into account, the bureaucracy is devoted to the state and is working on stabilizing social life. The radical steps aimed at weakening the influence of the former party bureaucracy (such as those undertaken not only in Tajikistan, but also in neighboring Kyrgyzia) threaten to paralyze state power.

The Collapse of the USSR and Tajikistan

Boris Yeltsin's victory and the failure of the August 1991 coup resulted in a new peak of political activity in Dushanbe. This time the opposition—more consolidated and backed by some apparatchiks from the top power echelons—began an anti-Communist campaign. But it did not take into account the force the republican Communist party possessed. Actually, by that time the party was no longer Communist as far as its ideology was concerned and was in reality a mighty economic structure possessing immovable property, joint ventures, and banks. The demands on abolishing this organization and confiscating its property remained just that—demands. The only concession made by the party was sacrificing its first secretary and president of the republic, K. Mahkamov, who was replaced in December 1991 by Rahman Nabiev, who had once been Mahkomov's predecessor as head of the party. Moreover, they are fellow countrymen, since both are from Leninabad (Khojent).

The presidential elections in Tajikistan in December 1991 reflected an aggravated political confrontation. The society's traditional divisions were observed on several levels: north vs. south, mountainous vs. valley Tajiks, Tajiks vs. non-Tajiks, and town vs. village. Almost all of the north and Kulyab (the government of the latter was promised high posts in the republican government), almost all non-Tajiks, and most of the urban population voted for Nabiev, that is, for the status quo in social life. The opposition candidate, D. Khodonazarov (Badakhshan), was backed by the mountaineers of Matchi (north), Garm, and Badakhshan.

After gaining power, Nabiev's administration began a planned attack on the opposition. The president himself tried not to advertise his backing of the the old structure, but it was quite obvious that he was not only its vivid representative but also its hostage. The model of a political system—common to many oriental countries—is still dominant in the republic: authoritarian power supports itself with the ruling party, fused with the state; the facade of governmental offices is carefully preserved; and the opposition is tolerated, but is not allowed to participate in deciding economic and political issues. As a result, the status of oppositional parties is not comparable to that of the state party, while the unequal conditions of political competition inevitably toughen the opposition, thus radicalizing it.

In April–June 1992 the opposition block, having used as a pretext the fixed resignation of the minister of Domestic Affairs (a Badakhshani, who was far from upholding democratic views himself), began a counteroffensive campaign. Using democratic slogans, those in power and their counterparts used all possible traditional means of mass mobilization: clan-paternalistic, fellow-countrymen, and religious. The peaceful development of the events culminating in the meetings on the two squares—Shahidon Square backing the opposition and Ozodi Square backing the government—was finally broken by the government. Having lost the support of the Soviet Union's repressive structures and power but still unwilling to give up control, the bureaucracy nevertheless had to lose part of it. The opposition got one-third of the seats in the Cabinet of Ministers and also broadened its representation in the Majles (Parliament). But the old structures were preponderant.

By autumn, after recovering from the shock, they began more aggressive activities, though they could not manage to control some southern and central regions. At the same time, the settlement of the military conflict seemed to be a long and difficult process with or without the intervention of Russian/CIS troops called into the republic for "peacekeeping operations." Neither side put down its arms. New small, independent armed groups emerged. Nabiev remained president, but only in name. The bureaucracy had previously supported him but was convinced of his inability to rule and acted on its own at the most crucial moments. As for the opposition, in which the main forces were the Islamic Renaissance party (IRP) and the Kaziyat, it had no doubts about the hypocrisy and unpopularity of the president. The conflict took the shape of regional war.

The "forced" resignation of President Nabiev, the ensuing bloody conflict in Kulyab, Kurgan Tyube, and in the "north" and "south" of the republic in September and October 1992, the eventual resignation of the post-Nabiyev leadership, and the Russian and CIS "peacekeeping" intervention were the latest manifestation and macrocosm of the socioeconomic and political malaise of the republic. The horrors of this especially brutal civil war will be a new chapter, one with lasting, negative implications adding to Tajikistan's already complex national picture—a picture, "nation," and "state" still in search of its identity and values.

The Civil War

The specificity of the political system in Tajikistan lies first in the bureaucratic character of the system and second in the preservation of the strong role played by the local "independent princes," that is, the heads of the local administration in the oblasts and rayons. Even if the republican leadership is paralyzed at a given moment, the local power, as a rule, remains effective and viable. These characteristics of power have a significant impact on the political process in the republic. The rules of the political game are such that neither ideology nor socioeconomic theories are of great importance. It is the regional or local factor that comes into the foreground during the struggle for power in a semi-traditional society. Thus, the patron-client model characteristic of Third World states applies here as well. The parties and social movements involved in the local bureaucratic game eventually act contrary to the ideological pronouncements of their programs and become mere instruments in the hands of the political elite, which is striving for power in different regions of the republic. Thus, the popular/journalistic depiction of the latest developments in Tajikistan as the struggle between democratic forces, or Muslims, with a Communist regime is wrong in its very essence. It is a regional war that has been under way in the republic.

While the military conflict exploded in May 1992, its political roots originated in the events of February 1990, the details of which were discussed earlier. The following is an analysis of the events that took place from autumn 1991 to the spring of 1992.

On the eve of the presidential election campaign of 1991, Khojent (former Leninabad) and Kulyab became sister cities. Thus a bureaucratic alliance was formed between the two largest oblasts of Tajikistan, the Kulyab oblast and the Khojent oblast. The population of the former is approximately two million people and the latter approximately one million. Together, they make up approximately 60 percent of the republic's population.

Kulyab appeared to be the most appropriate ally for Rahman Nabiev, a Leninabadi by origin and a candidate for the presidential post. There are several reasons for this:

1. At the end of the 1980s an energetic and influential Garmi-Badakhshani group that hoped to occupy the leading posts in the republic stood at the upper echelons of power. Among other things, the group planned to promote one of its members to the post of leader of the republic. Rahman Nabiev, being of northern origin, was definitely not suitable for the job. At the same time, a less numerous Kulyabi political elite seemed to have no intention to promote one of its members to the presidential post. Its appetite had been constantly restrained by Izatullo Khayoyev, a Kulyabi by origin, who had always been loyal to Khojent and who occupied the post of chairman of the Council of Ministers and later that of vice president when Kakhor Mahkamov was the head of state. It was in the interest of the Kulyabis to preserve for themselves the post of prime minister and also the leading position in the power system of the Kurgan Tyube oblast. They also hoped to strengthen their position in the republican Ministry of Internal Affairs in which Abdullo Khabibov, a Kulyabi, occupied a prominent post as head of the Political Department.

2. There is a traditional hostility between the Kulyabies and the

Badakhshanis. The animosity, which beginning in the 1970s manifested itself in mass street clashes between youngsters, could have been easily extended into the sphere of political struggle.

3. The Kulyabi local power, skillfully using traditional institutes (mosques and their attendants, sufi sheikhs, heads of respected families) and also mafia groups, succeeded in sufficiently limiting the influence of the Rastokhez movement, the Democratic party of Tajikistan (DPT), and the IRP.

All this attracted Rahman Nabiev's attention to Kulyab. Concluding a political alliance with Kulyab, Nabiev promised to leave the post of prime minister to Izatullo Khayoyev if he was successful. Another Kulyabi, director of the autotransport enterprise Nazrullo Dustov, was promised the vice presidency. Soon after Nabiev came to power, Akbar Mirzoyev, head of the Executive Committee of the Soviet of the Kulyab oblast and the main organizer of the support of the Leninabadi in Kulyab during the presidential election campaign, took over Izatullo Khayoyev's post. The political alliance was strengthened by an economic one. Large deliveries of food and industrial commodities were sent immediately from Khojent to the oblast of Kulyab.

The Garmi-Badakhshani began to be excluded from the power structure. The chairman of the Supreme Soviet, Kadriddin Aslonov, a Garmi, ceded his position to Safarali Kendjayev, who was from the north. There were plans to remove the minister of Internal Affairs, Mamadyoz Navjuvanov, a Badakhshani, as well as the Kazi Kalon and the mayor of Dushanbe Maksud Ikramov, both of whom backed the Garmi-Badakhshani group. It is important to recall that previously G. Pallayev (a Badakhshani and the former chairman of the Supreme Soviet), Buri Karimov (a Garmi and the former vice chairman of the Council of Ministers), and Nur Tabarov (also a Garmi and the former minister of Culture) had been deprived of their posts. Moreover, in the spring of 1992 the government began a planned offensive campaign against the opposition parties and movements. The trials of Shodmon Yusupov, head of the DPT, and Mirbobo Mirrakhimov, leader of Rastokhez, were expected to be held. Maksud Ikramov was accused of corruption and arrested, and in April 1992 government supporters held meetings at the Ozodi Square, where they called for the prohibition of the IRP.

The division of political forces according to regional loyalties became absolutely vivid in the political life of Tajikistan from April to early May 1992. The traditional mechanisms of involving the "masses," which had never been successfully tested, came into play. The masses from the north of the republic and from the Kulyab oblast backed Nabiev, Kendjayev, and their team. The citizens of Dushanbe and the majority of the non-Tajik population supported those who were holding meetings at the Ozodi Square in favor of the government.

The following event is a vivid example of the regional formation of the parties involved. One group emerged from a faction of the DPT ranks that was under the leadership of A. Otchilov, from the oblast of Leninabad. The faction served as a basis for the formation of the Republican party of Tajikistan, which backed the government, at the end of March 1992. The party's leadership accused the Democratic party of Tajikistan of attempts to divide the republic. By the end of April, Otchilov was at the head of the headquarters of the meeting at the Ozodi Square. It was then that the so-called detached batallion of the brigade of special purposes was formed from the Kulyabis in accordance with the president's order.

On the other hand, the opposition at the Ozodi Square appeared to be represented by the masses from the Garmi group and from Badakhshan. It was headed by the Kazi Kalon Khoja Akbar Turajonzods, by the Badakhshani organization "Lali Bakakhshon," the Rastokhez movement, and by the DPT (whose leader, Shodmon Yusupov, was from Garm). But the main organized, mass disciplined force was the IRP (its leader, Muhammadsharif Khimmatzoda, is also from Garm).

In May, the so-called Islamic-democratic block succeeded in forcing Nabiev to form a coalition government of National Reconciliation. In the new government, the Garmi-Badakhshani group again managed to press back the representatives of the north and Kulyab. One-third of the Cabinet of Ministers was renewed, but only two people in it did not represent the usual administrative-economic elite. The first of the two, vice chairman of the IRP, Davlat Usmon, occupied the post of vice prime minister. The other, Mirbobo Mirrakhimov, mentioned above, received the post of chairman of the State TV and Radio Committee. Parliament Speaker Safarali Kendjayev was removed from his post. Vice President Nazrullo Dustov was also forced to resign.

Naturally, such rearrangements were painfully taken in Kulyab. The armed Kulyabi detachment, having returned from Dushanbe, began repressions against differently minded fellow countrymen. The main blow was aimed at the Kulyabi branch of the IRP, the most well-organized opposition force at the time. According to statements by

Kulyabi officials, not a single Islamist was left in the oblast by the end of June.

After the activization of the military operation in the neighboring Kurgan Tyube oblast, the Kulyabi volunteer corps began to grow rapidly because it was joined by the Kulyabis who escaped from Kurgan Tyube and also by the Urgut Uzbeks and the Lakays. Local self-defense detachments began to be formed spontaneously in different regions of Kulyab. Under the circumstances, the chairman of the Executive Committee of the Kulyab oblast, Kurbon Mirzoaliyev, decided to unite all the detachments under one command, which practically meant under his own command, and also to strengthen their fighting efficiency at the expense of the Kulyab militia (police) forces. Mirzoaliyev's call for the implementation of martial law was backed by the heads of the executive committees of the towns in the oblast, by the head of the oblast's Department of Internal Affairs, Sh. Khusainov, and by the oblast's public procurator, Sh. Khabibov. The leadership of Kulyab accused the president of being indecisive, refused to follow the government's orders, and decided that it should itself bring order into its own patrimony and beyond its borders. According to a statement made by Sangak Safarov, a Kulyabi field commander, by the end of October 1992 there were already over thirty thousand people in the ranks of the Kulyabi resistance forces.

The oblast of Leninabad rendered moral, material, and also (according to unofficial data) military assistance to the Kulyabis. The chairman of the Executive Committee of the Leninabad oblast, Jure Shokirov, also refused to obey the central government and the presidential orders. He gave an order for the creation of the oblast's own military forces. The calls for the detachment of the Leninabad oblast began to be frequently heard at the meetings of the local executive committee.

The Islamic-Democratic block had been trying all summer long to strengthen its position, but to no avail. The central power's paralysis was evident. They could not manage to gain military superiority and merely felt support from foreign countries.

The Islamic Movement

The dissident movement in Central Asia has been mainly of a religious character. Actually, there were quite a few individuals among the secular intellectuals who dared to openly manifest their dissatisfaction with the totalitarian system. At the same time, there appeared in 1978 a more well-organized and purposeful opposition in the form of young, unofficial religious authorities.

This group of Muslims, being close to the traditional country masses, naturally protested against the lawless actions and despotism of those in power, against breaking traditional ethical norms, against the lack of spirituality in society, against the atheism which became part of the state policy, and against the conformism of the official *ulama*.

As for religious practice, these people propagated strict adherence to the Koranic regulations on prayer, fasting, and giving alms. They accused Muslims of spending large sums of money on different rituals and ceremonies. They began to call these Muslim dissidents "Vakhabis" by analogy to the "Puritan" trend in Islam which appeared in Saudi Arabia in the eighteenth century under the influence of the ideas of Muhammad ibn-Abdul Wahab. Nevertheless, most of them denied espousing the views of Wahabism.

The supporters of cleansing early Islam from later influences nevertheless seem to represent a moderate fundamentalist movement if we take into account their views on the possibility of combining the Islamic norms of everyday life with the contemporary juristic system, economic relations, and models of state development. To a great extent, their flexibility might be attributed to the specificity of Islam itself in the region.

The majority of Muslims in Central Asia adhere to the norms of the Khanifi *mazhaab* (a religious-legal school). It stands out among the four mazhaabs in Sunnism for its flexibility and capacity of adaptation to the modern conditions of life. It is also obvious that the outlook of the theoreticians of Islamic fundamentalism in Tajikistan was greatly influenced by the ideas of democratization of the state, multiparty political systems, human rights, and individual freedom—ideas that were gaining strength in the former Soviet Union. All these postulates are depicted in their program documents, which also express a great deal of other good intentions in the field of observing the rights of all peoples, rejecting national borders between people of one creed, defending women's rights, and concern over the ecological situation. Nevertheless, these people are idealists and romantics. Their views on the Islamic state have been rather vague. In different speeches and interviews, the fundamentalist leaders as a rule stressed the necessity of the balance between private and public interests in the system they proposed. They also pointed out that Western liberal-democratic or socialist systems are unacceptable for their own model of social development. At the same time, they asserted that their model is based upon Islamic and democratic principles that do not contradict one another and that it is not like the political models espoused by Pakistan, Saudi Arabia, Afghanistan, or Iran.

Islamic fundamentalists organized themselves into the Tajik branch of the all-union Islamic Renaissance party at the regional conference of the IRP that took place semilegally in Tajikistan on the 6th of October 1990. The IRP in Tajikistan (Renaissance Nahzati Islomi) has been acting as an independent organization since December 1991. Muhammadsharif Khimmatzoda is its chairman, and there are also two vice chairmen—Davlat Usmon and Saidibrohim Gadoyev.

According to a statement made by the party's leaders in the summer of 1992, the party consisted of twenty thousand members and counted on the support of thousands of Muslims. These were mainly peasants and part of the town population from the Garmi group of regions, or people who were originally from these regions who are now living in the Kurgan Tyube oblast, Hissar Valley, Leninsky rayon, and the city of Dushanbe.

The peak of the political activity of the IRP in spring 1992 was due, above all, to the fact that the domestic policy of President Nabiev and his supporters in the government was becoming more and more severe. The party was forced into activity by the Kaziyat, the DPT, and Rastokhez, all of which were well aware that they could not oppose the government's repression without the support of this well-organized force, which was backed by the masses.

The events of spring–autumn 1992 in Tajikistan showed the radicalization of the Islamic fundamentalist movement. The IRP, acting contrary to its program declarations, opted for nonconstitutional force methods in solving political problems. Its moderate wing, headed by Davlat Usmon, stopped playing the first fiddle in working out the tactics of the political struggle. Throughout the summer the party tried to gain military superiority, strengthen its political position, place under its own command the republic's repressive institutions, influence the placement of officials in the upper echelons of power, and consolidate itself in the structures of local power. It did not, however, succeed in getting the leading posts in the state. The majority of the population did not back it. Moreover, many religious authorities in the republic did not approve of the actions of Kazi Kalon and the IRP. In the Kulyab oblast, another Kaziyat independent of Dushanbe was created in June

1992. Khodji Haidar Sharifzoda, one of the spiritual fathers of the Kulyabi resistance movement, was elected Kazi Kalon of Kulyab.

To say the least, the IRP turned into a regionalistic, monoethnic organization that found itself associated with mafia and other corrupt groups. The good intentions of the Islamic revolutionary romantics were paved into the road leading to Hades.

Tajik Foreign Policy: Its Future Orientation

The opponents of the Islamic-Democratic block demonstrated their military strength and unity in October–November 1992. They took under their control the more populated areas, the strong points and roads in the Kurgan-Tyube oblast and Hissar Valley, blockaded the capital, and were able to hold out the railway routes connecting Tajikistan with the Surkhandarya oblast of Uzbekistan. At this time, mass deliveries of medicine, food, and arms from Uzbekistan to the regions under the control of the Kulyabis and the Hissar National Front headed by Safarali Kendjayev began.

On 16 November 1992 the sixteenth session of the Supreme Soviet of Tajikistan opened. At its opening it was obvious that the military-political superiority was not in the hands of the Islamic-Democratic block. Moreover, the block itself had begun to split. Thus, the Leninabadi-Kulyabi bureaucratic alliance spoke to its opponents at the session from a position of power and began placing personnel according to its own wishes. As was expected, the leading posts in the republic went to the representatives of the Kulyab and the Kurgan-Tyube oblasts. A Khojenti, Abdulmalik Abdullojanov, received the post of prime minister, and a Kulyabi, Imomali Rahmonov, that of speaker of the Parliament. The session expressed its distrust of deputy President Akbarshoh Iskandarov, a Badakhshani, by casting a majority of votes against him.

Another decisive step was taken by the Leninabad-Kulyab alliance in view of the long-term prospects of strengthening its position. The new prime minister's supporters insisted on abolishing the presidential form of power and on concentrating strong executive power in the hands of the prime minister. The Supreme Soviet, 95 percent of whom are representatives of the administrative economic nomenclature, was preserved. The representatives of the Islamic-Democratic block and of the Garmi groups are likely to always constitute a minority.

The next step is the formation of the new Council of Ministers and

Presidium of the Supreme Soviet. It can be confidently assumed that the Garmi-Badakhshani elite and its allies would be considerably pressed out of these institutes. It would be difficult to restrain the appetite of the leaders of the Leninabad-Kulyab alliance, who at the tide of a relative victory are in a hurry to occupy as many positions of power as possible. Under the circumstances, the separatist movement is likely to spread throughout Badakhshan and the Garmi group of regions, although it is likely to be delayed in coming to Leninabad. Thus, the prospects for settling the military conflict will remain pending.

Tajikistan's foreign policy orientation will depend largely on the apportion of political forces in Tajikistan. When Rahman Nabiev was in power (up to May 1992) the government's foreign policy credo could be characterized as "Both the West and the East." Development of economic, political, and cultural relations with the European countries, the United States, countries of the Near and Middle East, and with the CIS was taking place simultaneously. But relations with Russia, Uzbekistan, and Iran were of greater significance.

When the Government of National Reconciliation was in power from May to November 1992, relations between Dushanbe and Uzbekistan became strained. Tajikistan began to isolate itself from the CIS and consequently to dampen relations with Russia. The signing of the Tajik-Russian Treaty on Mutual Cooperation, which was planned for September, was postponed by the Tajik side. Meetings with anti-Western, anti-American, and anti-Russian slogans were becoming more and more frequent in Dushanbe. At the same time, sympathy for Iran was constantly growing.

But after the change in the republican leadership in November–December 1992 the pendulum of external orientation swung back. It is obvious that the cultural-ethnic attraction to Iran will remain and that relations in the economic and cultural realm will continue to develop. At the same time, the new power is actively containing the spread of the Islamic fundamentalist ideology. Moreover, Russia and Kazakhstan are attempting to restrain Iran on this question. Both states, especially Russia, are large suppliers of arms to Iran and both have strong interests of their own in Central Asia. Relations with Russia have since strengthened, and the economic dependence of Tajikistan on Russia is obvious. Russia's support of the government against the opposition throughout 1993–94 and the equally important support of the Russian military in protecting the Tajik-Afghan border underlie the continuous geopolitical significance of the republic for Russia in the post-Soviet period. In this regard Moscow has enjoyed the support of key Central Asian states, including Kazakhstan and Uzbekistan. Close economic and military relations are being developed especially with Uzbekistan, as the containment of the Islamic threat and keeping Tajikistan in its regional orbit have remained key to Tashkent regional foreign policy. Furthermore, the Tajik Ministry of Foreign Affairs has shown interest in developing multilateral ties with Saudi Arabia, the United Arab Emirates, Kuwait, Pakistan, and Turkey. The future foreign policy orientation of Tajikistan, as reflected in its short history since the independence, will continue to be decided to two internal and external factors, namely the political and regional makeup of the dominant forces in Dushanbe and the limitation imposed on the republic by the combined geopolitical interests of Russia and key regional players such as Uzbekistan. This internal and external mix will be better conditioned by the intricate links between Tajikistan and Afghanistan. The Soviet legacy in this regard will continue to be a relevant factor in the shaping of Tajikistan foreign policy at least in the near future.

Conclusion: Islam and the Intelligentsia

In post-Soviet Central Asia, broadly speaking, two forces are considered to be the leading magnets around which the nation-state building could eventually be accomplished; namely, the liberal intelligentsia and the custodians of the Islamic movement. What are the chances and prospects for these two forces to achieve such an undertaking in Tajikistan?

It is necessary to stress the role of the intelligentsia in the sociopolitical life of Tajikistan, which is largely predetermined by the peculiarities of its traditionally high status in the Muslim East. The social status of people of science, literature, art, religion, and academia in the East has always been high, though often in contradiction with their standard of living. The Tajik intelligentsia has a much greater influence than, for example, the Russian intelligentsia. It is necessary to stress that the backbone of the Democratic party and Rastokhez is represented mostly by the national intelligentsia.

It goes without saying that the Tajik intelligentsia is not homogeneous as far as its outlook, education, and economic conditions are concerned. Certain differences may be observed between the urban intellectual elite, rural and urban teachers, and the bureaucratic semi-intelligentsia. A difference is also quite noticeable between social scientists and natural scientists and engineers. The former are more active socially and head the new democratic movement, are more radical in their projects, and are more resolute in their attempts to give life to the ideas of national and cultural renaissance.

The intelligentsia has shown a strong tendency to focus on ethnic, nostalgic, and pseudonationalistic ideas. It has much in common with the Russian "patriotic block" and, like the latter, through its hypernationalism does much harm to the movement for national and cultural renaissance.

What is characteristic of the Tajik, as well as, probably, the intelligentsia in the other Central Asian Republics is its contradictory and ambiguous ideology. It easily combines traditional and modern thinking, idealism and realism, and modern scientific knowledge and superstition. In politics it combines Western democratic ideals with authoritarian outlook, the desire to serve people with exaggerated personal ambitions, cosmopolitanism with hypernationalism. The Tajik intelligentsia, born on the border of two worlds—the Oriental and the Soviet—personifies the cultural synthesis of everything of value (negative and positive) created by its own nation and other nations of the Soviet Union and may, in the future, serve as a vessel to channel the sociopolitical and cultural energy of the society en route toward national rebirth. The dual and contradictory nature of the intelligentsia, however, has been its major impediment for assuming leadership, as it has been unable to elevate itself above the existing and contradictory nature of Tajik society itself.

Would Islam take the lead? Will Tajikistan become an Islamic republic? There is much talk about the flourishing of Islamic fundamentalism in Tajikistan. The fear connected with the possibility of the establishment of an Islamic state has been rampant, both in the West and in Russia. The Tajik Islamic reality betrays such projection.

There is no doubt that the tendency to adapt Islam to political purposes has become stronger, but at the present stage in the religious movement educational activity and enlightment prevail; this is similar to the South Asian "Tabligh" or Arabian "Daawa" movements. The long Soviet legacy of atheistic education and secular life could only be reversed by emphasis on long-term educational activities purifying Islam from home-grown superstitions, and this is a task of enormous magnitude in terms of manpower, material need, and energy. This is not to

say that the Tajik Islamic leaders or movements have not been involved in the political process, as they have played an important role
in the current quagmire that engulfs the republic. Yet, the political participation and engagement in power struggle does not translate into
political leadership capable of shaping the nationally acceptable political model, for example, similar to the one which was established in
Iran. Tajik Islam lacks the historical relevancy, political richness, and
sophistication of Iranian Islam. In Tajikistan, as in the rest of Central
Asia, in addition to overcoming the legacies of Soviet atheistic totalitarianism, the absence of Islamic intellectual potential remains a key
handicap. Central Asia has yet to produce its own version of Iran's Ali
Shariati.

By and large, both the liberal nationalist intelligentsia and the Islam-
icists continue to reflect and be entrapped by the overpowering characteristics of Tajik society, that is, tribal-clan/regional loyalties, tensions,
and aspirations. Neither a Tajik nor an Islamic identity has been able
to provide a unifying and common ground for national unity and
statehood.

While a liberal democracy presents an ideal and viable political system capable of reflecting the diverse inner tensions and conflicting interests of the republic, the establishment of such a system is unlikely
in the near future. The authoritarian political culture will remain more
adaptable to the emergence of a strong leader capable of establishing
national unity.

Notes

1. Here are noted only a few of them: *Evolyutsiya vostochnykh obshchestv:
Sintez traditsionnogo e sovremennogo* [Evolution of Eastern societies: synthesis of traditional and modern] (Moscow: Nauka, 1984); *Ideologichskiye protsessi
i massovoe soznaniye v razvivayushchikhsya stranakh Azii i Afriki* [Ideologi-
cal processes and the mass consciousness in the developing countries of Asia
and Africa] (Moscow: Nauka, 1984); *Razvivayushchikhsyia strani traditsionnie
tsennosti i sovremennie institutie* [Developing countries: traditional values
and modern institutions] (Moscow: Nauka, 1986); A.V. Malashenko, *V Pois-
kakh alternativiye (Arabskiye kontseptsii pootiei razvitiya)* [Searching for alternatives (Arabic conceptions of the ways of development)] (Moscow: Nauka,
1991).

2. The main unit of the administrative-territorial division in tsarist Russia
was *guberniya*, which were divided into *uyezds*. The latter were divided into
volosts. After the Revolution, during the administrative-territorial reform of

1923–29, guberniyas were transformed into krays and oblasts or okrugs, and the uezds into rayons (derived from regions). Volosts then were completely abolished.

3. This data is taken from Materiali, podgotovlennie Akademiei Nauk Tadzhiksoy SSR dlya Plenooma TSK KPSS po mezhdoonarodnym otnosheniyam [Materials prepared by the Academy of Science of the Tajik SSR for the Plenary Meeting of the Central Committee of the CPSU on foreign relations] (Moscow: 1989).

4. The data on ethnic structure of these regions are full of inexactitudes. Thus, according to the census of 1920, there were 98,274 Tajiks and 30,487 Uzbeks and Sarts in the Samarkand Okrug—that is, practically in the city; as to the rural areas adjacent to Samarkand, there were 136,193 Tajiks and 441,515 Uzbeks and Sarts. The data is taken from *Ts GAOR SSSR* [Central state archives of the October Revolution upper state administration and government bodies], file 1318, vol. I, year 69. As to the census of 1923, there are no data at all on the Tajik population of towns and cities of Turkestan. The data of the census can be found in the book of articles *Na istoricheskom roobezhe* [At the historical boundary] (Tashkent: 1924), 22.

5. See the newspaper *Todzhikistoni sorkh* [Red Tajikistan], no. 196, 1 September 1930; and a magazine that was an organ of the Central Asian Bureau of the Central Committee of the All-Union Communist Party, *Za partiyo* [For the party], no. 1–2 (1929).

6. See the Uzbek language newspapers *Zeravshan* and *Turkistan* from December 1923 to February 1924.

7. The Jadid movement, which was first of an enlightment character, was finally divided into two main groups: a liberal-reformatory group that strove for the ideals of peaceful renovation of the society and which was later on formed into the "Shuro-i Islomiya" organization and a revolutionary-radical group, the representatives of which began to call themselves the "Young Bukharis." See R. Shookorv, *Neobkhodimost novogo videniya: Izvestiya Akademii Nauk Tadzhikskoy SSR. Seriya: Vostokovedeniye, Istoriya, Filosofiya* [The importance of a new outlook], News of the Academy of Science of the Tajik SSR Series: Oriental Studies, History, Philosophy, 20, no. 4 (1990): 75.

8. Thus, the donations to the budget of the Tajik ASSR were 1924, 46.5 percent; 1925, 61.7 percent; 1926, 84.4 percent; 1927, 92.2 percent. Of the national budget of 1929–30, which was 42 million rubles, 9 million came from the Tajik income. Thirty-three million rubles of deficit were paid from the all-union treasury. See *Tsentral'nyye Gosudarstvennyyi Arkhiv Tadzhikskoy SSR* [Central state archives of the Tajik SSR], folio I, description 3, affair 23, pp. 49–54.

9. The materials of the official and unofficial investigations testify to this. See, for example, *Tadzhikistani Sovieti*, 11 October 1990, 16 June 1990, 18 September 1990; *Kommunist Tadzhikistana*, 20 May 1990, 26 August 1990, 3 March 1990; *Kommunist Tadzhikistana*, 5 September 1990; *Pravda* 10–11 May

1990. In this respect, of special interest are shorthand reports of the work of the 17th and 18th plenary meetings of the Tajik Communist Party Central Committee, as well as the interview of the former Minister of Culture N. T. Tabarov in *Komsomolets Tadzhikistana,* 26 September 1990.

10. The list of members of the Provisional People's Committee and the positions they occupy is given in the newspaper *Bofanda,* 15 May 1990.

10

Turkmenistan

Andrei G. Nedvetsky

Turkmenistan is perhaps the most peaceful and stable state of the CIS. Although as a former member of the USSR it has been subjected to a gradual rate of change, it maintains a high degree of continuity in its various local structures and the growth of their impact on the regional situation. The peculiarities of the local processes thus reflect certain features of Turkmen culture and social life.

During seventy years of Soviet power, the Turkmen society has preserved quite a number of traditional structures, values, and even some aspects of political culture. The kin and tribal structure is one such feature that has not been eliminated by the process of modernization.

Turkmen tribes, including the Teke, Ersari, and Yomut, are heavily intermixed. Numerous Turkmen communities live abroad, especially in Iran and Pakistan. This may lead to interethnic or interstate conflicts. The Turkmen-Uzbek border dispute is a case in point.

The tribe is an ethnosocial structure that arranges and dominates the everyday life of individuals and social groups. It serves to make the political system rather stable on the one hand, yet potentially strained or even explosive on the other. As similar events in some Middle Eastern countries testify, the traditional division of Turkmen tribes into "strong" and "weak" might promote intertribal conflict.

Intertribal solidarity and loyalty are major factors of social life. Individuals who are successful in different fields (for example, commerce or art) are obliged to help their fellow tribesmen, since they owe their prosperity to the support of the tribe.

Because of tribal "intermixture," a new factor of Turkmen political life—the local or territorial communities—is gaining importance. Communal ties are increasingly supplementing tribal ties. When these coincide, individual life is doubly restricted by tribal and communal affiliation. These ethnocommunal cells will always affect individuals, regardless of whether they remain within their community or tribe. Thus, the centers of "Turkmen attraction" appear beyond the borders of Turkmenistan proper. The loyalty to one's tribe or territorial community is, as a rule, stronger than the new ties and affiliations at the place of work or study, especially when tribal and territorial ties coincide.

During the past two or three decades the tendency for self-identification on the all-national level has grown. Individuals increasingly consider themselves not only as members of a particular tribe but as representatives of a large, "modern" nation. This phenomenon was observed in the Soviet army during the 1960s and 1970s when enlisted men from Turkmenistan considered themselves not as Yomutis or Tekes, for example, but as Turkmen.

It is very likely that the consolidation on the all-national level will gain more importance as intertribal tensions ease, yet these contradictions will hardly vanish in the immediate future. In principle, this is possible only after the disintegration of traditional social structures and decisive changes in the individual and social psyche.

The idea of national consolidation is very popular with the ethnic Turkmen living beyond the borders of the CIS. Two factors are of major importance: (1) traditional kin and tribal loyalty, the natural desire to assist one's kinsmen; and (2) the purely economic considerations of Turkmen of the diaspora to make business on the land of their ancestors using its considerable natural resources.

Ethnicity and Political Culture

The political culture and political situation of Turkmenistan are formed in unequal proportions on three levels of loyalty: national, tribal, and communal. The transmission of the basic, traditional values of life and behavioral patterns is generated through the family. This principal social cell determines Turkmen attitudes to life, as well as their worldview. As a general rule, Turkmen families have many children. There were 473 per 1,000 Turkmen families with four to seven children in 1979. In 1989, only ten years later, this index reached 533. The fact that several generations of relatives often live together might account for the transmission of tribal and religious values within a family from generation to generation.

For Turkmen youth, family interests prevail over all others. According to a 1988 sociological finding, the family oversees the younger generation until marriage and even after. According to this survey, only

25 percent of rural high school graduates are free to choose where to live or whether to continue their education or work; in 75 percent of the cases the decisions are made by the parents. The family serves as an initiating stage or prerequisite to full membership in the tribe or territorial community.

Competition between different tribes and territorial or local communities has always played an important part in the political life of Turkmen society. As a rule, a balance of interests of different groups has been observed at the upper levels of power. The replacement of the leader of the republic has usually meant changes in the entire hierarchy. At the same time, there is a characteristic tendency in the process of the formation of the Turkmen political elite that makes it possible to understand the reasons for the present relative political stability, as well as its limits. After 1917 a number of causes led to the occupation of the highest national positions by those who did not belong to the tribal aristocracy. Moreover, they belonged to "weak" clans and tribes. This was the result of a compromise between the "strong" tribes on the one hand and the central power's policy of "divide and rule" on the other. It may be added that the "poor and deprived" could compensate for their low social status by administrative promotion.

In many cases the representatives of the political elite, though they did not owe their promotion to their kinsmen, took tribal and communal ties into consideration in making nominations to higher posts. Thus they might have upset the balance of "ethnocommunal" relations that had developed over decades. During the past few years, for example, representatives of the Teke tribe and of two major Turkmen cities—Kyzyl-Arvat and Mary—occupied more privileged positions. This irritated those who were not selected.

When there is a threat of competition from other ethnic groups, the tendency to look for support among kinsmen plays a unifying role. In such cases all Turkmen are considered kinsmen and fellow countrymen. When the external threat vanishes the intraethnic rivalry reappears. It is possible to attribute the absence of powerful nationalistic emotions, and the relative stability in interethnic relations resulting from it, to this lack of open solidarity on the all-national level. But in a situation of choice all the advantages belong to the kinsmen, excluding representatives of other ethnic groups. The fact that Turkmenistan of all of Central Asia has the highest percentage of representatives of the titular nation among the heads of enterprises might prove the case.[1]

Nevertheless, Turkmenistan possesses a considerable potential for tensions, as is seen by the wave of anti-Armenian riots in Turkmenistan in May 1989; the adoption of the national language law, causing serious disturbances in February 1990; and the fervently nationalistic shade of the Gök Tepe Battle holiday, in which the Turkmen inflicted a major, if not the only, defeat on the Russian army in the course of the colonization of Central Asia.

The preservation of the importance of kin, tribal, communal, family, and other traditional ties in Turkmen society does not mean that Turkmenistan managed to avoid the winds of change. In this respect it is necessary to refer to the process of active urbanization during the entire Soviet period. Between 1926 and 1991 the population of Turkmenistan increased from 1 million to 3.7 million (3.7 times), but the urban population reached 48 percent. In the 1960s and 1970s it fluctuated on the level of 47 to 48 percent, and later it began to decrease. In higher than the rate of growth of the population of Turkmenistan as a whole. The share of the urban population grew from 14 to 45 percent. This process was most active until the 1960s, when the share of the urban population reached 48 percent. In the 1960s and 1970s it fluctuated on the level of 47 to 48 percent, and later it began to decrease. In the 1970s and 1980s the share of industrial workers in Turkmenistan diminished from 19 to 14 percent, while the share of agrarian workers increased from 38 to 42 percent.

In the 1970s and 1980s the Russian-speaking population began to emigrate. (Contrary to widespread perceptions, this process began far before the disintegration of the USSR.) In 1979 there were 350,000 Russians in Turkmenistan; in ten years their numbers decreased by 5,300, or 1.5 percent. Even higher was the emigration of Ukrainians (4 percent) and Tatars (2.5 percent). The result was a lack of qualified workers and specialists in some branches of Turkmenistan's economy, where the share of Russians was especially high.

The rate of urbanization among the Turkmen population was also very high. In 1926 Turkmen constituted 7 percent of the urban population of Turkmenistan, while in 1989 their share was 54 percent. Thus, the share of the Turkmen urban population, as compared to all ethnic Turkmen of the republic, rose from 1.5 to 34 percent from 1926 to 1989. However, the share of industrial workers and builders as compared to all working Turkmen was 18 percent in 1979 and began to gradually decrease after that. The growth of the urban Turkmen population during the last three decades was due almost entirely to the natural increase of the already existing urban population, which was two times higher among the Turkmen than among other ethnic groups. Yet, the migration of the rural population to towns did not account for the growth of the population in the urban sector. From 1970 to 1989 the median growth of the urban population resulting from migration from rural areas did not exceed four thousand people per year.[2]

It is commonly assumed that a significant increase in industrial labor and large-scale migration from rural to urban areas are the main features confirming the reorientation of a population from the rural to the urban way of life. The above analysis proves that this has not been the case with the Turkmen. It can be assumed that this is the main cause not only of the sluggishness in the execution of economic reforms but also of the lack of anxiety among all social strata, as the population does not yet understand the necessity of reforms.

Domestic Politics

An *Izvestiya* observer wrote in his analysis of the situation in Central Asia: "At present, President Niyazov of Turkmenistan is in the most favorable situation. He has no opposition. There is no political life in Ashqabat. It is possible to say that 'the society is asleep.' And a very simple idea comes to mind: is it for the better? Niyazov has told me 'We don't need revolutions. We stand for evolution.'"[3]

Certainly, the situation is not exactly like this, though the opposition in Turkmenistan is possibly the weakest in all of Central Asia. Only an embryo of political opposition exists—the movement "Akzybirlik" and the Democratic party of Turkmenistan. These movements are scanty; they unite small groups of Westernized intellectuals of the titular nationality and have practically no influence on public opinion. Also, there is almost no way to get information about their activity. The opposition does not have the opportunity to publish newspapers or magazines or to express its position on television or radio. The main Ashkhabad newspaper, *Turkmenskaya Iskra* (The spark of Turkmenistan), has remained practically unchanged since the beginning of the 1980s. The authorities do not hesitate to use repression against differently minded individuals.

According to Alexei Maleshenko, the Turkmen opposition resembles by many parameters the Soviet dissidents of the Brezhnev era. The persecution of the opposition by Turkmen authorities also resembles measures taken by Soviet repressive organs against dissidents in the 1970s and 1980s. During U.S. Secretary of State James Baker's visit to

Ashkhabad in 1992, some opposition intellectuals were detained at police stations or placed under house arrest. According to members of democratic groups, there have been cases of persecution of opposition activists at the workplace or of their confinement in mental hospitals.

At the end of April 1992, Muhammedmurat Salamatov, the editor of Turkmenistan's first independent magazine, *Dayanch*, was detained in Ashkhabad's airport without official charges. All magazine copies had been confiscated. Salamatov's supporters believed that the persecution followed articles published in the magazine which were critical of President Niyazov and of Minister of Interior Serdar Charyiarov. There is no doubt that the authorities are checking the opposition's activities and will either suppress it or make it known that disciplinary measures will be taken if necessary.

As a whole, the present political regime in Turkmenistan may be characterized as soft authoritarian. The only known case of severe punishment is the sentence passed on the poet Sh. Murmamedov, who was sentenced to seven years in prison for a satire on President Niyazov. The official charge was blackmail and fraud. According to Sergei Panarin, Murmamedov's sentence was a retaliation for an attempt on the sacrosanct authority of the supreme power rather than a punishment for political dissent.

The leaders and the population are unanimous in condemning the violation of ancient religious, kin, and tribal traditions, including particular behavioral patterns of etiquette vis-à-vis supreme power. These features of social psychology and political culture will determine the political evolution of Turkmen society in the near future.

The punishment of those violating the traditional behavioral code is not limited to cases where the authority of supreme power is undermined. In June 1991 Niyazov organized a relentless purge of the corrupt leading bodies of the Kaakhin and Serakh regions after a group of angry peasants addressed a petition directly to the president. The protection of ordinary people from the tyranny of bureaucracy is one of the main means to ensure the leader the authority of a traditional patriarch. According to the tribal elders and to the mullahs, President Niyazov managed to win this authority among those who are forming public opinion and guarantee the preservation of traditional values of Turkmen society.

Islam occupies a central place among these values. Turkmen leaders appeal to Islam as one of the bases of the revival of Turkmen cultural identity. Niyazov is ahead of some other Central Asian leaders in his emphasis on the Muslim identity of the republic. This matches the changes in the orientation of Turkmen foreign policy and efforts to consolidate ties with Muslim countries, as the republican leaders are counting on their economic assistance. However, the president's attitude toward political Islam is restrained. He does not want to have a powerful rival with an Islamist platform. Incidentally, the Islamic Renaissance party (IRP), established in June 1990 on the then all-union level, has not managed to spread its activity to Turkmenistan, though according to certain sources a small cell of this party has been established there. N. Ovezov, a spokesman for the president, sharply criticized attempts to set up the IRP in Turkmenistan.

When Islamic values are used for purposes of enlightenment and not for political struggle, they obtain approval from the government. This is the case of the "Sunna" enlightenment society. The activity of this society is very close to the conservative principles of the administration. The "Sunna" society condemns the decline in morals caused by the new trends. It even demands a stop to the broadcast of Moscow TV in Turkmenistan because of its incompatibility with Islamic morals. Westernized liberal intellectuals trying to set up democratic movements in Turkmenistan are also condemned by the "Sunna" society. As a whole, it may be assumed that the Islamist political movement has no prospects in Turkmenistan in the near future.

Recent presidential elections demonstrate that President Niyazov has managed to gain strong support in the country despite all ethnic, tribal, and clan differences. According to the central election commission, 99.9 percent of all the voters took part in the last presidential elections. Saparmurad Niyazov was the only candidate, and he collected 99.5 percent of all votes, 1.2 percent more than in previous elections, which had taken place only six months before. The new elections were merely a protocol action held in compliance with Turkmenistan's new constitution, adopted by the *majlis* (parliament). These elections demonstrated the firmness of Niyazov's position. He has the full support of Turkmenistan's population. The Russian population of Turkmenistan also approves of Niyazov's national and economic policies.

According to some observers, after the consolidation of his political and economic position Niyazov eased his control over political life and opened the possibility for the political activism of the moderate opposition, connected to the independent newspaper *Turkmenistan Today*.

It is possible that the experience of Uzbek President Islam Karimov has been decisive in this respect.

The Economy, Trade, and Foreign Policy

Given the present economic situation, Turkmenistan possesses only one more or less reliable guarantee for a stable economy and a satisfactory consumer fund, and that is to ensure permanent growth in natural gas and raw cotton export. Turkmenistan is next only to Russia and the United States in natural gas reserves.

The easiest way to attain this goal has been to raise the price of gas. In 1992 this became a source of tensions between Turkmenistan and the Ukraine. At first Ashkhabad demanded a sharp increase in gas prices, but Kiev rejected this demand. The representatives of the Turkmenistan government declared that the republic would not sell gas to the CIS partners at prices lower than those fixed by Russia. The Turkmen leadership maintained a firm stand on this issue and ultimately ceased supplying gas to the Ukraine. Tensions were eased when President Kravchuk intervened. In mid-June it was announced that there had been an agreement to resume gas supplies, since the Ukrainian side expressed its readiness to make maximum efforts in order to reach an agreement about gas prices. Both presidents agreed to begin the preparation of an entire system of accords in order to regulate the economic relations between the two countries. But the press reported that even after the agreement was reached, transit foodstuff freights for Turkmenistan were being blocked in the Black Sea ports by Ukrainian customs.[4] There were comments that the agreements signed by Turkmenistan with Iran and Turkey made Kiev more compliant.

To realize an increase in the extraction of gas, Turkmenistan needs mass investments, modern technology, and highly qualified personnel. Turkmenistan hopes to resolve these problems by shifting a major part of its economic relations to the Middle East, particularly to Iran and Turkey. Apart from economic interests and geographical propinquity, Turkmenistan is drawn nearer to Turkey due to their common Turkic heritage and to Iran by the fact that there are ethnic Turkmen in Iran's province of Khorasan, and that the two states share an extensive border. This process reflects the general trend of the economic reorientation of the Central Asian and Transcaucasian states from the CIS to their southern neighbors.

Turkmenistan began the policy of active rapprochement with the

Muslim states in 1991. At the end of 1991, Turkmenistan, Azerbaijan, and Kazakhstan were admitted to the Organization of Islamic Conference. An agreement was reached with Iran that Iranian specialists would assist Turkmenistan with the modernization of oil refinery. A series of barter transactions with Iran were signed. Thus, since January 1992 Turkmenistan has sold cement, glass, motorcycles, and other goods to Iran in exchange for citrus fruits.

While explaining the reasons for the conclusion of the contract providing for the refining of Iranian oil in Turkmenistan and the concomitant refusal to refine Russian oil, President Niyazov declared in the beginning of 1992 that the oil pipeline from Russia crossed the territories of Kazakhstan and Uzbekistan. This has made oil supplies from Russia rather vulnerable since the disintegration of the USSR. Niyazov also added that the possible rise of prices for Russian oil might annul all interest to buy it. Nevertheless, Niyazov's declaration did not indicate his intention to stop economic and other relations with Russia, as was corroborated by the events that followed.

By the beginning of summer 1992 Turkmenistan announced its intention to increase in the near future deliveries of its gas to Iran and Turkey and to reduce gas supplies to the unified network of the CIS, as well as to some of the member-states of the CIS that used to be its stable partners. It was declared that by 1994 Turkmenistan would stop gas deliveries to Kazakhstan (by this time the pipelines from Turkmenistan to Iran and Turkey would be ready). According to the bilateral agreement, Turkey will get up to ten billion cubic meters of Turkmen natural gas per year.[5]

Turkmenistan's decision will provoke serious problems for Kazakhstan. According to the agreement for 1992, Turkmenistan had to supply Kazakhstan with 6.7 billion cubic meters of natural gas at the fixed price of 870 rubles per thousand cubic meters. The failure to fulfill this agreement will inflict the heaviest losses on the Mangyshlak region of Kazakhstan, as the local power stations and enterprises there depend on Turkmen gas. The situation is further aggravated by the decision of the Kazakhstan government to stop the nuclear reactor located in this region. As for the gas deposits discovered recently in Mangyshlak, their exploitation is nonprofitable.

On 14 April 1992 an agreement concerning the construction of the Turkmenistan-Iran-Turkey-Europe pipeline was signed in Ashkhabad, following the negotiations of Saparmurad Niyazov and the members of the republican government with Iranian oil minister Golaman Reza

Agazade. During the important visit of Iranian president Hashemi Raf-sanjani in October 1993, Iran and Turkmenistan reaffirmed the previous agreements on the pipeline project. The first echelon of the pipeline, with the carrying capacity of up to fifteen billion cubic meters per year, is scheduled to be ready by the end of 1994, and the second, with the carrying capacity of twenty-eight billion cubic meters per year, in 1997. As it was announced by the Turkmen president's press service, the construction on Iranian territory was carried out by the Iranian side, while Turkmenistan was an investor. Iranian demands for Turkmen gas were preliminarily estimated at three billion cubic meters per year, but the final, exact figure will be specified later. All these supplies will be at world prices.[6] In the beginning of August 1992, according to President Niyazov's decision, all the calculations of Turkmen gas supplies to CIS members were transferred into free prices.

Iran is paying much attention to the reorientation of the transport and communication network of the Central Asian states to the south. It emphasizes its role as a bridge connecting the world market with the Central Asian states, which have no direct access to it. There is now an agreement on the construction of the railway Tajan-Saraks-Meshkhed, which will connect Iran with Central Asia and Kazakhstan and give Turkmenistan access to Turkey and the Arab countries. Direct flights between Tehran and Ashkhabad are currently operating, and a joint Iranian-Turkmen air company has been established in Turkmenistan. The Iranian slogan "The Caspian Sea must be Islamic" is well known; according to this, the cooperation of all Islamic states bordering the Caspian Sea should include fishing, navigation, and protection of the environment. But in reality, measures taken by Iran to establish the Organization of Cooperation of Caspian States indicate that Iran has not thus far made any attempt to limit cooperation in these spheres to Islamic states alone. The idea of the creation of the Caspian cooperation zone was first forwarded by then–Russian vice president Alexander Rutskoy during his visit to Iran in December 1991. This goes against the interpretation that the Caspian cooperation plan is a kind of counterbalance to the Black Sea Association, initiated by Turkey.

According to numerous experts, Turkmenistan, as well as the majority of the other Central Asian states, prefers the Turkish secular pattern of development to the Iranian Islamic one. Incidentally, this is corroborated by the fact that President Niyazov's first visit abroad was to Turkey and not to Iran. During his talks in Turkey he asked Turkish leaders to send professors of Islam to Turkmenistan in order to prevent radical Iranian Islam from filling the existing vacuum. In 1991 Turkmen Foreign Minister A. Kuliev had already supported the idea of the development of political and economic relations with Turkey. Kuliev emphasized that his country is waiting for help from more developed Turkey.[7] In the summer of 1992 it was announced that two thousand graduates from Turkmen schools would be admitted to universities in Turkey. The idea of the transfer from Cyrillic to Roman script is also being discussed; this would bring Turkmenistan still closer to Turkey. Evidently having chosen the Turkish pattern, Ashkhabad intends to favor its relations with the West, though the ambiguity of this problem is obvious.

Thus Germany, which has a long tradition of close relations with Turkey, approves of the Turkish model for Central Asia and Transcaucasia. The Western countries are unanimous in this. At the same time, they express misgivings lest these states follow the Turkish pattern of "authoritarian modernization" too closely. According to an *Izvestiya* correspondent, Bonn considers the increase of Turkish influence in the region as a handicap to the human rights problem there.[8] In any case, the rights of ethnic minorities are an actual problem for all Central Asian and Transcaucasian republics. The Turkish pattern, despite its attraction, is hardly unblemished in this respect.

Some Russian experts believe that the Iranian pattern—presuming the state-regulated economy and strong, authoritarian power combined with the freedom of small-scale production and trade—fully corresponds to the interests of clan structures, which dominate the Central Asian republics. The henchmen of this idea are of the opinion that old "partocratic" structures are now fighting new "Islamist" clans in these republics. Under these conditions, the close relationship of their economy with Iran will strengthen these clans in their struggle against "partocrats." As to the latter, after their rupture with socialist ideas they are inclined to appeal to national slogans. The Iranian support is also favorable to them, since it might serve as a counterbalance to "Slav" states. At the same time, it makes the victory of "Islamist" clans more likely.[9]

Turkmenistan needs the help of its southern neighbors in resolving its ecological problems. During the last twelve years, public opinion in Turkmenistan has been very anxious about the heavy ecological consequences of the barrage that separated the Gulf of Kara-Bogaz-Gol from the Caspian Sea. In February 1992, at the Economic Cooperation Organization (ECO) conference in Tehran, the need to destroy the barrage was discussed. Niyazov declared that his country was ready to reopen the strait connecting the Gulf with the Caspian Sea, thus suspending negative ecological processes. At the same time—and against the opinion of the experts, who had advocated the construction of the barrage—the level of the Caspian Sea will not be affected. On the contrary, it is going up ten centimeters per year. The barrage was removed at the end of June 1992.

The establishment of diplomatic relations with Romania in July 1992 was significant for Turkmenistan. Romania has expressed its willingness to participate in at least six economic projects, including some in the oil and gas industry. Romania has also reaffirmed its intention to join the ECO. It emphasized the lack of an Islamic orientation of this organization. Romania probably considers the establishment of cooperation with Turkmenistan a step toward membership in the ECO.

It should be pointed out that the development of gas-extractive industry and oil refinery in Turkmenistan cannot be achieved with foreign financial and technical support alone. The overwhelming majority of the Turkmen population is not skilled to work in the extractive industry. This creates a gap between the structure of employment of the indigenous population and the labor power requirements in qualified personnel. It is hardly possible to satisfy these requirements with the help of the nonindigenous population because, first, it is numerically insufficient, and second, it will seriously threaten interethnic relations.

The Turkmenization of the administrative personnel of the republic is also a destabilizing factor. It is provoking discontent among nontitular ethnic groups because of infringement of their interests. It also affects adversely the general level of economic management.

A partial reorientation of Turkmen and other Central Asian countries' economic ties to the Middle East might be dangerous to Russia. According to certain Russian statesmen, it may deprive Russia of strategic raw materials, and it may also lead to the lowering of industrial potential, tightly connected to the entire CIS economic complex, as well as to the weakening of the transport network. The existence of the ferryboat communication with Azerbaijan across the Caspian Sea makes Turkmenistan an important bridge connecting Central Asia with Transcaucasia, as well as the bridge within "post-Soviet Turkestan."

Turkmenistan is not inclined to promote the consolidation of the CIS, preferring bilateral agreements with the members of the CIS. On 16 July 1992 a meeting of the ministers of foreign affairs and defense of eleven CIS states took place near Tashkent. Incidentally, the Central

Asian countries have played a decisive role in the adoption of decisions to create international forces for the maintenance of peace, as well as the adoption of the Charter of the CIS and an agreement on the development of cooperation in defense problems. Russian Foreign Minister Andrei Kozyrev emphasized the constructive spirit of the conference in an interview with the Uzbek national radio and television company. According to some observers, the success of the conference indicated a strengthening of the trend toward the consolidation of the CIS. Kazakhstan, Uzbekistan, and Kyrgyzstan were mentioned as its principal initiators.[10] The absence of Turkmenistan in this list is not significant, taking into consideration the already high level of cooperation existing between Turkmenistan and Russia, including the question of defense. Turkmenistan's position may be explained by various reasons, such as the diplomatic passivity of its government, orientation to bilateral agreements, or the reluctance to have too tight relations with the other Central Asian states because of their much worse economic and political situations.

Nevertheless, even before this conference President Niyazov announced that a strict plan to create a national army and frontier guard has been prepared. On 6 July 1992 the conference of the heads of state of the CIS abolished the interstate committee for the protection of state borders and the unified command of frontier guards, creating in its place the council of the commanders in chief of the CIS. This decision meant that the protection of the lengthy southern border of Turkmenistan came under the jurisdiction of Ashkhabad. Recently the leaders of the Central Asian states supported the principle of protecting their state frontiers. Now the situation has changed. Tajikistan's President Nabiev, who was a partisan of the frontier protection principle in March 1992, had to make concessions to the opposition by the beginning of the summer of 1992, proclaiming that "there is no need for protection against one's brothers." Turkmenistan's president, probably against his own will, followed suit. In June, the Turkestan military district (*okrug*), which carried out the high command of all armed forces on the territories of the four Central Asian republics and Kazakhstan, was abolished. In July the creation of the national army and guard was announced in Turkmenistan. The function of the one thousand strong national guard includes the protection of the presidential palace, ceremonial activities, and the support of order in mass events.

The signing of the treaty of friendship and cooperation between Turkmenistan and the Russian Federation in Moscow on 31 July 1992

was a major step in the further development of the bilateral relationship. A series of documents have also been signed regulating the relations of the two countries in the spheres of politics and economy and
in the resolution of diplomatic and military problems. President
Niyazov stated in connection with this: "For the first time in history
after the disintegration of the USSR an interstate bilateral agreement
has been signed, which takes into account the interest of both states in
full scale without infringing upon the national interests of any side."[11]

The security treaty with Russia, which entailed the important agreement for a joint defense effort on the southern border, signified the
continuous dependency of Turkmenistan on Moscow in the areas of
foreign policy and reflected the similarities of geopolitical perspectives
between Ashkhabad and Moscow, at least in the immediate future.

This dependency on security matters is also extended to the economic realm. Turkmenistan cannot provide its population with food
and many other consumer goods. The country is thus dependent on
supplies from Russia and other members of the CIS. Evidently, the
leaders of the republic want to lessen the level of this dependency by
developing the local economy.

As was stated above, Turkmenistan is a major producer and exporter
of cotton. Cotton is on a level with gas and oil as one of the main
sources of hard currency receipts for the republic. In 1991, 1,000,473
tons of cotton were gathered, constituting 20 percent of the gross yield
of cotton in the CIS. In 1992, 580,000 hectares have been sown with
cotton, as compared to 614,000 hectares in 1991 and 630,000 hectares
in 1990. These figures reflect the general tendency of reducing land
under cultivation of cotton in Central Asia and decreasing cotton production. During the Soviet period emphasis was placed on the cultivation of cotton, thus making Turkmenistan's economy largely dependent
on a single crop at the expense of the cultivation of cereals. According
to expert evaluations, this year's crop was estimated at 1.3 million tons.
Turkmenistan depends entirely on Russia for the sale of cotton. It is
very difficult for the republic to command new markets because of the
low quality of its cotton. Early attempts to improve the quality of
Turkmen cotton, however, have been successful. In the summer of 1992,
decrees granting preferences for the increase of land sown with cotton
were adopted.

The lack of foodstuffs induced the government of Turkmenistan to
grant preferential taxes for importers of foodstuffs. Deputy Prime Min-

ister Valeriy Otchertsov declared that the government was ready to ensure maximum assistance to private economic activity in this domain, as well as to draw in foreign investment.[12]

In 1992–93 Turkmenistan's approach toward the perspectives of and potential for economic development diverged markedly from that of most other Central Asian republics. Intensively diversifying its foreign economic ties, Ashkhabad tried to exploit to the fullest its advantages, the most important of which is its natural resources. Turkmenistan chose to follow the path of gradual reforms and prevented the decline of living standards by heavily subsidizing its food and consumer goods industries.

As far as the CIS is concerned, President Niyazov drifted toward clear predilection for bilateral agreements, disapproving of, like his Ukrainian counterpart, any collective treaties. In January 1993 Turkmenistan refused to sign the draft of the Charter of the CIS in Minsk. At the meeting with his ministers, Niyazov declared his full accord to the CIS membership, but "this membership must be strictly consultative. No single structure of the CIS of a supragovernmental nature that may infringe this country's legitimate interests will be adopted." The holding of the CIS summit in December of 1993 in Ashghabaul, however, indicated that while Turkmenistan's desire for independence of action remained strong, the economic and geopolitical reality will continue to push for a degree of integration within the CIS and especially for a closer relationship with Russia.

When in the autumn of 1992 the states of Central Asia and Russia decided to take joint steps to settle the crisis in Tajikistan, Turkmenistan was the only state that refused to even discuss the problem, regarding the Tajik conflict to be the internal affair of Tajikistan alone.

However, in the beginning of January 1993 Ashkhabad participated in the formation of the Commonwealth of Central Asia and closed a number of agreements on regional cooperation. By that time the government model chosen by Niyazov—now called "enlightened authoritarianism"—had become firmly established. The leader of Turkmenistan believes that strong personal power is in accordance with the Turkmen tradition and provides stability. Thus, the president views his having received the military rank of general and the honorary title "Hero of Labor," as well as the naming of the main street of Ashkhabad and the Kara-Kum canal after himself, as acknowledgment of his authority and as signs of respect from his people. He set up the People's Council (majlis), which holds no real power, but, according to the Council's spokesman, Sahat Muradov, "has roots in the Turkmen people's national tradition."

Conclusion

It is possible to project that Turkmenistan has a fair chance to preserve a stable domestic political situation and to obtain positive changes in the economy. At the same time, it might face problems caused by the inevitable social and economic transformations necessary for the building of a modern state. The transformation of traditional tribal and communal structures is also inevitable, since social groups, integrated into modern spheres of life, will emancipate themselves from these structures (without a total rupture from them). In other words, Turkmenistan is entering a period of social modernization with gradual change and disintegration of some traditional economic, political, and cultural structures and their amalgamation with new imported or locally developed structures.

Much will depend on the economic situation. The economic failure of the present leadership will provoke political and social unrest, as happened in Tajikistan. The general situation in the CIS and the development of new and equal relations between Turkmenistan and Russia are also of prime importance.[13]

Notes

1. The calculation is based on official statistical data.

2. According to the estimations of the scholars of the Institute of Oriental Studies, Russian Academy of Sciences.

3. *Izvestiya*, 24 June 1992.

4. Ibid., 17 June 1992.

5. "Oil, Gas, and Coal Report," *Interfax* 20, no. 13 (3 April 1992).

6. "Presidential Bulletin," *Interfax* 22, no. 15 (15 April 1992).

7. *Millieyet*, 25 November 1991.

8. *Izvestiya*, 15 July 1992.

9. E. Dunaeva and L. Sklyarov, *Musulmanskie Strany SNG vo vneshnei politiki Irana* [Muslim countries of the CIS in the foreign policy of Iran] (Moscow: Institute of Oriental Studies, Russian Academy of Sciences, 1992).

10. *Nezavisimaya Gazeta*, 18 July 1992.

11. *Izvestiya*, 6 August 1992.

12. "Food and Agricultural Report," *Interfax* 22, no. 15 (17 April 1992).

13. *Komsomol'skaya Pravda*, 29 January 1993.

Part 4

RUSSIA AND THE FORMER SOVIET SOUTH

The New Geopolitics

11

The Disintegration of the Soviet Eurasian Empire

An Ongoing Debate

Milan L. Hauner

With the establishment of Commonwealth No. 2—consisting of eleven out of fifteen of the original Soviet Union republics—in Alma-Ata on 21 December 1991, a dramatic new chapter of Eurasian history began. We have been accustomed to watching the Soviet Eurasian Empire crumble away for some time, especially since Gorbachev took over in the spring of 1985. Since then numerous speculations on what would happen and which form the gradual collapse would take filled many a learned journal.

The former Soviet Union has been undergoing a process of triple disintegration, caused by the simultaneous collapse of its political (and ideological), economic, and imperial structures. It is to the last one, woefully neglected by Western observers until December 1991, that I wish to turn my attention, for the fact has seldom been recognized that the former Soviet Union had been until recently the last great surviving colonial empire, one that tried to escape, among other things, the decolonization processes of the post–World War II era.

Reconstituted in the heartland of Eurasia, Commonwealth No. 2 has a better chance of survival than its short-lived predecessor, Commonwealth No. 1 (of three Slavic republics), which lasted only two weeks. The Central Asian birthplace of the new commonwealth, as the press did not fail to report, is in "the heart of a snow-decked mountainside city north of the Chinese border."[1] It is not, however, the exotic attraction that this symbolic center of Eurasia may evoke with which I am concerned. Rather, I am concerned here with its historical, ideological, and geopolitical significance. If all three dimensions are taken together, then the choice of Central Asia as the pivotal region of the new Eurasian Commonwealth makes sense. Moreover, some of the present pat-

terns of disintegration could also become more understandable if compared with the nearest historical analogy of imperial collapse in this
region, namely, the international and civil wars of 1914–22. It was during this period that the Central Eurasian pivot area became the scene of
great upheavals that could have shaped the future of "Greater Turkestan" in a way different from what we know today. As a consequence of
World War I and the Russian Civil War, the state of continuous flux
created in Central Eurasia multiple political options.

Patterns of Disintegration, 1917–1922

World War I and the two Russian revolutions of 1917 caused cataclys-
mic disruptions in western Eurasia: four empires collapsed and fifteen
successor states emerged in the segment stretching from the Baltic Sea
to the Indian Ocean. The entire geopolitical framework of the tsarist
empire collapsed, resulting in the cession of its borderlands (Finland,
Baltic provinces, Poland, Bessarabia, temporarily the Ukraine and the
Transcaucasian Federation). Russian Turkestan, too, seemed to be drift-
ing in the same direction of separation and disintegration. This state of
continuous flux in Central Asia created an unpredictable series of challenges and responses for all participants in the division of spoils.

The Bolshevik power in Turkestan rested solely on the maintenance
of the only through-rail connection with central Russia via Orenburg.
For most of the first two years of the civil war the rail link with Moscow was cut off and the Bolshevik power remained confined to Tashkent, the only larger Russified city in Turkestan. The central authority
in Petrograd, and later in Moscow, could hardly reach Turkestan, which
in any case occupied a low military priority in the eyes of a Bolshevik
government struggling to survive against a multitude of internal uprisings and foreign interventions.

From early on, however, the Bolsheviks possessed two major advantages. First, they were the only force in Central Asia capable of repair-
ing, maintaining, and using the railway network for their own military
aims. Second, they seized the only professional force of military value
available in Turkestan after the dissolution of the old Russian army.
These were the prisoners of war, mostly Austro-Hungarians, estimated
to number over forty thousand in the fall of 1917. As early as 1915
they constituted an important element in the calculations of German
schemers to unseat the British Raj in India by provoking a Muslim uprising.[2] In 1918 this remote threat suddenly became real. With a tacit

agreement with the Bolsheviks under the terms of the Brest-Litovsk Peace Treaty, it was not impossible to imagine a Turco-German sweep originating from Transcaucasia across Transcaspia, northern Persia, and Afghanistan. As these prisoners of war, suffering from malnutrition and boredom, were volunteering in increasing numbers to join as *internatsionalisty* the Red Guards in Turkestan, to constitute throughout 1918 the backbone of troops commanded by the Tashkent government, the British became greatly alarmed by the additional gloomy prospect of watching "these potential recruits of an army of world revolution" getting loose in the direction of India.[3]

Because there was no similar dramatic change in the region during the last two centuries since the last attempt (by Nadir Shah of Persia) to create a Central Asian empire, it might be useful to review those various options for political change in this vast region in more or less chronological order:

1. German imperialists' designs primarily concerned disrupting British control over India. By exploiting the Turkish connection, they hoped to stir up the Muslim population of India via Afghanistan through a mass tribal uprising on the northwest frontier. This would tie down the British Indian Army and thereby prevent reinforcements from India from reaching other theaters of war. As a useful vehicle of religious and ethnic propaganda for Turkestan, the Germans hoped to exploit the pan-Turanist movement (Enver Pasha). Although these German plans had been hatched since 1915 (for example, the Henting-Niedermayer Expedition), they took more concrete shape during the eastern conquest of the Russian "living space" (*Ostraum*) under the Hindenburg-Ludendorff military dictatorship. The Brest-Litovsk Peace Treaty of March 1918 forced the Bolsheviks to recognize the independence of the new Caucasian republics and the sovereignty of Iran and Afghanistan in Central Asia, hitherto considered Russian buffer states. The German threat vanished, of course, when Germany surrendered in November 1918.[4]

2. British interventionists entered Baku in late summer 1918 to prevent the oil fields from falling into German hands, and they occupied Transcaspia between 1918 and 1919 to deny to the Turco-German forces the control of "Russia's southeast passage" toward India. Although some prominent Muslims, such as the Aga Khan, wanted the British Empire (already "the greatest Muslim power in the world") to include additional Muslim states and stretch from the Bosphorus to Chinese Turkestan, the temptation was wisely avoided in London. The

fear of pan-Islamism was omnipresent. If the former Russian Empire were to disintegrate, the India Office reflected in a memorandum of December 1918, Turkestan "should look rather to Omsk than to Petrograd or Moscow as its focus." In other words, it was not in the British interest to encourage the reunification of the former Russian Eurasian Empire. If an Asiatic Russian government centered on Omsk and controlling all the railway systems up to Orenburg could survive the civil war, then Central Asia, the India Office reflected, should be divided into four autonomous units under Siberian suzerainty: Bukhara and Khiva should retain their nominal independence, and the rest of Turkestan should be organized into two local administrations, one based in Tashkent and the other in Kokand, with a mixed Muslim and European representation.[5]

3. Intermittent centrifugal and short-lived groupings of white settlers, such as the "Cossack Southeastern Union," were encouraged by the Germans and stretched from the Don region to Orenburg and Semirechie. The Cossacks might have significantly influenced events in Turkestan, pending the control and maintenance of the Orenburg-Tashkent Railway, which was beyond their capability.[6] The Cossack autonomists proved even less coherent than Admiral Kolchak's separatist government of Siberia.

4. The prospect of uncontrolled "Balkanization" of Central Asia might have led to the temporary extension of life for the former Russian protectorates, the khanates of Bukhara and Khiva.

5. Alternatively, the conservative khanates could have been replaced by the forces of modern Islamic revival (Jadids), as epitomized by the short-lived existence of the "Provisional Government of Autonomous Turkestan" under Mustafa Chokaiev in Kokand, which claimed authority over Russian Central Asia in competition with the Bolshevik Tashkent government (all-European). The Kokand experiment was crushed savagely by the Red Guards dispatched from Tashkent in February 1918.[7]

6. An attempt was made to create a larger Islamic federation in Central Asia, led by the ambitious Amir Amanullah. Apart from Afghanistan, it was to consist initially of Bukhara and Khiva. Since Persia was considered too weak, it was assumed that it would have to accept Kabul's leadership. Amanullah was hoping that further disintegration of the Russian Empire would increase his chances of incorporating the rest of Turkestan. In the event of British power collapsing in India,

Kabul would have undoubtedly tried to reclaim historic Afghan holdings across the Durand Line down to the Indus River to secure the integration of all Pashtun tribes—which Amanullah attempted in 1919
by launching the "Third" Anglo-Afghan War. An inseparable part of
Afghan territorial claims against British India was the maritime province of Sindh, with the port of Karachi. This projected Islamic federation, however, would have rested on the leadership of Iranian ethnic
elements and was bound to clash sooner or later with the pan-Turanist
movement, rallying all Turkic-speaking groups of Central Asia.[8]

7. A Muslim pan-Turanist federation in Central Asia was a lifelong
dream of Enver Pasha, who, after disastrously failing as a military
leader to lead Turkish troops to Central Asia through the Caucasus in
1915, was eventually to arrive with Lenin's encouragement in Turkestan via Moscow in November 1921. But instead of helping to promote
an anticolonial revolution near the Indian border and helping the Bolsheviks consolidate their control over the Muslims of Central Asia, as
he must have promised to Lenin, Enver Pasha used the first opportunity to join the anti-Bolshevik guerrillas (*basmachi*). Despite his superb
credentials (son-in-law of the last Turkish sultan, the *khalif*; former
minister of war, and so son), Enver's claim to overall leadership was
never recognized by the basmachi. After his death amidst fighting in
August 1922, the incoherent basmachi resistance would linger on into
the 1930s, incapable, however, of offering a constructive solution for a
viable political alternative in Central Asia.[9]

8. A "socialist pan-Turan" was envisaged by the "red" Tatar, Sultan
Galiev, Stalin's confidant in the Commissariat for Nationalities. This
option was exploited by the Bolsheviks during the civil war, especially
among the Tatars and Baskhirs. It was also useful as a propaganda vehicle for carrying antiimperialist slogans to rally non-European revolutionaries.[10]

9. Finally, there existed the option that materialized when all others
had failed or had been exhausted, namely, the return to the ante bel-
lum status quo, that is, the reconquista of Turkestan by the Bolsheviks,
the heirs of the Russian colonial administration in new clothes. The
khanates of Khiva and Bukhara, the former tsarist protectorates that
the Bolsheviks allowed to linger on while they were fighting elsewhere,
were finally absorbed into the People's Republic of Khorezm (February
1920) and the People's Republic of Bukhara (September 1920).[11] Furthermore, in May 1920 Bolshevik troops landed in the northern Persian

port of Enzeli; the region was soon proclaimed a "Soviet Republic of Gilan."[12]

Why did all of these attempts fail in the 1920s, and why did the Bolshevik reconquista of Central Asia succeed in the end? To sum up the complex reasons it will suffice to analyze briefly the two major historical categories, space and time, that epitomized the fate of Russian Central Asia in relationship to the wider Russian Empire and the outer world. Specifically, the spatial relationship between the center and periphery placed Russian Central Asia with its Turkestan core at an obvious disadvantage. Ultimately, any food, industrial goods, and military reinforcements could reach starving Tashkent, Samarkand, or Kokhand only from the northwest by rail. As events had convincingly demonstrated, this lifeline could not be maintained by the transitory anti-Bolshevik forces that had temporarily controlled Orenburg or Samara, but only by those in permanent control of Moscow, the strategic hub of the empire, which decided the outcome of the civil war. All other options for Central Asia proved fleeting and futile because no major power—neither Germany nor Great Britain, as we have seen—wished to make this pivotal region its strategic priority. In fact, not even the Bolsheviks did in 1920 when they faced more direct threats to their dictatorship in European Russia. Indeed, it seemed almost an afterthought when they turned to Central Asia with a relatively minor force to extend control of the recently repaired railway line from Moscow to its terminus in Tashkent.

With regard to the dimension of time, the new state formations emerging and disappearing in Central Asia, as well as the older ones such as Khiva and Bukhara, lacked the necessary basis for political stability in conditions of civil war. The process of decolonization had hardly begun in a world in which preferential treatment in terms of national self-determination was exclusively reserved for the Europeans. Consequently, it was difficult to translate this nonexistent stability in Central Asia into a recognition of political legitimacy by any member of the international community of states. Neither could the neighboring states of Turkey, Iran, and Afghanistan offer any viable basis for political stability in Central Asia that would at the same time terminate the civil war and begin the administrative and economic reconstruction. They were partly exhausted by war themselves, and partly their rival pan-Islamic propaganda was running at cross-purposes. To sum up, it seems that the lessons of the 1920s provide useful analogies for the painful process of imperial disintegration and formation of new states in the 1990s.

Patterns of Disintegration in the 1990s

In the summer of 1989, as I was finishing *What Is Asia to Us?*, I contemplated in my conclusions what state formations could replace the dying Soviet Eurasian Empire. Three options seemed to be in the offing:[13]

1. I considered a new confederation, a sort of commonwealth, the most optimistic variant. But this option was pregnant with the heavy mortgage of the past, which would make the continuous role of the center, now vigorously opposed by the independent republics on the periphery of the former empire, untenable and unworkable in the long run.

2. The growing tensions between the center and periphery might ultimately lead to a Great Russian reaction, a nationalist and military coup attempting desperately to hold together the disintegrating empire. A truly apocalyptic scenario for such a backlash, whereby the "New Russian Right," with all its wretched fascist past and hatred of the "Judeo-Masonic Conspiracy," would wrest power from the discredited Gorbachevites, is dramatically portrayed in Alexander Yanov's book, *The Russian Challenge and the Year 2000*.[14]

3. Finally, I thought of a middle course, with Moscow simply trying to muddle through (*durchwursteln*) one crisis to the next, as characterized the last decades of the Austro-Hungarian and Ottoman empires (but more of an "Ottomanization" than "Habsburgization," a term suggested for this wishful scenario by Timothy Garton Ash, one of the most perceptive observers of the East European scene).[15]

In August 1991 a half-baked military putsch was attempted. It failed for lack of determination and coordination on the part of the putschists and because of the spontaneous resistance of the democratic forces and the opposition group around Boris Yeltsin, who, in addition, received strong moral backing from the major Western powers. This does not mean that the worst card was played and lost forever, though. In fact, the worst could still happen. A military dictatorship under the banner of the most reactionary ideology and led by somebody like Vladimir Zhirinovsky, the present leader of an extremist Russian nationalist party, might still ravage the scene. Writing from the juncture of early 1992, one cannot help but see in the emergence of the two Commonwealths of Independent Nations an imperfect merger of options numbers one and three. Should a civil war situation similar to events between 1917 and 1922 again develop in Central Asia, the involvement of the border states stretching from Turkey to China could become very likely. In such a case the number of domestic options will multiply.

Is Kazakhstan Central Eurasia?

In spite of earlier attempts under Peter the Great in the Caucasus and across the Caspian Sea, Russian expansionism established itself in the core of Central Asia only some 130 years ago. The conquest of Turkestan was hailed, in the words of the noted explorer Colonel M.I. Venyukov, as the "return of the Slavs to the neighborhood of their prehistoric home . . . and the cradle of the Aryan or Indo-European race . . . at the sources of the Indus and Oxus whence our ancestors had been displaced by the Turko-Mongol invaders."[16] It may not be altogether farfetched to hear today appeals using the same vocabulary from somebody like Vladimir Zhirinovsky.

Although both the tsarist and Soviet regimes tried to fill the vast space of Central Asia with European settlers, this Russian version of Manifest Destiny was not successful in the end. The Kazakhstan Republic remains today an artificial creation of the Soviet system in the center of Eurasia, where it occupies an area nearly four times that of than Turkey and stretches some 2,500 kilometers from the Caspian Sea to Xinxiang. Can Kazakhstan become an important buffer holding the balance between European and Asian Russia to the north and the more densely settled Muslim republics of the former Soviet Union situated to the south along the Iran-Afghan border? In these trying days when ethnic passions are running high, Kazakhstan's multinational population provides little comfort. Its population of seventeen million is divided between Europeans and Asians, the native Kazakhs accounting for roughly two-fifths, with an almost equal number of Russians, who are intermingled with large minorities of Ukrainians, Uzbeks, Tatars, Uighurs, and deported Germans, Crimean Tatars, and Koreans.[17] Because of its location, size, presence of nuclear weapons and major testing sites, and major railways and pipelines, Kazakhstan holds a pivotal strategic position in the very center of Eurasia, bearing weight to the east, west, and south of the dual Eurasian continent. In contrast to the

strong tendency to separate from the center, which has been most conspicuous in the Baltic republics, Kazakhstan's political and cultural
elites (for example, President Nursultan Nazarbaev and leading poet
Olzhas Suleimenov) do not desire partition for the time being.[18] For all
these reasons, Kazakhstan must be considered the decisive litmus test
for the survival of the new Eurasian commonwealth. If it can survive as
a miniature multiethnic commonwealth of its own, within which "Rus-
istan" and "Islamistan" could coexist, then the larger Eurasian commonwealth might survive too.

Tatarstan and Bashkiria, the smaller autonomous republics within
the Russian Federation, filling out the space further westward to the
Volga, are potentially even more explosive than Kazakhstan because
their Muslim population is encircled by Russians on virtually all sides.
Further east, Siberian autonomists, already strong and vocal before
World War I, have reappeared on the political scene.[19] This is not a
movement founded on ethnic emancipation. The proud Siberians consider themselves true Russian patriots, but their ethos of pioneers in
the wilderness suffered for a long time from St. Petersburg's and Moscow's arrogance, which treated Siberia as a mere raw material append-
age of the metropolis. Here the spatial relationship between the center
and the vast periphery requires a political solution for mutual economic benefit. Similarly, the inhabitants of the Russian Far East are
demanding autonomy from Moscow, but at the same time require protection against the enormous population pressure of the Chinese world
and the technological superiority of the Japanese. Here, at the easternmost extremity of the former Soviet Empire, the fiasco of the Russian
colonial model, magnified by the Soviet era, becomes conspicuous for
all to see. It is the second and third generations of Russian settlers
themselves, in Vladivostok or in the Kurils, who, when confronted
with Japanese or Korean tourists brandishing their video cameras, must
feel like inhabitants of the Third World.

Where Does Europe Begin, Where Does
Asia End, and What Is Eurasia?

In order to appreciate some of the major issues in the ongoing quest
toward "New Russia," which ultimately implies Eurasia, some recurrent
spatial problems of political geography should be mentioned.

Just as the former USSR underwent two major metamorphoses during the month of December 1991, the *Daily Report* for the Soviet

Union, published by FBIS since 1941, decided on its fiftieth anniversary on 1 January 1992 to change its title from "Soviet Union" to "Central Eurasia." Unable to learn about the official motives behind this abrupt change of title, one is free to dig into the rich annals of Russian history to find out more about the ambiguity of the term *Eurasia*.

The uncertainty about what Eurasia is begins with the dilemma of where to draw a dividing line between Western and Eastern Europe, as well as between "Europe" proper and "Asia" as a whole. For many centuries the eastern limits of Europe remained determined by the dominant Catholic religion and thus corresponded to those of the *Sacrum Imperium Romanum*. The Orthodox Christians of the Byzantine Empire and of Russia, as well as the splinter Christian churches in Asia Minor, were simply ignored. Only after the conquest of Constantinople by the Ottomans in 1453 did Europe readmit the Orthodox Christians in the East as cobelievers. In the ensuing centuries the border of "Europe" moved back and forth following the movable demarcation line between the Turco-Arabic sphere of control on the one hand and the Christian on the other; Europe's easternmost border remained for many centuries the river Don. Following the Russian eastward expansion under Ivan the Terrible, the Volga River became considered the natural borderline between the two continents. The Urals mountain range was first described as Europe's easternmost frontier in 1730 by a Swedish officer, Strahlenberg,[20] though later as an extreme alternative the river frontier of Yenisei or Ob/Irtysh/Tobol in the center of Siberia was also discussed.[21]

During the nineteenth century, when the notion of Eastern Europe became more accurately defined, it continued to carry with it the prejudiced association with a half-Asiatic region, for centuries exposed to raids by wild nomads from the East, and hence a region not genuinely belonging to Europe. Russia, of course, would constitute the bulk of uncivilized Eastern Europe. The Bolshevik Revolution caused another retreat of Russia, in Western European popular opinion, from Europe to "Asian barbarism."[22] However, the term *Eastern Europe* could not acquire its fullest political meaning before the disintegration in 1918 of the four empires overlapping in this region, and the foundation of independent states as buffers separating Bolshevik Russia from revisionist Germany in this "Europe in between" (*Zwischeneuropa*).[23] It was not only the Reformation that split the German Empire and ultimately Europe united hitherto in Catholic faith, but also the long-term impact of Renaissance and Enlightenment, which continued to reach the East

European region and ultimately Russia itself. The most important change, however, was brought by the radical "opening of the window into Europe," the process of one-sided Westernization of Russia itself, its westward expansion and the transfer of its capital from Moscow to St. Petersburg by Peter the Great. Catherine the Great was obsessed with the idea of making the Russian Empire acceptable to Europe: "La Russie est une puissance européenne," the German-born tsarina insisted.

The systematic shrinking of the Ottoman realm in Eastern Europe, achieved mainly by Russian arms, created the notion of temporary solidarity between the Orthodox, Catholic, and Protestant rulers.[24] In the second half of the nineteenth century a number of Russian intellectuals began to publish views on and interpretations of Asia which were highly original. One must mention at least the visionary Nikolai Ya. Danilevsky, who in his *Russia and Europe* (1869) boldly reversed the relationship between Europe and Asia by declaring the former a mere appendix of the latter. The accidental Ural boundary had to be rejected, and self-contained Russia emerged from this inquiry as a geographical world of its own. Danilevsky challenged the Western type of colonization with a Russian countermodel, allegedly less brutal because proceeding "organically" through gradual assimilation through Russian settlers.[25]

The true Russian genius, with a grand spatial vision far ahead of his time, was the celebrated scientist Dimitriy I. Mendeleev (1834–1907), whose *Toward Understanding Russia* will remain one of the most original geopolitical texts, though still hardly known in the West.[26] Mendeleev, along with his generation of scientists, profited from the massive statistical materials collected since 1897 in the course of the first really scientific census ever conducted in and about the Russian Empire. More than anyone else in Russia at that time, Mendeleev tried to correlate population with space. He was planning a spatially more balanced reorientation of the future Russian Eurasian Empire to augment from 150 million (1906) to 600 million inhabitants by the end of the century, and to 1.280 billion by 2026 (if the net annual population growth could be maintained at 1.8 percent). He predicted that Russia's mean center of population would gravitate irresistibly eastward into Asia and suggested that all inhabitants of the empire should get used to a new focal point in the center of Eurasia instead of looking from or to St. Petersburg. The conservative reaction against him was furious and unsparing even after his death. "There was a Russia of Petersburg," wrote one critic indignantly, "but there can be no Russia of Omsk!"[27]

If Mendeleev's imperial projection advocated equilibrium between the eastern and western parts of the empire, the renowned climatologist Alexander Voeikov was more skeptical about the possibility of transforming Russia's Eurasian landmass into flourishing zones of commerce. In his pioneering 1904 article "Will the Pacific Ocean Become the World's Main Trade Route?" Voeikov tried to demonstrate that the dominant maritime trade would encourage the development of coastlands rather than of the Eurasian heartland, which found itself outside the seven major world trading zones. Although Voeikov did not deny the potential significance of the Trans-Siberian Railway connecting Russia and China by land, he did not believe it could successfully compete with maritime transport. The Trans-Siberian, which was just about to be completed, could carry passengers and mail faster across Eurasia, Voeikov conceded, but never heavy goods.[28]

In comparison, the geopolitical ideas of Veniamin P. Semyonov Tyan-Shansky were closer to those of Mendeleev. He believed in the future of the Russian Eurasian Empire stretching "from sea to sea," but radically restructured so that the existing severe imbalances between its western and eastern extremities could be reduced. Semyonov saw an analogy with the empire of Alexander the Great that once stretched from the Greek Archipelago to the Indian Ocean; he was even more inspired by the contemporary American effort to achieve "Manifest Destiny from coast to coast" through improved communications and internal colonization. Semyonov's stimulating typology of colonial empires distinguished among three types: "circular," like ancient Rome and Carthage in the Mediterranean; "scattered," like the overseas empires of Portugal, Spain, or England; and "from sea to sea," modeled on Alexander the Great and adopted by Russia, the United States, and Great Britain in the northern hemisphere. The Russians, however, were facing a much more arduous task because of the size of the space and the harsh climate. There were also many more yellow Asians opposing the Russian colonizers, Semyonov admitted, than there were Indian inhabitants in North America.

Like Mendeleev, Semyonov vehemently opposed the artificial division between Europe and Asia along the Urals, but unlike Mendeleev, Semyonov did not feel confident about Russia's future in the vast spaces of East Asia where the European settlers would always be outnumbered by the yellow race demanding "Asia for the Asians." He suggested restructuring the empire into nineteen "states and territories" organized like the British dominions of Australia and Canada.[29]

Despite the terrible setbacks caused by World War I, the Bolshevik Revolution, and civil war, the intellectual quest for a special relationship with Asia continued with unabated intensity among the Russian intelligentsia. During the 1920s the most brilliant minds among the Russian exiles created the Eurasianist movement, which defended the complete cultural symbiosis between the European and Asian parts of the former Russian Empire. In their first manifesto, *Exodus to the East* (1921), R.O. Jakobson, N.S. Trubetskoy, P.N. Savitsky, G.V. Florovsky, and G.V. Vernadsky advocated a Eurasian association of languages and cultures. The Eurasianists saw in Marxism and Bolshevism the worst manifestations of Western culture, while the revolution itself was seen as the great and necessary catalyst that had destroyed the old world and aroused the passive Russian masses and the peoples of the Orient. For instance, Trubetskoy's *Europe and Mankind* (1920) denounces an exclusively Eurocentric approach to Asia. Russia's humiliation in the wake of war and revolution, he argued, could provide a unique opportunity for a radical transformation of attitudes toward non-Russian peoples. A colonial power herself, Russia could lead other colonial countries, in particular her "Asiatic sisters," in a decisive struggle against the "Romano-Germanic colonizers."

The discussion has not ceased today. Compromise continues to be sought between the notion of geographical suitability and Russian political control. A breakthrough in the acceptance of the term *Eurasia* was represented by the geopolitical theories of the British geographer Halford Mackinder, formulated at the beginning of the twentieth century, when the Trans-Siberian Railroad was completed—the iron link that gave a new practical meaning to the cohesion of Russian Eurasia. Mackinder opened his fascinating interpretation in his 1904 lecture by telling his listeners that they should try "for a moment to look upon Europe and European history as subordinate to Asia and Asiatic history, for European civilization is, in a very real sense, the outcome of the secular struggle against Asiatic invasion."[30] He announced the ascendancy of the new "geographical pivot of history" in the "Heart-land" of "Euro-Asia," which he described as the natural fortress in the middle of the dual continent, measuring some nine million square miles (out of some twenty-one million in the whole of Eurasia), whose main feature was that it lacked access to the seas. The geographical location of the heartland coincided with its singular historical and cultural significance. To the east, south, and west it was surrounded in a vast crescent by marginal regions, sorts of dependent subcontinents that were,

nevertheless, accessible to maritime traffic. Four in number, these regions corresponded to the great world religions: Buddhism, Hinduism,
Islam, and Judeo-Christianity. The center of gravity of this new, strategic heartland was identical with the autocratic Russian Eurasian Empire. Mackinder saw it as an almost perfect symbiosis between its
harsh natural environment and crude political organization, unlikely
to be changed by "any possible social revolution," which itself could
never alter the empire's "essential relations to the great geographical
limits of its [Russia's] existence."[31]

Mackinder certainly saw in the victory of Bolshevism in Russia yet
another confirmation of his "correlation thesis." And yet, in contrast to
the geostrategic tendency his latter-day acolytes (Spykman, Collins)
emphasized most, Mackinder's own significance lies more in the geo-
historical sphere. During the Soviet era the term *Eurasia* was freely
used by geographers to describe climatic and physical features of the
dual continent but was frowned upon with regard to geopolitical theories. This radically changed under Gorbachev, who frequently used the
term *Eurasia* in his book *Perestroika* and in his public speeches.[32]
Among his advisers is the geopolitically minded Igor Malashenko, who
has been devoted to the concept.[33]

The next step in the debate, not really clarified until now, was the
fundamental question of whether Western Europe should accept Russia
(or, however much of the Russian Empire) as part of Europe. This old
problem reappeared in a new guise in 1987 when Gorbachev launched
his campaign claiming that "Russia" belonged to the "Common European
House." He supported his claim on two grounds: a common Christian
heritage and the rescue of Western Europe from two usurpers in the
last two hundred years. Later, Gorbachev appropriated General de
Gaulle's slogan "Europe from the Atlantic to the Urals."[34] In retrospect,
Western sympathy for Gorbachev's idealistic drive must now be interpreted as a visible demonstration of support for the former Soviet
leader rated as "pro-Western" (*zapadnik*) in the long tradition of Westernizers from Peter the Great and Lenin. Moreover, in the face of the
recent violent strife inside the former Soviet Union and the Balkans,
what might be seen as calculated offensive of Soviet foreign and security policy in order to split the West and separate Europe from the
United States will now be regarded with certain nostalgia as a manifestation of Russia's desire to return to Western civilization. If this is true,
how did Gorbachev reconcile his vision of the "Common European
Home" with the fact that three-quarters of the Soviet Union's territory

and eighty million of its subjects lived in "Asia"? Although the bulk of Soviet Union's manufacturing capacity and population are in the cis-Ural regions (between 70 and 75 percent in both cases), nearly 90 percent of its energy and mineral resources are found in the Trans-Ural territories. Gorbachev solved the geographical dilemma of the Soviet Eurasian Empire by declaring in his Vladivostok speech of July 1986 that the Soviet Union was also an Asian country and the Asia-Pacific region its natural sphere of influence. How many more "Common Homes" did Gorbachev have in mind?

Numerous Soviet think tanks tried to conceptualize in geopolitical terms Gorbachev's ideological obsession with the "Common European Home." The "New Thinking" (*novoie myshlenie*), which reached its climax in 1988, was a joint effort to make the transition from an ideologically overburdened jargon to a geopolitical language that Gorbachev's major international partners could clearly recognize as their own. At the outcome of a truly mammoth Foreign Ministry conference between 25 and 27 July 1988 of more than one thousand experts drawn in from various think tanks, one of the deputy foreign ministers, Anatolii Kovalyov, outlined for the future the three principal directions of Soviet foreign policy: American, European, and Asian-Pacific. On the strength of its unique geostrategic position, Kovalyov implied, the Soviet Union could serve as a kind of "bridge between Europe and the Asian-Pacific Region."[35] The Central Asian factor obviously became submerged under the imaginary bridge linking Europe with the desirable Asian-Pacific region. This new direction of Soviet foreign policy during the imperial sunset is not without certain historical irony, which the advocates of "New Thinking" probably did not realize. It is virtually identical with an older geopolitical model of the Russian Empire functioning as the "Eurasian land bridge," which was pioneered by the founder of German geopolitics, Karl Haushofer.[36]

Exactly three years later, in the summer of 1991, undisturbed by the approaching military putsch, a similar conference was held by the Russian Foreign Ministry, the successor institution to the former "imperial" ministry. It was amazing to notice that several alternative concepts to the old-fashioned geostrategic vision of Eurasian Russia as a bridge between Europe and the Pacific emerged at the conference, such as Russia as a distinct entity from Europe, reminding the initiated of Danilevsky; unique "Eurasian state," which recalled the Eurasianists.[37] It was impossible to declare a "winner" among these visions. One commentator summed up his views in a warning that "an extremely dramatic period laid ahead of Russia" and that only the avoidance of disintegration and the preservation of some union structure made sense; the world needed "a Russia which was democratic and powerful" at the same time.[38] Whether the Russians can pursue both aims remains highly disputed and one of the key questions of the 1990s.

What Is Asia to Russians?

> What is the need of the future seizure of Asia? What's our business there? This is necessary because Russia is not only in Europe, but also in Asia, because the Russian is not only a European, but also an Asiatic. Not only that: in our coming destiny, perhaps it is precisely Asia that represents our main way out.
>
> F. M. Dostoevsky, 1881

It has become almost routine to refer to the great Dostoevsky whenever the innermost of the Russian soul is to be revealed. I am afraid this is also true about Asia. Just weeks before his death, Dostoevsky published the essay "What Is Asia to Us?" as an apology of the Russian military conquest of Central Asia. To him, Asia was like the undiscovered America waiting for the Russian colonizer to seize it.[39]

Because of the unique amalgam of history and geography that blended the European and Asian portions of the Russian Empire, Russians have long claimed a close and intimate relationship with Asia. Like the Americans following the call of Manifest Destiny "to overspread the Continent allotted by Providence for the free development of our yearly multiplying millions" (John L. O'Sullivan, 1845), the Russians felt predestined to rule over Asia. Not so long ago, before being pushed out by the Cossack and tsarist conquests, the banks of the Volga, the Kuban, and the Ural rivers were inhabited by peoples originating from Asia. These nomads penetrated Russia's steppes much further west than today's settlements of Asiatic population of the former Soviet Union would indicate. Until the fourteenth century these nomads were also supplied with the fruits of higher civilizations through the traditional trade routes connecting Constantinople with Peking (the Silk Road). With the collapse of the greatest land-based Central Asian empire, assembled by Genghis Khan, the major transportation axis between Europe and Asia, and the only land-based alternative to the sea route, was closed. According to the fascinating interpretation of Janet Abu-Lughod, this was the longest of eight trade circuits that constituted, until the thirteenth century, an integrated "world system" connecting three continents. The turning point in world history, argues Abu-Lughod, occurred between 1250 and 1350, when in terms of space, "the Middle East heartland region, . . . constituted a geographic fulcrum on which West and East were then roughly balanced, . . . and there was no inherent historical necessity that shifted the system to favor the West rather than the East."[40]

The Russian occupation of the Central Asian pivot did not lead to the reconstruction of the lost land route from Europe to Asia. Russian imperialism pursued autarchy; it did not seek to reconstitute the vanished world system but to remain outside it with its special spiritual mission. The Russian masters did not exploit the Central Asian nexus; instead they were inspired by military guidelines to build further north the Trans-Siberian Railway. Following the victory in the Second Patriotic War (1941–45), the pursuit of autarchy reached its zenith with Stalin's two-camp theory, to be gradually undermined after the dictator's death under Khrushchev and his successors. The final implosion was to occur under the rule of Gorbachev.

It is still too early to predict whether the dramatic transition from Gorbachev's *perestroika* to Yeltsin's *demokratizatsiya* will generate enough energy and inspiration in spatial terms among the Russians to get the former Soviet Eurasian Empire, hitherto governed by the tradition of political autocracy and economic autarchy, back into the world system worthy of the thirteenth-century precedent, then composed of eight interlocked subsystems, the largest of which consisted of Central Eurasia. Conditions in the post–Cold War world of the 1990s are indeed very different from those at the beginning of the century when Mendeleev, Voeikov, Semyonov-Tyan Shansky, and other outstanding Russian authors tried to lead the discussion about the modernization of the Russian Eurasian Empire.

Can the European and Asian parts of the former Soviet Eurasian Empire still coexist within one "Commonwealth"? Most geographers will agree that separating Europe from Asia does not make sense. The perfect continuity of the Eurasian plain over a distance of several thousand miles is only interrupted in the middle by the Ural range. The Eurasian area seems to be an almost closed world of relatively easy internal water transportation in the limited north-south direction following the course of the major rivers, characterized by their interior drainage and therefore cut off from access to warm ocean waters in the south where the natural border is formed by high ranges and plateaus considered impassable until the encroachment of modern twentieth-century transport technology.[41] In the north there are the even more impervious barriers of the ice-covered Arctic Ocean and the vast, uninhabitable territories subject to permafrost. Thus, some of the greatest rivers of the world, such as the Ob, the Yenisei, and the Lena, are practically useless for year-round internal and coastal navigation; whereas other rivers of Inner Eurasia, such as the Volga, the Amu and Syr Daryas, the Tarim and the Helmund, fail to reach the ocean altogether. The access to sea for the Eurasian world opens only by the narrow windows from the Pacific Ocean, and more broadly on Europe, which appears to be a mere appendix of the colossal Asian continent. In terms of physical geography the *Encyclopaedia Britannica* describes Central Eurasia as "the island part of Asia, farthest removed from the world oceans, in the midst of the greatest landmass on earth." Is this the chosen land and people about which the FBIS promised to inform us every day since January 1992?

From the geostrategic standpoint, the Russians tended to view the central portion of Eurasia throughout the last decades of the tsarist empire as falling into three parts: the Middle East, namely, the middle sector between the Near East, stretching from the Maghreb to the head of the Persian Gulf, and the Far East, which faced the Pacific Ocean. Hence the Middle East would begin at the great divide between the Caucasus and the Persian Gulf, which not only separated geographically the Black Sea and the Mediterranean from the Caspian Sea and the Indian Ocean, but also served as the great, historic divide between the former Ottoman realm and those of Iran and India. Less clear was the Russian answer to the questions of how far east or south this Central Eurasia should stretch. How much of the Indian subcontinent, or of Mongolia, should it incorporate? General Andrei E. Snesarev, the remarkable military geographer and orientalist, defined Central Asia in 1906 as consisting of Turkestan, Khiva, Bukhara, north of India, Kashgaria, the Pamirs, Tibet, Afghanistan, Baluchistan, and eastern Persia.[42]

So far, we have heard what Asia, specifically Central Asia, meant to the Russians in the recent past. What does it mean today?

Conclusions

We might start with the premise that the definition of where Europe ends and Asia starts is a matter of sheer convenience for the onlooker. For the politician and ideologue, however, the demarcation of the easternmost boundaries of Europe was, and still is, of considerable importance. During the early euphoria of 1989–90, when perestroika and glasnost seemed to have prevailed over the violent outbursts of ethnocultural nationalism, conventional geopolitical thinking appeared inadequate to provide the answer. For a moment it looked as if the traditional instrument of geopolitics, determined almost exclusively by military-strategic criteria stemming from the era of high imperialism, of which the late Soviet Union was the anachronistic lone survivor, was to be radically revised and complemented by a new discipline called "geoculture," which appeared more suited to the post–Cold War world.[43]

However, given the continuing violent character of disintegration of the former Soviet Eurasian Empire in its many regions, the discussion is likely to still be conducted within the bounds of conventional geopolitics. Two parallel scenarios for this stage could be suggested. One is the traditional but reformed geopolitical approach contemplating the "New World Order" as a mere upgrade of the old one. Such is, for example, Henry Kissinger's vision of the post–Cold War modeled on the European state system of the late eighteenth and nineteenth centuries, in which five or six major powers will take care of the international equilibrium: the United States, Europe, China, Japan, the former Soviet Union ("or whatever emerges to replace it," suggests Kissinger), and probably India.[44]

The rival scenario could be devised differently. It should, on the one hand, reflect the resurrected legacy of the integrated thirteenth-century world system, so beautifully argued in Janet Abu-Lughod's book. Its peaceful variant would most probably envisage the emergence of six larger zones in the process of the empire's further decolonization and recontruction: (1) the Baltic belt (Kaliningrad, Baltic republics, St. Petersburg) connected with Scandinavia; (2) Russia proper; (3) the Black Sea zone, including Moldavia, Crimea, southern Ukraine, southern Russia, and western Caucasia, including Armenia and part of Georgia (and Turkey, of course); (4) the Central Asian zone, spreading from eastern Caucasia and the Caspian Sea, Turkestan, and as far as Semirechie (Yeti Su), and resuming cross-border relations with all the neighboring states from Turkey to western China; (5) Central Siberia from the Urals to Lake Baykal; and (6) the Far Eastern and Pacific region. The basic assumption for such a scenario is, of course, the control of such imponderables as the ethnocultural factor in the sphere of domestic, regional, and international relations.

Will such an organic reconstruction of former Russian/Soviet Eurasia ever take place, and if it does, will it predominantly be peaceful and nonviolent? It is too early to define a new common "Eurasian" identity when it is still unclear whether the Russians and non- Russians wish to share the same space. The pivotal importance of Kazakhstan was underlined earlier. The return to the ethnocultural identities of the prerevolutionary era, either through outspokenly violent (Abkhazia, Nagorno-Karabakh, Tajikistan) or less violent upheavals, appears for the time being to be the determining factor among the non-Russian nationalities of the former empire. In conjunction with the local mafias, who are often involved in superficial dealings with one of the Muslim countries across the border, a ruthless power struggle has led to internal paralysis of important regions of Transcaucasia and Central Asia. There is an acute danger within the Russian Federation itself of a further crumbling into more than twenty ethnic republics and probably a dozen regions, calling themselves "the Republic of the Urals," centered on Yekaterinburg (former Sverdlov), or "the Maritime Republic of Vladivostok," or the "East Siberian Republic," stretching between Krasnoyarsk and Irkutsk.[45] Since the economic power of these regions is far larger than that of many republics, they are bound to test Moscow's centralism to the last. The results are predictable: not having an accepted federal constitutional framework for the new Russian Federation and Commonwealth, the former republics, autonomous republics, and regions of the former Soviet Eurasian Empire are slipping into further anarchy and decomposition. In the preliminary discussion on the new draft constitution for the Russian Federation, about eighty-eight "subject units," ranging from regions, ethnic republics, and major cities, have been recognized as autonomous subjects. For Central Asian nationalists and regionalists there is an additional temptation to jump on the bandwagon of a superficial alliance with one of the cross-border Muslim states, be it Pakistan, Iran, or Turkey (Afghanistan is at the moment completely paralyzed as a subject in international politics). This would be the final blow for any prospects of survival for the CIS in Central Asia and the Caucasus.

   That such upheavals are having the most disastrous consequences for the entire economic life of the Caucasian and Central Asian economies is at the moment of secondary importance to those ambitious nationalists and regionalists who have been absorbed in the power struggle. The economic costs have been threefold: (1) the termination of budgetary subsidies from Moscow (which also kept in power the old, indigenous Communist establishments); (2) the acceleration of migration of European professionals and technicians from the region; and (3) the decline in trade between the former Soviet republics.[46]

If more than one hundred years ago Dostoevsky envisaged Central Asia as an exclusive sanctuary for the Russian *Mission Civilisatrice* and spiritual regeneration, we have seen this legacy transpiring through Igor Malashenko's soft language. Unlike Mackinder, who ignored the ethnic factor, Malashenko has tried to integrate geopolitical and ethnocultural elements in a new supraregional framework, in spite of the strong forces of secession. "Russia is by no means an imperial State only, having mechanically united an incredibly multifarious conglomerate of lands," he claims. "It is an ethnically and culturally unique country, lying in Europe and Asia, that is, an Eurasian country in the true sense of the word, which was not only an instrument of expansionism, but also a powerful center of attraction for numerous *ethnoses.*"[47] Naturally, in case this kind of wishful reconstruction of the old Eurasian empire is not followed, Malashenko envisages a horrible future in the heartland of Eurasia, paralyzed by nationalistic upheavals, "beside which even the most macabre variations of the German question will have paled into insignificance." The Cold War may have ended with the defeat of the old Russian Eurasian Empire. This defeat, Malashenko predicts with confidence, "has been the starting point of the regeneration of Russia and of a new geopolitical round."

However, it seems unlikely that the non-Russian people of former Soviet Eurasia will follow Malashenko's advice, and for several reasons. Judging by the intensity of intraethnic fighting, the former empire will first have to traverse a brutal and difficult stage of falling apart before some of its parts could reintegrate again. As during the Russian Civil War of 1918–22, the new reintegration will have to wait until after the excesses and frenzy of the present ethnocultural friction are overcome. This could be delayed by the rise of the new Russian nationalism, whose spokespersons are, naturally, passionately interested in the preservation of the empire, of the old values of Imperial and Orthodox Russia, and will not accept the present-day "Americanization" of Russia under Gorbachev and Yeltsin.[48] The nationalists view the year 1991 as a "geopolitical catastrophe," and the whole process of imperial disintegration as a Russian national tragedy.

The year 1992 saw the emergence of a peculiar branch of Russian nationalist imperialists, those advocating "Neo-Eurasianism." Choosing selectively from the legacy of Eurasianism of the 1920s described earlier, they seem to be greatly attracted by Mackinder's vision of the heartland, stretching from "Rhine to Novosibirsk," and like to quote from his best-known prophecy: "He who rules the Heartland commands Eurasia, he who rules Eurasia commands the world."[49] "Traditional" Eurasianists of the post-Brezhnev era, such as Alexander Prokhanov,[50] are being joined by younger "Neo-Eurasianists" such as the eloquent Tatar writer Shamil Sultanov (1952), who believes in the inevitability of confrontation between Eurasianism on the one hand, and Atlanticism, displaying all the sins of the "decadent, hypocritical and atheistic" American civilization, on the other. Sultanov, unwittingly reproducing the familiar arguments of prerevolutionary Eurasianists, is of course arguing ecstatically in favor of a Slavo-Turkic and Orthodox-Islamic alliance.[51] The writer Alexander Dugin, who describes himself as "metaphysicist and geopolitician," preaches the rehabilitation of the old grandiose dream of a "Euro-Soviet Empire from Vladivostok to Dublin," founded on the invincible geopolitical alliance of "Russia, Germany and China."[52] Their infectious ideas have already reached the highest echelons of Russian executive and legislative power. How else should one interpret statements advocating a kind of "Russian Monroe Doctrine" by Sergei Stankevich,[53] political adviser to President Yeltsin, or Andrei Kozyrev's mysterious pro-Asia and pro-Serbia statements at the Stockholm CSCE (Conference on Security and Cooperation in Europe) meeting in December 1992?[54]

Notes

1. Francis Clines reporting from Alma-Ata for the *New York Times*, 22 December 1991.

2. U. Gehrke, *Persien in der deutschen Orientpolitik während des Ersten Welkrieges* [Persia in Germany's Oriental policy during World War I], vol. 1 (Stuttgart: Kohlhammer, 1960), 2–3; Gregorii Safarov, *Kolonialnaya Revolyutsiya (Opyt Turkestana)* [Colonial revolution: the case of Turkestan] (Moscow: Gosizdat, 1921).

3. Compiled from the *Journal of the Royal Central Asian Society* 6 (1919): 3–11, 119–36; 7 (1920): 42–58; 8 (1921): 46–69; 9 (1922): 96–110.

4. W. Baumgart, *Deutsche Ostpolitik* 1918 [Germany's eastern policy 1918] (Vienna: Oldenbourg, 1966). Andreas Hillgruber, in his penetrating chapter "New German Foreign Policy Objectives, 1914–1918," in *Germany and the Two World Wars* (Cambridge: Harvard University Press, 1981), 41–48, maintains that with the establishment of the new Ostraum the Hidenburg-Ludendorff Army Command went far beyond the original idea of Mitteleuropa, limited in 1914 to German domination of Central Europe.

5. L.C. Dunsterville, *The Adventures of Dunsterforce* (London: 1920); F.M. Bailey, *Mission to Tashkent* (London: Cape, 1946). Quotes from "The Future of Russian Central Asia," memorandum by the India Office, 3 December 1918, India Office records: L/P&S/18/C 186.

6. Anonymous, "Russia, Germany and Asia," *The Round Table* (London) 8 (1917–18): 526–64; Safarov, *Kolonialnaya Revolyutsiya*, 121–28.

7. M. Chokaiev, "Turkistan and the Soviet Regime," *Journal of the Royal Central Asian Society* 18 (1931): 403–20.

8. Ikbal Ali Shah, "The Federation of the Central Asian States," *Journal of the Royal Central Asian Society* 7 (1920): 29–49. See also L.W. Adamec, *Afghanistan 1900–1923. A Diplomatic History* (Berkeley: University of California Press, 1967), 108–68.

9. Essad Bey, *Die Verschwörung gegen die Welt* [The conspiracy against the world] (Berlin: 1932); Azade-Ayse Rorlich, "Fellow Travellers: Enver Pasha and the Bolshevik Government 1918–1920," *Asian Affairs* (October 1982): 288–97.

10. A. Bennigsen and S.E. Wimbush, *Muslim National Communism in the Soviet Union: A Revolutionary Strategy for the Colonial World* (Chicago: University of Chicago Press, 1979); Mehmet E. Rasul-Zade, *O Panturanizme v svyazi s kavkazskoy problemoi* [About Panturanism in connection with the Caucasus problem] (Paris: 1930; reprint by the Society for Central Asian Studies, no. 7, Oxford, 1985); Mir Said Sultan-Galiev, *Stati* [Articles] (reprint by the Society for Central Asian Studies, no. 1, Oxford, 1984). The classic treatment remains the work of the former president of the Bashkir Republic, Ahmed Zeki Validi Togan, *Begünkü Türkli (Türkistan) ve yakin tarihi* (Istanbul: 1947).

11. Richard Pipes, *The Formation of the Soviet Union. Communism and Nationalism 1917–1923* (Cambridge: Harvard University Press, 1954), 174–84.

12. D. Geyer, *Die Sowjetunion und Iran, 1917–1954* (Tübingen: Böhlau, 1995), 14–16.

13. M. Hauner, *What Is Asia to Us?* (London & Boston: Unwin Hyman, 1990), 248.

14. A. Yanov, *The Russian Challenge and the Year 2000* (Oxford: Basil Blackwell, 1987).

15. T.G. Ash, "The Empire in Decay," *New York Review of Books*, 29 September 1988.

16. M.I. Venyukov, "Postupatel'noe dvizhenie Rossii v Srednei Azii" [Russia's gradual advance in Central Asia], *Sbornik gosudarstvennykh znaniy* 3 (St. Petersburg: 1877).

17. James Critchlow, "Kazakstan and Nazarbaev: Political Prospects," *Prepublication from RFE/RL Research Institute*, 2 January 1992.

18. Ibid. It may be of interest to know that in his speech at Georgetown University on 26 September 1991, Olzhas Suleimenov strongly defended the present status quo in Kazakhstan.

19. Aleksei Manannikov, "Novosibirskie Neformaly: Prizyv k bor'be za avto-nomiyu Sibirii" [Neformaly from Novosibirsk: summons to struggle for Siberian autonomy], *Radio Svoboda*, RL/PC, 3/89. TASS from Novosibirsk, 17 November 1990.

20. W.H. Parker, "Europe: How Far?" *Geographical Journal* 126 (1960): 285–86.

21. F.G. Hahn, "Zur Geschichte der Grenze zwischen Europa und Asien" [History of the boundary between Europe and Asia], *Mitteilungen des Vereins für Erdkunde zu Leipzig* 1 (1881): 91, 104.

22. Egbert Jahn, "Wo befindet sich Osteuropa?" [Is Eastern Europe to be found?] *Osteuropa* (May 1990): 422, 427.

23. Ibid., 429; Halford J. Mackinder, *Democratic Ideals and Reality* (London: Constable, 1919); Giselher Wirsing, *Zwischeneuropa und die Deutsche Zukunft* [Europe-in-between and Germany's future] (Jena: Diederichs Verlag, 1932).

24. Jahn, "Wo befindet sich Osteuropa?," 423.

25. See the excellent summary by Mark Bassin, "Russia between Europe and Asia: Its Ideological Construction of Geographical Space," *Slavic Review* 50, no. 1 (Spring 1991): 9–11.

26. D.I. Mendeleev, *K poznaniyu Rossii* (St. Petersburg: 1906).

27. Hauner, *What Is Asia to Us?*, 153.

28. A.I. Voeikov, "Budet-li Tikhyi Okean glavnym torgovym putyom zem-nogo shara?" *Izvestiya Imperatorskogo Russkago Geograficheskago Obshchestva* 40, no. 4 (1904): 482–556. Voeikov's interpretation comes closes to Nicholas Spykman's "rimlandic" view of Eurasia, which was formulated forty years later.

29. V.P. Semyonov Tyan-Shansky, "O moguchestvennom territorial'nom vladenii primenitel'no k Rossii" [About the great-power dominion applicable to Russia], *Izvestiya Imperatorskogo Russkago Geograficheskago Obshchestva*, 51, no. 8 (1915): 425–57.

30. Halford J. Mackinder, "The Geographical Pivot of History," *Geographical Journal* 23, no. 4 (1904): 421–44.

31. Ibid.

32. Hauner, *What Is Asia to Us?*, 249.

33. Igor Malashenko, "Russia: The Earth's Heartland," *International Affairs* (Moscow) 34 (July 1990): 46–54.

34. M.S. Gorbachev, *Perestroika: New Thinking for Our Country and the World* (New York: Harper & Row, 1987): 191–98.

35. *Mezhdunarodnaya zhizn* (Moscow) 34, no. 9 (1988): 36–39.

36. Haushofer's scheme consisted of three major geopolitical realms: western Europe under German hegemony, the Indo-Pacific region under Japan, and the Russian Eurasian Empire functioning as the bridge between the two. All three "have nots" were to be linked through an alliance and directed against the satu-rated western colonial empires headed by the Anglo-American bloc. See Hauner, *What Is Asia to Us?*, 165–190.

37. For a full discussion see Ibid., 23–24, 150, and 60–65.

38. A. Lapshin, "From the Russian Point of View," *International Affairs* (Moscow) 37, no. 10 (October 1991): 79–81.

39. F.M. Dostoevsky, *The Diary of a Writer*, vol. 2 (New York: C. Scribner, 1949), 1043–52.

40. Janet L. Abu-Lughod, *Before European Hegemony: The World System A.D. 1250–1350* (Oxford: Oxford University Press, 1989), 12, 34, 359–67. I am not certain whether this book has been cited or reviewed within the former Soviet Union.

41. See the 1986 conference papers, published in M. Hauner and R.L. Canfield, eds., *Afghanistan and the Soviet Union: Collision and Transformation* (Boulder: Westview Press, 1989).

42. A.E. Snesarev, *Indiya kak glavnyi faktor v sredneaziatskom voprose* [India as the main factor in the Central Asian question] (St. Petersburg: 1906), 7–13.

43. See, for instance, Immanuel Wallerstein, *Geopolitics and Geoculture* (Cambridge: Cambridge University Press, 1991).

44. H. Kissinger, "What Kind of New World Order?" *Washington Post*, 3 December 1991.

45. See Serge Schmemann in the *New York Times*, 13 July 1993.

46. Michael Kaser and Santosh Mehrotra, *The Central Asian Economies after Independence* (London: RIIA, 1992).

47. Malashenko, "Russia: The Earth's Heartland," 52–54. The "ethnos theory" (*etnos in Russian*) was developed by Soviet ethnographers in the early 1970s; see Yuriy V. Bromlei, *Etnos i etnografiya* (Moscow: Nauka, 1973).

48. See Walter Laqueur in *Foreign Affairs* (Winter 1992/93): 103–16.

49. Halford Mackinder, *Democratic Ideals and Reality* (London: Constable, 1919), 194. For the contemporary views of Russian "Neoeurasianists," see Igor Torbakov, "The Ideology of Russian Imperial Nationalism," Draft research paper, RFE/RL Research Institute, Munich, 12 November 1992; Vera Tolz, "Russia: Westernizers Continue to Challenge National Patriots," *RFE/RL Research Report* 1, no. 49 (11 December 1992).

50. See Hauner, *What Is Asia to Us?*, 221–25.

51. Shamil Sultanov, "Dukh evraziitsa" [The spirit of Eurasia], *Nash Sovremennik* 36 (July 1992): 143–48.

52. See the roundtable discussion in Prokhanov's weekly *Den* 30, no. 2 (1992): 2–3; Helen von Ssachno, "Der grosse Krieg der Kontinente" [The Great War of the continents], *Süddeutsche Zeitung*, no. 18 (23 January 1993).

53. See *Nezavisymaya Gazeta*, 26 March and 19 August 1992; *Izvestiya*, 7 August 1992. See also Stankevich's article, "Russia in Search of Itself," *National Interest* (Summer 1992).

54. The foreign minister of the Russian Republic, Andrei Kozyrev, spoke in Stockholm at the session of the CSCE Council of 14 December 1992.

12

Great Power Ideology and the Muslim Nations of the CIS

Arthur Sagadeev

The process of disintegration in the Soviet Union, specifically the emergence of newly independent Muslim states, may reshape the political map of Muslim-dominated Southwest Asia and its relationships with the non-Muslim world. It is obvious, however, that the immediate and more distant consequences of this process will largely depend on the further development of relations between Moscow and the Muslim nations of the CIS. From the ideological point of view, this will depend on the willingness of both sides to revise historically established mutual perceptions.

This chapter will discuss the enduring role of Russian great power ideology in shaping the perception and policies of the Kremlin toward the Muslim nations of the former USSR. This ideology has shown remarkable resilience and longevity as it has survived the Bolshevik Revolution (socialist internationalism), perestroika, and, indeed, the collapse of the Soviet Union.

Great Power Ideology in History

In 1552 Tsar Ivan the Terrible conquered Kazan, the capital of the Volga Tatars. This historical event marked the beginning of the rise of the Russian empire. By the end of the nineteenth century the Russians seized 4.5 million square kilometers of Muslim lands, including vast territories of Kazakhstan, Central Asia, the Caucasus, Azerbaijan, Tatarstan, Bashkortostan, and the Crimea. Since then the political and ideological orientations of Moscow have undergone numerous and substantial changes. Regardless of these changes, however, the non-Russians were deprived of their national sovereignty and independence. Despite official Communist propaganda that maintained that almost all these lands joined Russia voluntarily, the Muslims have viewed the annexation of their countries as a coercive and purely colonial act.

It should be noted that many Muslim champions of national liberation believed that the Bolshevik Revolution of 1917 would serve to elevate their nations to an equal status with the Russian nation. But soon after the revolution they were compelled to relinquish those hopes. In 1923 Mirsaid Sultan Galiev, the most prominent Muslim Communist in the Soviet Union and the first victim of Stalin, was arrested on suspicion of "counter-revolutionary nationalist conspiracy against the power of the Soviets." In a letter he wrote while in prison he confessed that he had been merely a "slave-revolutionary" and that his "deviation" from the party line had consisted primarily of the fact that he had come out against the nationality policy of the party, a policy aimed at conserving the non-Russian peoples in a "colonial state vis-à-vis the Central Great Russian part of the Republic."[1] Sultan Galiev's arrest and show trial were followed by an antinationalist offensive that eventually led to the liquidation of all Muslim national leaders. By the late 1930s, thousands of Tatars, Bahkirs, Turkestanis, Azeris, and others—high-ranking officials, "clerics," scholars, and literary figures—had disappeared in the purges under the indictments of "Sultan-Galievists," "bourgeois-nationalists," "pan-Turkists," "pan-Islamicists," "anti-Communists," "spies," and "traitors."

> During this period, Stalin liquidated nearly all of the nationalist Muslim intellectuals, as well as nearly all of the pre-revolutionary Muslim intelligentsia, regardless of whether or not they opposed the Bolshevik regime. In 1928 he augmented the systematic elimination of the Muslim intellectual elite with a frontal assault on the USSR's Islamic infrastructure. Mosques were closed and destroyed by the thousands, clerics were arrested and liquidated as "saboteurs" and, after 1935, as spies. By 1941, of the 25,000–30,000 mosques open in 1920, only about 1000 remained. Moreover, all of the 14,500 Islamic religious schools were forcibly shut down; and fewer than 2000 of the approximately 47,000 clerics survived. By the outbreak of World War II, the traditional Muslim religious establishment in Central Asia and the Caucasus had been destroyed.[2]

These actions, coupled with an antireligious campaign, led to the eventual deprivation of the Muslim peoples of essential attributes of their cultural legacy and barred communication with the rest of the Muslim world. The situation was aggravated in the late 1920s when Soviet Muslims were forced to adopt the Latin alphabet, which was then replaced in the late 1930s with the Cyrillic alphabet. Manifested in the latter change was an increased effort by the Bolshevik leaders to facilitate the process of Russification in the regions of the Soviet Union inhabited by the Muslim peoples.

For several centuries, starting with the conquest of Kazan, Russian rulers made numerous attempts to convert their Muslim subjects to Christianity but did not try to Russify them. Their Bolshevik successors tried not only to convert all Soviet peoples to the Communist "religion" but also to forge a new national entity into which Muslim peoples, equipped with the Russian language as their second mother tongue, would be included. Under Stalin, given that Great Russian nationalism became one of the principal driving forces of the society, the internationalist ideology directed toward creating a genuine *Homo Sovieticus* was used as a suitable tool for Russification. To facilitate this process, Soviet propaganda encouraged marriages between Russians and non-Russians, under the assumption that the children would be more likely to adopt the Russian identity if one parent was Russian.

After Stalin, the Communist regime intensified its Russification policy. Under Khrushchev, the 22nd Congress of the Soviet Communist party advanced a radical concept of "fusion" of the Soviet peoples, implying their biological merger and homogenization. At the 26th Party Congress, in 1981, Brezhnev urged in his speech that the linguistic and cultural needs of migrant workers should be properly met. However, from other statements in the same speech it became clear that he was encouraging the migration of Muslim workers from Central Asia and the Transcaucasus to the Russian Federation for the purpose of assimilation.[3]

By the time of perestroika, the nationality policy of the Soviet Communist party had undergone considerable changes. In the 1920s, Stalin and his allies

> grasped that the minority intelligentsia, which occupied leading roles in the republics, constituted an unreliable and threatening potential for the future. Their very existence along with the fact that the regime lacked support from the

masses threatened the future of the Communist Party. To defuse the unrest and mollify the intelligentsia it was necessary to make concessions in language policy and nativization of the *apparatus* of the republics. This nativization would provide the means for promoting workers, who were less educated and more dependent upon Stalin's machine, into leadership roles where they could then supplant the more obstreperous intelligentsia. Referring to the promotion of new Marxist cadres, Stalin observed that the Party had to struggle on two fronts, against the left and the right. Until then the Central Committee had dealt only with organizational leaders and relatively loyal elements. Now the local parties themselves had to discover the best means of converting local cadres into a mass Party. Party organs had to draw closer to the masses by speaking their languages and by purging chauvinists who opposed them. Linguistic equality and nativization were essential if strife in the parties of Kazakhstan, Tatarstan, and Bahkiria was to be averted.[4]

In addition, the Russians living in the Muslim republics were required to learn native languages.

Now, in the early 1990s, the subsequent policy of Russification, based on the concepts of "drawing together," "rapprochement," "full unity," "merger," and "fusion" of the nations, as well as the suggestion that the study of local tongues by Russians living amidst Muslims should be optional, has led to flagrant linguistic asymmetry. At present only tiny groups of Russians living in a Muslim environment (for example, 0.9 percent of Russians living in Kazakhstan) claim to have fluency in the native language, whereas, for example, the number of Tatars declaring the language of their nationality as their mother tongue has been gradually decreasing, and cases of total psychological assimilation (emotional self-identification with Russians) are common. As the result of increasing urbanization, some ethnic groups are decidedly doomed to steady annihilation.

Many scholars, observers, and political analysts have indicated a continuity between the policy of Russification and the great power ideology of the tsarist regime. As early expectations of a worldwide proletarian revolution faded, Soviet Communism became a respectable legitimization for the Soviet system. This system was seen as a reconstituted version of the prerevolutionary Russian empire. The old utopian idea of Russia as the Third Rome may be paralleled with the "scientifically sanctioned" concept of Soviet power as "the Fatherland of Communism," historically predestined to world leadership. Under the guise of social justice and an internationalist ideology, Communist rulers carried out policies that were purely imperialistic. Expansionism, strict centralization of economic, political, and ideological life, dena-tionalization and assimilation of non-Russian peoples, domination of ethnic Russians in the Soviet political system, implementation of Rus-sian nationalism as a way to secure popular support, physical extermi-nation and deportation of thousands and thousands of "nationals," a mystical fear of the increasing Muslim population, and the colonial character of their republics' economy are visible manifestations of asser-tive Russian nationalism and great power ideology.

The most characteristic feature of this policy, however, was that it provided no material benefits for the Russian masses. As a result, many Russians expressed their displeasure with the fact that their republic subsidized the economies of the Muslim republics. These republics, on the other hand, complained that Russia plundered their natural re-sources. The real control of the Soviet empire was in the hands of the Kremlin, not the Russian people.

Great Power Ideology after the Soviet Collapse

The implicit great power ideology underlying the policies of Moscow toward Muslim nations became explicit during the period of perestroika, glasnost, and new political thinking. New Soviet leaders abandoned the principle of proletarian internationalism and replaced it with the prin-ciples of democracy and human rights. However, the great power ideol-ogy remained unchanged. Moscow exerted every effort to hinder all attempts of the non-Russian republics to exercise their right to self-determination. In particular, Soviet policymakers have interpreted the principle of democracy as implying the minority's subordination to the majority. These policymakers also carried out an all-union referendum to ascertain the attitude of Soviet citizens toward the further existence of the USSR as an integral entity. The majority of respondents sup-ported the idea of its indivisibility and thereby made the right of na-tions to self-determination null and void.

The dissolution of the Soviet Union after the failure of a coup or-ganized by a clique of ardent defenders of the Soviet Empire in August 1991 compelled the advocates of great power ideology to revise their attitude toward democracy. Given the fact that Russians make up the overwhelming majority of the population of the Russian Federation, the above-mentioned understanding of democracy was retained in order to prevent the breakaway of former autonomous republics from Russia. But, since Russians constitute a minority in the republics of the former Soviet Union, human rights have been interpreted by writers by placing them in opposition to the rights of nations.

Such opposition is expressed, for instance, in an article published in an issue of *Moscow News*, a weekly noted for its democratic orientation. According to the article's author, a great deal of "the highly acute problems" now arising in the country is the result of the "pleasure" the independent republics of the former Soviet Union experience from "having got rid of the center." In this context he complains about the fact that too many people underestimate the liberal conception of democracy as "recognition of the individual's inalienable rights over the prerogatives of 'ethnos' and any other 'communal body.'"[5] But in actuality, when the Russian media made allegations about "Russian honor and dignity" being jeopardized they were referring only to the fact that in the non-Russian republics Russians are compelled to learn the indigenous language.

The policies and attitudes of Russian leaders toward non-Russian nations and states of the CIS are highly inconsistent. At times they reassert the principle of their territorial integrity, and at other times they lay claim to the Crimea, an integral part of the Ukrainian republic. First they promise the deported Germans that they will restore their autonomous republic, then they declare that the republic may be reestablished, provided that the Germans constitute no less than 90 percent of its population (it should be noted that the native population in Russia's autonomous republics constitutes, as a rule, an ethnic minority). At one moment they assure that every nation may enjoy as much independence as it can bear or digest, at another they declare that Russia is one indivisible whole.

The incoherence of the actions and attitudes of the Russian leadership can easily be explained by the lack of unanimity inside the Russian White House. Outside the White House this state of affairs may be paralleled with controversies among spokesmen of various political and ideological trends, observers, and other opinionmakers.

One trend is represented by politicians, publicists, writers, and military figures who strive for the restoration of the former empire. This trend brings together hard-line advocates of Russian nationalism and great power ideology, including neo-Communist and neo-Fascist elements, otherwise known as Reds and Browns.

The opposite trend is represented by intellectuals of genuine democratic orientation who criticize the great power ideology of the Russian nationalists as a manifestation of political megalomania. In their opinion, a "normal great power" is primarily a rich and democratic state, not simply a state endowed with vast territory, densely populated, and possessing military power and cultural traditions. The United Kingdom is a model of such a "normal great power."[6]

The third trend represents an opinion fairly similar to the position of the present-day Russian leadership, and it considers the Russian Federation the only successor to the collapsed empire. A spokesman of this opinion also holds the United Kingdom as an example, but in quite a different context. He argues that "Britain managed not only to preserve, but even strengthened its influence over countries making up the former British Empire," as the result of its neocolonialist policy toward them.

> The term *neocolonialism*, unless used for vulgar propagandist purposes, merely amounts to an accurate description of the present-day relations between strong and weak countries. The biological uniformity—the strong subordinates the weak—is still valid in world politics with the inexorability of world gravitational laws. The novelty of this colonialism consists in the fact that the forms and methods of subordination have been changed: bayonets and gunboats have given way to loans, custom tariffs and immigration quotas. It has been found that in the 20th century these means are more effective than any others."[7]

The author of these words believes that newly independent republics, unable to become true sovereign states, must enter Russia's sphere of attraction. The Muslim republics are advised to satisfy the Russian economy's perpetual love for their warm ports, oil deposits, and cotton. "Russia's dominance is an inevitability. The whole question is at what price. One can't become a superpower using the methods of the tsarist or Communist regime. Those times are over! We thus need to learn civilized and neocolonialist ways of influencing others. Russia will become the center of a colonial empire."[8]

These ideas may be said to conform to superpatriotic feelings experienced and/or exploited by the majority of the members of the Russian Supreme Soviet, as well as by some personalities surrounding President Yeltsin. The then–vice president Rutskoy, one of the prominent heroes of the Afghan War, has often been characterized as a personification of assertive Russian patriotism and great power ideology.

> With vigour far exceeding competence, Rutskoy lashed out at the liberal intelligentsia for their indifference toward the disintegration of the USSR, little suspecting that the people he refers to, with some irony, as the "Soviet nation" have always been against the empire and for the right to self-determination. He referred to the lawfully elected presidents as "new gang leaders," which isn't by any stretch of the imagination a friendly reference. . . . Ruskoi crudely charged the government with the economic genocide of the Russian people.[9]

Rutskoy's practical moves vis-à-vis the Chechen Republic and the Republic of Moldova was in full accordance with his above-mentioned description of the heads of the non-Russian sovereign states of the CIS.

It is almost impossible to imagine manifestations of great power ideology as not linked with one form or another of xenophobia. For decades the latter was associated with the concept of the "capitalist encirclement"; later it expressed itself as overt anti-Semitism and in a campaign against imaginary supporters of "Russophobia." For some time now, after the breakup of the Soviet Union, it has involved Islamophobia and the intimidation of people with tales about the growing threat of Islamic fundamentalism allegedly spreading throughout Central Asia, Kazakhstan, the Caucasus, and Azerbaijan.

In the Russian media, Islamic fundamentalism has become a sheer bugaboo, the term "fundamentalism" always remaining vague and obscure not only for readers, but, most likely, for the writers using it. True, some articles on recent developments in the Muslim world outside the CIS can provide us with certain information on the subject. We are told, for instance, that Algerian fundamentalists from the Islamic Salvation Front (FIS) advocate the remaking of society based on Islamic law and the ensuring of the purity of Islamic thought (other points of their program are not peculiar to Islam or have nothing to do with it, aiming at reorganization of the country's parliament and local governments, restoring land to its true owners, encouragement of foreign investments, and so on). Still, some questions arise. For example, is there in any CIS member state a single party whose program targets the creation of a state entirely based on *Shari'a* as the only source of legislation? And can we consider the traditionalist Islamic Renaissance party, whose activity is concentrated in the Republic of Tajikistan, as a true fundamentalist organization aspiring for the preservation of Islamic thought in its initial purity? (Keeping in mind, of course, that its leaders take pride in Islam as the only religion that can conserve the spirit of Plato's and Aristotle's teachings.)

Cock-and-bull stories concerning the threat of Islamic fundamentalism spreading in the southern republics of the CIS under the influence of Iran are surely addressed to an unsophisticated and naive audience. When U.S. Secretary of State James Baker toured Central Asia in February 1992 to visit Tajikistan, Turkmenistan, and Uzbekistan, he discovered that there were no Irans in the making there. Rather than spreading an anti-Western fundamentalist revolution, these three republics were "interested primarily in developing their backward economies."[10]

The same can be said about the situation in Azerbaijan. It has been alleged that the country is threatened by both Islamic fundamentalism and the restoration of pan-Turkism. Valter Shonia, Russia's ambassador to Baku, said recently:

> The fears regarding the restoration of pan-Turkism as I, an expert in Turkic studies, see them are based not so much on facts as on inference deduction. . . . Today it is just as difficult to imagine the revival of pan-Turkism as, say, the revival of pan-Slavism. Turkic-speaking countries of the former Soviet Union are looking for new partners enjoying equal rights, but not new suzerains. This is by no means national selfishness but normal cooperation which exists for their mutual benefit.
>
> Almost the same can be said regarding Islamic fundamentalism in Azerbaijan. It boasts orthodox Muslims who deserve every respect. Islamic fundamentalism is politics based on Islam. But this is something I did not notice in Azerbaijan and consider it quite inappropriate to make a good deal about it. I also disagree with statements that Iran is allegedly concerned about exporting Islam to Azerbaijan.[11]

It is true that many of the presidents from the Muslim republics are former Communist leaders and have little interest in strengthening political Islam in their countries. But one must not exaggerate its role in the grass roots movements either. There are reasons to doubt that even the popularity of the Islamic-oriented forces of Tajikistan compared to that of the former Communist leaders should be considered as an unqualified endorsement of their quasifundamentalist program on the part of the Muslim masses. Those oppositional forces may be viewed as incidental beneficiaries of antiregime sentiments (this observation is also applicable to the FIS in Algeria). In any case, fears that some extremist kind of Islam may dominate politics in the Muslim republics of the CIS have yet to materialize.

These fears have partly originated due to the fact that substantial differences in cultural situations and in interconfessional relations in the former Soviet Muslim republics and in their neighboring countries to the south have been neglected. The integration of the present-day CIS member-states into the Russian-dominated Soviet system produced two factors that have diminished the possibility of an aggressive anti-Western Islamic fundamentalism surfacing in Central Asia. First, the social changes that the Soviet Muslim republics have undergone in the past seven decades have created social circumstances conducive to their cultural renaissance and modernization. Industrialization, urbanization, and increasing literacy (now Soviet Muslims are almost 100 percent literate, an exception to any other Muslim nation in the world) have contributed to an increase in a universalistic worldview, alien to any kind of religious fanaticism. Second, as a corollary to cultural development and due to longstanding coexistence with Russians and other Europeans in their own land, Soviet Muslims, as a rule, have not nurtured hostility toward them in everyday life. The Muslim people understand that it was not ordinary Russians who oppressed and exploited them and that the Russians were not treated any better than other ethnic groups. That is why, in contrast to the "classical" situation of colonized countries, there have been no socioeconomic grounds for interconfessional conflicts in the area in question that could propel the rise and spread of extremist Islamic fundamentalism. As for the departure of Russians from the southern republics after the collapse of the USSR, those people left for Russia mainly to avoid troubles caused by local conflicts among Muslims themselves and in the absence of clear prospects, but not because of any pressure on the part of the native population.

As stated above, predictions concerning the forthcoming triumph of Islamic fundamentalism, implying the possibility of a north-south confrontation, have not come true. Moscow, for its part, declared that Russia had resolutely abandoned the imperial ambitions held by the Soviet Union. Yet, the national liberation movement of Muslim peoples continued. They considered the Russian Federation to be an indivisible whole for the advocates of great power ideology and an empire, like that of the Soviet Union.

In August 1991 the Supreme Soviet of Tatarstan, a republic situated on the middle Volga River, declared its sovereignty. That was done after President Yeltsin had made his famous statement in Tatarstan's capital, Kazan: "Take as much sovereignty as you can cope with." But when the leaders of Tatarstan demonstrated their resoluteness to translate their declaration into reality, some supporters of the idea of Russia's indivisibility demanded that a referendum on sovereignty be held in the republic, taking into account that out of about 3.7 million of the republic's population only 1.8 million are Tatars, the rest being made up of Russians (1.6 million) and of various other nationalities (the total number of Tatars in the republics of the former USSR amounts to about 7 million, out of which nearly 5.5 million live in the Russian Federation).

The referendum was held on 21 March 1992. The majority of the republic's population said yes in response to the question put to the vote: "Do you agree that the Republic of Tatarstan is a sovereign state, a subject of international law whose relations with the Russian Federation and the other republics and states are based on equal treaties?" The battle for independence was nominally won, but the victory was not easy. The referendum was held in spite of Moscow's campaign to misrepresent it and attempts to intimidate the voters and the people of Tatarstan in general. On the eve of the referendum, for instance, the Constitutional Court of Russia declared the referendum anticonstitutional, and Tatarstan's procurator demanded that the head of the Central Electoral Commission close the commission and its offices in the towns and villages. It is noteworthy that after the referendum some advocates of great power ideology argued that the referendum as such cannot express the will of the people, or, if it does, the tyranny of the people it sanctifies is no better than the tyranny of the dictators.

The referendum held in Tatarstan encouraged its neighbor, the Republic of Bashkortostan, to follow suit. Taking into consideration Tatarstan's experience, the Supreme Soviet of Bashkortostan suspended, on the territory of its republic, the implementation of the Russian Constitutional Court's decisions until a bilateral agreement on relations between the Russian Federation and the Republic of Bashkortostan had been signed.

The Tatarstan and Bashkortostan governments said their republics would not leave Russia (the activists of the Tatar national movement, for their part, argued that Tatarstan was not leaving Russia because it never joined Russia—it was conquered by Ivan the Terrible). Nevertheless, in both republics, "Russian-speaking" communities formed associations "to defend their rights and to offset the actions of the national separatists."

The so-called "separatist actions" of Tatarstan and Bashkortostan corresponded to the International Covenant on Economic, Social and Cultural Rights signed by the USSR in 1966 and to the Concluding Act of the Declaration on Security and Cooperation in Europe adopted in Helsinki in 1975. They were also confirmed by the countries undersigning the Vienna Document in 1989. With this fact taken into account, in the campaign against the two republics' sovereignty emphasis was placed on the alleged possibility of jeopardizing the rights of the "Russian-speaking" communities living in these republics. Once again human rights were placed in opposition to the right of nations and peoples to self-determination.

A question arises: Is it correct to oppose human rights to the right of nations and peoples to self-determination? This problem has been discussed in the UN. In the course of preparing the drafts of the International Covenants on Human Rights in 1952, it was stressed that the right of nations and peoples to self-determination was essential for the enjoyment of all other human rights because it affected every individual and was the natural corollary of the principle of individual freedom and dignity. And in resolution 637 A (VII) of 16 December 1952 the General Assembly recognized that "the right of peoples and nations to self-determination is a prerequisite to the full enjoyment of all fundamental human rights." In the same resolution, it was stated that all members of the UN should facilitate the exercise of this right by peoples "according to the principles and spirit of the Charter of the United Nations in regard to each Territory and to the freely expressed wishes of the peoples concerned, the wishes of the people being ascertained through plebiscites or other recognized democratic means."[12]

The great defender of human rights A. Sakharov, speaking about the Union Treaty, suggested the introduction of flexible membership, whereby subjects of the Federation delegate a range of powers to the federal center. The "separatist actions" of Tatarstan and Bashkortostan are in full accordance with this suggestion of the Russian humanist, as well as with the principles of international law.

Moscow has recognized the independence of the Central Asian and other former republics of the Soviet Union. But a double standard outside Russia and inside Russia is not permissible. If, in accordance with international standards, we recognize the right of nations to self-determination, we also must recognize it inside Russia.

The use of human rights slogans by the advocates of great power ideology is very dangerous, particularly when those advocates are military figures. The developments in Moldova have demonstrated to what tragedy the defense of "honor and dignity of Russians" in sovereign republics can lead. And it is quite natural that the Democratic Congress of the republics of Central Asia and Kazakhstan, held in Bishkek, Kyrgyzstan, on 30–31 May 1992, condemned the developments in Moldova as an open interference by Russia in the internal affairs of that republic.

The prospects for great power ideology in the near future cannot be optimistic. All depends on the political course chosen by the Russian government. Meanwhile, all groupings of the present-day Russian Supreme Soviet are overtly or covertly trying to exploit the "Russian idea," that is, supporting the same great power ideology. Besides "patriots" and Communists, who formed an explosive national-socialist mixture, other movements are calling a crusade under the same "patriotic" banner and are forming paramilitary troops. They include, among others, Pamyat's tough guys, National Republican party "volunteers," the Russian Communist Workers' party, "workers' troops," and the Russian Popular Assembly of Cossacks.

Finally, at the beginning of 1993 two political congresses were convened almost simultaneously. One of these, held in St. Petersburg, proclaimed the establishment of a party of Russian Fascists. The other, held in the environs of Moscow, proclaimed the foundation of a united party of Russian Communists. Reds and Browns have redoubled their efforts to attain their political ambitions by reaching positions of power through legal means.

While all these facts may appear insignificant, they reflect the increasing impact of Russian nationalism and great power ideology on Russia's political life. This may be perceived in Russian policymakers' moves and positions toward political developments that concern Muslim peoples, including events in the Chechen Republic, Tatarstan, and the former Yugoslavia.

The fate of the great power ideology depends on the destiny of Russian democracy, and on the reforms it is trying to realize. Thus far, however, its ability to influence the federal legislative and executive bodies' activities has been substantially limited.

1. M. Sultan Galiev, "Kto Ya?" [Who am I?] *Tatarstan*, no. 1 (1991): 51–52.

2. A. Bennigsen, P.B. Henze, G.K. Tanham, and S.E. Wimbush, "The Soviet Islamic Establishment as a Strategic Instrument," in *Soviet Strategy and Islam*, ed. A. Bennigsen, P.B. Henze, G.K. Tanham, S.E. Wimbush, and S. Enders (New York: St. Martin's Press, 1989), 22.

3. See J.B. Dunlop, "Language, Culture, Religion, and National Awareness," in *The Last Empire: Nationality and the Soviet Future*, ed. R. Conquest (Stanford: Hoover Institution Press, 1986), 265–89; M. Agyrsky, "Soviet Communism and Russian Nationalism: Amalgamation or Conflict?" in *The Soviet Union and the Challenge of the Future*, vol. 3: *Ideology, Culture and Nationality*, ed. A. Shtromas and M.A. Kaplan (New York: Paragon House, 1989), 139–60.

4. S. Blank, "Stalin's First Victim: The Trial of Sultan Galiev," *Russian History/Histoire Russe* 17, no. 2 (Summer 1990): 174.

5. A. Rubtsov, "Legendy i Mify Novogo Sovka" [The new Sovok's legends and myths], *Moskovskiye Novosti*, no. 4 (1992): 18.

6. M. Pavlova-Silvanskaya "U Rossiyi Yest' Shans Ostat'sya Valikoy Derzhavoy" [Russia has a chance of remaining a great power], *Izvestiya*, 21 February 1992, p. 3.

7. M. Shevelev, "Za Nashu i Vashu Metropoliyu" [For a mother-country of ours and yours], *Moskovskiye Novosti*, no. 4 (1992): 8.

8. Ibid.

9. L. Ovrutsky, "Ruskoism" *Moscow News*, no. 12 (1992): 7.

10. R. S. Greenberger, "Baker Tours Central Asia Seeking Promises and Ties," *Wall Street Journal Europe*, 14–15 February 1992, p. 12.

11. V. Shonia, "Azerbaijan: Its Relations with Russia Are Overlasting," *Moscow News*, no. 24 (1992): 5.

12. *United Nations Actions in the Field of Human Rights*, vol. 35 (New York: United Nations, 1989), 16.

13

Central Asia and the Middle East

The Emerging Links

Anthony Hyman

The Muslim republics of Central Asia, long artificially isolated under Russian and Soviet rule, are now rediscovering their Muslim neighbors and the wider Muslim world of which they are a part. Rivalry for influence and control over Central Asia and the Caucasus was strong four centuries ago between the two great Middle Eastern empires of the time, Saffavid Persia and Ottoman Turkey, before the rise of Russian and British power. In the 1990s competition for influence is much more open.

Under Soviet rule, links between the Central Asian republics and the Middle East were extremely limited and carefully controlled from Moscow. Imam al-Bukhari Islamic Institute in Tashkent (founded in 1971) was the main center of training for Muslim clergy in the USSR, and naturally had links with the outside Muslim world. Most of its teachers studied at Al-Azhar in Egypt or in Syria, Jordan, Libya, or Morocco. The size of the official *muftiate* (spiritual directorate) in the USSR, however, remained extremely small, and its influence in society was certainly restricted.

Islam was not an important component of Soviet Middle East policy under Stalin or in the period from 1955 to 1967, but gradually more stress began to be placed on Islam.[1] In practice, the official Soviet Islamic establishment during the Brezhnev era was coopted, becoming active in foreign travel, hosting delegations from foreign Muslim lands, and holding international conferences in Tashkent and other cities. One analysis of activities by Soviet front organizations, the Communist party, and government organizations with Middle Eastern countries in the 1970s concluded that Algeria, Iraq, Syria, Turkey, Jordan, and Egypt were most favored targets in what has been described as "a coherent and powerful Islamic strategy."[2]

To a lesser degree, Libya, Saudi Arabia, South Yemen, and Morocco were also wooed. Alone among Arab states, Libya even maintained a consulate in Tashkent, the capital of Uzbekistan, though its precise function was far from clear, since Libya had and has minimal interests in Central Asia beyond a small number of students in institutes in Tashkent.

Military links between the USSR and the Middle East had a small but significant Central Asian component in personnel, which has been often overlooked. According to the Military Balance (1982–83) of the International Institute for Strategic Studies, Soviet advisers and troop deployments in the Middle East were composed of the following: Libya, 1,750; South Yemen, 1,500; North Yemen, 500; Syria, 2,500; and Iraq, 1,000. In Afghanistan 95,000 Soviet troops—some of them Muslims— were serving during most of the decade, together with an array of translators and specialists, many of them drawn from Uzbekistan and Tajikistan.

Many of the Arabic and Persian interpreters attached to Soviet military units in these countries were Muslims from the Central Asian republics, often students of oriental faculties at Tashkent and other universities of the USSR. However, their exposure to Arab societies (typically for periods of two years) had little impact. Rather few of the many hundreds of young men working as interpreters continued after military service in this field. They saved money from their earnings and went on to other things. Only now, after independence and the opening up to private trade, are quite a few Arabic speakers in the republics finding jobs relevant to their experience.

For the purposes of this analysis, Pakistan and Afghanistan will be treated as a special part of the Middle East. Pakistan's links with the Gulf Cooperation Council states in particular (especially in military and manpower areas) have become close since the early 1970s. The legacy of involvement of key Middle East states such as Iran, Saudi Arabia, and Egypt in Afghanistan during the Soviet intervention and after the collapse of the USSR, in addition to the ongoing crisis in the Afghan-Tajik border, will inevitably link Afghanistan to the dynamics of Central Asian-Middle East relations. Likewise, Kazakhstan will be included in the Central Asia region, though according to some definitions (and standard Russian terminology) Kazakhstan is a separate region and distinct from "Srednyaya Aziya" (Middle Asia). The Kazakhs are a Turkic people related to those of the four Central Asian republics proper, sharing many features of history, society, and economy, though the recent mass settlement of Europeans distinguishes it, and the sheer size of Kazakhstan dwarfs the rest of Central Asia.

Some of the transborder ethnic, tribal, or national connections of Central Asia with the Middle East are important. The Kurdish communities of the former Soviet Union, though relatively small and scattered across Central Asia and the Transcaucasus, are nonetheless well known to the Kurds of the Middle East, though they are settled far from the Kurdish heartlands. There is a large Turkmen minority in Iraq that settled, like the Kurds, in the northern border areas until they were forcibly resettled by the Baghdad government.

In Turkey there are large Turkic migrant communities originally from Central Asia and the Caucasus (notably Daghestan). Many of those whose ancestors fled as refugees from Russian rule during the nineteenth century or in the 1920s have become assimilated into the host society, but others retain interest in and sympathy with their respective homelands, the various former Soviet republics.

The same is true of Turkic and Daghestani Muslim communities settled in Saudi Arabia, Jordan, and Egypt. Entrepreneurial members of these emigrant communities, often of the third or fourth generation, are currently engaged in starting joint ventures or trading with Central Asia. In Uzbekistan, for example, numerous visitors of this category from Saudi Arabia as well as Turkey have come in recent years to visit Tashkent, Fergana, and other areas from which their families originated.

As for the Gulf states, they had very restricted contacts with the republics of Central Asia, mostly indirect in the religious-cultural field. Only a tiny number of officially selected Muslims from Soviet Central Asia were permitted to go as pilgrims on the annual hajj. Both Saudi Arabia and Kuwait were forced to rely on Muslim organizations and institutions based in India, Pakistan, and other countries in the 1970s to channel any help. Only at the end of the 1980s, and notably after de facto independence at the end of 1991, did this situation change. The Saudi Foreign Minister Prince Saud Al-Faisal made the first official visit to four Muslim republics (Azerbaijan, Uzbekistan, Turkmenistan, and Tajikistan), three in Central Asia, in February 1992.

In the field of cultural and religious relations, Saudi Arabia has become active. Rather modest (but certainly large in local terms, given the devalued ruble currency) financial help has been given by Gulf countries for building new mosques and restoring old buildings as mosques and *madrassas* (theological colleges) together with establishing Muslim missions in the cities. Help in enabling Muslims from Central Asia to perform the hajj in much larger numbers has come from Saudi Arabia, together with gifts of copies of the Koran for distribution through the muftiates.

Only small numbers of Saudi citizens are active in this "missionary" field in Central Asia, though considerable funding is being given by Saudi Arabia. Reliance is being placed in Islamic preachers and scholars from al-Azhar and other Muslim centers in Egypt. In the terse words of a critical Egyptian scholar, "it is a case of Saudi money hiring Egyptian brains."

With the relaxation of religious freedoms in the former USSR from the mid-1980s, a process that amounts to an Islamic revival began in the Muslim republics, along with a virtual rediscovery of Islam after decades of Communist repression and persecution. This has served as a major stimulus to Saudi sponsorship of Islamic missions for the Central Asian republics. Like the rest of the USSR, they had been effectively closed off because atheism was the official doctrine. However, a further stimulus to undertaking this religious mission has been competition with Iran. Iran, for its part, has sent numerous preachers of Islam from its religious training centers to Azerbaijan and Central Asia in recent years to preach in the various republics.

Frequent media speculation about the attraction of the Turkish, Korean, or Iranian models of society and economy for contemporary Central Asia tends to overlook one basic point. The ruling elites are prepared to look anywhere and everywhere for guidance and help in solving their severe problems of development. They are by no means restricted to one country or model, let alone to societies claiming to be exemplars of Islam. In some key respects, indeed, the contemporary Iranian or Saudi Arabian models of society on offer seem remote, deficient, or even irrelevant to the secular-oriented members of the ruling elites of Central Asia. The basic orientation to building a better society in the republics is secular and modernist, with a considerable inheritance from socialist ideas of the Soviet state.

The Asian republics are naturally eager to foster contacts with other large and particularly influential states, notably Egypt. In Uzbekistan, for example, the Uzbek-Arab Friendship Society (officially promoted and with a former Soviet ambassador to various Muslim countries as its head) has been formed with the specific aim of fostering closer links with all the major Arab countries.

Semiofficial organizations of the Persian Gulf states have become active in building bilateral relations with the Central Asian republics. A number of Islamic missions and organizations of Saudi Arabia linked to the Wahhabi preaching movement have sent delegations and representatives to Central Asian capitals to assess local needs and the potential for cooperation. Gifts of printed Korans were followed by gifts of money, often small, toward construction of new mosques, which has been a notable feature of the scene since the mid-1980s in the former Soviet Union. Saudi religious organizations also gave funds for expanding madrassas and generally improving the standards of religious education in the Central Asian republics, and toward providing scholarships for study in Saudi Arabia.

The Kuwait-based "Committee for Muslims in Asia" sent missions to Tatarstan and Moscow as well as Central Asian capitals from late 1992 to assess the viability of projects. The committee offered financial help to numerous educational institutions, besides offering to sponsor students for higher studies in Arab states and to pay for translation of more than one hundred books from Arabic into Russian and other Turkic languages. Sponsorship of films about the national culture of the Uzbek and Kyrgyz people was also envisaged, with contracts signed in 1993 for four films to be made in Tashkent and Bishkek studios. The same committee was also engaged in planning to open specialized institutes for learning foreign languages (Arabic, English, German, and French) in various cities of Central Asia.[3]

It should be pointed out that Islamic influences are by no means having it all their own way in Central Asia. In stressing here the Middle Eastern and Asian dimensions, we should certainly not lose sight of a strong Central Asian interest in the West, evidenced at a popular level in choice of sweatshirts and the universal pop culture of youth. At the official level, Western interest can be seen in the embassies established in the main Central Asian capitals by the United States, Germany, France, Italy, and Britain.

Central Asian Republics and Their Muslim Neighbors

Muslim states are among the most eager to develop their relations with the former USSR's Muslim republics. The most prominent are Iran, Turkey, Saudi Arabia, Pakistan, the Persian Gulf states, and some other Arab states. Each clearly has specific priorities and interests in Central Asia. For most, Uzbekistan and Kazakhstan, because of their large populations (twenty-one and seventeen million, respectively), sheer size, and natural resources, are the obvious prizes in terms of investment and trading of the five Central Asian republics.

Uzbekistan, the cultural heartland of Central Asia with its historic capitals Samarkand and Bukhara, has a bigger population than Turkmenistan, Tajikistan, and Kyrgyzstan combined. It ranks as one of the world's major cotton exporters and gold producers. Its gas production is considerable, though only half that of Turkmenistan. Since 1992, discoveries of large oil fields in Uzbekistan have encouraged hopes that oil and gas exports will soon prove to be a major asset.[4]

Iran is essentially concerned with fostering relations with four Muslim republics: Azerbaijan, Tajikistan, Turkmenistan, and Uzbekistan. Both for Iran and Turkey, relations with Central Asia cannot be disentangled from those with the Transcaucasus (and, arguably, with the CIS as a whole). For Iran, relations with Azerbaijan are of particular importance, being a newly independent republic of Azeri Turks who are ethnically and culturally close to those living in the adjoining Iranian provinces based on Tabriz and Ardebil. The Azeri Turks form Iran's largest national minority.

Azerbaijan lies much closer to Turkey than Central Asia, with Nakhichevan ASSR, an Azeri enclave on the border of Armenia, being the only point at which a narrow land border exists with Turkey. Like Iran, Turkey has to consider its future relations with the Transcaucasus as a whole. Both Georgia and Armenia have borders with Turkey, and irredentist claims as well as historical grievances of Armenian nationalists remain to be dealt with.

Azerbaijan also happens to be the sole former Soviet southern republic where Twelver (*imami*) Shia Muslims are in the majority, with 70 percent of its 6.5 million population. Elsewhere in the Caucasus and Central Asia, small Shia communities exist, with some 100,000 Ismailis living in the remote Badakhshan region of Tajikistan. However, the great majority of some fifty-five million Muslims in the CIS belong to the Hanafi school (*mazhaab*).[5]

A series of Iranian agreements signed with Azerbaijan in 1992 and 1993 include joint ventures and joint exploitation of rich oil and gas deposits in the Caspian Sea region. Cultural-religious links include training in Iran's madrassas for Azeri clerical students. Twelver Shia Muslims are in the majority in Azerbaijan, unlike all the other republics. There has been considerable wariness in Tehran over the rapprochement between Tabriz and Baku, capitals of the two halves of Azerbaijan, which went their separate ways after Russia took Baku in

1806. However faint it is at present, the prospect of Azeri Turkish irredentism in the form of a movement to unite the two parts of Azerbaijan into one independent state based on the Caspian must be alarming to Tehran.

Tajikistan has much less to offer Iran in economic terms, being far poorer in natural resources than either Azerbaijan or Turkmenistan. But Iranian influence and prestige is undeniably high in Tajikistan, helped by the Tajiks being Persian speakers and looking to Iran in cultural matters even more than the other peoples of Central Asia. The ideal of creating an Islamic republic in Tajikistan won some popular backing before setbacks in the civil war that began in April 1992. However, it is clearly questionable how far most Tajiks understand what is implied by the Iranian postrevolutionary model of society, or necessarily want to see this implemented in Tajikistan.

Rather than Iran, it is Turkey's image that is more potent for all the Turkic-speaking peoples of Central Asia. A more developed, populous country than any of them are or can hope to be in the medium term, Turkey has developed a strong industrial base. Turkish managerial expertise and industrial know-how are valued. Turkey also represents other things desired by many in Central Asia—a secular society along with a successful market economy. As a member of NATO and the Council of Europe and a big trading partner with the European Community (EC) states, Turkey may be able to help the Asian republics obtain concessional terms of trade with the EC. So at least it is hoped in the Central Asian capitals.

After decades of neglect, the emphasis on developments in Central Asia has had definite political repercussions in Turkey, too, resulting in a revival of pan-Turkic ideas and hopes. Some ultranationalist circles in Turkey see their country as the obvious patron and champion of all the Turkic-speaking peoples in the vast region stretching from Azerbaijan to Xinjiang in China.

Formation of the Economic Cooperation Organization

Ten countries are linked in the Economic Cooperation Organization (ECO), enlarged last year by Iran, Turkey, and Pakistan to take in five Muslim republics of the CIS as well as Afghanistan, with a combined population of over sixty-five million people. Having a total population of some three hundred million, the ECO countries have considerable

economic potential that can be better exploited by their close cooperation.

Is this the first stage toward creating an "Islamic Common Market"?
Is it a contemporary pan-Islamic initiative, or rather a purely commer-
cial and economic bloc of regional states? Such questions are natural,
but the answers depend very much on the ideological perspectives of
the inquirer. Official circles in Iran and Turkey are poles apart on this,
while Pakistan stands somewhere in between.[6] As for the republics of
Central Asia, none of the governments desire their shared Muslim religion to intrude as a factor in their relations with neighbors.

It is clear that a contest for influence is going on between Iran,
Turkey, and Pakistan in spite of their being partners in ECO. Turkey
has deliberately emphasized all along that this is a secular initiative,
but one that has political significance for the future. Nationalist circles
in Turkey take great pride in Ankara's efforts to woo the Turks of Central Asia, efforts that include satellite TV and alphabet reforms away
from Cyrillic to Latin, like Turkey.

Pan-Turkic sympathies exist throughout Central Asia, but their political influence is uncertain. "Anadoly is the motherland for us, while
Kazakhstan is the land of our ancestors," claimed Turgut Ozal, the late
president of Turkey, in a widely quoted speech during his second and,
as it turned out, final official visit to Kazakhstan in April 1993.

Turkey is currently training over one thousand students from Kazakhstan alone in its universities in a program that takes in students at
all grades from six republics. A total of ten thousand students were reportedly studying in Turkey at the beginning of 1993. In the fields of
telephone communications, infrastructure, transport, and technical
training, besides general trading, Turkish business interests are extremely active.

In areas requiring larger-scale investment, though, and notably in the
gas and oil sectors, Turkish companies have found it difficult or impossible to compete. Instead, it is the large Western multinationals that
are making the run. Chevron, British Gas, Agip, Lonhro, and Mercedes
Benz are among big companies prominent in joint ventures, along with
those of South Korea and China.

In the cultural field, Turkish help and advice is much appreciated.
For substituting the Cyrillic script in which the various Central Asian
languages are written, the choice lies with either the Arabic or Latin
alphabets. The Cyrillic alphabet, along with the Russian language, is

now well established, effectively the sole lingua franca.[7] If Cyrillic is to be abandoned, the modified Latin alphabet system adopted by Turkey under Kamal Ataturk appears to be a frontrunner. For many Central Asian politicians and the intelligentsia, the Latin alphabet is the obvious choice, bringing them out of the Russian sphere of cultural influence and closer to Turkey as well as the West. In September 1991 the Turkish Standards Institute began a series of meetings intended to coordinate work on agreeing on a common alphabet for all the Turkic-speaking nationalities.

The Arabic script was in use throughout Central Asia until half a century ago. Because earlier literature was in Arabic script, it has a certain prestige and attraction. This helped push Tajikistan to adopt the Arabic alphabet in 1992 for Tajiki, its form of Persian, akin to the national language of Iran. Yet realistically, the Arabic alphabet cannot compare with the allure of the Latin alphabet used for English, German, and all the other major European languages, in addition to modern Turkish. In October 1993 Uzbekistan followed Azerbaijan in adopting a Latin alphabet similar to that used in Turkey. The transition would be a gradual one, with Cyrillic due to be phased out by the year 2000.

This enlarged regional grouping of the Muslim republics of the former Soviet Union with their neighbors Iran, Turkey, Pakistan, and Afghanistan has far-reaching geopolitical implications. The four Central Asian republics, together with Kazakhstan, Azerbaijan, and Afghanistan, formally joined ECO in November 1992. ECO had been dormant, originally set up as the economic (specifically development-oriented) counterpart of the Central Treaty Organization (CENTO), the military grouping of conservative, pro-Western Middle Eastern states.

There is an obvious disparity between the boundless ambitions of the leading states in ECO and practical limitations of finance and technology. ECO will not provide instant riches or immediate benefits for the neighbors, but if illusions are shed solid progress and mutual benefits will eventually flow from it. A new Investment Development Bank for ECO is intended to fund joint projects, yet the bank's capital of $400 million is tiny in comparison to the republics' needs. The big potential sources of foreign investment are in Japan and the Far East, the West, and the Gulf Arab states.

The formation of an Asian "Common Market" in which Iran would have predominant influence over weaker or poorer neighbor states such as Afghanistan and Pakistan was the goal of the late shah of Iran.

Even though its economy is stagnant, Iran still has more hard currency available than its partners because of its earnings from oil and gas exports. Iran's influence in Turkmenistan has been increased by its geographic position, offering an alternative to reliance for trade routes on Russia and the increasingly problematic railway/port routes through the Transcaucasus.

Iran can help by providing alternative routes for foreign trade for Azerbaijan, Turkmenistan, and the other landlocked Central Asian republics via Iran's Gulf ports, expanding the existing railway network or, conceivably, by trucking across Iran to the Gulf coast. However, the formidable costs of building a gas pipeline from Turkmenistan would be prohibitive in Iran's difficult economic climate, and there is little sign of outside funding for this scheme.

Iran has had troubled relations, though, with both Uzbekistan and Azerbaijan, both of whose governments suspect Iran of meddling in the region. However, an official visit by Uzbekistan's President Karimov to Iran in November 1992 broke the ice and led to the signing of bilateral agreements in specific fields of banking, insurance, staging of exhibitions, and exchanges of official delegations.

The joint communiqué issued by the two presidents stressed the need for an end to fighting in both Afghanistan and Tajikistan and called for noninterference in the affairs of neighboring states, as well as respect for all existing borders. Uzbekistan, like the Kyrgyz and Turkmen governments, had often claimed that Iran was at the root of the civil war in Tajikistan and deliberately stirring up political instability in the name of Islamic revolution. But these suspicions had clearly eased by October 1993, when Iran's president, Ali Akbar Rafsanjani, visited five republics of the former Soviet Union and met with a very cordial reception.

Claims by Iranian newspapers that Tehran represents "a second home" for the leaders of the former Soviet Muslim republics are little more than flowery compliments. Moscow remains more familiar, and Istanbul certainly much more alluring, than Tehran to all the Central Asian leaders.

Though Turkey itself has little hard currency available for foreign investment, its expertise in industry and manufacturing is more impressive than either Iran's or Pakistan's. In addition to Turkish credits offered for a total of $1.2 billion in 1992, many private Turkish companies are investing and trading in the region. The Turkish model of development is the common reference point. Effusive sentiments have been expressed for Turkey. Typical was Azerbaijan's Foreign Minister Tofik Gasymov, who declared in Ankara in August 1992, "Turkey is our greatest helper. We want Turkey's aid in establishing links with the world."[8]

Turkey is standing out as big brother to the smaller Turkic republics. Its Avrasia TV satellite broadcasts are watched each day by audiences throughout Central Asia and Azerbaijan. Extremist circles in Turkey dream not of mere influence but of a pan-Turkic "empire" in which Ankara would extend its power over a vast region of Central Asia. The term "New Ottomanism" has been coined to indicate the new sphere of influence, actual and potential, that the successors of the Ottoman Empire are in the process of gaining through recent years' developments not only in the former Soviet Union but also in the Balkans and in northern Iraq.

This vision, though, has no official backing in Ankara. President Turgut Ozal was quick to repudiate the claim of one of his ministers (Ercument Konukman in January 1990) that "several states in the Soviet Union and in China will be under the Turkish flag in the next century."[9] Nor are there echoes of these sentiments in the region. Nationalists in Central Asia itself are not eager to swap their Russian big brother for another from Turkey.

The sudden death of Ozal in April 1993 after his hectic tour of Central Asian capitals could well be followed by a revision of Turkey's Central Asian policy followed under this figure, who was a visionary statesman as well as a flamboyant politician. Significantly, Turkey's Prime Minister Suleyman Demirel, elected president in May 1993, recently declared: "In Central Asia we are the emissaries of Europe. We are Europeans who are taking European values to Central Asia. We want to remain Europeans." Evidently repudiating the ultranationalist vision of a Turkish "empire" in Turkestan, Demirel stated, "Pan-Turkism, the goal of uniting all Turkic-speaking nations, is Utopian."[10]

There are many grounds for thinking that the rivalry for influence between Turkey and Iran is less intense than some sensational or simplistic press reports have claimed. Turkey and Iran have shown themselves prepared to cooperate in ECO, and it should be remembered that even Iran's interest is by no means restricted to the Muslim republics of the CIS. Iran signed a trade accord worth up to $7 billion with Ukraine in January 1992, and Russia itself is a big trading partner.

Like Pakistan, Iran has pledged help in providing alternative routes for foreign trade. This is most useful for Azerbaijan and Turkmenistan, which have long land borders with Iran. Turkmenistan's big gas production needs alternative routes for exports, while freight from the other states of Central Asia as well could go via Iranian Gulf ports, using Iran's existing railway network or, conceivably, by trucking across Iran to the coast. But Iran can do little on its own without international financing to pay for building a gas pipeline and highway from Central Asia down to the Gulf.

Turkey and Iran's relations with another important neighbor, Azerbaijan, on the western side of the Caspian Sea, are also important and relevant to their policy toward Central Asia. Turkish business interests have become prominent in Azerbaijan, though the oil and gas sector is dominated by British Petroleum along with other Western multinationals.

Iran is active in the oil and gas sector, with joint developments planned in the Caspian Sea region, which it shares with Azerbaijan. And in November 1992 Iran signed a far-ranging agreement for bilateral trade and closer economic cooperation with Azerbaijan. This may help end a troubled period during which Baku blamed Tehran for supporting the Armenian side in the intractable dispute over Nagorno-Karabakh.

Expanding and improving communications between ECO member states is the agreed priority. Companies from Turkey and Pakistan are helping the Central Asian republics modernize and improve the flawed system inherited from the Soviet era. The new system via Pakistan is for an investment of $175 million. Uzbekistan, for its part, is eager to extend its communications links with Iran and wants a railway extension to connect the Central Asian rail network to Mashad in Iran's Khorasan province. Another planned route from Central Asia across Afghanistan will create a highway to Pakistan and enable surplus gas and electrical power from Central Asia to be exported to Pakistan.

Typical of the fast-changing regional scene is an air transport accord under which joint transport companies will be created. Iran leased aircraft and crews from the large fleet of Uzbekistan Hava Yollari in 1993, and regular flights between Tehran and Tashkent began early in the year. Tashkent is already linked by air to Islamabad, Karachi, Istanbul, Kabul, and other Central Asian capitals.

Pakistan, the third original member of ECO, faces formidable obstacles in developing trading links with Central Asia. Direct access by a projected highway, and possibly by completion of a railway line in the future, must be through Afghanistan's mountain terrain, and the viability of any route will be dependent on stability there.

Pakistan's Foreign Minister Momammad Siddiq Khan Kanju typified the emotional or romantic approach to Central Asia commonly seen in Pakistan when he declared, at the inaugural ceremony of the ECO Cultural Association in Islamabad in November 1992, "it is like long lost brothers meeting once again and joining in a deep embrace." Kanju declared that ECO was not complete without the Central Asian states. He chose to emphasize the common links: "Central Asia has been the main home of *all* our people and by joining with them we are reaching back to the original homeland of many amongst us."[11]

In Pakistan there is undeniable interest in developing trade, cultural, and other links with Central Asia. Many eminent families in Pakistan claim descent from ancestors in Bukhara, Fergana, and other areas of Central Asia, which makes the region more attractive, as well as exotic for having been so long restricted. Another factor is Pakistan's acute rivalry with India. The Indians already have well-established trading links as well as cultural prestige at a popular level throughout former Soviet Central Asia.

In both Pakistan and Turkey, cotton is also an important crop and export item, even though cotton growing never dominated their agriculture to the extent that it did in Turkmenistan and Uzbekistan. Not surprisingly, the first joint venture registered in Uzbekistan is by a Turkish company active in the cotton sector. Pakistani and Turkish entrepreneurs—if they are willing to risk capital—are well placed to help develop weak textile manufacturing industries. For many foreign entrepreneurs, trading will be the soft option, as for numerous Afghan businessmen who are conducting trade not only from Kabul but from Tashkent, Dushanbe, and Moscow itself, as well as Dubai and Hamburg, on a surprisingly large scale.

Trends in Middle East Relations with Central Asia

According to some observers, private sector links may eventually become as important as official aid and investment from Gulf states, but private firms have been cautious to commit themselves. The most prominent Saudi business group to display interest in the region has been al-Baraka Investment Company of Jeddah, whose chairman is the dynamic Sheikh Saleh Kamel. Al-Baraka has set up a joint venture bank in Alma-Ata and is negotiating for a second bank in Tashkent. Al-Baraka also runs training courses for banking staff from Central Asia.

Other Gulf companies doing business with Central Asia include

Saudi Marble Company of Jeddah (in Uzbekistan), Sabic, and Saudi Cable Company. In the Gulf states there are business circles that, like those in Turkey, see in the CIS and in Central Asia a valuable market for their petrochemical and industrial exports. A sign of this was a feasibility study commissioned in 1992 by the Export Development Centre of the Council of Saudi Chambers of Commerce to explore the scope for exports in CIS markets as a whole by Saudi Arabia.

It is quite clear that greatly exaggerated hopes of the Uzbekistan government have been placed in manpower export, in particular to Gulf states. Protocols of intent to cooperate with the United Arab Emirates, Saudi Arabia, and Kuwait were specified in reports published in *Pravda* at the end of 1991 that claimed that manpower export would earn the republic more hard currency than cotton, by far its biggest export item. These hopes were quickly shown to be unrealistic. But a modest agreement on exporting specialists and qualified workers to Saudi Arabia was signed in December 1991 between Uzbekistan's Ministry of Labour and the Ismail Harun Dahlawi corporation of Saudi Arabia.[12]

At the end of 1991 Saudi Arabia agreed to give generous aid to the Central Asian republics. Uzbekistan's regular large shortfall in wheat was helped by Saudi Arabia's agreement to deliver 800,000 tons of grain in 1992. The official visit to Saudi Arabia by President Karimov in 1992 was dwelt on in unusual detail on state TV of Uzbekistan, giving some indication of how important it was judged to be by his government.[13]

Large-scale investment by Gulf states in Central Asia has been slow to develop, but Oman announced in July 1992 a giant oil pipeline project from Kazakhstan, known as the Caspian Pipeline Consortium. Oman is to be a partner with Kazakhstan, Azerbaijan, and Russia in building a pipeline from landlocked Kazakhstan to world markets.[14]

Another important field of regional relations with the Middle East since independence has been air communications, which have opened up rapidly. Turkey (Istanbul), Pakistan (Karachi and Islamabad), and Afghanistan (Kabul) are served from Tashkent, still the main hub of communications in Central Asia. In opening up communications, Iran, Turkey, Pakistan, and Israel are all active. Regular air flights between Tashkent, Islamabad, and Karachi in Pakistan opened in 1992 by PIA (Pakistan International Airlines) and Uzbekistan Hava Yollari. Contacts are growing rather quickly between cities of the two regions.[15] The United Arab Emirates are now attracting tourists from Uzbekistan, who take package holidays there from Tashkent, while groups of Arab visitors fly to Uzbekistan. Bahrain is now linked by air with Ashkhabad, capital of Turkmenistan, in flights by the national airline Turkmen Aria, which started up in 1993.

One of the less likely Middle Eastern states to be involved in Central Asia is Israel. Israeli successes in Central Asia are noteworthy given the policy of the Islamic Conference Organization states to block all Muslim states' trading and diplomatic links with Israel. Israel quickly established links with the Central Asian republics. It is part of a bold Israeli policy of building up relations with all the former Soviet republics, Muslim as well as Christian.

Growing trade links between Israel and the Central Asian republics have been greatly helped by recent emigration of many Soviet Jews to Israel and the presence of established Jewish communities in Bukhara, Tashkent, and other cities of Central Asia. Israeli business initiatives were not by any means limited to Uzbekistan, where most Central Asian Jews lived. To many people's surprise, the Eisenberg group of Tel Aviv claimed to have letters of intent for upgrading oil refineries and other projects worth a total of $2 billion for Kazakhstan alone in January 1993.[16]

Israeli scientific expertise in developing agriculture in arid lands is considered of particular relevance to Central Asia, where the water crisis is recognized as extremely serious but where effective government action to repair some of the environmental damage has not been taken. Israeli expertise, so it is claimed, could help with the Aral Sea tragedy, which arose through reckless exploitation of the two great rivers—Syr Darya and Amu Darya—to increase Central Asia's cotton crop.

It is not only Muslim or Middle Eastern states of the wider region that are becoming involved. For the future, China represents a key potential partner in development, as well as for access for trade, for Kazakhstan and Kyrgyzstan in particular. China has relevant industrial and mining experience available, as well as technology.

In addition to Russia, China represents another regional alternative to the Middle Eastern states for influence in Central Asia. Future good relations with China are bound to turn on the stability of Xinjiang (the adjacent region that used to be known as "Chinese Turkestan"), which has a varied population of mainly Turkic-speaking Muslims of related ethnic and tribal origins to those across the borders. Tensions are largely due to resentment over Beijing's policy of sending more and more Han Chinese to effectively colonize this huge outlying province, by far the biggest in China. It is important to note that China's interest in Central Asia is also, in a broader context, linked with China's renewed interest in the Middle East in recent years. Central Asia not only provides the logistical links to the Middle East, that is, through the revitalized "Silk Road," but further provides China with instrumentalities for affecting and utilizing Central Asian relations with the Middle East in promoting her own geopolitical and economic interests in the region.[17]

The Asian republics arguably have certain strengths in spite of their appalling ecological problems. Educational levels are generally high, and literacy is widespread among women as well as men. Even though industrialization has procccdcd very unevenly, there are sectors of heavy industry, notably in Kazakhstan, where there is a highly skilled work force. However, this remains in the case of all five republics highly dependent upon Russians, Ukrainians, Volga Germans, and other non-Muslims.

Each of the governments is well aware of the danger of compromising its newly gained independence by overconcentration of economic links with one foreign state. They have all learned this from bitter experience with the Soviet system, often denounced today as a veiled form of Russian neocolonialist exploitation by imposition of a cotton monoculture. That is one good reason why the Central Asians are eager to develop their problem-ridden economies by attracting trade, investment, and aid from as diverse sources as possible.

In any discussion of foreign relations, the residual importance of Central Asia's relationship with Russia must be taken into account. This relationship is close and extremely complex, with much depending on the viability of Russia itself and the presence of substantial Russian minorities in all the republics. For all the Central Asian states, a major concern is that Moscow may try to regain control of the region. Russia retains enormous residual power to affect events in the former Soviet republics. This residual power is most felt in the area of security, where the virtually defenseless Central Asian states remain totally dependent on the direct or indirect Russian presence and help.[18] Thus the new Muslim states of the former Soviet Union will remain cognizant of their delicate position between Russia and their Muslim brothers in the South. In other words, Moscow's interests and preferences will be an important consideration in shaping the attitudes of Central Asian states toward the Middle East.

Quite apart from foreign pressures and dangers, the regional scene presents some obvious dangers. The sudden coming of independence has served to sharpen economic and political rivalries between the republics.[19] The ideal of regional unity, or even confederation, of Central Asia survives among the intelligentsia (especially of Uzbekistan) in the form of one "Turkestan," yet the reality is five separate and rival republics. Even though closer collaboration is vital between the republics, notably on environmental issues, it is proving very difficult to achieve.

Consideration of Central Asia's regional stability has to take due note of Afghanistan, which has long land borders with Turkmenistan, Tajikistan, and Uzbekistan. The long-standing conflict inside Afghanistan is creating a real prospect of collapse of Afghanistan as a state, together with total or partial disintegration into its various regional and ethnic components. The continuation of foreign intervention, with backing for rival parties and interest groups in this civil war, is another factor. No longer a superpower proxy war, the Afghan conflict is in part fueled by four powerful neighboring states of the Middle East as well as Central Asia with stakes in Afghanistan: Pakistan, Iran, Saudi Arabia, and Uzbekistan.

The worst-case scenario is that Afghanistan, a fragile state even before the civil war, will simply unravel. If it disintegrates, what is likely to succeed? Often described as a "museum of peoples" or an empire, Afghanistan's diverse ethnic elements were particularly notable in the northern half and central region of the country. North of the Hindu Kush were not only Hazaras, Aimaq, and Pushtuns, but Uzbeks, Tajiks, and Turkmen (even a small number of Kazakh and Kyrgyz), all of the same ethnic groups as the peoples whose names were given to the Asian republics to the north of the river Amu Darya.

It is through Afghanistan that the newly independent republics of Central Asia are likely to be drawn into the politics of their Muslim neighbors. This is especially true of the three republics having borders with Afghanistan—Tajikistan, Uzbekistan, and Turkmenistan. The interaction and interdependence of events in Afghanistan and Tajikistan from the middle of 1992, with the civil war inside Tajikistan, became obvious. One way of measuring this is the flow of weapons between militias or *mujahidin* groups in northern Afghanistan and the opposition parties in Tajikistan.

The repeated accusation from Moscow, Tashkent, and Dushanbe—that fanatical Afghan mujahidin were trying to foment a jihad against the former Communist rulers of Tajikistan and all the Central Asian republics—had a certain superficial plausibility. But it has to reckon with the fact that Afghanistan itself is too devastated by war and too absorbed with its own domestic problems for this to be a serious option for any Kabul "government," which in any case lacks authority outside the capital. Direct intervention by Afghan mujahidin across the Amu Darya was arguably marginal to the civil war taking place inside Tajikistan from mid-1992.

Probably more important than weapons or military backing by any local guerrilla commanders in northern Afghanistan was the inspiration among Muslims of Central Asia from the Afghan resistance and "victory of Islam" against Communism. Moreover, the impact of ethnic and tribal issues is seen markedly in Afghan politics and, by extension, in Tajikistan at the present time. This actually represents a strategic factor for the whole of Central Asia through the reinforcement of existing ethnic identities and centrifugal forces.

The scenario of anarchy inside Afghanistan, together with prolonged civil war, could have distinct geopolitical consequences for Central Asia. It could well result in governments or nationalist groups sympathizing with their kinsmen across the Amu Darya and lending them support. In the event of the development of a strong separatist movement of Uzbeks or another ethnic group of northern Afghanistan, there could well be backing for it from a Central Asian capital in the future, even if at present each government maintains that existing state borders must be respected.

With independence for the Central Asian republics and a political vacuum in Kabul, it is legitimate to inquire into the potential appeal of irredentist ideas to unite peoples or nationalities across existing state borders. If such a political rearrangement takes place in the northern half of Afghanistan, the impact would undoubtedly amount to a great challenge or opportunity for Pakistan, and probably also for Iran, both having ethnic minorities with close links across their borders. It would fundamentally alter the political scene in Pakistan's Northwest Frontier Province and Baluchistan and raise the prospect of one united "Pukhtunistan," or the merger of the Pukhtun regions of Afghanistan with Pakistan.

In conclusion, it is safe to assume that the relations between the Middle East and Central Asia will grow considerably closer, having developed rapidly since de facto independence at the end of 1991. They are still in the process of evolving. Priorities in foreign relations naturally differ for all the governments of the Central Asian republics. They are all eager to strengthen links with the outside world, but their focus varies according to their geographic situation. For the three republics having land borders with Iran and Afghanistan (Uzbekistan, Turkmenistan, and Tajikistan), relations with Middle Eastern states are certainly judged more important than is the case for either Kazakhstan or Kyrgyzstan.

Turkey, Iran, and Pakistan are likely to remain the most important partners from the Middle East, as the embassies these countries have opened throughout the region indicate. As for the Arab states, there is a distinct possibility that Saudi Arabia will open embassies in Tashkent, Ashkhabad, and Baku in early 1994. There is little incentive, though, for an urgent decision on this, given that none of the Central Asian republics is in a position to open more than a handful of embassies, and the priorities are clearly elsewhere than the Arab world.

The alternative will continue to be appointing a wealthy private citizen living abroad as honorary consul, or as a more or less symbolic "envoy" to Saudi Arabia, Kuwait, or Egypt. Stringent financial problems of the republics will restrict their existing embassies to Moscow and, at best, a few capitals in the immediate region, together with Washington and some of the major European cities. Relations with other Middle Eastern states will count more in Central Asia when the leading countries demonstrate unequivocally their interest and greater involvement in the region.

Notes

1. Karen Dawisha and Helene Carrere d'Encausse, "Islam in the Foreign Policy of the Soviet Union: A Double-Edged Sword?" in *Islam in Foreign Policy*, ed. Adeed Dawisha (Cambridge: 1983).

2. A. Bennigsen and C. Lemercier-Quelquejay, *Islam in the Soviet Union* (London: 1967); and A. Bennigsen and P. Henze, eds., *Soviet Strategy and Islam* (London, 1989), chapter 3.

3. See *Central Asia Brief*, no. 1 (Leicester, UK: Islamic Foundation, 1993).

4. See also M. Kaser and S. Mehrotra, *The Central Asian Economies after Independence* (London: Royal Institute of International Affairs, 1992).

5. Background information can be found in A. Bennigsen and E. Wimbush, *Muslims of the Soviet Empire: A Guide* (London: 1985).

6. See, for example, *ECO: Looking to the Future, Special Issues of "Strategic Studies,"* vol. 15, no. 2 (Islamabad, Pakistan: 1992).

7. Recent studies of the Central Asia region as a whole include: W. Fierman, ed., *Soviet Central Asia: The Failed Transformation* (Boulder, Colo.: Westview Press, 1992); and Robert Lewis, ed., *Geographic Perspectives on Soviet Central Asia* (London: Routledge, 1992).

8. *FBIS-Central Eurasia*, 23 August 1993, p. 23.

9. *FBIS-NES*, 26 January 1990, p. 24.

10. Ibid., 27 May 1993, p. 45.

11. Ibid., 21 November 1992.

12. See Edmund O'Sullivan's article in *Middle East Economic Digest* (London), 30 October 1992.

13. For coverage of this visit see *FBIS-NES*, 14–15 November 1992.

14. *FBIS-NES*, 21 July 1992, pp. 11–12.

15. *FBIS-Central Eurasia*, 20 September 1992.

16. See Hugh Carnegy's article in *Financial Times* (London), 28 January 1993.

17. In addition to China, Japan and both North and South Korea are actively pursuing trade and investment with the Asian republics. The presence of substantial ethnic Korean communitics in Kazakhstan and Uzbekistan, including many thriving private entrepreneurs, has aided this process.

18. See Maxim Shashenkov, *Security Issues of the ex-Soviet Central Asian Republics* (London: Center for Defence Studies, 1992).

19. See Shirin Akiner, *Central Asia: New Arc of Crisis?* (London: Whitehall Paper Series, Royal United Services Institute for Defence Studies, 1993).

14

Russia and the Geopolitics of the Muslim South

Mohiaddin Mesbahi

The most important and enduring change in the strategic environment of what has historically been referred to as the "southern flank" is the introduction of a fundamental change in the concept of "flank" itself and the resultant confusion over conceptualization of security by both the old and the newly emerged actors.

As in Europe, the Middle East/Persian Gulf's historical geopolitical fix on presumed Soviet threat and its counterpart, the Western containment, has basically disappeared. The convenience and conceptual simplicity of the Cold War—notwithstanding its negative and dangerous potentials—has now been replaced by a broad chaos and confusion over how to define security, threats, doctrines, and strategies. Every single actor—both extraterritorial, such as the United States, and now Russia and the old regionals, Turkey, Iran, Afghanistan, Pakistan, and the "new" kids in the bloc, the Central Asian republics—is struggling to adapt to the shockingly sudden strategic shift in their security environment.

This picture has become further complicated by the addition of other actors—those who belong to the outer layer of the old southern flank—the Persian Gulf states, India, China, Egypt, Syria, and Israel. True, proclamations from Washington, Moscow, and all the regional capitals are pointing to some esoteric uniformity in political intentions and designs. New ideas abound, such as the renunciation of the use of force and reliance on political means to solve conflict; collective security; defensive military doctrines; rejection of imperial and hegemonic ambitions; and criticism of bloc policy. While these lofty aims might partially reflect the responsiveness of the actors to an air of optimism and cooperation in the post–Cold War international system, it also, and more seriously, reflects the uncertainties of the actors regarding their foreign policy and security objectives and their corresponding national strategy.

The second and equally profound change resulting from the collapse of the Soviet Union has been the sudden inclusion of the newly independent states of Central Asia and Azerbaijan in the geopolitical landscape of the Middle East and the Islamic world. As if the old Middle East lacked in strategic complexity and tension, Central Asia and the Caucasus brought with them an additional myriad of security-related problems ranging from ancient land disputes, artificial borders, ethnonationalism, and a new flank of weak nation-states presenting a symbiosis of tempting opportunities and endless conflict scenarios.

The key factor in shaping the future and ultimate makeup of the security in the region is obviously the future security arrangement within the CIS, in particular the nature of the relationship between Russia and the Central Asian republics and Moscow's place in influencing the contextual elements of the geopolitics of these new states. In the following pages we will first address the emerging Russian foreign policy concepts in the region and then discuss Russia's and the CIS's security issues. Finally, we will address the impact on and the reaction of regional actors to the emerging realities of the region.

Russian Foreign Policy: Concepts and Paradigms

Russian foreign policy since December 1991, like other aspects of the Russian polity, has gone through considerable fluctuations in both formulation and implementation. A lack of clear-cut foreign policy concepts has been the common criticism laid on the Russian Foreign Ministry by almost every political force in Moscow. From the "red and brown" media to the influential speaker of the Parliament and academia, the unanimous critique has been the inability or unwillingness of Foreign Minister Andrei Kozyrov's team to identify the key concepts of Russian national interests and develop a strategy for their implementation. Kozyrov's repetitive comments on the removal of ideology and the real end of the Cold War have not been enough to answer the critics. Now, a few years since the collapse of the Soviet Union, though the critique has not diminished, the overall parameters of the debate or trends in Russian foreign policy are emerging.

It is important to note that these emerging parameters are trends taking shape within the official establishment of Russian foreign policy. The nonofficial positions may be similar or may deviate from these official trends, but they usually find some common ground within the official lines. While a microscopic analysis of the official trends might lead to the identification of several trends in thinking on foreign policy, a more general and sweeping approach will point to two broad trends, "schools of thought," or, more accurately, two perspectives. The first of these, which I have termed *Euro-Atlanticist*, has been represented primarily by Andrei Kozyrov and some of his younger advisers in the foreign ministry. It was backed in the cabinet by powerful personalities such as Yegor Gayder (until his removal), and has enjoyed the overall support of Boris Yeltsin. This perspective has until recently been the prevailing mode of thinking in Russian foreign policy. The second school of thought, here termed *Neo-Eurasianist*, which has increasingly been dominating Russian foreign policy since late 1992, has been advocated by a powerful coalition of influential interest groups, such as the military-industrial complex, the army, and, until their removal from power, individuals such as Vice President Alexander Rutskoy, Speaker of the Parliament Ruslin Khasbulatov, and Russia's National Security Council secretary Yuri Skokov. It is also being reluctantly supported by President Yeltsin.

From the outset it is important to clarify that this division of perspectives is not meant necessarily to imply a clear dichotomy or the presence of visible and institutionally well-defined and well-entrenched foreign policy groupings, for the intellectual and institutional scenery of post-Soviet Russian foreign policy has remained fluid and flexible. People and ideas of both camps interact and at times synthesize. Yet, the division of perspectives will be an analytically useful tool for identifying both the key elements of the current debate and for further contextualizing the intellectual setting of Russian foreign policy practices and performance in the initial two years of post-Soviet foreign policy.

The Euro-Atlanticist Perspective

An elaborate discussion of the roots and "sociology" of this perspective is beyond the scope of this study. Here we may identify the key concepts, especially as they relate to Russia's relations with Central Asia and the Caucasus.

First, and perhaps the very philosophical underpinning of this school, is the predominance of domestic considerations in the shaping of foreign policy. According to proponents of this view, not only are domestic and foreign policy closely interrelated, but domestic considerations and, in this case, the success of economic reform in Russia, carry the greatest weight in the making of Russian foreign policy. The most important function of Russian foreign policy is creating an international environment and relations that will enable Russia to become a "democratic, market oriented, civilized nation." "The country's greatness, particularly on the threshold of the 21st century is determined not by the scale of its empire, but above all by the level of its people's well being," declared Foreign Minister Andrei Kozyrov.[1] The Russian foreign minister approvingly recalled Charles de Gaulle's statement on France's foreign policy objective ("when every French woman came home from the market content and smiling") when identifying what he considers Russia's foreign policy "supertask": "The Russian Foreign Ministry will feel that it has been useful when Russian women no longer wait in line for hours thinking of how to feed their families, but are able to spend more time thinking of how to use their charms to please their replete Russian men."[2]

Second, the only logical approach to achieve this objective is for Russia to become a permanent member of the "civilized" world; more specifically, and to use Kozyrov's phrase, "a special civilized club," that is, the G-7.[3] The Russian inclusion in this "club" could only take place through renunciation of any ideological vestiges of the Russian past, both tsarist and Soviet; Russia has to achieve a psychological breakthrough by overcoming messianic temptations and "excessive Russianness."

Once and for all, Russia has to accept the fact that only by following the Western model can it find its proper place in the emerging pan-European home. Western democratic values and, above all, respect for the principles enunciated in the UN Charter, the Helsinki declarations (CSCE Charter), and the Paris Charter on human rights should be used as a guide for the formulation of Russian foreign policy.[4] Western principles are not lofty aims and empty proclamations, but should be taken as serious criteria for Russian foreign policy to set the Russian national objectives. This will bring Russian foreign policy in line with global trends. Further, it will generate respect and trust and will be the only available mechanism to protect the basic human rights of the Russian minorities now living outside the borders of the Russian Federation in the former republics.[5] While Russia understands the difficulty of full membership in the civilized club (the G-7) in the current transitional phase, and might tolerate a 7 + 1 formula for now, the ultimate objective is to achieve full membership by being part of the G-8. "It is important to give up the formula, 7 + 1, of major democratic economic powers and work toward the formula of 8. Russia is for alliance with the United States and the West," declared Andrei Kozyrov in his speech in September 1992 at Columbia University.[6]

Third, Russia will remain a great but "normal power."[7] It will carry the "historical responsibility" granted by the possession of nuclear weapons and the seat in the UN Security Council. The key new concept here is that of "normal" power, implying the absence of global ambitions of Soviet scale and no traditional superpower status, much as the Euro-Atlanticists advocate multipolarity and politely ignore U.S. claims of a unipolar world. An additional theoretical issue here is the concept of Russia as a "continuer state" (*Gosudarstvo-prodolzhatel*) as opposed to "successor state" (*Gosudarstvo-preyemnik*). Both Yeltsin and Kozyrov have repeatedly argued that Russia is a continuation of the USSR as it relates to its international responsibility and privileges of being a big power, thus the exclusive claim over nuclear weapons and occupation of the security council seat.[8] These concepts have important ramifications for Russia's relations with the rest of the CIS republics, as Russia will have the exclusive right over the global privileges of the former Soviet Union while it will share with the rest all the obligations, including the USSR's international debt and adherence to nuclear arms cuts and disarmament measures.

Fourth, this "civilized," "continuer," and "normal power" has, of course, the distinct geographic characteristic of being situated both in Europe and Asia. This would give it a *Eurasian character*, acting as a linkage or bridge between Europe and Asia. What distinguishes this Eurasian concept from the traditional one is that Russia as a Eurasian state is not a static, self-contained link but a modern, Westernized, and dynamic agent of change.[9] This modern Russia, while transforming itself, would also change the "Asian wing" of the Eurasian entity into a pan–Euro-Atlantic one. The "immature" states of the former Soviet Union (that is, Central Asia), which, to use Kozyrov's words, "belong to another world,"[10] will by the persistence and dynamism of "an enlightened Russian big brother" become part of this Euro-Atlantic "family."[11] The "continuer state"—now "civilized" and "normal"—will shed not only its own Asiatic baggage but will become the bridge that transforms the Central Asian part of the former Soviet Union. The key mechanism for this transformation will be Russia's and Central Asia's active participation in a new, invigorated, and expanded CSCE process.

Fifth, the issue of security in the Euro-Atlanticist school is guaranteed for the most part by the unique historical opportunity that Russia now has, being without an enemy for the first time in its history, though some other forms and sources of potential danger persist.

Two components of Russia's security system, according to the Euro-Atlanticists, are (1) the "partnership" (or eventual alliance) with the United States and Europe through confidence-building measures, disarmament, and a global collective security system that stretches from Vladivostok to Vancouver; and (2) the collective CIS security system in which Russia, for all practical purposes, will be a guarantor and dominant player. The CIS collective security will be part and parcel of the global system.[12] This vision was clearly defined in the Charter of Russo-American Partnership and Friendship signed by Boris Yeltsin and President George Bush on 17 July 1992 in Washington.[13]

The Euro-Atlanticists and the Islamic Threat. Two fundamental and largely interconnected sources of threat have been identified by this view. First are ethnonationalist regional conflicts that might jeopardize the security of twenty-five million Russians living in other republics, extraterritorial but ethnically driven conflicts that might involve a CIS member and necessitate Russian intervention. Second is the real concern over the spread of "Islamic radicalism," both in Russia proper and in Central Asia. The primary sources of the "Islamic" threat are identified as being both internal and external. The external sources of this Islamic threat have been perceived as emanating specifically from the south, that is, Iran, Afghanistan, the Middle East, and so on. In this context, Central Asia is intimately connected with the political and security dynamics of the old southern flank, and thus its security and defense now occupy a significant place in the Euro-Atlanticist view.

What is important is that the Euro-Atlanticists and the West have identical views of the Islamic threat, and one can deduce that Russia will provide the front line of defense against the perceived threat of Islamic fundamentalism. The Euro-Atlanticists will delegate to Russia the role of "container" of the Islamic threat on behalf of the "civilized world," that is, the West, in Central Asia.[14] Both the religious and ethnonationalist dimensions of the threat will be tamed by the rapid incorporation of the Central Asian states into the CSCE process. These states, though geographically distant, have all expressed their desire to participate in the process and have in principle accepted the CSCE charter. It is hoped that Russia will be the catalyst of this inclusion and the "educational" source for the "Asian wing."

The "continuer" state, according to Kozyrov, is "the primary thread of communication of the CIS to the outside world." Russia will shed its

Asiatic baggage and pull Central Asia in the direction of the civilized Western world. All Central Asian republics and Azerbaijan have expressed on record their concern over the Islamic threat and share the Euro-Atlanticist general view that they should neutralize the domestic dimension of the Islamic challenge by increasing contact with the West and especially the pan-European process.

Perhaps the most important policy ramification of this view will be a much closer overall security relationship with the West and a rather cooperative policy in the Persian Gulf/Southwest Asian region. The U.S. preponderance in the Persian Gulf will not be questioned, and Iran will be kept under a watchful eye, while the role of Turkey as the Western-endorsed model for the region will, with some reservation, be accepted. No controversial and "out of line" stand will be adopted that might jeopardize the strategic direction of Russia for inclusion in the "civilized club." Russia wants to be treated as a normal Western great power with identical interests.

The Neo-Eurasianist Perspective

This second trend or "school of thought" became increasingly relevant during late 1992 and more prominently in 1993. What is significant is that although this trend was initially developing on the periphery of the Euro-Atlanticist view, it now has considerable voice within the official establishment at the foreign policy circles, cabinet level, the army, and, obviously, in the Supreme Soviet. It was embraced by such persons as then vice president Alexander Rutskoy, former speaker of the Supreme Soviet Ruslan Khasbulatov, Russia's State Council Sergei Steinkevich, Secretary of Russian Security Council Yuri Skokov, Commander of the CIS Joint Armed Forces General Shaposhniko, General Samsanov of the CIS, Russian Defense Minister General Pavel Grachev, and the powerful centrist political forces gathered under the umbrella of the "Civic Union," which collectively presented a considerable force in the Russian political establishment. An increasingly vocal number of Foreign Ministry advisers, scholars from the Russian Academy of Sciences, and other think tanks severely criticized some of the fundamentals of the Euro-Atlanticist school and have individually or collectively elaborated a more "realist" vision of Russian foreign policy.

The emergence of Russia's "Security Council" and its enhanced and perhaps predominant position in the formulation of foreign policy signified a dramatic change. The dominant centrist/realist makeup of the Security Council, both in personnel and ideology, led to the gradual emergence of a competitive—if not prevailing—Neo-Eurasianist perspective on Russian foreign policy vis-à-vis the Euro-Atlanticist.[15] The combination of the "Security Council" and the forces represented in the "Civic Union" was a powerful symbiosis of domestic and foreign policy forces that became the foundation of the Neo-Eurasianist foreign policy. The following are some of the key arguments of the Neo-Eurasianist view.

First, the philosophical underpinning and objective of Russian foreign policy—to provide a conducive international environment for the Russian transformation and reforms—remains largely similar to the Euro-Atlanticist school. This fundamental similarity in the main objective should not, however, obscure some key differences. The Neo-Eurasianists believe that the success of reform depends to a large extent on the reassertion of Russian statehood and the recovery of some of the ground lost with the collapse of the USSR. This view also sharply differs on the ideology, strategy, and tactics of reform, and thus in its foreign policy/international dimensions, aspects, and requirements. The recent alternative economic reform plan offered by the "Civic Union" has laid down a more centrist evolutionary socioeconomic plan, a plan closer, for example, to the Chinese model.[16]

Yegor Gayder's downfall and the emergence of a new Cabinet led by Viktor Chernomyrdin—a trusted technocrat from the old system—signaled the end of the ideological certainty and conviction that surrounded the issue of economic reform in the early days of Yeltsin's rule and further pointed to the realignment of economic and political forces in Russia. The new premier, who came to office after the stormy Seventh Russian Congress of People's Deputies, favors a market reform with a "human face," one with clear commitment to the "strengthening of the social orientation of reforms."[17]

While transformation market economy is accepted in principle, the extent, scope, and method of change have been questioned. "Primitive Capitalism," the "shock therapy" of the "Chicago school of economics" and the IMF program, is sharply criticized,[18] not only because it has not worked but also because it has put undue pressure on Russian foreign policy to become excessively one dimensional, focusing on the West as the primary source of aid and inspiration. This has led to a "concessionary," "naive," and "confused" foreign policy that has neglected other actors and, above all, the CIS members, Asia, and the Middle East. A different and more centrist reform model preferred by the Neo-Eurasianists will have more centrist/realist foreign policy requirements. Further, the

Neo-Eurasianists do not share with the Euro-Atlanticists the view that foreign policy is an extension of domestic factors, but consider foreign policy an equally important pole of an interdependent dynamic. While the Euro-Atlanticist vision of Russia is an "enlarged Switzerland," the Neo-Eurasianist view reflects a modern, yet unique, great power.

Second, within this vision the West (the "civilized world") does not enjoy the same status. Although close and friendly relations with the West are strongly encouraged, its "romanticism" is being rejected.[19] "Permanent interests, not permanent friends" is the favorite catchphrase of the proponents of this school. Kozyrov's idealized vision of the "civilized West" is being replaced by a vision of the West that will pursue its own interest based on cold calculation. The West, warns Ednan Agayev, a Russian foreign ministry advisor, is not interested in a strong Russia.[20] Russian Defense Minister General Pavel Grachev believes deep and unnecessarily rushed concessions have been made to the West without extracting a comparable price for the enormous political investment made by the Soviet Union in the last two decades.[21] Even Russia's U.S. Ambassador Vladimir Lukin, a man apparently in the Euro-Atlanticist camp, has raised questions about America's intentions, calling them contradictory. According to the Neo-Eurasianist school, relations with the West must be devoid of Kozyrov's "messianic illusions" of shared values and should instead be put on the firm and more predictable foundation of an enlightened realpolitik.

It is important not to overlook the subtle yet significant shift in the perception of the West in general and of the United States in particular. While the earlier phase of the nascent Russian foreign policy after the collapse of the Soviet Union reflected a severe self-criticism and a complete embrace of the United States' international role and posture, the current phase reflects a more critical attitude toward the United States and a rediscovery of realism as the philosophical foundation of Russia's perspective on international relations. The Neo-Eurasianist perspective rejects the notion that a qualitative shift and transformation has taken place in the nature of interstate relations—a belief that was characteristic of Gorbachev's new thinking and shared to a considerable degree by the Euro-Atlanticist view of the international system.

While acknowledging the relative decline of the role of military power in international relations and the increasing interdependence and significance of economic power, the Neo-Eurasianists maintain that the underlying philosophy in international relations has remained intact. Speaker of the Supreme Soviet Ruslan Khusbolatev argues: "We must always bear in mind that the struggle for economic and political influence is continuing in the world. There remains a complex hierarchy of relations conditioned by the real power of this or that country."[22] The struggle for influence has taken "more civilized, as well as more complicated forms than before."[23]

On a similar theme, Yevgeny Primakov, head of Russia's Foreign Intelligence, has reflected that "geopolitical factors continue playing a very big role in the framing of Russia's foreign policy." Russia's geopolitical realities, according to Primakov, cannot but be *global*. Russia's greatness could only be realized in a global setting that encompasses China, India, Japan, the United States, Europe, the Middle East, and also the Third World: "Russia cannot be great, it cannot play the positive role it is destined to in the absence of such a wide geopolitical scope. In promoting relations with all those countries, *we must remember that history never nullifies geopolitical values"* (emphasis added).[24]

One of the most telling "official" indications of the Neo-Eurasianist perspective on Russia's global position—and especially the role of the United States—emerged from a "scientific conference" held in Moscow in early November 1992 in which the General Headquarters of the CIS, representatives of all the CIS states, think tanks, and leading military scientists participated. This historic conference, according to the spokesperson of the joint armed forces of the CIS, Lieutenant General Valery Manilov, laid down the "foundation for consolidating the military and strategic thought of the CIS." The conference identified two sets of *stabilizing* and *destabilizing* factors in the current international system. The "most serious destabilizing factor" was considered "the attempts to use the disintegration of the former Soviet Union in order to create a unipolar structure of the world. Laws of natural sciences teach us that a stable system must be balanced. The absence of the balance that kept the world together and the attempt to reduce world order to the priority of the U.S.'s objectives may lead to the destabilization of the situation [and] . . . escalation of armed conflicts throughout the world."[25] The conference also called for "the formation of a military-political alliance as a counterbalance to destabilizing factors."[26]

Further indication of the official shift in the perception of the United States was reflected in the official draft of Russian foreign policy concepts released in 1992. The draft, which was prepared by the Russian Foreign Ministry, though giving development of ties with the United States a top priority, points to the intention of "leading Western countries to maintain their dominance" and the U.S. attempt "to ensure unilateral advantages" in the process of disarmament negotiations, thus undermining "Russia's military related technical potential." The document also warns that "the United States might try to replace Russia in the countries of its traditional influence," a clear reference not only to Eastern Europe but also Central Asia.[27]

Third, Russia will have to play its proper role as a great power. Comparing Russia with other "normal" powers such as France and Britain ignores the geopolitical realities of this unique Eurasian state. Russia differs from the Euro-Atlanticist conception of it, as it does not gravitate toward the Western pole; it is not looking for a "fitting place in the civilized club." Its destiny does not belong to either Europe or Asia, West or East. It is a self-contained, "independent," and unique entity. In the words of Sergei Stankevich, it is "one of the fundamental geopolitical realities of the world" that touches Christian, Islamic, Chinese, and Indian civilization; it is a stabilizing pole by itself.

Thus, as Primakov has argued, Russia's foreign policy context should remain global. Regional confinement of Russia to a "Western" or "Asian" context—or even simply a geopolitical linkage between the two—simply ignores its unique geopolitical realities, potentials, and historical responsibilities.[28]

To be sure, the Neo-Eurasianist view of the West is not hostile, but it is noneuphoric and "nonfraternal." The absence of a fundamental hostility toward the West and the willingness to cooperate with it separate this modern version of Eurasianism from the traditional one, which took as its main characteristic not only being distinct from the West but being distant and generally hostile. The modern version, the Neo-Eurasianist perspective, carries some of the baggage of the past, but is more firmly informed by the realistic view of power and security and some of the elements of the historical continuity of the Russian experience. It is concerned about the "utopian" nature of the Westernization trends and fears the subsequent alienation of the rest of Russia's contiguous world, Asia, and the Muslim world.

The Neo-Eurasianists and the Islamic Threat. The most immediate objective of Russian foreign policy must be to secure both the interior and the exterior borders of the CIS. To have a belt of "good neighbors"— especially along the southern flank—is considered most essential.[29] Accordingly, Russia's relations with the CIS members must be the number one priority. Central Asian republics play a pivotal role in this regard, as their domestic and international stability remains essential to the overall security of Russia. Russia's interest in this region could be undermined by overlapping ethnoterritorial nationalism, in which local conflicts might jeopardize the Russian minority population, creating the nightmarish trap of intervention by the Russian armed forces.

The influence of Islam, or the "threat of Islamic fundamentalism," is another concern that this school of thought has taken seriously. A vulnerable southern flank will be an invitation for regional actors such as Iran, Pakistan, and Afghanistan to effectively interfere in the sociopolitical dynamics of the Central Asian republics. Thus, a strong and increasingly integrated collective security process within the CIS, and an activist Russian role in it, seems essential to protect the vulnerable social and political borders of the Eurasian entity.

It is important to note that, although the fear of Islamic revivalism is shared by both trends, a subtle yet important difference separates them. While the Euro-Atlanticists have adopted Western perceptions of the threat and the need for its containment, the Neo-Eurasianists prefer a more subtle and sophisticated approach. First, their containment of the Islamic threat should not lead to wholesale opposition and hostility toward Islam and the Islamic world, and thus must be presented in the form of a legitimate security concern. According to Alexei Maleshenko, a leading Russian specialist on Islam, "Proximity with the Muslim world had always determined Russia's geopolitical position and diversified its international relations."[30]

Second, and equally important, this containment should not be part of the Russian conspiracy and partnership with the West against Islam and the Muslim world.[31] Russia's geographical contiguity with the Islamic world, its own Muslim population, and its close relations with the Central Asian republics should be used to maintain friendly relations with the countries of the Middle East and especially with the southern flank states. A united Russian-Western anti-Islamic front—a view seemingly advocated by the Euro-Atlanticists—could be detrimental to the interests of Russia and the CIS as a whole.

It is important to note that the ideological underpinnings of the Neo-Eurasianist perception of Islam carries a historical ambiguity and contradiction. The fear of being "encircled" by an Islamic-Turkic world, which preoccupied the traditional Eurasianists of the nineteenth century, still resonates among the Neo-Eurasianists. This fear is now reflected in Russia's policy in the North Caucasus, Tatarstan, and the Chechnia and Ingush republics. The Neo-Eurasianists, nevertheless, look to the Islamic world as a potential—if not necessary—friend, required both for maintaining Russian and Central Asian domestic stability and for counterbalancing the Western world.

The potential for friendship with the Islamic world—especially in view of the increasing power of the Islamic states in the world and the continuous tension between Islam and the West—might present Russia with a historical opportunity. Sergei Stankevich, the influential state counselor of the Russian Federation and one of the most vocal of the Neo-Eurasianists, has recently called for the "revival of the Eastern question in Russian foreign policy" and the enhancement of Russia's "unifying, reconciling role" in bringing together the Turkic and Muslim elements. He argues that "Russia has always been a mix of Slavic and Turkic components, of Orthodoxy and Islam."[32]

The Neo-Eurasianists' historical distaste for the spiritual ills of Westernization can provide a potential element of commonality with the Islamic world, which has displayed similar tendencies. The removal of Marxism-Leninism and its atheistic vestiges could remove a critical obstacle for a closer spiritual/cultural relationship with the Islamic world. In an interview with *Al-Hayat*, Viktor Posovalek, head of the Middle East and African Desk at the Russian Foreign Ministry, underlined the potential significance of this cultural affinity: "When the Communist covers are removed, the ring of spiritual attraction between the Russians and the people of the region [the Middle East] can be restored." Pasovalek, a leading authority within the Russian foreign policy establishment, considers the Islamic world "a belt extending from Kazakhstan to Mauritania," a region among the top priorities of Russian foreign policy in the coming decades and one that will witness Russia's multilayered military, diplomatic, economic, and spiritual presence.[33] The new draft of Russian foreign policy concepts also emphasizes the importance of the Arab world and Southwest Asian states for Russia and stresses that, notwithstanding cooperation with the United States, Russia intends "to maintain its own initiative" in the region.[34]

The challenge facing the Neo-Eurasianists' relations with the Islamic world, however, will be their ability to balance the historical legacy of Russia's fear of an Islamic encirclement, the treatment of its "internal Islam" on the one hand and the common areas of mutual interest with the Islamic world—especially in its relations with the West—on the other. This balance is as much a function of Neo-Eurasianist policies as it is of the internal dynamics of the Islamic world, and Central Asia in particular.

The Neo-Eurasianists would need the assistance and active participation of their Central Asian allies—especially Kazakhstan—for a meaningful rapprochement with the Islamic world. Just as the Soviet Union tried to utilize Central Asia as a conduit of influence with the

Islamic world, there are indications that Russia might use its Central Asian connection in the same way. Kazakhstan's recent initiatives might indicate its willingness to become the bridge between Russia, the CIS, and Muslim states. As the leading Central Asian state, and one with considerable prestige among the Islamic states, Kazakhstan might be suited to play such a role. Nursultan Nazarbaev's recent call for the creation of a "Conference on Mutual Action and Confidence Building Measures in Asia"—a replica of the CSCE—might be an initiative along this line. This conference would incorporate the Central Asian states, in addition to Turkey, Iran, and Pakistan. Kazakhstan, the quintessential Slavic-Turkic state in the CIS and the one with the closest relationship with Russia, might be able to play the role of bridge between the CIS and the Islamic states, a role that Russia itself finds difficult to perform.[35]

Russia, the CIS, and the Southern Flank: From Theory to Policy

In the short life span of the CIS, Russian policy toward its southern flank has gone through two phases. In the first phase, which began in December 1991, the prevailing attitude in Russian foreign policy, with its heavily Western orientation, reflected the views of the Euro-Atlanticists. The initial move of creating the short-lived "Slavic Union" in the absence of the Central Asian republics set the atmosphere and the mood for the first phase of Russian foreign policy: a nearly complete neglect of Central Asia, the Caucasus, and adjacent regions such as the Persian Gulf, and total immersion into relations with the West.

The Russian neglect of Central Asia was perceived as a clear message to the new Central Asian states and other regional actors, such as Iran, Pakistan, and Turkey, that a historical shift in Moscow's strategic perception had taken place, and a power vacuum that had been filled by Russia for the last two hundred years was now open to penetration. The regional reaction was twofold. In Central Asia, ideas of an "Asian Turkic Islamic bloc" were toyed with. In several consecutive meetings in Alma-Ata, Bishkek, and Tashkent, general aspects of this bloc were discussed. Meanwhile, the two dynamic regional actors with clear interest in the region, Iran and Turkey, responded to the apparent vacuum. The obscure names of Central Asian capitals—Alma-Ata, Dushanbe, Bishkek, Ashkhabad, and Tashkent—became "household" names for the media, politicians, and analysts of these two countries, and series of diplomatic initiatives led to numerous economic, cultural, and political agreements among the new Central Asian states, Iran, and Turkey.

The Economic Cooperation Organization (ECO) summit in Tehran was attended by its new members—the Central Asian states and Azerbaijan—as well as its original members—Turkey, Iran, and Pakistan. The Ashkhabad summit meeting, which brought together the leaders of Iran, Turkey, Pakistan, and all heads of Central Asian states, highlighted the new activism and showed that Central Asia will now have a much more intimate relationship with its southern neighbors. It has brought the region, with all of its complexities, closer to Russia's heartland.

While the eastern borders of the southern flank witnessed intense diplomatic activity, the western border—the Caucasus—was engulfed in the explosive issue of Nagorno-Karabakh. Again, Iran and Turkey were the most active actors. Iran's mediation efforts in Karabakh and its apparent initial success was matched by Turkey's overt support for Azerbaijan and an open discussion about possible military intervention in Nakhichevan and Nagorno-Karabakh.

What was perhaps more remarkable in this phase, which lasted until mid-1992, was the uncharacteristic passivity of Russian foreign policy toward the region and lack of any concern for the shrinking of Russia's underbelly. Russian Defense Minister General Grachev bitterly complained, "We are now facing a truly unprecedented situation, the Moscow Military District has essentially become a frontline location. This is altogether mind boggling."[36] The apparent U.S. interest in Central Asia and the Caucasus and the high-visibility diplomacy of Secretary of State James Baker's Central Asian tour was perceived by Russian critics as a clear indication of the lack of direction in Moscow's policy toward its southern region. While Kozyrov argued that U.S. diplomacy in the region and contacts with the Asian republics and Azerbaijan were normal developments within the rights of the new sovereign states, others believed that Russia's bias against or indifference vis-à-vis the southern region was a clear signal and invitation for both regional and extraregional actors to expand their influence in the region at Russia's expense.

The Policy Shift

A discernible shift in Russian policy toward Central Asia and the southern flank has taken place since mid-1992. Several reasons and—

viewed from Moscow—several dynamics have contributed to this adjustment. First is the realization that the security of Russia and the Central Asian states are interdependent, as these young states with weak economies, unstable political systems, and no independent defense capability have become vulnerable to external pressure and penetration. Russia's comprehensive and long-standing relations with Central Asia—notwithstanding prevailing nationalism—are deeper than could be overcome overnight.

Second, the growing concern over the ethnic factor in the overall security of the CIS—and Russia in particular—was another and essential factor in refocusing Russian policy. Protection of the basic rights of Russian minorities "left behind" and the real possibility of military clashes with the republics over this issue demanded much closer relations with these republics. The CIS and its collective security arrangements were to be taken more seriously.

Third, the growing influence of more centrist conservative political forces in the Russian government and, especially, the reassertion of the army's role in defining Russia's general security requirements were important changes that brought new input to the formulation of Russian security policy and demanded a renewed and focused attention toward Russia's southern border. What was perhaps more significant was the fact that this Neo-Eurasianist position was at least partially supported by Yeltsin himself. Rejecting the accusation of Russia's pro-West policy, Yeltsin, in a major interview, reaffirmed the new shift in Russian foreign policy: "The time for the Eastward move has arrived."[37]

Fourth, the demand for Russian activism was not confined to political forces in Moscow but was coming from Central Asia itself. Without exception, all Central Asian states (though with varying degrees of emphasis) preferred and insisted on a substantive collective security system with active Russian participation. The Central Asian elites were not satisfied with the token gesture of the nuclear umbrella of the CIS for their security, demanding instead a more comprehensive, meaningful security system that included practical measures for dealing with the conventional defense of their security and their borders. Early optimism over the formation of an "Asian-Turkic/Islamic bloc" was fading in the face of the realities of historical interdependence with Russia. Commenting on the pivotal role of Russia in the security of Central Asia, President Askar Akaev of Kyrgyzstan argued, "The Eurasian entity hinged on Russia would collapse if it [Russia] ceased to be a world power, with painful implications for Kyrgyzstan as well. That's why we must make our contribution to Russia's revival."[38]

Fifth, the concern over the Islamic threat, while all along present in Russia and Central Asia, now demanded some practical measures. A long-term view of the problem meant that although the domestic dimension of the threat was driven by internal instabilities, a *containment* of its external dimension meant the protection of the exterior borders of the CIS—and especially Central Asia—along the southern flank. If Islam was to penetrate the CIS, the main direction of its external route would be the Southwest Asia/Persian Gulf region, particularly Iran, Afghanistan, and Pakistan. The security of southern borders would not only have enhanced the physical security of the new Central Asian republics, but it was loaded with a clear political message of Russian sensitivity to all regional actors regarding this issue.

Finally, the Russian recognition of Western limitations in effecting reforms in the former USSR and the excessiveness of the earlier one-dimensional and Western-oriented foreign policy was a further impetus in promoting the shift. An overall wariness over a romantic foreign policy driven by "shared values" with the civilized West and "values common to mankind"—ideas that for the critics echoed the Gorbachev era—was now visible in Russian foreign policy circles. A more balanced policy based on realism and more traditional realities of a Eurasian power seemed to be needed. This mood was perhaps captured best by General V. Samsanov, chief of the CIS Joint Armed Forces General Staff, on the eve of the summit of the CIS in Moscow in July 1992: "We must realistically grasp that the principles of relations between states that have prevailed throughout mankind's history remain mostly unchanged. As 100 and 200 years ago, they are based on certain principles—a state's strength ensures that it enjoys complete independence and freedom of development along whatever path it believes necessary. After all, even Karamazin wrote in the 'History of the Russian State': 'There is no freedom where there is no strength to defend it.' "[39]

This policy shift away from the Euro-Atlanticist to a Neo-Eurasianist outlook should not be taken as a complete victory of one view over the other, yet it clearly indicated a serious accommodation of and adjustment to the emerging realities facing Russia and the new Central Asian states. The fact that Yeltsin elevated himself above the debate and gave support to both perspectives indicates that a certain synthesis of both views—albeit with the Neo-Eurasianist view increasingly dominating—might be the overall guide to and framework for Russia's policy in the near future.

Russia's Southern Flank: Collective and Bilateral Security

The Russian policy shift in Central Asia and the Caucasus has been reflected in a two-prong strategy of advocating (1) the reintegration of Central Asian, Caucasian, and Russian security within the institutional context of the CIS; and (2) simultaneously pursuing bilateral security arrangements with individual states in Central Asia and the Caucasus.

Russia and the CIS: Collective Security

The most significant dynamic within the CIS with potentially far-reaching security implications is the Treaty on Collective Security signed between Kazakhstan, Russia, Kyrgyzstan, Tajikistan, Uzbekistan, and Armenia in Tashkent on 15 May 1992. Although the treaty was initially perceived as a mere rhetorical stand and another "declaration of divorce" in the commonwealth life, subsequent meetings in Moscow and Tashkent provide substance for a more serious and perhaps an eventually enduring security system. A discussion of all aspects of the collective security agreement is beyond the scope of this essay, but what is critical for our purposes are articles 1 and 4, which state,

> If one of the participating states is subjected to aggression by any state or group of states, this will be perceived as an aggression against all participating states to the treaty. In the event of an act of aggression being committed against any of the participating states, all the other participating states will give it the necessary assistance, including military assistance, and will also give support with the means at their disposal by way of exercising the right to collective defense in accordance with article 51 of the UN charter.[40]

Articles 1 and 4 under collective security prohibit the participating states from entering "into any military alliances" or taking part in "any groupings of states or actions directed against another participating state."[41] General Leonid Ivashov, head of the working group on defense issues and one of the key participants preparing the documents for the Tashkent Summit in May 1992, argued that the treaty "confirms already established views, particularly within the military circles of the Commonwealth governments, that the establishment of a system of collective security, *or more accurately, its preservation,* is a practical necessity and an objective requirement" (emphasis added).[42] General Samsanov, in an article published by *Krasnaya Zvezda,* pointed to the political significance of the treaty: "The Treaty on Collective Security is the basis for forming a defense alliance . . . the first and probably the most complex step toward creating an effective *military and political structure* capable of being a guarantee of security for the *successful political and economic development* of the subjects that form the CIS" (emphasis added).[43]

Equally significant were the agreements reached among the participant states in Moscow (6 July 1992) and Tashkent (16 July 1992), which gave more substance to the collective security agreement reached in mid-May. The two meetings addressed the twin issues of the creation of a CIS "blue helmet" force (Moscow Summit) for rapid deployment in the area of regional conflict within the CIS and the issue of security of the southern border of the CIS (Tashkent meeting). The Moscow Summit also witnessed discussion and reached agreements on missile attack early warning systems, operational principles of the Supreme Command of CIS Joint Armed Forces, and the approval of the Statute of the CIS State Border Security Committee.[44]

What was especially noteworthy was the insistence of the Central Asian states in putting the two critical issues of "blue helmet" forces and the security of the southern borders of Central Asia on the agenda. President Islam Karimov of Uzbekistan put the rest of the participants on the spot by his relentless pressure to put the issue of border security along the southern republics—especially those facing Iran and Afghanistan—on the agendas of the Moscow Summit and the Tashkent meeting.

The Treaty on Collective Security defined the exterior border of "the participant states" as the border of the CIS, and its defense is within the jurisdiction of CIS armed forces. "We now have common external borders within the framework of the Commonwealth—land, air and sea borders," declared General Leonid Ivanshov.[45] Both Marshal Shaposhnikov, commander in chief of the CIS Joint Armed Forces, and General Samsanov reaffirmed that the quick reaction to the threat posed against the "outside borders of the Commonwealth" is one of the key tasks of the CIS collective security arrangement.[46]

After the discussion of the ethnic conflict and border issues in the Moscow Summit—a discussion characterized by Askar Akaev as of "supreme importance and in depth" and by Boris Yeltsin as "emotional"[47]—further decision was set for the Tashkent meetings of foreign and defense ministers in mid-July 1992. Uzbekistan's forceful presentation of the border and ethnic conflict issues in Moscow was reinforced by a critical report given by President Rahman Nabiev of Tajikistan on the border problem with Afghanistan. The Tashkent meeting in mid-July 1992 of foreign and defense ministries of the CIS came to general agreement on the mechanism of creation of the CIS peacekeeping force ("blue helmet") and, more importantly, the necessity of reinforcing the security of the southern border, especially the border of Tajikistan with Afghanistan.

The subsequent meetings of the CIS in Moscow and Central Asian capitals have, with different degrees of precision or success, dealt with the complicated issues of policy implementation and members' force contribution to the collective security arrangements. The eventual success or failure of collective security awaits the resolution of the political aspects of intra-CIS dynamics. While some Central Asian states, such as Kazakhstan, Kyrgyzstan, and Uzbekistan, have been more eager to solidify the collective aspects of security, others, such as Turkmenistan and the Ukraine, and to a certain degree, Byelarus, have remained vague on the merits of this security system. The Ukraine continued to look at CIS structures as being transitional, while Turkmenistan has emphasized its neutrality and lack of interest in being a member of any security alliance, and Byelorus continues to show hesitation concerning entanglement in CIS regional conflicts. The ardent supporters of collective security, namely Kazakhstan, Kyrgyzstan, and Uzbekistan, have also shown signs of internal constraint, such as the real ability to participate both in manpower and material in supporting peacekeeping forces. The future of collective security, nevertheless, might have gone beyond just being a cover-up for the "divorce process."

The preliminary meeting of CIS defense ministers that took place in Moscow on 26 February 1993 allowed for a discussion of serious issues and for the presentation of a draft agreement on issues such as creating a collective security council for the CIS and the integration of the defense industry. The meeting's discussion for the alternative organization of the CIS supreme command on NATO or Warsaw Pact models was further indication that the Treaty on Collective Security—against all military and political impediments—has moved beyond mere rhetoric, being presented as the only existing base for collective regional security, and might prove with further modification to become a viable alliance system in the region.[48]

Russia and the Central Asian Republics: Bilateral Security

While the Treaty on Collective Security provided the security umbrella for the Central Asian republics and must be considered a significant step in sculpting the ultimate shape of the region, it has still to face major political, economic, and operational challenges in the implementation phase. The chances of this collective security for survival and endurance have, however, been greatly enhanced by the series of bilateral "friendship treaties" that Russia has signed with all of the Central Asian republics. It is this "bilateral level" that provides the additional and perhaps real substance to the "collective level" security.

Kazakhstan. Among the Central Asian republics, Kazakhstan took the lead on 25 May 1992. Following his trip to the United States, Nursultan Nazarbaev arrived in Moscow to sign the "Treaty on Friendship, Cooperation and Mutual Assistance." The two sides agreed that the two countries will form a "united military and strategic zone and will jointly use the military bases, test sites and other military infrastructures."[49] The treaty was characterized by Yeltsin's press office as "a kind of political test site, and verifying philosophy" of relations between newly independent states.[50] Yeltsin and Nazarbaev expressed hope that other CIS states would take the treaty as a model to be followed.

This first experiment in bilateral security ties within the CIS had an additional regional significance, as it took place after the Ashkhabad Summit, in which Central Asian leaders, as well as the leaders of Iran, Turkey, and Pakistan, contemplated an "Asian bloc" formation. This summit signified the height of Russia's indifference or passivity on the geopolitics of the southern republics. The treaty with Kazakhstan was the beginning of Russia's "Eurasian/Eastern" shift and of the regaining of some of the lost ground in the region. The communiqué issued after Yeltsin and Nazerbaev's summit on 26 February 1993 reiterated the commitment of both states to the implementation of the bilateral treaty signed in May 1992 and the enhancement of the treaty on collective security by a Kazakh-Russian decision to "sign a treaty on military co-operation in order to set up a united defense space and make joint use of military capabilities."[51]

Uzbekistan. Uzbekistan was next to follow the model. On 30 May 1992, Russia and Uzbekistan signed the "Treaty on the Fundamentals of Interstate Relations, Friendship and Cooperation." The two sides agreed that the "territories of Russia and Uzbekistan will form a common military strategic area." They also granted each other "the right to use military facilities situated on their territories in case of necessity on the basis of mutual agreement."[52]

In subsequent agreements the two states have gradually moved toward planning and implementing the bilateral treaty. In February 1993 a Russian military delegation headed by Minister of Defense Pavel Grachev met with President Islam Karimov to discuss the integration of the two states' positions in the spheres of military-technical cooperation; joint utilization of strategic anti-aircraft, intelligence-gathering, and space-monitoring facilities; and joint plans for combat, mobilization, training, and military exercises of the Russian and Uzbek armed forces. This, in addition to the continuous presence of Russian officers, who constitute more than 80 percent of the officer corps of Uzbekistan's armed forces, also points to the close military relationship between Russia and Uzbekistan and its possible development into one of the pillars of security in Central Asia. This *might provide the military arm of a Russian-Uzbek political consensus in the* region, especially in view of Uzbekistan's willingness to perform an active role in dealing with regional ethnic conflicts, as in the case of Tajikistan.[53]

Kyrgyzstan. Askar Akaev of Kyrgyzstan was the next Central Asian leader to go to Moscow for a similar treaty with Russia. The two countries signed the "Friendship and Cooperation Treaty" on 10 June 1992, a treaty that, according to Yeltsin, raised the bilateral relations to a new level, putting the two states "on an absolutely equal footing" and thus signifying the end to Russia's "imperial ambitions."[54] Russia's role as the guarantor of Kyrgyzstan's security was reaffirmed. Kyrgyzstan's economic difficulties and inability to handle the financial responsibility of taking part in supporting CIS formations in Kyrgyzstan made this bilateral arrangement with Russia more appealing and more necessary.

Turkmenistan. Russia's bilateral security treaties with Turkmenistan and Tajikistan were the most significant of all because they dealt directly with the future security of the southern borders of the CIS. The significance of the treaty with Turkmenistan was underscored by the

intimate involvement of Russian Defense Minister General Pavel Grachev, who personally negotiated the agreement with Turkmen defense
officials and President Saparmorad Niyazov. The treaty with Turkmenistan was a unique one that envisioned the formation of a national
army for Turkmenistan under the joint command. The armed forces
will be composed of the two existing divisions (Kushka and Kizylarvat)
and other military units of the former Soviet Union still stationed in
Turkmenistan. The control of air force and air defense systems will be
entirely with the Russian armed forces (with some limited control by
Turkmenistan).[55] While logistics, training, and exercise will be in Russia's hands, the Turkmen will share the costs and will contribute in
manpower. It is noteworthy that Russian servicemen will retain the
oath of loyalty to Russia, not Turkmenistan, though the option of
changing the oath is envisioned. The strength of the army will be approximately forty-two thousand.[56]

This treaty was an important geopolitical agreement for both Russia
and Turkmenistan. For Turkmenistan, the financial burden and the
structural impediment of creating a national army seemed insurmountable.[57] In the opinion of Valeriy Otchertsov, member of the Turkmenistan Presidential Council, "for small Turkmenia surrounded on all sides
by larger neighbors, the creation of its own armed forces guaranteeing
the reliable defense of its sovereignty from outside aggression would be
highly dubious."[58] Turkmenistan's Vice Premier Nazar Soyonov pointed
to the significance of the treaty for Russia: it strengthened Russia's
southern flank by maintaining its defensive flank and not changing the
strength of its armed forces, and allowed Russia "not to build its defense
lines in the South of the Urals."[59] The political significance of the
agreement for Russia was understood by Colonel O. Falichev, military
observer of *Krasnaya Zvezda*: "Turkmenistan is choosing Russia rather
than any of its southern neighbors as guarantor of its security, its prosperity, and stability in the region."[60] During the CIS summit in Ashkhabad in December 1993, Turkmenistan joined the new CIS Economic
Union and through a series of bilateral agreements solidified its military
relations with Russia.[61] According to these agreements, 2,000 Russian
officers now stationed in the republic will officially take part in building the new army starting in January 1994.[62]

Obviously, among Turkmenistan's neighbors, Iran will be most concerned about the nature and thrust of the treaty, as it will continue to
affect Iran's overall geostrategic position. In order to neutralize Iranian
concerns, Turkmenistan has tried to maintain a posture of neutrality

toward the CIS by raising doubt on its viability as a military bloc and emphasizing its role as a political and economic structure and forum, rather than a military alliance. Rhetorically, Turkmenistan continues to portray its foreign policy as neutral, a clear message designed for the Iranians in the aftermath of signing the joint security agreement with Russia.[63]

Turkmenistan's politico-military posture will continue to reflect the two key realities and preoccupations of its post-Soviet positions. First is its continuous and direct dependency on Russia for security of the new state vis-à-vis its neighbors (at least until Turkmenistan's economic and technical potentials allow for the development of an independent and viable army). Second is the political desire and commitment to remain as independent as possible from Moscow and to avoid meaningful commitment in any regional politico-military bloc (that is, the CIS) that could undermine its newly acquired independence and become a source of provocation and concern for its southern neighbors, especially Iran. Turkmenistan's ongoing effort to enhance the political weight of its position in the command structure and decision-making mechanisms of the "joint command" of the army and its persistently reluctant policy within the CIS—rejecting any notion of creating a "supra-state" structure for the commonwealth—are a reflection of its predicament. Russia's forward politico-military position in Turkmenistan will thus continue to be affected by the inherent tension between Russian security designs and Turkmenistan's independent "neutralist" regional posture.[64]

Tajikistan. The Russian-Tajikistan security arrangement was more complex. Although Tajikistan was a signatory of the CIS Collective Security Treaty, on the bilateral level close relations with Moscow remained in the shadow of—and at times hostage to—the ongoing political struggle in Dushanbe between President Rahman Nabiev and the democratic and Islamic opposition. What made the Tajik case especially significant was the collapse of the Afghan regime and victory of Islamic forces in that country. The vulnerability of Tajikistan to mujahidin influence and border penetration increasingly captured the attention of both Moscow and—especially—the Central Asian states. The ensuing "civil war" between northern and southern parts of Tajikistan after the victory of the democratic and Islamic coalition in Dushanbe and after the collapse of the Tajik border troops formation made the infiltration of arms and bandit groups from Afghanistan a potentially explosive issue. With a clear stake in the security of the southern flank,

Uzbekistan took the lead in addressing the issue in both the Tashkent and Moscow summits. In an interview with *Nezavesmaya Gazeta* on the eve of the Tashkent meeting, Uzbek President Islam Karimov gave a frank account of this issue:

> It goes without saying that the ongoing events in Afghanistan, the uncertainty there is an object of close scrutiny on our part. And they can hardly fail to influence the socio-political situation in Uzbekistan and the other republics of Central Asia. When I spoke recently about signing the mutual security document and the fact that *Russia ought to be the guarantor of security* it was this problem that I had in mind. When I was in Ashqhabad I made a statement whose gist was that *Tajikistan is an inseparable part of Central Asia*, and that to assert that Tajikistan might suddenly find itself under the sphere of influence or under any protection of Afghanistan's Mujaheddin is absolutely unacceptable" (emphasis added).[65]

Tajikistan's security problem was raised again in the foreign and defense ministries meeting in Tashkent in mid-July 1992, and a decision was made to immediately enhance the strength of the troops on the border with Afghanistan. Marshal Shaposhnikov reiterated the now common theme that "without Russia's assistance, the people of the south will not cope." The commander in chief of the CIS forces announced the dispatch of twelve hundred additional troops to the border of Afghanistan.[66] The stage was set for a broader security agreement with Russia.

A draft of a treaty with principles of bilateral relations between Russia and Tajikistan was initiated on 21 July 1992 in Dushanbe. Russian Vice Premier Alexander Shokhin, the head of the Russian delegation, announced after the meeting with President Nabiev that given the inability of Tajikistan to maintain its border security, Russia will take the border troops of the CIS under its jurisdiction.[67] Deputy commander of the Central Asian border district, General Anatoly Martovitsky, confirmed that the border troops will be brought to full strength.[68]

Tajikistan's further incorporation into the security agreements was underscored by the request of President Nabiev for deployment of CIS "blue helmets" in Tajikistan's "conflict zones" to dismantle "the so-called 'popular front'" and "to take over the task of ensuring the activities of the national economy's facilities and protection of the population."[69] Russian security relations with Tajikistan, however, remained subject to complicated domestic pressures generated by opposition forces in Tajikistan. Democratic and Islamic groups continued to be suspicious of Russian intentions and policies in the republic and feared that the Russian military presence, disguised as "peacekeeping forces," would in reality be used to tip the balance of political power in the republic toward pro-Moscow forces, that is, the supporters of Rahman Nabiev. The Committee for National Salvation, for example, strongly protested against the presence of the "foreign military contingent."[70]

The ensuing civil war in Tajikistan, especially after the forced resignation of Nabiev in September of 1992, highlighted the complicated Russian political and security role in Tajikistan and Russia's essential role in defining both the internal political dynamics and its external security. The full and accurate story of Russia's role in the Tajikistan civil war is yet to be told, as the barrage of accusation, counteraccusation, and denial makes it difficult to discern the real picture.[71] But what could be discerned was a pattern of behavior that may provide indications of Moscow's attitude toward other regional conflicts in the territory of the former USSR, a pattern that has shown the following characteristics: a balancing act among opposing forces; guarded sympathy toward pro-Moscow groups, including former-Communist elites; an initial reluctance to become involved; and the patient period of waiting for an invitation to intervene as the only possible "peacekeeper."

There have been numerous accusations that the Russian military, and especially the 201st Motorized Rifle Division, provided support to the opposition groups and to the supporters of the deposed President Nabiev. Initially, the Russian military refused to participate in disarming Nabiev's sympathizers, who left the Ozodi Square in Dushanbe fully armed. Further, the four "stolen" or "sold" T-72 tanks and the armored vehicles and artillery pieces used by the opposition in Kulyab and Kurgan Tyube to overrun the government forces and reach Dushanbe in late October set the stage for Russian intervention and control of the city. Russia was indeed responding to the call of the Central Asian leaders gathered in Alma-Ata to perform the "peacekeeping role" envisioned in the collective security agreement. The need for Russian intervention was echoed without hesitation or ambiguity by the leaders of the besieged government of Tajikistan, headed by Akbarshoh Iskandarov. What is critical here is the discussion of two intertwined issues: (1) the presence of a general consensus for Russian politico-military intervention both at the regional—that is, Central Asian—and republic, that is, Tajikistan—levels; and (2) continuity of Russian willingness for politico-military intervention in Tajikistan, as in other republics. The consensus for Russian involvement has been instrumental in neutralizing the charges of Russian imperialism. Moscow's reluctance to intervene undermines the effectiveness of nationalist charges of Russia's aggressive interventionist policy and further confirms the existence of a "structural dependency" between Tajikistan (and, for that matter, most of the Central Asian republics) and Russia.

I have used the term *structural* to indicate the enduring elements of continuity of Central Asia's—and in this case Tajikistan's—organic and multidimensional economic, political, and military dependency on Russia, in spite of a genuine Tajik desire to create a full-fledged, independent nation-state. Russian leaders and foreign ministry officials have been cognizant of this "structural dependency," and expressed confidence in the continuity of the Russian presence amidst Moscow's erosion of power and the tide of ethnonationalist movements in Central Asia. Shelov-Kovedyaev, until mid-1992 deputy foreign minister and the official in charge of CIS affairs, in an important interview with *Nezavisimaya Gazeta* in July 1992, argued that Tajik domestic problems, including "the rivalry of North and South," which "did not arise yesterday and will not disappear tomorrow," will not have a major bearing on the essential understanding that Russian-Tajik relations will remain close as "all political forces would welcome the significance of a treaty with Russia and would recognize its legal validity regardless of the development of the situation."[72]

The reality of Tajik structural dependency did not escape even the forces that are, by political orientation and philosophy, not friendly to Moscow. "We are still connected with Russia like this," said presidential advisor Davlat Khodanazarov as he interlaced his fingers, "but I have nothing against being dependent, if it works to help people survive."[73] Davlat Usmon, Tajikistan's vice premier and deputy chairman of the Islamic Renaissance Party, also indicated that stability in Tajikistan without the help of Russia and the CIS will be "rather problematic."[74] The invocation of a collective security agreement in the case of Tajikistan by the Alma-Ata meeting[75] on 4 November 1992 was a clear indication that Russia and the Central Asian partners—regardless of their intra-CIS differences—will continue to hold the former Soviet Union's southern borders as the border of the CIS and of Russia's sphere of influence. More significantly, it also indicated that the maintenance of the domestic stability of the republic has been considered a legitimate security concern of the member states, one that falls within the jurisdiction of the collective security agreements.

This was a clear message to all regional actors, including Iran, that notwithstanding the collapse of the Soviet Union, its geopolitical legacy will remain largely unchanged. Sergei Yastrzhembskiy, head of the Foreign Ministry Press and Information Department, in a news briefing in early September 1992, characterized Moscow's position rather frankly:

> The Russian Ministry proceeds from the premise that interference in the internal affairs of *Tajikistan that is located in the area of the Russian Federation's important and versatile interest,* cannot be justified no matter from where it comes and what it is motivated by . . . Russia is ready to take all necessary measures to provide assistance to the fraternal Tajik people in stabilizing the situation in the country, to help it shore up its sovereignty and territorial integrity and *ensure the security of the CIS's southern borders.* (emphasis added)[76]

Returning from his three-day trip to Iran on 4 November 1992, N. Nazarbaev echoed the sensitivity over the role of the external factor in the crisis in Tajikistan and pointed to the assurance received from the Iranian president of "nonintervention" in the internal affairs of Tajikistan.[77]

The downfall of the "democratic-Islamic" coalition government in December 1992 and the consolidation of "pro-Communist" forces in Tajikistan, headed by Imomali Rahmonov, was not only a watershed in the Tajikistan civil war, but also signaled a qualitatively new stage in the involvement of Russia and its primary regional ally, Uzbekistan, in shaping the political and security dynamics of the region. Uzbekistan's direct involvement in providing political, logistical, and military backing for the "pro-Communist" forces, namely, the "People's Front," was crucial in changing the balance of power among the contending parties. As discussed earlier, Uzbek President Islam Karimov has been, from the early days of the Soviet collapse, the most outspoken Central Asian leader in promoting a regional security arrangement that would not only safeguard the external borders of Central Asia (for example, borders with Afghanistan) but, more significantly, would allow a flexible intrusive policy of intervention in the domestic politics of the republics with seemingly threatening dynamics.

While concerns over the instability in Tajikistan were usually couched in terms of anxiety over Afghan infiltration or Iranian influence, the real fear of Uzbek, Russian, and other Central Asian leaders was the threat of an anti–status quo political alternative, be it "Islamic," "democratic," or otherwise, that might successfully unseat the existing elite and have contagious political ramifications for the adjacent republics, including Uzbekistan. Thus, Tajikistan's domestic stability—meaning the existence of a political model and leadership acceptable to Uzbekistan, Russia, and others—was an implicit but important justification and rationale for politico-military intervention.

Uzbek and Russian intervention in Tajikistan's civil war was both direct and indirect. Uzbekistan not only provided logistical supplies for the pro-Communist forces throughout the conflict, but it was more specifically involved in the military aspects of the civil war. Uzbek officers literally formed and trained a brigade of Tajik troops in Termez, a small Uzbek border town. In addition, pro-Communist forces were provided with armored vehicles and air support.[78]

Uzbekistan's intimate role in the Tajik civil war may point to a potentially significant regional development with far-reaching implications for the security of Central Asia; namely, whether Uzbekistan and its leader have assumed the role of a regional policeman. Uzbekistan's interest in Tajikistan's developments cannot be overstated. Among the key components of Tashkent security and foreign policy concerns are cross-border ethnoterritorial conflict, especially in view of the Tajik-Uzbek ethnic mix of both states; the threat of radical political change in Tajikistan that might set a new precedent for post-Communist transition in Central Asia; hegemonic ambition of perpetuating an Uzbek-Centric regional order; improving Uzbekistan's power and leverage vis-à-vis Russia and other regional powers such as Kazakhstan; and the security of the CIS's southern borders.

Russia's preoccupation with its own deepening political-economic crisis and its explosive entanglement in the North Caucasus conflict, as well as concern over charges of neo-imperial policies, were factors that collectively encouraged an activist security role for Uzbekistan in Tajikistan. This is not the first time that a great power, itself in crisis, has deliberately or reluctantly solicited or supported the efforts of a junior ally. Allowing a degree of generalization in the following analogy, the role of Karimov in Central Asia could be compared to the role of the shah as the policeman of the Persian Gulf in the 1970s. As in the Russian-Uzbek case, American-Iranian security understanding was based on an overall shared perception of threat, that is, political instability emanating from revolutionary and unwelcome political alternatives.

And as the United States was uncomfortable with Iran's regional hegemonic ambitions, so too has Russia refused to endorse the ambitions of a "Greater Uzbekistan." Yet, Russia's post-Soviet realities have encouraged coordination of interests and modification of differences between Moscow and Tashkent, as American post-Vietnam realities encouraged Washington's accommodation to the shah's policies. And as Russia itself is moving away from its early enthusiasm over democracy and human rights, these political irritants of earlier months in Russian-Uzbek relations have faded into the background. Uzbekistan's leadership has not only ignored the issues of democracy and suppressed its own domestic opponents and their occasional Moscow supporters, but moreover has openly rejected the inclusion of a human rights clause in the latest CIS charter, discussed in the recent summit at Minsk. (The shah was also notorious for ignoring occasional American democratic "reminders.")

Russia's direct involvement in Tajikistan, nevertheless, indicated that Moscow may not be willing to delegate total responsibility to Uzbek regional policing. Furthermore, a sustained and effective politicomilitary intervention in the Tajik crisis seemed impractical without direct Russian engagement. Russian direct participation has taken two forms. First was a gradual abandonment of the position of "positive neutrality," which had been adopted during the earlier stages of the crisis, in favor of active support of "pro-Communist" forces in the latter and crucial stages of the conflict. After the downfall of the "democratic-Islamic" coalition government in Dushanbe, the Russian airborne units took part in a series of antiguerrilla campaigns in Garm, Navabad, and Komsomolabad, while the Russian (CIS) air force and helicopter gunships bombed opposition forces in these regions.[79]

Second, Russia has practically taken over the task of creating a new army for Tajikistan. Participation of General Pavel Grachev and top CIS military officials, such as CIS deputy Chief of Staff Major-General Farrokh Niyazov, in planning the formation of the new army only signified the importance of security arrangements in the republic. Thirty-one Russian officers who arrived in Dushanbe on 4 February 1993 as part of the Russian military delegation will assist the new government in building the army. While initially the Russian 201st Rifle Division was to become the nucleus of the new army,[80] a subsequent decision indicated the use of the division as the independent Russian "forward position" in Tajikistan (the division also recruits Tajik conscripts only from the pro-government stronghold in the northern region of the republics).

The armed formations of the "People's Front," instead, will be used as the foundation of the new Tajik military.[81]

According to Major-General Niyazov, who also acts as the permanent representative of Tajikistan in the CIS, the new Tajik army will be built based on the strategic location of the republic and "special local features of the republic such as its mountainous terrain," which requires "a mobile and flexible army equipped with up to date equipment."[82] Ironically, Niyazov's suggestion echoes what Mikhail Tukachevsky, the father of Russian mobile warfare, had suggested to the Bolshevik leadership seventy years earlier regarding what was needed to fight the *basmachi*-type challenges in Central Asia.

The civil war in Tajikistan may not be over, as the fight has continued and potential problems for future conflict have increased, not only among the Tajik's themselves but between Uzbeks and Tajiks. The Uzbek Turks' participation in the civil war has given rise to a Tajik version of the "Armenian syndrome" for the defeated regions of the republic.[83] The deployment of Russian/CIS troops in the Tajik-Afghan border and the ensuing clashes between Russian troops and the Tajik opposition forces stationed in Afghanistan signified the security importance of Central Asia and its southern border for Russia. The participation of Russia, Uzbekistan, and other CIS members in the conflict indicates that any future security challenge in the republic, either from internal or external sources, will have to anticipate the politico-military response of Russia and its Central Asian allies. In the words of Imomali Rahmonov, the leader of the new government in Dushanbe, Russian and Uzbek involvement in Tajikistan's conflict was the first successful test of the collective security agreements.[84]

Azerbaijan. Russia's security on the western side of the southern flank, the Caucasus, became much more complex as the region was engulfed in the bloody ethnic conflict in Nagorno-Karabakh and the undeclared war between Armenia and Azerbaijan. The involvement of the two powerful neighboring states—Turkey and Iran—in the conflict underlined the extreme fluidity of the geopolitical environment of the western side of the flank. Moscow's initial vacillation between supporting Armenia and doing nothing undermined Russia's position in the region. The following months, however, witnessed some change in the policy and a sense of direction.

While Russia's diplomacy anxiously awaited the Iranian failure to mediate, it focused its own conflict resolution strategy on promoting the CSCE mechanism and providing parallel unilateral mediation. The collapse of Azeri defense in Nagorno-Karabakh and victory of Armenia, which to no small scale was the result of Russian arms and equipment (mainly from the 7th Army) and apparent participation of certain Russian army and military units (366th Brigade), undermined the balance of power in the Caucasus and also set the dangerous precedent of change of borders by force. Turkey's support for Azerbaijan and its threat of military intervention on Azerbaijan's behalf brought the sharp reaction by Marshal Shaposhnikov and the warning of the "possibility of a global war."

Shaposhnikov's remarks, although considered a bit overstated by the Russian Foreign Ministry, marked Russia's anxiety and also the beginning of the shift in Moscow's policy. The initial pro-Armenian position was gradually modified by a subtle military move in providing Azerbaijan with the arms and equipment and some actual military support (allowing the Russian officers to perform their duty!)[85] by transferring equipment of the 4th Army to Azeri authority.[86] It should be noted that some of this equipment had already been confiscated or stolen by "informal Azeri groups"; however, the main decision for official transfer, especially the air force in Baku, played a critical role in redressing the balance of power between the two sides.

The Russian balancing act seemed to be geared not only toward demonstrating evenhandedness but probably also to allowing Azerbaijan to regain some of the ground lost in Nagorno-Karabakh. A closer politico-military relationship with both sides provided a more flexible environment for Russian policy in the Caucasus. The total alienation of Azerbaijan, a state that had refused to join the CIS, would have carried the twin dangers of creating a power vacuum that might have been justifiably filled by Turkey or Iran and, thus, creating the possibility of Turkey's intervention against Armenia. This latter possibility has been especially acute in the Nakhichevan Autonomous Republic, which borders Turkey and was under Armenian military pressure during 1993. In such a scenario, Armenia as a "participant state" in CIS collective security could have drawn Russia into a major regional conflict.

Russia's balancing strategy has paid some tangible, though not decisive, dividends. Armenia, clearly unhappy about Russia's involvement in strengthening Azerbaijan militarily, had little option but to rely on its fundamental security guarantee, namely, its membership in the CIS collective security system and Russia's principal role in the system.[87] Furthermore, Armenia's continuous exercise of military power relies heavily on Russia's continuous goodwill—or at least lack of opposition—

to have access to military hardware and units of the 7th Army.[88] Moreover, Russia's diplomatic support or "positive neutrality" will continuously be needed in the complex and uncertain dynamics of the conflict. Azerbaijan, though not a member of the CIS (it maintains an observer status), also needs a benevolent Russian military policy and diplomatic support. Though the anti-Russian hostility and ill feeling generated by the events of January 1990 in Baku and Russia's subsequent pro-Armenian policy still remain, the realpolitik of the Russian factor is casting a heavy shadow over the emotional dimension of the relations.[89] Furthermore, and perhaps decisively, the Azeri leadership's concern over its relations with Iran and the protection of its southern border mitigates a closer security relationship with Russia.

It is interesting to note that in spite of Azerbaijan's public position regarding the CIS, some initial contact as early as late May 1992 was made between the Russian and Azerbaijani military. General Grachev had discussed the issue of arms transfers and the possibility of Azerbaijan joining the CIS with Azerbaijan's defense minister.[90] Although Azerbaijan's participation in the CIS process remains a possibility, it runs into both domestic and regional obstacles. Domestically, the Popular Front, the dominant political force in the republic, and President Abulfez Elchibey have campaigned against the idea of joining the CIS and have equated true nationalism and independence as contradictory with such participation. Furthermore, given the growing influence of Turkey in Azerbaijan in both the political and military spheres, Baku's participation in CIS collective security may not have the blessing of Ankara. This might be especially pertinent in view of the de facto protectorate position of the Nakhichevan Autonomous Republic vis-à-vis Turkey, a position that had been nurtured by the disintegration of the Russian military presence in Nakhichevan and the increasing isolation of Nakhichevan from Azerbaijan and ensuing vulnerability vis-à-vis Armenia. Thus, instead of a problematic collective security arrangement with the CIS, Azerbaijan opted for bilateral security relations with Russia.

There are several reasons for this move. First is the inability of Azerbaijan, like other republics of the former USSR, to field its own army. This is an especially acute problem for Azerbaijan as it has been engaged in a major local war in Nagorno-Karabakh and was in 1993 in a state of undeclared war with Armenia. Without a good relationship with Russia, the existing military capabilities are hardly sustainable. Second, the close relations with Turkey, while flourishing and developing, may have their drawbacks. In the minds of nationalist Azeris, their relations with the "elder brothers" in Turkey also run the risk of entrapping them in an unequal relationship between a weak and ruined former republic and the most formidable military actor in the region, one with rekindled pan-Turkic and possibly hegemonic tendencies. Russia will be a possible balancer over the horizon. Third, relations with Iran are perhaps the key factor in promoting closer military relations between Azerbaijan and Russia. In spite of religious, historical, and ethnic ties between the two countries, the Azerbaijani leadership maintained a cool and at times hostile attitude toward Iran. The most serious potential problem between Iran and Azerbaijan was the "irredentist claim" for unification of Iranian Azerbaijan with the new Azerbaijani state. On numerous occasions, the leader of Azerbaijan, Abulfez Elchibey, made open and at times provocative remarks about the eventual unification with its southern Azeri brother. He has also gone so far as to predict that Iran as a multiethnic entity will no longer exist at the end of the decade and that it will be divided into several ministates. In addition, and as a norm, the threat of "Islamic fundamentalism" was presented as the main factor.

Iran's alleged support for Armenia—or to put it more accurately, Iran's unwillingness to abandon its neutrality in the Nagorno-Karabakh conflict—has been an important source of Azeri irritation. How could a neighboring Muslim country with more than fifteen million Azeris not support Azerbaijan against the aggressive Christian Armenia? Furthermore, Turkey's strong opposition and displeasure over any gains by Iran in the Caucasus is the additional contributing factor in promoting the anti-Iranian position of Azerbaijan. The tougher attitudes toward Iran will also fit into the prevailing U.S. policy in the region, as was brought home to the Azeri leadership during Secretary of State Baker's trip to Azerbaijan. Iran, as the embodiment of the Islamic threat, should be contained. On this the Turks, Americans, and Russians share Azerbaijan's concern.

The combination of these factors provided a basis for a Russian-Azeri security military arrangement dealing with the southern borders. This agreement, though not as far-reaching as those Russia reached with the Central Asian republics, allowed Russia's participation and protection of Azerbaijan's border with Iran and Turkey, including the continuous control of air defense systems, reconnaissance, and missile early warning systems. According to a press report in Moscow, Azerbaijani Foreign Minister Tofik Gasymov was quoted as saying that "the northern border of Azerbaijan might not have to be closed after all." On the contrary, it is the southern border of the republic that will have to be strengthened.[91] He anticipated a treaty with Russia that "would solve issues of mutual interest, including the protection of state borders and the status of border troops."[92] On 29 July 1992, Azerbaijan and Russia finally agreed on the joint guarding of Azerbaijan's southern borders with Iran and Turkey for a two-year term. The agreement also envisioned that the Azerbaijani army personnel would be trained in "specialist schools" in Russia.[93]

The possibility of joining the CIS was also raised by some Azerbaijani officials, such as Isa Kamberov, who argued that observer status at CIS summits is not effective for the conduct of the Azerbaijani policy with the former republics of the Soviet Union. This was especially the case in view of the warning by some members of the CIS that Azerbaijan's observer status might be terminated, demanding a more concrete approach by the republic toward the CIS.[94]

Russia's enhanced position in Azerbaijan and the critical role it played in balancing relations between Azerbaijan and Armenia—and the presence of the similar "structural dependency"—led to the creation of the politico-military environment that gave Russia, in spite of its early weakness, the key role in the Nagorno-Karabakh problem. An internationalized conflict that brought actors of different capabilities and objectives into competition for influence and "peace-making" finally had to be addressed by the Russians. Many actors, including the United States, Turkey, Iran, the UN, and the European Community, have attempted individually or collectively to solve the problem of Nagorno-Karabakh, all with little or no success. The CSCE-sponsored conference in Rome was the most serious extraregional attempt that ended in complete failure. Against this background, the announcement of the *Sochi* cease-fire agreement between Armenia and Azerbaijan, designed and negotiated by Russian Defense Minister Pavel Grachev in late September 1992, took most observers by surprise.

What was perhaps most significant about the cease-fire was not only its scope and detailed military protocol (for example, demarcation lines, nonmilitary zones, demilitarization) but the unprecedented role of the Russian military in single-handedly negotiating it. In a remarkable interview with *Kraznaya Zvesda*, Defense Minister Grachev provided the details of the top-secret negotiations that had been ordered by Yeltsin sometime in May 1992. What is most interesting about the process of negotiations was the preeminence of the role of the military establishment of all sides of the conflict and the central and guiding role of the Russian military in pressuring the Armenians and Azerbaijanis to ratify an agreement. Grachev, "the elder brother"[95] in the negotiations, in a moment of frankness reflected on the underlying causes that forced the Azeris and Armenians to come to the negotiation table, namely the dependence of both republics on Russia. He explained that he had forecasted several months earlier that the military exhaustion and the need for spare parts would force a negotiation in which Russia would play a central role: "And who will they turn to for specialists and spare parts? Russia? We know what Russia's answer will be."[96]

The Nagorno-Karabakh problem and the Azeri-Armenian conflict are far from over, but the Russian policy reflected an intense desire and determination to remain involved, not as a peripheral observer but as the principal shaper of its eventual politico-military development and outcome. The downfall of the Elchibey government in Baku in June 1993 and the reemergence of Haider Aliev, the former CPSU Politburo member, was, at least for the time being, a welcome development for Moscow. The removal of an overtly pro-Turkish Elchibey and his replacement by more centrist forces could only further consolidate the Russian position in Azerbaijan and its ability to influence the internal and external dynamics of the republic. "The Caucasus region is a traditional sphere of Russian interest and we do not intend to abandon it," declared Russian Foreign Minister Andrei Kozyrov.[97] Azerbaijan's Deputy Premier Abbas Abbasov, emphasizing the transparency of the Russian-Azeri border, echoed a similar sentiment: "Azerbaijan is in the zone of Russia's military-strategic protection," for in addition to being an "economic nucleus," Russia remains "the political and military nucleus of our entire region."[98] Azerbaijan's severe economic, political, and security crisis, along with the absence of a powerful alternative in the region (either Turkey or Iran), will continue to provide the structural basis for Russia's influential position in the republic. Furthermore, Azerbaijan—regardless of which political force is in charge—faces a national crisis of existential proportions in Nagorno-Karabakh. An honorable and acceptable solution to this dilemma will be critical to the evolution of the republic as a nation-state; unfortunately for Azerbaijan, the dispute appears to be intractable, not unlike the Israeli-Palestinian conflict. Initiatives undertaken by Aliev during the latter half of 1993 have been designed to provide Baku with badly needed leverage in its conflict with Armenia. Azerbaijan's acceptance of Russia's mediation, its demand for modification of provisions of the Treaty on

Collective Security (to address member-states' agressions against one another), and growing military cooperation with Russia all indicate that Azerbaijan has calculated that Russia will play the central role in the shaping of the republic's security for the foreseeable future.[99]

Toward a Russian Monroe Doctrine?

A general overview of the Russian foreign policy debate and actual policy during the two years after the collapse of the Soviet Union indicates a clear Russian desire and willingness to protect its historical politico-strategic interests in Central Asia and the Caucasus. The ascendancy of the Neo-Eurasianist thinking and policy in Moscow also indicates that notwithstanding the Soviet collapse and the emergence of new independent states, Russia has been able to partially recover the apparent strategic vacuum through measures such as the Treaty on Collective Security and bilateral security agreements with the new Central Asian and Caucasian states. Thus, the entire border of the former Soviet Union with the states of the traditional southern flank (that is, Iran, Afghanistan, Turkey) remains within the realm of Russian and CIS strategic reach. The treaty-bound presence of Russian troops in the border republics points to a major element of strategic *continuity* in the midst of drastic changes in the region.

What are the key ingredients of this apparent continuity? Why can Russia, in the midst of its own deep political and economic crisis, still count on the preservation of its historical interests and influence in Central Asia and the Caucasus? The answer to these questions lies in the enduring military, economic, and political legacies of the Soviet Union. Although the Russian "center" has been severely weakened on all three levels, it still outweighs the Central Asian and Caucasian "periphery." Between the Russian "center" and its Asian "periphery" there exists a level of *structural dependency/interdependence* that will not be overcome overnight.

Militarily, Russian foreign policy is increasingly driven by the belief that Russian security is inherently linked with the security of its Asian periphery, so the vigorous protection of Russia's historical geopolitical environment will remain fundamental to Russia's foreign and security policy. In fact, a careful reading of Russian thinking and policy points to the emergence of what could be called the "Russian Monroe Doctrine" in Central Asia and the Caucasus. The draft of the "Russian foreign policy concept" has called the protection of the "Commonwealth's outer border" an urgent task in Russian foreign policy. The document also clearly warns other international actors, regional or otherwise, that Moscow will vigorously oppose all attempts to build up the political or military presence of third countries in the states adjoining Russia.[100]

This "strategic denial" to "third countries" accompanies and fits conveniently within the Neo-Eurasianist vision of Russia as the sole guarantor of security in the territory of the former Soviet Union. In a speech to the Civic Union on 28 February 1993, Yeltsin reiterated this critical point: "Stopping all armed conflicts in the territory of the former USSR is Russia's vital interest. The world community sees more and more clearly Russia's special responsibility in this difficult undertaking." Cognizant of charges of neoimperialism and also of the importance of the UN in the post–Cold War world, Yeltsin went on to ask for the international endorsement and legitimization of Russia's interest: "I believe the time has come for distinguished international organizations, including the UN, to grant Russia special powers of a guarantor of peace and stability in the region of the former USSR."[101]

The Russian military has to overcome enormous political, financial, and organizational difficulties to be able to perform its function in Moscow's overall strategy. Yet Russian military activism in Tajikistan and similar efforts in other regions, including the creation of the North Caucasus Military District and the deployment of troops in the Tajik-Afghan border, indicate the commitment of the Russian military to perform its role.[102]

The Soviet economic legacy and the continuous interstate dependency further perpetuate Russia's dominant position. Not only do the new states still need each other and Russia for their continuous flow of production and trade (on average 25–30 percent of production downfall in Russia and the republics is due to broken economic ties!), but equally significant, the similarity of challenges facing economic reforms in Russia and the Central Asian states points to a level of convergence in the economic models of these states in their post-Communist transition. As the enthusiasm over Russia's experiment with overnight market transition through "shock therapy" fades into the background and Russia's new cabinet attempts a more centrist economic policy (reflected mostly in practice though not in words), Central Asian states find their gradualist, conservative approach toward economic reform vindicated, and might have acquired a new conservative model partner in Moscow.

Chernomyrdin's "market with a human face,"[103] Nazarbaev's "socio-market economy,"[104] Karimov's "market with strong social policy" with the state as the "main reformer,"[105] and Niyazov's "socialist-market without ideology" all indicate a degree of economic interdependence/convergence not only on economic ties but also on the level of intellectual consensus for post-Soviet transition. Free from the ritualistic ideological baggage of Communism, Russia and Central Asia still share the socialist legacies of the Soviet experience.

The political dimension of structural dependency/interdependence between Russia and the new states follows a similar pattern. As Moscow's democratic hype and its claim of becoming an agent of democratic change in the former USSR fades into the background, the Central Asian authoritarian elite may find in the new Russia not only vindication of their political model but also a new, model partner in substance, though not in form. The struggle between President Yeltsin and the Russian Congress has failed to be the struggle between democrats and nationalists, but rather of who will rule Russia; an essential authoritarianism runs through the body politics of both camps. There is little debate in Moscow about real democracy. The Neo-Eurasianist political model for Russia essentially values stability and a strong state as key requirements of socioeconomic reform and security, and in that there is little disagreement between the Central Asian capitals and Moscow. Thus, convergence of the Russian and Central Asian economic models in the post-Soviet transition phase follows parallel political models required to implement reforms. Furthermore, a shared political vision on the key threat to the existing order, namely an Islamic threat, also provides a significant common area of interest between the Central Asian elite and Moscow.

The military, economic, and political dimension of Russian–Central Asian interdependence seems even more significant if analyzed in the context of real alternative sources of competition from outside. Much has been written about the United States, the West, Turkey, Iran, and others in relation to Central Asia regarding their attempt to fill the vacuum left by the Soviet collapse. The realities of these actors' relations with the new states, however, indicate that given the enormity of Central Asian needs and the military, economic, and political limitation of these actors, Russia's chance of being the most important actor remains promising. Thus, will the 1990s witness the reassertion of Russia's dominant "center" in its Asian "periphery"? Are there any mitigating factors that might signal that Russia will not be able to repeat the remarkable imperial comeback similar to the post-1917 period?

One might argue that the presence of such a formidable superpower as the United States and other factors such as the Russian economic crisis and the nationalistic-Islamic fervor of the new states have formed a powerful combination that will not allow the reassertion of Russian dominance. Indeed, these are considerable challenges, yet Russia has not been unfamiliar with similar obstacles in the past, and its power base, both at home and abroad, is much more favorable in 1993 than it was in 1917.

The key mitigating factor against Russia's reassertion in the long term will be of a subjective nature, namely, the absence of a dynamic, forward-looking neoimperial vision and zeal. Russia's "great power ideology" lacks the religiously based "third Rome" of the tsars and the equally fanatical Marxian-Utopian conviction of the Bolsheviks. The most devastating implications of the current Russian crisis are not its economic problems but an emerging national psyche that is largely shaken by doubt about its glorious past and is devoid of real hope and vision for the future. The messianic elements of the enlightened Euro-Atlanticist perspective are defeatist in nature, as they look primarily to the West for salvation and inspiration, while the Neo-Eurasianist's realpolitik is inherently cynical and lacking ideological conviction and thus is not equipped with the visionary impulses required to supplement and inspire Russia's objective (that is, military power). Gorbachev's "new political thinking" was too little and too late of an attempt to revitalize the needed ideological backup of the empire.

Will Russia's nationalism provide the ideological substitute for Communism? The outdated, nostalgic, and inherently exclusivist currency of Russian nationalism that presently inspires nationalist-Communist factions in Russia will be a dangerous and poor substitute, as it will engulf Russia in a bloodbath of civil war varieties at "home" and wars of national liberation in its "nearby foreign parts."

In the absence of an all-embracing visionary ideology and in the context of the current deep crisis, Russia must rely on ordinary instruments of power, that is, military coercion and diplomacy of accommodation and maneuver, a symbiosis that may prove inadequate for the repetition of the post-1917 imperial revival.

Conclusion: Greater Central Asia and Its Contextual Security Elements

Any specific and certain conclusion on the overall direction of security in the southern flank—or, to be more precise, in Greater Central

Asia—must take into consideration the depth of the changes that are taking place and many yet to come. The current security environment is transitional; actors are still coping with the immediate impacts of the Soviet collapse and grappling with more long-term challenges. What could be attempted here is to identify some of the general issues around which the post-Soviet politico-military environment of this region would evolve. With this in view, the following are some of the fundamental components of the new geopolitics of the region.

Islamic Geopolitics and the New Containment

In the post–Cold War era the main ideologically driven security threat was the Soviet Union, but today a new threat, different in shape and character, has been identified as the primary source of menace to the region and its current top security priorities. The Islamic threat, exaggerated or not, has shaped the geopolitics of international and regional actors since the early 1980s, and now, in the absence of Communism, will be the major factor in future developments. From China's Xinjiang Muslim region to India's Kashmir and to Algeria in North Africa, the Islamic factor has occupied a key place in all geopolitical calculations. The inclusion of Central Asia in the Middle East and the prospects of its cooperation on ideological and military levels with nearby Muslim countries has only enhanced the significance, complexity, and endurance of "Islamic geopolitics." The announcement of the "dual containment" doctrine in the Persian Gulf by the Clinton Administration will have its domino effect in Central Asia and the Caucasus. As Iran and its Islamic threat remains the focus of dual containment, the chasing and containing of Iran and Islam in the Middle East by the United States will be echoed and followed also in Central Asia and the Caucasus. Thus, the attitude toward Iran and Islam will be an important factor affecting the behavior of the big powers—especially the United States and Russia—in Central Asia. The West, and particularly the United States, faced with choices of a post-Soviet secular authoritarianism or Islamic Central Asia, will support the first option. U.S. acquiescence in Russia's suppression of Islamic forces in the Tajik civil war is perhaps an indication of future trends in the region.

The military dimension of this ideological threat has been encapsulated in the concern over the so-called "Islamic bomb": nuclear proliferation, chemical weapons, and missile technology. In fact, the Western security thinking in the post–Cold War has shifted to two dimensions: nuclear proliferation and relations with Islam;[106] the Greater Central Asian region happens to encapsulate both.

The significance of attitudes toward the Islamic threat for the region's security cannot be overstated. The Iraqi invasion of Kuwait and the subsequent military intervention by the United States and its allies was to a large extent an indirect by-product of Western and Soviet fear of Islam in the 1980s. The emergence of Saddam Hussein's Iraq as a regional leader was the direct result of the unconditional support given to the Baghdad regime by the big and small powers during the 1980s out of fear of victory of "fundamentalist Iran" and the "Islamic domino effect." Religion and oil—a combination of the masses' frustration and their temptation to return to the puritan and the glorious Islamic past and its confrontation with Western/Russian containment—are the explosive ingredients of Islamic geopolitics that will continue to dominate the security of the region in the 1990s.

A Besieged Nation-State System

The second trend affecting the security of this region is the systemic pressure on the nation-state system through the emergence of the new nations and rekindled ethnoterritorial and religious nationalism. New nations of Central Asia are welcome additions to the region, yet the ethnoterritorial nature of new nation-building trends might lead to a long, bloody process of breakdown of other states in the region, such as Iran, Iraq, Afghanistan, Pakistan, and Turkey, along ethnic and religious lines. Cross-border ethnic and religious affiliation and preemptive strategies to prevent disintegration could easily lead to Balkanization or Lebanization of the region. A Yugoslav-type scenario is not too farfetched. Dynamic and independent-minded ethnic groups like Azeris, Kurds, Baluch, Tajik, Uzbek, and Turkmen are spread among Turkey, Iraq, Iran, Pakistan, Afghanistan, Azerbaijan, Tajikistan, and Uzbekistan, all contiguous states with political maps that betray ethnic realities. Scenarios of instability are endless, and the possibilities of intervention and counterintervention abound.

The Balance of Power

The balance of power in the region has clearly shifted in favor of the West, and particularly the United States. Supported by key regional allies—Turkey and Saudi Arabia—with direct (permanent) and over-the-horizon military presence, the United States enjoys, at least for now, a politico-military preponderance. The key objective of the United States in Greater Central Asia remains constant: stability, the containment of the Islamic threat, access to "reasonably priced oil," protection of key allies, and prevention of domination by regional leaders.

As one of the main beneficiaries of the Soviet collapse, Turkey enjoys the support of the United States and basically has been given the role of promoting the interests of the West in Central Asia. Of course, this does not exclude the fact that Turkey lacks its own Central Asian agenda, an agenda optimized by Turkey's cultural and political ties to the "Turkic world."

Iran, the other key regional power, has and will continue to have the most complicated and taxing geopolitical environment in the region. As the subject of Islamic containment, feared by its neighbors for its "subversive" and dynamic Islamic message, Iran's geopolitical environment is encircled. To the north are cautious and at times hostile Russia and anxious Central Asian republics, to the west are hostile Iraq and competitive Turkey, to the east are unstable and "ungrateful" Afghanistan and Pakistan, and to the south are the hostile United States and its Gulf allies. Never before has such a tight geopolitical environment been imposed on Iran. This geopolitical "fishbowl" is being compounded by the overtly multiethnic nature of the Iranian state, situated in the geographical heart of an irredentist, ethnonationalist region. Maintaining its territorial integrity will be the number one priority of Iran. The most potentially dangerous development would be the introduction of a Turko-Iranian conflict in Central Asia and the Caucasus, which could have both regional and global consequences; both Russia and the United States will be affected by this competition, and might be drawn into conflicts emanating from it. Iran's Islamic threat and its alleged search for the "Islamic bomb" will be the focus of U.S.-Iranian tension.

Russia and Central Asia's approach to the region will be affected mostly by the domestic requirements of the transitional period. The future orientation of Russia's approach depends not only on the degree of success in avoiding further domestic crisis but also on its overall foreign policy orientation or preference. A Euro-Atlanticist view will follow the Western lead in the region and will closely coordinate its policy with the overall policy of the United States. A Neo-Eurasianist view will have a more independent, "self-contained" policy, mostly cooperative, yet at times competitive with the United States, and will opt for closer relations with Iran, for example. Russia will attempt to limit both Iranian and Turkish influence in the Caucasus and Central Asia, and it will be vigilant in protecting the border of the CIS in the southern flank. Russian diplomacy will be active in the Persian Gulf, and arms sales will be increasingly used to both make money and facilitate influence.[107]

Russia and the CIS's military doctrine toward the South has yet to be elaborated. There has been considerable talk in Russian military circles, however, regarding the preference of a flexible doctrine that envisions a "forward base" deployment in which the main force would be based in the Russian heartland during peacetime but would be able to deploy rapidly to a "forward position" if real threat of an attack emerges from the South.[108] Russian and CIS military officials have envisioned a meaner and leaner army, "something no less than NATO," for the future defense of the CIS and Russia.[109]

Although weakened and mired in domestic reform, Russia—for its sheer size and military power—remains the most important factor, along with the United States, in affecting the geopolitics of greater Central Asia. Though its power has eroded, its desires remain. In a comprehensive presidential news conferences on Russian foreign policy in July 1992, President Yeltsin provided a general overview of Russia's interest in the region. While rejecting the accusation of following a pro-Western policy, he argued that the time for more "balance" and "constant eastward movement" in Russian foreign policy has arrived. He emphasized the need for much closer relations with China, Turkey, and Iran, and elaborated, "One must bear in mind that an alliance seemed to be emerging between the Central Asian republics and Islam in the East—at the cost of a break with Russia—[but] both sides have come to the conclusion that it would be a strategic mistake. We ourselves did not exert influence here. They—in particular Iran, Turkey and our Central Asian states—realized themselves that the answer was no. *One has to bear in mind that Russia is a mighty power*" (emphasis added).[110] Almost two years later, in January 1994, Andrei Kozyrov, the Russian foreign minister—a person usually associated with the Euro-Atlanticist view—echoed Yeltsin's view on Russia's dominant position in Central Asia and the Caucasus. Addressing a meeting of Russian ambassadors in the former Soviet republics, Kozyrov argued that it would be necessary to keep the Russian military in the former republics in order to avoid a "security vacuum." Dismissing criticism of Russia's military presence, Kozyrov stated, "We should not withdraw from those regions which have been the sphere of Russia's interests for centuries, and we should not fear these words about the military presence."[111]

Although the debate over the ultimate orientation of the Russian approach toward its South is far from over, the Neo-Eurasianist overtone of Yeltsin's remark is unmistakable. The most formidable challenge facing Russian foreign policy is Moscow's ability to overcome the temptation of an imperial power, benevolent or otherwise, as Central Asian societies on the threshold of their transition to self-realization will continue to be suspicious of Moscow's intentions of imperial reassertion. Russia's relations with Central Asia, ironically as in the past, remain a showcase of Moscow's intentions toward the old southern flank.[112]

Notes

Author's note: This chapter draws particularly from the author's previous article, "Russian Foreign Policy and Security in Central Asia and the Caucasus," *Central Asian Survey* 12, no. 2 (1993).

1. See Andrei Kozyrov, "Transformed Russia in a New World," *Izvestiya*, 2 January 1992, p. 3.

2. Ibid.

3. See Kozyrov's interview with *Le Monde*, 8 June 1992, pp. 1–5, *FBIS-SOV* 92-111, 9 June 1992, pp. 14–16.

4. For an official and theoretical discussion of this issue and an overview of the Euro-Atlanticist view, see Yevgeniy Gusarov, "Towards a Europe of Democracy and Unity," in *Rossiyskaya Gazeta*, 5 March 1992, p. 7; and Andrei Kozyrov, "Challenge of Transformation," *Izvestiya*, 1 April 1992, p. 6.

5. According to Gusarov (ibid.), one of the main architects of the Euro-Atlanticist view, the "humanitarian sphere must not be bound by considerations of state sovereignty and non-interference in internal affairs."

6. For a review of Kozyrov's lecture at Columbia University see *ITAR-TASS*, 25 September 1992, in *FBIS-SOV*, 28 September 1992, pp. 7–8.

7. See Kozyrov, "Challenge of Transformation," and his interview with *Le Monde*, 8 June 1992.

8. For an early discussion on the "continuer state" concept, see Kozyrov's interview in *Rossiyskaya Gazeta*, 21 January 1992, p. 5; and also his interview with *Al-Hayat* in Arabic, 28 January 1992, in *FBIS-SOV* 92-020, 30 January 1992, pp. 31–33.

9. See Kozyrov's interview with *TASS*, 26 March 1992, *FBIS-SOV* 92-060, 27 March 1992, pp. 19–20; and Gusarov, "Towards a Europe of Democracy and Unity."

10. Kozyrov's interview with *TASS*, 26 March 1992; and Kozyrov's interview with *Le Monde*, 8 June 1992. In the latter the Russian foreign minister makes the point that European republics of the former USSR are in the CSCE sphere and will belong to the civilized world. On the other hand, "the Asian republics belong to a different world and although at first they had illusions, they backpedaled when faced with the reality of Asia. Those republics realized that it

was better to conclude the political and military alliance with Russia in one form or another."

11. Gusarov, "Towards a Europe of Democracy and Unity."

12. Ibid.

13. The Charter contains many elements of the Euro-Atlanticist view and particularly carries the language of the Russian theorists of this school of thought. For the full text of the Charter see *ITAR-TASS World Service,* 17 June 1992, in *FBIS-SOV* 92-118, 18 June 1992, pp. 18–22.

14. For an expression of this view see, for example, Yu. B. Solomonov's report on a roundtable discussion on this issue with Foreign Ministry officials, including F.V. Shelov-Kovedyayev, A.A. Avdeyev, and others in *Literaturnaya Gazeta,* no. 18, 29 April 1992, p. 11, *FBIS-USR* 92-057, 13 May 1992, pp. 12–13; Alexei Pushkov, "Is Alliance with the West Feasible?" *Moscow News,* no. 9, 1–8 March 1992, p. 12; and Sergei Strokan, "Russia-India: The Pause to Extend," *Moscow News,* no. 10, 8–15 March 1992, p. 13, in *FBIS-USR* 92-044, 20 April 1992, pp. 2–3.

15. For a review of the importance of the Security Council and the predominant role of centrist forces in it, see *ITAR-TASS,* 11 September 1992, *FBIS-SOV,* 11 September 1992, p. 4; *Moscow Russian Television Network,* 11 September 1992, *FBIS-SOV,* 14 September 1992, pp. 4–6; and *Moscow Radio Television Network,* 7 September 1992, in *FBIS-SOV,* 9 September 1992, pp. 28–29.

16. For this important economic program, which was offered as an alternative to Gayder's plan by the Civic Union, see A. Volskiy, "The Crisis Isn't So Terrible if We Don't Lose Our Heads," *Robochaya Tribuna,* 29 September 1992, pp. 2–3.

17. *ITAR-TASS* Chernomyrdin interview with *Moscow World Service,* 5 January 1993, cited in *BBC-Monitoring: Summary of World Broadcasts (SWB),* 7 January 1993.

18. For a powerful critique of the Russian economic reform, see the interview with Arkadiy Volskiy, president of the Russian Union of Industrialists and Entrepreneurs and a prominent member of the Civic Union, in *Pravda,* 9 September 1992, pp. 1–2; and *La Republica,* 3 October 1992, p. 19, cited in *FBIS-SOV,* 8 October 1992, pp. 29–30.

19. "The end of ideological and political confrontation with the West, does not mean that we want to embrace it with reckless abandonment. There is a limit to everything. There is no 'fraternity' in international relations, any policy worthy of being called a policy must be based on cold calculation and nothing else" (Ednan Agayev, "Russia Above All Else," *Moskovskiye Novosti,* no. 18, 3 May 1992, p. 12).

20. Ibid.

21. Interview with *Izvestiya,* 2 June 1992, pp. 1, 3.

22. *International Affairs* (Moscow), no. 4–5 (April–May 1992): 82.

23. Ibid.

24. Ibid., 92.

25. Cited in *Federal Information System Corporation, Federal News Service,* 6 November 1992.

26. Ibid.

27. This draft was delivered to the Supreme Soviet for further discussion, though according to Russian Foreign Ministry officials no drastic modifications were expected. For a brief version of the document see *INTERFAX,* 2 November 1992, in *FBIS-SOV,* 2 November 1992, pp. 11–13.

28. *International Affairs* (Moscow), no. 4–5 (April–May 1992): 82.

29. Ibid.; see also Giorgiy Arbatov interview with *Moscow Radio,* 18 February 1992, *FBIS-SOV* 92-035, 21 February 1992, pp. 49–50.

30. Alexei Maleshenko, "Russia and Islam: Will We Cross Ourselves in Time?" *Nezavisimaya Gazeta,* 22 February 1992, p. 3, *FBIS-USR* 92-037, 2 April 1992, pp. 1–2.

31. Ibid. Maleshenko approvingly cites another Russian observer, Dubrovsky, who argues that America may permit itself to regard the Islamic world as a scarecrow, but we must remember that this is a complex, heterogeneous structure in which there are perfectly realistic spheres of mutual understanding and cooperation. See also a very interesting discussion of a pragmatic approach toward Islam and the danger of its alienation by Sergei Nikolayvich Goncharov, a leading Russian foreign policy specialist, "The Special Interest of Russia," *Izvestiya,* 26 February 1992, p. 3, *FBIS-USR* 92-028, 12 March 1992, pp. 94–96.

32. See Sergei Stankevich's lecture at Moscow Institute of International Relations, published in *International Affairs* (Moscow), no. 4–5 (April–May 1992): 94. A similar view concerning the unity of the Turkic-Islamic world has also been expressed by Vladimir Lukin, who served as the Russian Ambassador in the United States. See the same source.

33. See *Al-Hayat* in Arabic, 17 September 1992, cited in *FBIS-USR,* 2 October 1992, p. 49.

34. For this document see *INTERFAX,* 2 November 1992, cited in *FBIS-SOV,* 2 November 1992, p. 12.

35. *Nezavisimaya Gazeta,* 18 September 1992, p. 3.

36. Interview with *Izvestiya,* 2 June 1992, pp. 1, 3.

37. *Moscow Russian Television,* interview with Boris Yeltsin by *Izvestiya, Literaturnaya Gazeta,* 15 July 1992, *FBIS-SOV* 92-137, 16 July 1992, pp. 18–22.

38. *INTERFAX,* 15 July 1992, in *FBIS-SOV* 92-138, 17 July 1992, p. 59.

39. *Krasnaya Zvezda,* 3 July 1992, p. 1.

40. *Rossiyskaya Gazeta,* 23 May 1992, p. 2; also see *Kazakhstanskaya Pravda,* 23 May 1992, p. 2.

41. Ibid.

42. Moscow Central Television, 4 May 1992, cited in *FBIS-SOV* 92-099, 21 May 1992, p. 31.

43. *Krasnaya Zvezda,* 3 July 1992, pp. 1–2.

44. *INTERFAX,* 6 July 1992, cited in *FBIS-SOV* 92-130, 7 July 1992, p. 7.

45. Interview with General Leonid Ivashov, Moscow Central Television, 19 May 1992, cited in *FBIS-SOV* 92-099, 21 May 1992, p. 31.

46. See Yevgeniy Shaposhnikov's interview with *Krasnaya Zvezda,* 29 May 1992, pp. 1–2; and V. Samsanov's article "A Collective Security System Is an Objective Necessity," *Krasnaya Zvezda,* 3 July 1992, pp. 1–2. This is a particularly interesting article, for the chief of the CIS Joint Armed Forces General Staff provides a conceptual analysis of key tasks of the CIS Strategic and General Purpose Forces. See and compare with Marshal Yevgeniy Shaposhnikov, "Military Aspects of Collective Security," *Izvestiya,* 4 July 1992, *FBIS-SOV* 92-131, 8 July 1992, pp. 12–14. These two articles are perhaps among the most authoritative discussion of CIS military practices and doctrine.

47. See the post-Summit News Conference *FBIS- SOV* 92-130, 7 July 1992, pp. 8–10.

48. In the press conference after the meeting, the CIS Commander in Chief Yevgeniy Shapashnikov told the audience that neither NATO nor the Warsaw Pact in "their pure form" could be adopted as the model for the CIS, and that a new organizational scheme should be developed in the near future. It is noteworthy that Russia and Uzbekistan both supported the Warsaw Pact model as the future pattern of CIS politico-military command structure. See *INTERFAX,* 25 February 1982, in *BBC Monitoring: Summary of World Broadcasts,* 1 March 1993, p. C2/1; and *INTERFAX,* 1 March 1993, in Ibid., 3 March 1993, p. C2/3.

49. Moscow *ITAR-TASS,* 25 May 1992, in *FBIS-SOV* 92-101, 26 May 1992, p. 14.

50. Moscow Mayak Radio Network citing the Russian president's press secretary, Vyacheslav Kostikov, comments made to *INTERFAX, FBIS-SOV* 92-101, 26 May 1992, p. 14.

51. A draft treaty to that effect was to be prepared by the defense ministries of Kazakhstan and Russia by the end of April 1993. See *ITAR-TASS,* 26 and 27 February 1993, in *BBC Monitoring: Summary of World Broadcasts,* 3 March 1993, pp. B/1 and B/2. Both sides signed additional bilateral treaties on military-technical cooperation during the Ashkhabad CIS summit in December 1993. See *FBIS-Central Eurasia,* 27 December 1993, p. 22.

52. See especially President Islam Karimov of Uzbekistan interview with *Pravda,* 2 June 1992, pp. 1–2, *FBIS-SOV* 92-107, 3 June 1992, p. 23; also for Yeltsin's comments see *Rossiyskaya Gazeta,* 1 June 1992, p. 3, *FBIS-SOV* 92-107, 3 June 1992, p. 21.

53. For a report of the Grachev-Karmov meeting see *ITAR-TASS,* 3 February 1993, in *BBC Monitoring: Summary of World Broadcast,* 5 February 1993, p. C3/2.

54. *INTERFAX,* 11 June 1992 in *FBIS-SOV* 92-114, June 1992, p. 13. Further agreements on bilateral military-technical cooperation between Russia and Kyrgyzstan were signed in Ashkhabad during the CIS summit in December 1993.

55. See interview with Valeriy Otchertsov, member of Turkmen Presidential Council, *Nezavisimaya Gazeta*, 16 June 1992, p. 3, *FBIS-SOV* 92-117, 17 June 1992, pp. 53–54.

56. For this figure and also details of the agreement see *INTERFAX*, 11 June 1992, in *FBIS-SOV* 92-114, 12 June 1992, pp. 82–83.

57. "We cannot afford maintaining an army guaranteeing the defense of the republic's sovereignty" (Valeriy Otchertsov, member of Turkmenistan Presidential Council, quoted in *INTERFAX*, 11 June 1992, in *FBIS-SOV* 92-114, 12 June 1992, p. 83).

58. *Nezavisimaya Gazeta*, 16 June 1992, p. 3.

59. Ibid.

60. *Krasnaya Zvezda*, 10 June 1992, p. 1.

61. For the details of the new military-technical provisions the previous Russian-Turkmen treaties, see *FBIS-Central Eurasia*, 27 December 1993, pp. 14–24. In an interview with *Izvestia* (31 December 1993), Niyazov pointed to the Turkmenistan decision to join the new CIS Economic Union and the joint military cooperation with Russia as key political developments for Turkmenistan in 1993.

62. See Pavel Grachev's interview with *INTERFAX*, 27 December 1993, in *FBIS-Central Eurasia*, 28 December 1993, p. 1.

63. In a remarkable gesture of sensitivity and goodwill, President Saparmorad Niyazov, in a low-key, half-day trip to Tehran immediately after the signing of the treaty, met with President Rafsanjani to explain the defensive and nonaggressive nature of the security treaty with Russia and handed him a copy of the agreement. This information was provided to the author in an interview with A. Va'ezi, Iranian Deputy Foreign Minister, 7 October 1992, New York.

64. For an indication of Turkmenistan's reluctant approach toward the CIS, see the coverage of the CIS Summit meeting in Minsk that took place in January 1993 in *FBIS-Central Eurasia*, 22 January 1993, pp. 5–14. After the CIS summit in Ashkhabad in December 1993 and the signing of the military agreements between Turkmenistan and Russia, S. Niyazov was quick to elaborate on Turkmenistan's intent to pursue peaceful relations with Iran. See *ITAR-TASS*, 10 January 1994, in *FBIS-Central Eurasia*, 11 January 1994.

65. *Nesavisimaya Gazeta*, 15 May 1992, pp. 1–3, *FBIS-USR* 92-063, 19 May 1992, p. 86.

66. Interview with *Moscow Mayak Radio Network*, 16 July 1992, *FBIS-SOV*, 92-138, 17 July 1992, pp. 9–10.

67. *Moscow Radio Rossi Network*, 21 and 22 July 1992, *FBIS-SOV* 92-141, 22 July 1992, p. 72.

68. *INTERFAX*, 23 July 1992, *FBIS-SOV* 92-143, 24 July 1992, pp. 61–62.

69. Nabiev's remark was part of his address to an extraordinary joint session of the parliament's Presidium and Cabinet of Ministers; see *ITAR-TASS*, 20 July 1992, in *FBIS-SOV* 92-139, 20 July 1992, pp. 60–61.

70. Moscow *ITAR-TASS World Service*, 2 August 92, *FBIS-SOV* 92-150, 4 August 1992, p. 73. In the interview, Shodmon Yusupov, chairman of the Committee for National Salvation and leader of the Tajik Democrats, argued that the democratic forces of Tajikistan have convincing proof of the participation by subunits of the Russian motorized rifle division in the armed clash between the conflicting groups that took place in a settlement in Bokhtar Rayon in Kurgan-Tyube Oblast on 27 July 1992.

71. Akbar Iskandarov, acting president of Tajikistan shortly before his resignation, in a letter to the UN general secretary, indicated that the "illegal armed units of one of the sides have secured the backing of some Russian officers" (*ITAR-TASS*, *FBIS-SOV*, 3 November 1992, p. 63). For a series of reports on Russian military forces supporting the opposition forces, especially in Kurgan-Tyube, see several reports by *INTERFAX* in *FBIS-SOV* 92, 28 September 1992, pp. 40–45.

72. Interview with *Nezavisimaya Gazeta*, 30 July 1992, pp. 1, 5. This interesting interview reflects the general view of the Russian Foreign Ministry on Central Asia.

73. *Washington Post*, 3 November 1992, p. A14.

74. *INTERFAX*, 3 November 1992, *FBIS-SOV*, 4 November 1992, p. 60.

75. For the earlier statement issued by Russia and the Central Asian states concerning the need for intervention in Tajikistan, see *INTERFAX*, 4 September 1992, in *FBIS-SOV*, 8 September 1992, pp. 4–5. For the new statement see *Komsomolskaya Pravda*, 5 November 1992, p. 1.

76. Moscow *ITAR-TASS* in *FBIS-SOV*, 9 September 1992, p. 11.

77. *ITAR-TASS* reported by *Agence France Press*, 4 November 1992.

78. For an interesting account of Uzbekistan's role in the Tajik civil war, see Mark Frankland, "Old Style Party Boss Turns the Tide of Islam," *Observer*, 7 February 1993, p. 12.

79. *International Herald Tribune*, 22 February 1993, p. 4.

80. During the commemorations of the fiftieth anniversary of the battle of Stalingrad, Grachev had indicated such options. See *ITAR-TASS, Moscow World Service*, 2 February 1993.

81. *ITAR-TASS, Moscow World Service*, 6 February 1993.

82. *ITAR-TASS, Moscow World Service*, in *BBC Monitoring*, 5 February 1993, p. C2/2.

83. I am indebted to Marie Broxup for bringing this point to my attention. Apparently the anti-Turk (anti-Uzbek) feeling among Tajik refugees in Afghanistan is most prevalent.

84. *Izvestiya*, 12 January 1993.

85. According to a Moscow Television report, the Nagorno-Karabakh headquarters has obtained photographs of Russian servicemen who died in Karabakh while serving in the Azerbaijan army. This report put the Russian casualties at about three hundred (Moscow Ostankino Television, 19 June 1992, *FBIS-SOV* 92-120, 22 June 1992, p. 82).

86. On the equipment of the 4th and 7th armies, see Ostankino Television, 28 June 1992, and *FBIS-SOV* 92-125, 29 June 1992, p. 13.

87. For the Armenian view of Russia's balance of power game see interview with Georgiy Petrosyan, acting chairman of Nagorno-Karabakh Supreme Soviet in *Nezavisimaya Gazeta*, 16 July 1992, p. 3 in *FBIS-SOV* 92-138, 17 July 1992, pp. 64–65.

88. According to a report by *Nezavisimaya Gazeta*, 18 July 1992, based on a personal agreement between Russia and Armenia presidents, the Yerevan motor rifle division, including two hundred tanks, was turned over to Armenia in early July.

89. In an interview with Moscow Television, Azerbaijan President Abulfez Elchibey expressed satisfaction over the relations with the Russian army units stationed in Azerbaijan. See *FBIS-SOV* 92-130, 7 July 1992, pp. 66–69.

90. See Grachev interview with *Nezarisimaya Gazeta*, 9 June 1992, pp. 1–2.

91. *Moscow Radio Rossii Network*, 17 July 1992, *FBIS-SOV* 92-139, 20 July 1992.

92. *ITAR-TASS*, 22 July 1992, *FBIS-SOV* 92-142, 23 July 1992, p. 62.

93. Baku *ASSA-IRADA*, 29 July 92, in *FBIS-SOV* 92-147, 30 July 1992, p. 53.

94. *ITAR-TASS*, 23 July 1992, *FBIS-SOV* 92-14, 27 July 1992, p. 66.

95. During the negotiations, according to Grachev's account, he was repeatedly called "the elder brother" by the defense ministers of Azerbaijan and Armenia (*Krasnaya Zvesda*, 24 September 1992, p. 1).

96. Ibid.

97. *Rossiyskiye Vesti* in *FBIS*, 10 September 1992, p. 17.

98. *Nezavisimaya Gazeta*, 5 September 1992, p. 3 in *FBIS*, 25 September 1992, pp. 115–16.

99. For coverage of Azerbaijan's political moves toward Russia and the CIS and of related issues, see *FBIS-Central Eurasia*, 28 December 1993, pp. 14–24; and *FBIS-Central Eurasia*, 4 January 1994, p. 48.

100. *INTERFAX*, 2 November 1992, in *FBIS-Central Eurasia*, 2 November 1991, p. 12.

101. For the text of Yeltsin's speech to the Civic Union, see "Russia" TV Channel, Moscow, 28 February 1993, in *BBC Monitoring: Summary of World Broadcasts*, 2 March 1993, pp. B1/B3.

102. For Grachev's comments on the role of the Russian army in regional conflict and also the North Caucasus Military District, see interviews with "Russia" TV, 28 February 1993, in *BBC Monitoring: Summary of World Broadcasts*, 3 March 1993, p. C2/1, and *ITAR-TASS*, 26 February 1993, in Ibid., 1 March 1993, p. B7/B8.

103. See Chernomyrdin interview with *ITAR-TASS*, 5 January 1993.

104. See Kazakh Minister of Economics Besenbay Iztelevov's interview with *Izvestiya*, 30 January 1993.

105. See Islam Karimov's interview in *Rossiskaya Gazeta*, 24 February 1993.

106. Shahram Chubin, "The Geopolitics of the Southern Republics of the CIS" (unpublished paper).

107. For an economic rationale of Russian arms sales to the Persian Gulf region, see the interview with Peter Avon, Russia's minister in foreign economic relations, with Radio Moscow World Service, 13 July 1992, *FBIS-SOV* 92-137, 16 July 1992, p. 33.

108. "From the military-technical standpoint," the forward-based deployment was argued to be appropriate, as it assumes "technological superiority of the Russian armed forces over potential aggressors" from the south. For this and a more elaborate discussion of Russia's defensive doctrine, see A. Savelyev (vice president of the Institute of National Security and Strategic Studies), "Does Russia Need a Potential Enemy?" *Krasnaya Zvezda*, 19 March 1992, p. 2.

109. For a discussion of Russian military doctrine and the issue of rapid-deployment forces, see, for example, the interview with Pavel Grachev in *Nezavisimaya Gazeta*, 9 June 1992, pp. 1–2. See also the articles by General V. Samsanov, "A Collective Security System Is an Objective Necessity," *Krasnaya Zvezda*, 3 July 1992, pp. 1–2; Yegeniy Shepashnikov, "Military Aspects of Collective Security," *Izvestiya*, 4 July 1992, pp. 1–2.

110. *Moscow Russian Television*, interview with Boris Yeltsin by *Izvestiya, Litraturnaya Gazeta*, 15 July 1992, *FBIS-SOV* 92-137, 16 July 1992, pp. 18–22.

111. For reports of Kozyov's meeting see *ITAR-TASS*, 18 January 1994, in *FBIS-Central Eurasia*, 18 Janury 1994, pp. 1–2.

112. Both the Euro-Atlanticist's and the Neo-Eurasianist's views are prone to imperial temptations. Yet, while the Neo-Eurasianists are less ideologically driven and rely on realities of power relations, the Euro-Atlanticists, contrary to their claim, and perhaps subconsciously, are more ideological, as they have assumed the role of an enlightened big brother to educate and transform the "immature states of Central Asia." This modern version of a messianic approach is not that different from the views espoused by tsarist foreign minister, Prince Alexandre Mikhailovich Gorchakov, who in his landmark dispatch of 21 November/3 December 1864 wrote, "The position of Russia in Central Asia is that of all civilized states which are brought into contact with half savage, nomad populations, possessing no fixed social organization" (F. Kazemzadeh, *Russia and Britain in Persia* [Yale University Press, 1968], p. 8). Perhaps it is not coincidental that Gorchakov is Kozyrov's idol in matters of foreign policy. For an expression of the modern version of this messianic approach, see, for example, Yevgeniy Gusarov, "Towards a Europe of Democracy and Unity," *Rossiyskaya Gazeta*, 5 March 1992, p. 7; and Andrei Kozyrov, "Challenge of Transformation," *Izvestiya*, 1 April 1992, p. 6, interview with *Le Monde*, 8 June 1992, pp. 1–5, and other sources regarding Kozyrov that have been cited elsewhere in the text.

Contributors

MARIE BENNIGSEN BROXUP is the director of the Society for Central Asian Studies and editor of *Central Asian Survey*. She has written numerous journal articles and book chapters. Her main publications include *The Islamic Threat to the Soviet State*, coauthored with Alexandre Bennigsen (Croom Helm, 1983), and *The North Caucasus Barrier: The Russian Advance Towards the Muslim World* (C. Hurst and Co., 1991).

ALEXANDER O. FILONYK is a senior fellow at the Institute of Oriental Studies, Russian Academy of Sciences. His areas of interest are the socioeconomic development of Arab states and Central Asia. He has published over sixty articles and chapters. His most recent books are *Agrarian Problems of Modern Syria* (Moscow: Nauka, 1982) and *Jordan: Contours of Change* (Moscow: Nauka, 1987).

MILAN L. HAUNER is the visiting professor of history at the Center for German and European Studies, Georgetown University. He has written extensively in English and Czech. His most recent scholarly contributions are *What Is Asia to Us?: Russia's Asian Heartland Yesterday and Today* (Boston/London: Unwin & Hyman, 1990) and *Afghanistan and the Soviet Union: Collision and Transformation*, coedited with Robert L. Canfield (Boulder: Westview Press, 1989).

ANTHONY HYMAN has been a senior fellow of the Social Science Research Council/MacArthur Foundation of New York, working on a research project focusing on geopolitical changes in the Central Asia region. He was a visiting fellow at Queen Elizabeth House, University of Oxford, during 1991–92 and has traveled widely in the region. He is associate editor of *Central Asian Survey*, journal of the Society for Central Asian Studies (London). His latest books include *Afghanistan under Soviet Domination: 1964–1991* (London: Macmillan, 1992) and *Nations and Nationalism in Central Asia* (Cambridge: Cambridge University Press, forthcoming).

ALEXEI V. MALESHENKO is a researcher at the Institute of Oriental Studies, Russian Academy of Sciences. He has published extensively in

Russian and English. Among his most recent works are *The Soviet Union and the Muslim Nations,* coauthored with L. Polonskaia (New Delhi, 1988), and his articles "Islam i novaya Rossiya" [Islam and new Russia], *Svobodnaya Mysl,* no. 10 (July 1992); and "Kommunizm v teni Islam [Communism in the shadow of Islam], *Vostok,* no. 2 (1993).

MOHIADDIN MESBAHI is an associate professor at the Department of International Relations, Florida International University. He is the author of several studies on Soviet-Iranian relations and Central Asian security. His most recent works include, as editor, *Russia and the Third World in the Post-Soviet Era* (Gainesville: University Press of Florida, 1994), and *Russia and Iran: From the Islamic Revolution to the Collapse of Communism* (forthcoming). He is currently a Visiting Fellow at St. Antony's College, Oxford University.

ZAHID I. MUNAVVAROV is a senior researcher at the Institute of Oriental Studies of the Russian Academy of Sciences and a professor in the Faculty of Oriental Studies of Tashkent State University. He has published numerous scholarly works on the history of Arab states. His latest work is "Traibalizm i evolutsiya sotsialnyh i Politicheskih structur v yozhnoaraviyaskih obtshestvah" [Tribalism and the evolution of social and political structures in South Arabian societies].

EDEN NABY is an affiliate at the Center for Middle Eastern Studies at Harvard University. Her numerous publications include *The Modernization of Inner Asia* with Cyril Black et al. (Armonk: M. E. Sharpe, 1990); "The Ethnic Factor in Afghanistan's Future," in E. Jansson, ed., *Afghanistan: A Threatened Culture* (London: Croom Helm, 1987); and "Political and Cultural Forces among the Uighurs: The Struggle for Change—1930s," in *American Asian Review* 5, no. 2 (Summer 1987).

ANDREI G. NEDVETSKY is a researcher at the Institute of Oriental Studies, Russian Academy of Sciences, and professor at the College of Afro-Asian Studies in Moscow University. He is a specialist on Arab and Islamic history and culture. His most recent works have focused on Central Asian history and the post-Soviet developments in the area.

AZIZ NIYAZI is a researcher at the Institute of Oriental Studies, Russian Academy of Sciences. His primary areas of interest are the sociopolitical problems of the South Asian states and the former Central Asian republics. He has published extensively on these topics.

MARTHA BRILL OLCOTT is a professor of political science at Colgate University. She has published numerous articles in academic journals and books. Among her recent books are: *Soviet Central Asia in Modern Times* (forthcoming) and *The Kazakhs* (Hoover Institution, Stanford University Press, 1987).

SERGEI A. PANARIN is a leading researcher at the Institute of Oriental Studies at the Russian Academy of Sciences. He is the author of *The Role of Urbanization in the Social Evolution of the Orient* (1980) and *Rural Communities in the Orient* (1990), among numerous other publications.

ARTHUR SAGADEEV is a leading researcher at the Institute of Scientific Information for Social Sciences, Russian Academy of Sciences, department of Oriental and African Studies. He is also a professor at the Faculty of Philosophy of Patrice Lumumba State University, Moscow. His many publications include *Classical Islamic Philosophy* in collaboration with Taufic Ibrahim (Moscow: Progress, 1991) and *Mirsaid Sultan-Galiev* (Moscow: INION, 1990).

M. NAZIF SHAHRANI is a professor of anthropology and Central Asian Studies and the director of the Middle Eastern Studies Program at Indiana University, Bloomington. He has published many book chapters and journal articles and is the author of *The Kirghiz and Wakhi of Afghanistan: Adaptation to Closed Frontiers* (1979) and senior editor of and contributor to *Revolutions and Rebellions in Afghanistan: Anthropological Perspectives* (1984).

YURI N. ZININ is the chief editor of the journal *Islamski Vestnik* (Islamic Herald). He is a specialist on the Middle East, particularly on Russian policy in the Middle East. His publications include numerous articles and a book titled *The USSR and Algeria: Economic and Political Ties* (Moscow: Progress, 1987).

INDEX

Abazin (lang.), 24
Abazin (region), 17
Abbasov, Abbas, 303
Abdullojanov, Abdulmalik, 184
Abkhaz(ia)(ns), 18, 90, 228
Abkhazo-Adygei (lang.), 24
Abkhazian (lang.), 24
Abu Abdallah Makhammad bin Abi
    at-Tirmizi, Al-Khakim, 146
Abu Bakr, 148
Abu-l-Kassim as-Zamakhsharis,
    Makhmud bin Umar, 146
Abu-l-Kassim as-Zamakhsharis,
    Nakshbandis, 146
Abu-Lughod, Janet, 224–25, 227
Adygeis, 20, 22, 24
Adygeya, 17, 20, 21, 31
Adzharia, 18
Aerospace industry, Azeri, 103
Afghanistan, 36, 51; Central Asia and,
    46, 214, 226, 265, 279, 292, 309;
    Central Asians of, 309; conflict in,
    41, 257, 264, 265 (see also
    Afghanistan, Soviet Union and);
    and ECO, 254, 256; German focus
    on, 211; India and, 213;
    international traders of, 260; and
    Iran, 264, 265; Ismailis of, 43, 44,
    54n.13; Kazakhs of, 264; Kyrgyz of,
    264; Kyrgyzstan and, 161; and
    Middle East, 249; muhajirs of, 42;
    Naby in, 35; and Pakistan, 264, 265;
    population of, 264; post–Cold War,
    268; railway of, 259; and Russian
    Federation, 304; and Saudi Arabia,
    264; Soviet Union and, 52, 76, 81,
    93, 101, 211, 241, 249, 265;
    Tajikistan and, 52, 185, 186, 249,

264–65, 291–92, 295; Tajiks of, 264,
    317n.83; today, 228; Turkmen of,
    264; Uzbekistan and, 261, 264, 286,
    292; Uzbeks of, 264
Aga Khan, 211
Agayev, Ednan, 276
Agazade, Golaman Reza, 199–200
Agha Khan, 43
Agip, 255
Agriculture: of Azerbaijan, 100; Israeli
    expertise in, 262; in Kyrgyzstan, 7
Aimaq, 264
Aini, Kamoluddin Sadriddinovich,
    53n.11
Akaev, Askar, 48, 54n.21, 87, 149, 152,
    154–55, 157–59, 162, 283, 287, 289
Akhmadov, Sharipuddin B., 96n.11
Akims, Kyrgyz, 158
Akzybirlik, 195
Alash (Kazakh progenitor), 129,
    132n.32
Alash (party), 129
Al-Baraka Investment Bank, 260
Alexander the Great, 220
Al-Faisal, Saud, 250
Algeria, 241–43, 248, 308
Ali-al-Barr, Mukhammad, 135
Aliev, Geider, 113, 114
Aliev, Haider, 303
Alim Khan, 166
Alma-Ata, Kaz., 121
Alphabet(s): Arabic, 26, 47, 54n.19, 64,
    159, 255, 256; Azerbaijan shift of,
    112; Cyrillic, 26, 47, 48, 64, 201,
    236, 255, 256; language and, 45–48;
    Latin, 47, 48, 64, 201, 236, 255, 256;
    Soviet doctoring of Central Asian,
    64

Judaism, 145
Judeo-Christianity, 222. *See also*
   Christianity; Judaism
Juybar, the, 42

Kaakhin region, Turkm., 196
Kabadiyan, 165
Kabarda, 76
Kabardian (lang.), 24
Kabardians, 98n.30
Kabardino-Balkaria, 17, 20, 21
Kaliningrad, 227
Kalmyks, 96n.17
Kamal Ataturk, 256
Kamalov, Sakykjanhadji, 160
Kamberov, Isa, 302
Kamel, Saleh, 260
Kamirov, Buri, 173
Kanibadam, 165
Kanju, Mohammad Siddiq Khan, 260
Karabakh, 105–13, 317n.85. *See also*
   Nagorno-Karabakh Autonomous
   Region
Kara-Bogaz-Gol, Gulf of, 201–202
Karachai, 17
Karachai (lang.), 24
Karachayevo-Circassia, 17, 20, 21
Karachays, 85
Karaganda, Kaz., 122
Karakalpak (lang.), 24
Karakalpak Autonomous Soviet
   Socialist Republic, 18, 37
Karakalpaks, 24
Karakhanids, 165
Kara-Kyrgyz (term), 37
Kara-Kyrgyz autonomous area, 160
Karategin, 165
Karimov, Buri, 179
Karimov, Islam, 136, 147nn.5,8, 198,
   286, 295, 306; and Central Asia,
   296; and Grachev, 289; and
   Khojand, 54n.16; in Middle East,
   257, 261; on Tajikistan, 292

Kashgar, Turkestan, 40
Kashgaria, 226
Kashmir, 308
Kazakh (lang.), 24, 119, 124
Kazakh (term), 37
Kazakhs, 6, 24; of Afghanistan, 264;
   culture of, 249–50; diaspora of, 29;
   history of, 119–20; of Kyrgyzstan,
   149; language of, 71n.19
Kazakh Soviet Socialist Republic, 119
Kazakhstan, 3, 18, 21, 92, 104, 119–32,
   249–50; Azerbaijanis of, 122; as
   buffer, 216–17; challenge facing,
   129, 131; China and, 130–31, 262;
   and CIS, 203, 287; and Collective
   Security treaty, 285; Communist
   party of, 125, 126; Cossack
   separatists of, 124, 125;
   Daghestanis of, 122; and ECO, 256;
   economic patterns in, 121–27;
   ethnic patterns in, 28; as Eurasian
   apex, 216; Germans of, 48, 216;
   immigration to, 48; importance of,
   228; independence for, 6, 64, 120,
   123, 126; industrialization of, 263;
   and Iran, 130, 185; and Islamic
   Conference, 199; and Korea,
   130–31; Koreans of, 216, 267n.17;
   Kyrgyzstan and, 120, 149; language
   patterns in, 46; minerals of, 48, 123;
   muftiate of, 129; and Oman, 261;
   and perestroika, 121; pipelines of,
   104, 216, 261; population patterns
   of, 36, 53n.5, 95n.1, 119, 216, 252;
   prestige of, 281; railways of, 216;
   refineries of, 262; Russian Empire
   and, 77, 234; Russian Federation
   and, 125, 186, 280–82, 288–89,
   315n.51 (*see also* Treaty on
   Friendship, Cooperation and
   Mutual Assistance); Russians of,
   48, 119–22, 124, 126, 128, 129,
   132n.31, 216, 237; as "Russified,"

Manchu, 36
Manchuria, 93
Manghit, 38
Mangyshlak region, Kaz., 199
Manilov, Valery, 277
Mansur Ushurma, 84, 89, 96n.11
Maris, 91
Martovitsky, Anatoly, 292
Marv, 42
Marxism-Leninism, 63, 66, 76, 139,
    221, 280. *See also* Communism
Mary, Turkm., 193
Masons, 215
Masov, Rahim, 54n.14
Massaliev (Kyrgyz politico), 157
Matchi, 165, 172, 176
Materialism, as central to
    communism, 66
Mausoleums, 159
Maverannahr, 22
Mazhaabs, 22, 182
Mecca, Saudi A., 141. *See also* Hajj
Media: effect on rural Asians of, 49;
    government control of
    Turkmenistan, 195; Islam via, 146;
    Russian, 239; Tajik, 47. *See also*
    Films; Press; Television
Medina, Saudi A., 141. *See also* Hajj
Mediterranean Sea, 104
Mehkamov, Kakhor, 178
Mendeleev, Dimitriy, 219–20, 225
Mercedes Benz, 255
Mesbahi, Mohiaddin, 322
Microregions, Tajik, 170–71
Middle Asia. *See* Central Asia
Middle East, 21; and Afghanistan, 249;
    Central Asia and, 2, 9, 248–67, 269,
    308; China and, 263; defined, 226;
    Israel isolated in, 262; Kurds of,
    250; Pakistan and, 249; and Russian
    Federation, 275, 277, 279, 280;
    Soviet Union and, 249–49, 268; and
    Tajikistan, 185, 186, 266; and

Turkmenistan, 198, 266; U.S. and,
    308; and Uzbekistan, 250, 266; as
    world fulcrum, 225. *See also*
    Bahrain; Iran; Iraq; Israel; Jordan;
    Kuwait; North Yemen; Oman;
    Palestinians; Persian Gulf; Persian
    Gulf states; Saudi Arabia; South
    Yemen; Syria; Turkey; United Arab
    Emirates
Milli Majles, 91
Mineral springs, Central Asian, 138
Minsk, Belarus, 134
Mirrakhimov, Mirbobo, 179, 180
Mirzoaliyev, Kurbon, 181
Mirzoyev, Akbar, 179
Mission(arie)s, Muslim, 160, 251, 252
Moldavia, 227
Moldova, 134, 241, 246
Mongolia, 36, 226
Mongols, 37, 159, 216
Mordvins, 91
Morocco, 248, 249
Moscow, Rus., 219
Moscow News, 239
Mosques: of Azerbaijan, 109; of
    Bukhara, 43, 53n.12; construction
    of, 250, 252; of Kyrgyzstan, 159;
    return of, 23, 50, 55n.26, 250;
    Soviets vs., 65, 78, 85, 101, 109, 235;
    Tajik, 179; teahouses as substitute
    for, 50; of Uzbekistan, 141, 148n.17.
    See also *Husayniya*
Mountain Republic, 85, 92
Muftiates, 248, 251
Muhajirs, 41
Mujahidin, Afghan, 264–65, 292, 293
Mullahs, 160
Munavvarov, Zahid I., 6, 322
Muradov, Sahat, 206
Murder, as Soviet technique, 238. *See
    also* Pogroms; Purges
Murghab, 165
Muridism, 84, 85

Saudi Arabia, 250; and Afghanistan,
264; and Central Asia, 9, 252,
260–61, 266, 309; and CIS, 261;
Daghestanis of, 250; Islamic
factionalism in, 182; and
Kazakhstan, 130, 260; and
Kyrgyzstan, 162; Muslim activism
of, 250–51; and Soviet-Afghan war,
249; Soviet focus on, 249; and
Tajikistan, 186; and Uzbekistan,
136, 260–61; Uzbeks of, 250
Saudi Cable Company, 261
Saudi Marble Company, 261
Savitsky, P.N., 221
Scandinavia, 227
Self-determination, human rights vs.,
245
Seljuks, 99
Semirechie, 227
Semirech'ye, 20
Semyonov Tyan-Shansky, Veniamin,
220, 225
Serakh region, Turkm. 196
Shahrani, M. Nazif, 4–5, 323
Shakhanov, Mukhtar, 126
Shamil, Imam, 76, 84, 85, 89
Shanibev, Musa, 98n.30
Shaposhnikov, Yevgeniy, 274, 286,
292, 299, 315nn.46,48
Shari'a, 65, 242
Shariat, 25
Shariati, Ali, 188
Sharifzoda, Khodji Haidar, 184
Shaymiyev, Mintimer, 82, 94, 95nn.8,9
Sheep, 150
Sheikhs, Tajik Sufi, 179
Shelov-Kovedyaev (Tajik statesman),
294
Shiites, 21, 40, 42; of Azerbaijan, 5–6,
109–11, 253; of Central Asia, 37, 43,
53n.12, 253; of Iran, 109, 112; of
Iraq, 109; moderate Muslim fear of,
110. *See also* Ismailis; Ithna Ash'ara

Shokhin, Alexander, 292
Shokirov, Jure, 181
Shonia, Valter, 242
Shugnan (lang.), 24
Shugnan (place), 165
Shugni (lang.), 43
Shuro-i Islomiya, 189n.7
Shusha, Az., 107
Siberia, 61, 93, 102, 119, 152, 212, 227,
228; Kazakhs of, 120; Russo-Soviet
domination of, 76, 217; Tatars to,
78, 91. *See also* Trans-Siberian
Railway
Silk, fine-fiber cotton and, 135
Silk Road, 224, 263
Sindh, 213
Skobolev (Russian general), 77
Skokov, Yuri, 270, 274
Slavery, in Central Asia, 42
Slavic Union, 281
Slavs, Turks and, 128–29
Snesarev, Andrei, 226
Solto, 157
South Africa, 134
Southern Ossitiya, 18
South Korea, 130–31, 136, 137, 162,
255, 267n.17
Southwest Asia, 280
South Yemen, 249
Soviet Union: accomplishments of,
56, 69–70n.2; administrative units
of, 188–89n.2; and Afghanistan, 52,
76, 81, 93, 101, 211, 241, 249, 265;
and All-Union referendum, 95n.7;
and Azerbaijan, 99–102, 103, 106,
109; and Central Asia (*see* Central
Asia, Russo-Soviet domination of);
collapse of, 1–5, 7, 9–11, 32, 39, 51,
56, 57, 66–67, 75, 89, 111–13, 120,
127, 133–35, 137, 142, 150, 153,
161, 167, 199, 204, 209, 217, 234,
238, 241, 249, 268–69, 275–77, 295,
304, 306, 308, 310; and Dushanbe,

Turkestan—*continued*
on, 212; Chinese (*see* Xinjiang);
Cossacks in, 212; Russian conquest
of, 216; settlement patterns in, 29;
Soviet clout in, 210–11; Tajiks of,
189n.4; Tatars to, 78; Turks and,
258; as unified ideal, 264; after
World War I, 210. *See also* Bukhara;
Samarkand; Tashkent; Western
Turkestan
Turkestanis, 235
Turkey, 41, 227, 281; air traffic to
Central Asia from, 261; alphabet of,
256; Armenia and, 253; and
Armenia/Azerbaijan conflict, 298,
299; Armenians of, 105, 108; and
"Asian bloc" possibility, 288; and
Azerbaijan, 6, 104, 109, 111–13,
128, 130, 253, 258, 282, 299–301;
and Caucasus, 3, 93, 130, 253; and
Central Asia, 3, 10, 37, 46, 47, 64,
130, 201, 214, 228, 252–56, 258,
259, 266, 281–82, 306, 309–10 (*see
also* Pan-Turkism); Central Asians
of, 309; and China, 258; and CIS,
253; and ECO, 9, 254, 255, 282;
genocide in, 108; and Georgia, 253;
and Germany, 201, 211; and Iran, 9,
258, 301, 310; and Iraq, 258; and
Kazakhstan, 130, 255; and Latin
alphabet, 47; and Kyrgyzstan, 161,
162; and Mountain Republic, 90;
Muslim migrants of, 250; and
Nagorno-Karabakh crisis, 302; and
NATO, 112, 254; and Organization
of Regional Development, 136;
pipeline to, 199–200; post–Cold
War, 268; prosperity in, 257–58;
Russian Empire and, 99; Russian
fear of, 89; Russian Federation and,
94, 130, 274, 304, 311; Soviet focus
on, 100, 248; and Tajikistan, 186;
and Transcaucasus, 201; and

Turkestan, 258; and Turkmenistan,
8, 198–201; U.S. and, 310; and
Uzbekistan, 135–36, 260, 261;
Uzbeks of, 250. *See also* Ottoman
Empire; Pan-Turkism; Turks
Turki(c) (lang.), 24, 26, 39–40, 64,
71n.19, 166, 256
Turkish (lang.), 46, 64, 71n.19. *See also*
Turki(c)
Turki-Uzbek (lang.), 37
Turkmen, 71n.19, 77, 191–94, 309
Turkmen Aria, 262
Turkmenistan(-menia), 3, 8, 18, 36,
191–206; air traffic to Bahrain from,
262; Al-Faisal in, 250; Armenians
of, 194; and Azerbaijan, 202; Baker
in, 242; challenge facing, 206; children of, 192; and CIS, 199, 202–203,
205, 287, 291, 316n.64; and ECO,
256; ecological problems of,
201–202; economy of, 194, 198,
204–206; ethnic patterns in, 28;
exports/imports of, 199; foreign
policy of, 197–206, 291;
independence for, 64; and Iran, 8,
198–201, 253, 257–59, 290–91,
316nn.63,64; and Islamic
Conference, 199; and Kazakhstan,
120, 199; language problems of,
194; media controlled in, 195; and
Middle East, 198, 266; pipelines
from, 199–200, 257; political patterns of, 191, 192, 193, 195–98, 206;
population patterns of, 53n.5,
194–95, 202; purge as policy of, 196;
refineries of, 199, 202; riots in, 194;
and Romania, 202; Russian citizens
of, 194, 197; and Russian
Federation, 8, 203–205,
316nn.61,63,64; settlement patterns
in, 30, 37; Soviet control of, 191,
194, 204; Tatars of, 194; tribes of,
191–93; Turkey and, 8, 198–201;